MONTANA'S MANY-SPLENDORED
GLACIERLAND

Grinnell Lake and 9,541 ft. Mt. Gould

MONTANA'S MANY-SPLENDORED
GLACIERLAND

By Warren L. Hanna

Published by

The University of North Dakota Foundation
P.O. Box 8157, University Station
Grand Forks, ND 58202

First published in 1976 by
Superior Publishing Company
Seattle, Washington

Library of Congress Cataloging in Publication Data

Hanna, Warren Leonard, 1898-
Montana's many splendored glacier land.

Includes index.
1. Glacier National Park. I. Title.
F737.G5H36 978.6'52 76-3614
ISBN 0-87564-622-0

Second printing of the first edition

Printed and Bound in the United States of America

SONNETS TO A
WILDERNESS PARK

Northwest careening like a wind-whipped tide,
  A hundred peaks thrust upward to the sky
In reckless disarray, yet somehow guide
  The streams descending from their summits
    high
To distant seas, north, south and west. And all
  Of winter's snow defies the summer sun
On cliffs or cirque along the Garden Wall—
  In glacial prisons locked till time is done.

  Here sapphire lakes and tarns, a full ten
    score,
    Beget a host of dashing rills that flow
  Cascading downward with torrential roar
    To flow'r-kissed valleys where the stag and
      doe
  Supplied the ancient hunter with a more
    Attractive target for his eager bow.

High on a gale-swept crag or distant peak
  The shy goat pauses, then is lost to sight.
The bighorn nimbly treads his outpost bleak,
  The grizzly prowls the timber's upper height,
The black bear shuffles to his berry patch;
  While, far above, the golden eagles sail,
Intently peering down, a glimpse to catch,
  Of cowering creature hid by rock or trail.

  Ah trails, indeed, along whose pathways
    flow
    The threads of romance, and from ev'ry
    vale
  Lead onward, upward, as they proudly show
    Majestic skyland scenes that cannot fail
  To thrill. The charm of Glacier is to know
    The secrets of her thousand miles of trail.

                      —W.L.H.

TABLE OF CONTENTS
Message from the Governor of Montana
Foreword: Horace M. Albright, Director of the National Park Service
1929-1933

Lake Josephine and the Garden Wall—"A perfect scenic symphony"

Photo by Hileman

THOMAS L. JUDGE
GOVERNOR

State of Montana
Office of The Governor
Helena 59601

The State of Montana can claim the distinction of having within its spacious borders parts of two of the most thrilling and attractive recreational areas in the world. Astride our southern boundary, shared with sister state Wyoming, is the fantastic Yellowstone, not only the world's first national park, but also its most unusual and best known. On our northern border, shared with our sister nation of Canada, is the Waterton-Glacier International Peace Park. This magnificent mountain wilderness and geological showcase comprise the world's first international park.

The concept of national parks is no longer a novel one. In fact, with the advent of the 1970's, those in this country may be said to have attained a certain maturity. Yellowstone has recently reached its centennial year, and the beauty and importance of all wilderness parks were celebrated by the issuance in 1972 of a marvelously illustrated text called simply "YELLOWSTONE". Its publication was a notable event.

Glacier National Park, although established much later, has already completed nearly two-thirds of the years toward its first century. The admirers of this wonderful place are legion. It seems, somehow, to possess the strange power of making ardent fans out of many of its visitors - from George Grinnell to George Ruhle, from James W. Schultz to Henry L. Stimson, and from Mary Roberts Rinehart to Mel Ruder. These and thousands of others have at least two things in common: their abiding affection for, and unabashed loyalty to, the region that is Glacier. There has to be something beyond mere scenery and beauty about a place that can thus touch the lives and feelings of so many people.

Now, at last, for the benefit of those who would like to have the complete story of the Park, with special emphasis on all of the fascinating factors that contribute to its mysterious charm, such a book has been written by one who has known the Park almost from the date of its establishment. Lovers of our national parks should peruse with pleasure this comprehensive story of Glacier and its Canadian neighbor, Waterton Lakes Park.

Sincerely,

THOMAS L. JUDGE
Governor of Montana

FOREWORD

In my sixty years of participation in national park affairs, successively as administrator, advisor and consultant, I have never seen a book of the dimensions of this one about Glacier National Park.

The author worked there intermittently in his college days. The beauty of its natural features and the romance of its human history, including that of its neighbors, the Blackfeet Indian tribe, so interested, excited and inspired him that, beyond his profession, they influenced powerfully his life and that of his family.

His knowledge of this magnificent national park, third largest in the United States system and larger than the State of Rhode Island, is indeed profound, yet his book is easily read and appreciated. No feature of the great park's natural or historical heritage has escaped his keen observation. His vast store of information has been acquired through personal travels through every part of its domain, through personal contacts with scores of Park personalities. All of these enhance his recording of every phase of the Galcier Park story from early explorations to its enjoyment now in the last quarter of the twentieth century by hundreds of thousands of visitors each season from all over the world.

A good book may be rare because it was written long ago and is now difficult or nearly impossible to find; or it may be rare from the day it was written. This book falls in the latter category because it is unlikely that another will ever be written by one who, in an adult lifetime, has never wavered in his or her devotion to Glacier National Park, yet has been endowed with the memory to retain all he has seen, heard or read, and with the skill to write a perfect narrative that so captures the imagination and holds the interest of the reader.

The literature of Glacier National Park and the National Park Service has been greatly enriched by this splendid volume. Our indebtedness to the author is enormous.

HORACE M. ALBRIGHT
Director of the National
Park Service, 1929-1933

PREFACE

Incredible as it may seem, the original draft of this story of Glacier Park was completed in 1925. Conditions for publication not then being propitious, the project was laid aside and now, after an unintended number of years, it makes a belated bow. In its present form, however, its resemblance to the original text is something less than marked, not only because of the revisions and additions needed to make it relevant to the Park of today, but also because its orientation has changed from a largely personal odyssey to that of an account of the essential facts, special events and interesting personalities that have combined to make Glacier a source of never-ending fascination. From the beginning it has been a labor of love by reason of the thousands of enjoyable and carefree hours spent within Park environs and the happy marriage that grew out of a romance that blossomed there.

A deep interest in the Park began with my good fortune in securing summer employment there in 1918, while a law student at the University of Minnesota. For three summers in all, my position was that of "transportation agent" at the Many Glacier Hotel with the duty of arranging saddle horse and bus trips from that point, and serving on rare occasions as guide for a saddle horse party. Prior to this time I had never seen a mountain or a glacier. But since it was obvious that an important part of my stock in trade would have to be information concerning the area, I soon proceeded to cover, on foot or horseback, most of the Park's trails and, ultimately, all of its roads and highways.

When I first arrived at Many Glacier on June 20, 1918, the great hotel was only three years old and the Park itself had been established as such for barely eight. Now, with the passage of more than half a century, the ranks of those familiar with the Park's early years grow thin, and it seems increasingly important that those with first-hand knowledge do what they can to preserve, as fully as possible, the intriguing story of this extraordinary "pleasuring ground" for the people.

At the outset it should be emphasized that this volume does not purport to be a guidebook. For those in need of this kind of assistance, the Park is fortunate to have available a number of superior publications, including Robert Scharff's "Glacier National Park," J. Gordon Edwards' "A Climber's Guide To Glacier National Park," and the latest edition of George C. Ruhle's handbook entitled "Roads And Trails Of Waterton-Glacier National Parks." The book between these covers has been designed with the idea of presenting a series of chapters, each telling the story of some one of the Park's special features or attractions, with all of them combining to provide a comprehensive view, both textually and photographically, of Glacier and the many reasons for its greatness.

In putting together a work of this scope, the assistance of many people has been indispensable. Appreciation is owing to Francis H. Elmore, former Chief Naturalist of the Park, to Edwin L. Rothfuss, his successor, and to Ruben Hart, former Chief Ranger, for their friendly cooperation in supplying pertinent information. I am also obligated to the Glacier Natural History Association for permission to make use of material from their many fine publications. Acknowledgment is due to special friend and advisor, Mel Ruder; to Hugh Black, the major domo of St. Mary's; and to Ian B. Tippet, manager of the Many Glacier Hotel as well as personnel director for Glacier Park, Inc., for their generosity with time, information and advice.

To the National Geographic Magazine I am indebted for their kind permission to borrow, for use as part of the book's name, the title of the marvelous lead article of their May, 1956 issue. I am especially grateful to Professor J. Gordon Edwards, of the California State University at San Jose, for a critical reading of the manuscript, and for many helpful comments and suggestions. Particular thanks are also due my wife, Frances, for her cheerful cooperation in the making of many trips to the Park, and for her unswerving support and encouragement in bringing the book into final form.

There have been a number of publications without which this book could not have been what it is. These include that excellent work by Donald H. Robinson entitled "Through The Years In Glacier National Park," the 1948 edition of the "Drivers' Manual" (described at note 15 of Chapter 6 of the text), and the various publications, in pamphlet form, of the Glacier Natural History Association, each dealing with a particular aspect of the Park's make-up and development. Their substantial contributions to this volume are hereby gratefully acknowledged.

For the fine photography that accompanies the written text, acknowledgment is due to Marion Lacy, master photographer of Whitefish, Montana; to Mel Ruder, editor and publisher of the Hungry Horse News, prize-winning newspaper of Columbia Falls, Montana; to the National Park Service, and Glacier National Park; to Bob and Ira Spring; and to the Burlington Northern and its director of public relations, Frank Perrin, for their more than gracious cooperation. The outstanding pictures from all of these sources tell the story of "Montana's Many-Splendored Glacierland" in graphic form.

—WARREN L. HANNA

Along the highways and byways of goatland

Photo by Hileman

Part I
THE HANDIWORK
OF NATURE

Chapter 1
THE SECRET OF
GLACIER'S CHARM

For those who come to know it well, Glacier National Park holds a special fascination. Aficionados of the Park have described it as "many-splendored glacierland,"[1] as "wonderland of the great northwest,"[2] and as "the park with everything."[3] Other enthusiasts have declared that "when we found Glacier, we stopped looking."[4] Perhaps the ultimate accolade came from John Muir, distinguished California naturalist and authority on mountain country, who called it "the best care-killing scenery on the continent" and urged—

"Give a month at least to this precious reserve. The time will not be taken from the sum of your life. Instead of shortening, it will indefinitely lengthen it and make you truly immortal."[5]

Sometimes called "the crown of the continent," this paragon of parks sits astride the Rocky Mountains in the northwest corner of Montana. Stretching from the Canadian boundary south fifty miles to the main line of the Burlington Northern, and from the North Fork of the Flathead River east to the borders of the Blackfeet Indian Reservation, it encompasses more than fifteen hundred square miles of tumbled mountains, verdant valleys and azure lakes. Compared to the giant bulk of Montana, it appears deceptively small on the map; actually it is one-third larger than the state of Rhode Island, and is our fifth largest national park after Yellowstone, Mt. McKinley, the Everglades and the Grand Canyon.

In conjunction with Canada's Waterton Lakes National Park immediately to the north, it forms a part of the larger Waterton-Glacier International Peace Park. The latter was created in 1932 when the two great nations pooled their scenic borderland treasures as a means of "permanently commemorating the relationship of peace and good will long existing between the peoples and governments of Canada and the United States."[6] First of its kind in the world, this unique park is joint in name and spirit, although not in ownership or administration.

Attractions Of The American Alps

Here the mountains career off to the northwest, tumbling and frothing like a windswept tide—twin ranges that exchange the continental divide between them across the forested tableland of Flattop Mountain. Here is the ridgepole of the continent and here, with sources relatively close to each other, are tiny streams that, leagues to the north, the south and the west, flow as mighty rivers into Hudson Bay, the Gulf of Mexico and the Pacific Ocean.

Here a score of valleys display an extraordinarily beautiful, though individually dissimilar charm, ranging from the delectable vale of the Two Medicine to the rugged grandeur of the Waterton Lakes country, and from the magnificence of the St. Mary Valley, with its superb array of painted peaks, to the celebrated panorama of the Swiftcurrent, with its complicated system of majestic cirques.

Here peak after peak, named and unnamed, rear their sawtooth summits toward the clouds. Half a hundred glaciers are inexorably grinding away at their epochal tasks. Two hundred and fifty lakes in slender valleys and mountain cirques give back to the sky its changing colors. A thousand waterfalls cascade from perpetual snow in misty torrents or milk-white traceries. Rainbows flicker and vanish in the everlasting play of waters, while the clear Montana sun does tricks of light and shade upon pine and rock.

Here, in the pleasant summers of long ago, was a mysterious mountainland where the tribes that lived along its borders would pitch their tepees in the high meadows or on the shores of glacial lakes and stalk the elk or deer that ranged the pine-clad valleys. Here, too, in this most delightful of all hunting grounds, were the sacred places where they gathered for their religious ceremonies, and about which they wove many of their tribal legends.

Belated Appreciation

To the region's early visitors, however, these were matters of little moment. They had not ventured this far off the beaten track in quest of beauty; rather they were thinking of such materialistic things as furs, minerals or possible railroad routes. Their explorations were usually brief in character and confined to limited sections of the area. Not until the latter part of the 19th century did the future Park come to be visited by men who were knowledgeable in reference to scenic splendor, as well as skilled in the art of describing it.

Among those in this category were three rather notable men: Professor Raphael Pumpelly, George Bird Grinnell, and Dr. Lyman B. Sperry, all of whom visited the area two or more times in the years between 1882 and 1900. Pumpelly explored the south and the southeastern area, Grinnell visited the St. Mary and Swiftcurrent regions, while Sperry confined his explorations to the western slope and particularly to the Lake McDonald and Sperry Glacier areas.

Professor Pumpelly, eminent geologist, world explorer and nature lover, who headed up expeditions that twice visited the region of Cut Bank Pass, left the following description of the area:

"Among these limestone mountains—from lofty crest and in cirque—you will see the grandest scenery in the United States; and the best time to see it is when, from high-lying snow fields, water falls are plunging 2,000 feet down almost vertical steps."[7]

George Bird Grinnell, distinguished sportsman, conservationist, explorer, mountain climber, editor, publisher and prolific author, after many summer visits to the present park region, wrote:

"No words can describe the grandeur and majesty of these mountains, and even photographs seem hopelessly to dwarf and belittle the most impressive peaks."[8]

Dr. Lyman B. Sperry, a lecturer at Minnesota's Carleton College, and enthusiastic explorer of the western slope of the continental divide of the future park, wrote:

"The views from Chaney Glacier down the Belly River valley, and for miles southeastward, beggar description . . . I have never seen elsewhere, either in the Rockies, the Cascades, the Sierras, or the Alps, mountain scenery surpassing in real grandeur that which forms 'The Crown of the Continent'."[9]

Impact Upon Visitors To The New National Park

Some decades later, when Glacier had become a part of the national park system, and its portals had been opened to the general public, the visitors included many distinguished travelers who began to report their reactions and impressions. For Franklin K. Lane, a member of Woodrow Wilson's cabinet, the sublime moment came when, from the shores of Upper Lake St. Mary, he gazed upon the magnificence of the incredible peaks that tower above its waters and commented that here you would find—

" . . . the one thing on the North American continent that would inspire you most and make you feel properly humble."[10]

For Mary Roberts Rinehart, well-known writer and novelist, who visited the Park during the summers of 1915 and 1916 and published a book about each visit,[11] the impact was even more personal:

"There is no voice in all the world so insistent to me as the wordless call of these mountains. I shall go back. Those who go once always hope to go back. The lure of the great free spaces is in their blood."[12]

Katherine Bemis, travel writer of the early part of the century, also visited the Park in 1916 and came away equally impressed with its beauty and wonder, saying:

"He who traverses this mountain land park enriches his memory with a wealth of beautiful pictures. This is a dream world, a land of enchantment. It is Nature's great art gallery and sculpture hall."

The Park's Mystic Allure

These ecstatic comments of early explorers and later travelers provide an indication of the Park's tremendous appeal, but really tell us little about what makes these mountains so differently attractive. Visitors sense the environmental magnetism of the region, but rarely comprehend the reasons for it; hence they are mute, or express their praise in generalities or vague superlatives.

This mysterious attraction of the Park seems to grow on those who linger long enough to succumb to its influence, be they seasoned travelers or seasonal employees. Why, otherwise, are so many of the Park's visitors repeaters?[14] And why do hundreds of employees of the Park and its hotel company return, summer after summer, to work for a modest remuneration, some of them traveling thousands of miles at their own expense to do so?[15] What, in short, is the secret of Glacier's charm?

Unquestionably there are parts of America quite as distinguished as Glacier: Mt. McKinley, with its enormous snowy mass and stature; Yosemite, for the quality of its valley's beauty; Mt. Rainier, with its massive radiating glaciers; Crater Lake, with its distinctive cone and incredible deep blue; and the Grand Canyon, with its stupendous painted gulf. But there is no part of America, or of the world, to match it of its kind. At Glacier one sees what he never saw before, and will never see again—except at Glacier.[16]

Sources Of Mystique

The elements of the Park's potent appeal are provided by a constellation of features. Its remarkable mountains are like no others in the world in their fantastic shapes, their attractive coloration, and their unique geology. Its glaciers, because of their number, accessibility and relative rarity in our Rocky Mountain states, are obviously entitled to equal billing with its mountains as the Park's headliners.

To those who know the Park well, however, it is clear that a substantial part of its illusive charm is to be found in its unique history, in the legends of its native peoples, in the magificent character of its setting, in its incomparable cirques and valleys, in the beauty of its sensational passes, in its great profusion of water, in the luxuriance of its vegetation, in the unusual variations and abundance of its wild life, in the attractiveness of its visitor facilities and, above all, for many, in the interesting variety of fascinating trails.

Land Of Shining Mountains[17]

To begin with, the glamour of Glacier owes much to its fascinating history. Tales of such a mysterious land were among the earliest legends of the old West, and explorers began to be intrigued by them long before Lewis and Clark made their memorable trek to the Pacific. Not until then, however, were the actual existence and location of the "shining mountains" verified through the journal and maps of Captain Lewis identifying them as a part of the Rockies in what is now northwestern Montana.[18] This, it would seem, was the picturesque name for a glistening range which, according to the folklore of many of the tribes of mid-America, supposedly lay on the way to a western sea.

It is said to have been tales of such mountains and of such a sea that fired the imagination of the early French-Canadian explorer, Pierre Gaultier de Varennes, Sieur de la Verendrye, and provided much of the motivation for the 1742-1743 expedition led by his sons, Pierre and Francois, which culminated in their being the first white men to glimpse the Rocky Mountains.[19] A quarter of a century later similar reports from Cree Indians of the Minnesota country came to the ears of Jonathan Carver, soldier, explorer and writer.[20]

"Among these mountains," wrote Carver glibly, "those that lie to the west of the River St. Pierre (the Minnesota River of today) are called the Shining mountains, from an infinite number of chrystal stones, of an amazing size, with which they are covered, and which, when the sun shines full upon them, sparkle so as to be seen from a very great distance." And he went on to speculate that ". . . probably in future ages they may be found to contain more riches . . . than those of Indostan or Malabar, or than are produced on the golden coast of Guinea; nor will I except even the Peruvian mines."[21]

Neither the Verendryes nor Carver ever saw northwestern Montana,[22] yet it appears in retrospect, that the latter's fanciful tale of its mountains may have been more nearly right than he knew. Conceivably, his "chrystal stones of an amazing size," may have been none other than the living glaciers of Montana's future Park, and even his visions of extraordinary "riches" may have turned out to be "not so wild a dream,"[23] since it is now apparent that about these "shining mountains" lies a region of unequalled richness in its wealth of life-giving water as well as its fantastic and unforgettable beauty.

Physical Features Of Special Interest

Glacier enjoys an unique setting. A wilderness park itself, it is virtually surrounded by national forests and other wilderness areas. Adding further to its interest are the features—both natural and man-made—which constitute its perimeter. For example, its western boundary is formed by a fast-flowing stream that rises in Canada,[24] while every mile of its eastern boundary represents a segment of the western border of the Blackfeet Indian Reservation. On the south, it is bounded in part by the main line of a major railroad[25] and in part by another brisk mountain stream,[26] While a degree of geographic latitude, to wit, the 49th parallel,[27] is its northern boundary. This imaginary line serves also to divide the United States from Canada, and the two sectors of the international park from each other.[28] Who can say how much of Glacier's fascination is ascribable to the cosmopolitan aura arising from this happy sharing of a common boundary with its delightful Canadian neighbor, the Waterton Lakes National Park!

Glacier is preeminently the park of lakes. When all is said and done, they constitute its most distinguished single element of beauty.[29] Its wealth of water is everywhere repeated in the wilderness music of hundreds of rills and torrents. Its waterfalls are innumerable—mysterious ones that appear to gush forth from the rock wall, lacy ribbons that descend from lofty hanging valleys, and thunderous cascades that rush tumultuously through narrow gorges.

Rocks Of Distinction

In its rock formations, Glacier is also unique. Its cliffs are abrupt and sheer. Its peaks are clustered in propinquitous disarray—two magnificent ranges of them. There are saw-tooth ridges that separate great valleys and rock-walled amphitheatres that shelter pine-encircled lakes. Gabled promontories vie with pointed peaks that out-pyramid Egypt. Its multitude of precipice-walled cirques and lake-studded valleys are a heritage from the glaciers of old. They constitute one of Glacier's outstanding features and make it incomparable of its kind.[30]

Many of the rock formations are over a billion years old, some with strata that have been exposed to view by the singular upheaval in the vicinity known as the Lewis Overthrust. In them may be read a classical geological story that dates back to the dawn of earth's history when most of the western United States was covered by a shallow sea. These ancient sedimentary rocks, thus brought into view, are richly colored, their maroon, green and buff shades contrasting pleasantly with the dull hues of ordinary country rock.

Flora and Fauna

A profusion of wildflowers literally carpets the Park, converting it into a million-acre flower garden. In lakeside meadows and by alpine snows they bloom alike, their countless numbers rivaled only by their brilliant beauty. As a matter of fact, Glacier is distinctive in its many types of plant life and is becoming a classic field for botany just as it already is for geology. As the southern limit for many plants of Canada, and the eastern limit of many Pacific Coast forms, it is little wonder that botanists come from all over the world to study its flora.[31]

As a national park, Glacier is also a game preserve and frequent glimpses are caught of the fifty-seven species of wild creatures that make the Park their home. It is one of the last strongholds of the grizzly. Black bears, moose, elk, deer and beaver abound, as do mountain lions and coyotes. The country above timberline is the habitat of the bighorn sheep and the Rocky Mountain goat. The lakes and streams are teeming with gamy trout, while the forests provide homes for two hundred and ten species of birdlife.

Hikers' and Horsemen's Paradise

For many, the most important element of Glacier's lure lies in its mountain trails, taking one up to the high places and imparting the thrills of such dizzy heights, while embracing few of the dangers. The proximity of objectives, whether on horseback or afoot, is pleasant. There are no foothills. No long trips need to be undertaken to be among the peaks. The change from plains to summits is abrupt—and delightful. The wilderness is there, much as it was a thousand years ago, its sacred fastnesses reserved chiefly for the horseman and the hiker. The network of trails leads from valley to valley, back and forth across the continental divide, threading every pass, ascending and descending seemingly unscalable walls, solving the riddle of a challenging wilderness. Of the trails, a veteran hiker has said:

"They are irresistible. They are veritable threads of romance. They spell recreation in capital letters. They spell escape from the stress of a workaday world. They mean days under the bluest of skies; and if you like, night under the stars. Every switchback has a fresh thrill to offer. One can even cover the same trail over and over and never grow tired of it. For trail travel 'gets' you; the more you do, the more you want to do. The most phlegmatic become enthusiasts. You never talk with anyone on the trail whose conversation isn't sprinkled with exclamation points. Superlatives seem quite inadequate."[32]

All of these many factors combine to make the spell of Glacier a powerful and mysteriously delightful influence. It has been well said, in comparing Glacier with other parks, that its charm lingers longer in memory and is more easily recaptured in imagination, but that one must go there himself to find it for photographs cannot convey it, artists fail to catch and imprison it and words cannot describe it.

A Mountaineer Sums It Up

Despite this depairing view of the inadequacies of art and language, at least two writers have succeeded in painting word pictures that go far toward revealing the elusive secret of Glacier's charm. George H. Harvey, Jr., former president of the Colorado Mountain Club, soon after the return of himself and wife from a 30-day trek over Park trails with the Sierra Club in the season of 1924, summarized their adventure in these delightful paragraphs:

"As the weeks have crowded in between us and this outing, we are more and more impressed with the greatness and beauty, the charm and majesty, the lure and delightfulness of this wonderful park . . . We think of the countless lakes, gems of glowing and changeable blues and greens, surpassingly lovely whether asleep in the moonlight or rippling under the noonday sun; whether smiling up into the blue with the glassy surface of dawn, or sponged by the low-hung clouds of afternoon. We think of the deep-forested trails—those of the north, dim, overgrown and upended, those of the more developed section, wide, well-graded and easy. We think of the mighty forests, tall and silent, a perfect cover for the teeming wildlife—the scolding squirrels and trusting marmots; the deer, timid but almost unafraid; the bears, seldom seen and of bad repute.

"We think of the passes with their sweeping views; we see again the mountain sheep and the fearless goats skirting the dizzy cliffs above them. We think of the scores of tiny glaciers, and others not so tiny, that cling to the shoulders or sprawl at the feet of great painted cliffs, and send down their milky torrents with roaring rapids and impetuous falls to swell and color the lakes below. And always we think of the colorful rocks of which the park is made, marvelous at all times, but especially brilliant on a rainy day or when broken up to form the mosaic bed of some crystal stream; and the great peaks, like colossal upturned boats, from which these rocks came, huge roof-like masses of green and maroon and buff, belted here and there with black, towering a mile or more high in bright terraces of color – these are the source of all this beauty, its original material laid down on the ocean's floor millions of years ago, now lifted to be cut, carved and polished by wind, water and ice into one of the world's great spectacles."[33]

Twenty years later beloved Ernie Pyle, with his superlative ability to put great meaning into a few words, said it more simply:

"Glacier is my favorite of all the national parks. With the exception of Carlsbad Caverns, I wouldn't trade one square mile of Glacier for all the other parks put together. The vast valleys that you look down into, and the unbelievably great peaks and ridges rising above you, and the hidden passes, and the surprising banks of snow, and the incongruous meadows on the high flats, and the tumbling white streams, and the flowers and the silent little lakes around a bend—all have an isolation and a calm majesty that to me make Glacier Park more than just a place."[34]

Notes For Chapter 1

[1]Article by George W. Long entitled "Many-Spendored Glacierland" in the National Geographic Magazine for May, 1956.

[2]Articles by Agnes C. Laut entitled "Wonderland Of The Great Northwest," in Travel Magazine for January-May, 1926.

[3]Article by E. A. Bauer entitled "Glacier: The Park With Everything," in Field and Stream Magazine for June, 1964.

[4]Article entitled "When We Found Glacier, We Stopped Looking," in Sunset Magazine for June, 1958.

[5]Article by John Muir in the Atlantic Monthly Magazine for January, 1898 on the subject of our national parks and forest reserves, Volume 81, pages 21-22. Had Muir been able also to visit the eastern section of the future national park, his comments might have been even more ecstatic.

[6]An excerpt from the language of Chapter 157, Laws of 1931-1932 (approved May 2, 1932 (HR 4752 introduced by Congressman Scott Leavitt of Montana) authorizing United States participation in the creation of the Waterton-Glacier International Peace Park.

[7]See "My Reminiscences" by Raphael Pumpelly, Volume II, published in New York in 1918 by Henry Holt & Company, at page 644.

[8]Article entitled "The Crown Of The Continent," by George Bird Grinnell, in Century Magazine for September, 1901, at page 663. The article was prepared and submitted in 1891 or 1892, but was not published until nearly a decade later for unknown reasons.

[9]Article entitled "In The Montana Rockies," by Lyman B. Sperry, in "Appalachia," Vol. VIII, No. 1, January, 1896, at page 66.

[10]Article entitled "A Mind's Eye Map Of America," by Franklin K. Lane, then Secretary of the Interior, appearing in the National Geographic Magazine for June, 1920, at page 501.

[11]These books were respectively entitled "Through Glacier Park: Seeing America First With Howard Eaton," published in May, 1916 by Houghton Mifflin Company, and "Tenting Tonight," published in 1918 in book form by Farrar & Rinehart, Inc., after appearing serially in magazine form in 1917.

[12]Article entitled "An Appreciation Of Glacier National Park," by Mary Roberts Rinehart, written especially for the United States Railroad Administration circa 1920.

[13]See the foreword to "Glacier National Park, Its Trails and Treasures," by Holtz and Bemis, published in 1917 by George H. Doran Company.

[14]One visitor, for example, had spent a total of 1197 days in the Park by the summer of 1954. This was Mrs. Frank Oastler who, over a period of 40 years, averaged nearly 30 days a season, mostly as a guest at the Many Glacier Hotel. See the story of the Oastlers at pages 153-154 of Chapter 18, infra, entitled "Visitors: Distinguished And Otherwise."

[15]For one employee, Ray Kinley, a California resident, the summer of 1975 marked half a century of service in the Park. He was first employed at Many Glacier in 1922, and thereafter missed only the summer of 1964 and three summers during World War II, when the Park hotels were closed.

[16]"The Book Of The National Parks," by Robert Sterling Yard, at page 252.

[17]A colorful name frequently applied to the Park, with an origin antedating the advent of the white man in that area.

[18]Captain Lewis' journal, under date of July 2, 1805, contains this description of the snow-covered mountains of the northwestern Montana: "They glisten with great beauty when the sun shines on them in a particular direction, and most probably from this glittering appearance have derived the name of the Shining mountains." See page 401 of Volume II of "History of the Expeditions under the Command of Lewis and Clark," edited by Elliott Coues and published in 1965 by Dover Publications, Inc. of New York. On the map by Captain Lewis accompanying the above-mentioned publication, and prepared in 1805 principally from Indian information in reference to the country west of Fort Mandan (in present day North Dakota), the range in

the vicinity of what is now Glacier Park is designated as the "Shining Mountains."

[19]A story of the Verendrye discovery of "The Shining Mountains" will be found at pages 31-41 of "Land of the Dacotahs," by Bruce Nelson, University of Nebraska Press, 1964. However, a review of the original "Journals and Letters of Pierre Verendrye and Sons" does not disclose any use of the phrase "shining mountains"; and the same is true of the chapter entitled "The Discovery Of The Rocky Mountains" at pages 72-91 of "Pathfinders Of The Great Plains: A Chronicle Of La Verendrye And His Sons," by Lawrence J. Burpee, published by Glasgow, Brock & Co. in 1922. See, also, "Through The Years In Glacier National Park," by Donald H. Robinson, at page 6.

[20]See pages 76-77 of the text of "Three Years Travels Throughout The Interior Parts of North America For More Than Five Thousand Miles, 1766-1768," by Captain Jonathan Carver of the Provincial Troops In America, 1802 edition printed by Samuel Etheridge for West and Greenleaf, No. 56 Cornhill, Boston.

[21]Idem, at page 77. See, also, "Trails Of The Pathfinders" by George Bird Grinnell, and especially Chapter IV, entitled "Jonathan Carver." The quoted material will be found at page 70.

[22]Carver never reached any point west of present day Minnesota (see notes 20 and 21 above). The Verendryes, however (see "Pathfinders Of The Great Plains," supra, at pages 83-86 of the chapter entitled "The Discovery Of The Rocky Mountains," prepared by Lawrence J. Burpee from the journal of Francois de la Verendrye), obtained their first view of the mountains on January 1, 1743, while traveling with a large party of Bow Indians. Continuing westward or southwestward for another 12 days, they finally arrived at what Burpee described as "the foot of the Rocky Mountains . . . those silent snow-capped peaks upon which . . . Europeans had never looked before." These were probably the Big Horn Mountains in what is now the north central part of Wyoming.

[23]To borrow a phrase from the title of Eric Severeid's delightful book published in 1946 by Alfred A. Knopf.

[24]This is the North Fork of the Flathead River.

[25]The Great Northern Railway, now a part of the Burlington Northern System, completed construction of its right of way in 1891 along a route which was later to become, in part, the southern boundary of the Park.

[26]This is the Middle Fork of the Flathead River.

[27]For a more complete story of the international boundary, see Chapter 11, infra, entitled "Advent Of The White Man" at page 90.

[28]For a more complete story of the international peace park, see Chapter 21, infra, entitled "Our Canadian Neighbor," at page 172.

[29]See "The Book Of The National Parks," by Robert Sterling Yard, at page 256.

[30]Idem, at page 251.

[31]See article entitled "How The Trees Came To Glacier Park," by Ranger Naturalist H. E. Bailey, published in "Glacial Drift," Volume V, for July/August, 1932, at page 41.

[32]"High Trails Of Glacier National Park," by Margaret Thompson, published in 1938 by the Caxton Printers, Ltd., at page 16.

[33]Article entitled "Our First Sierra Club Outing," by George H. Harvey, Jr., at pages 158-162 of the Sierra Club Bulletin, Volume XII, No. 2

[34]From "Home Country," by Ernie Pyle, published posthumously in 1947, at page 415.

Iceberg Lake—"A pocket edition polar sea"

Photo by Hileman

Chapter 2
A ROMANCE IN ROCKS

The story of the creation of Glacier National Park is one of great fascination to every student of geology.[1] Yet, even for those who profess no interest in matters scientific, the message contained in the rocks, cliffs and peaks of the Park is one with potent appeal because of its dramatic character and the light which it sheds upon the sources of the region's superlative beauty. Its rocks are among the most ancient known to man, with billion-year-old ripple marks plainly visible on many of them. And the titanic uplifting of its peaks along the continental crest, followed by their horizontal movement eastward for several miles in what has been termed a classic among overthrusts, represents a scientific phenomenon of extraordinary dimensions.

Most of our national parks have been established as such because they contain striking examples of Nature's handiwork; several offer exhibits of prime geological interest, notably the Grand Canyon, Bryce Canyon, Zion National Park and the Yosemite. It is interesting, accordingly, to learn that within the boundaries of Glacier Park there is exhibited a greater variety of geologic features than in any other of our national parks.[2] Furthermore, much of Glacier lies above timberline, so that the rocks comprising its superb mountains are generously exposed to view. To decipher the message that they bear requires only the interpreting mind of the geologist.

The Geology Of Glacier

The tale of Glacier's creation can logically be divided into three periods, each of millions of years of duration, which might be alliteratively described as periods of deposition, deformation and delineation. The first of these was an era of **deposition** of almost unending layers of sandstone, mudstone and limestone. Known to geologists as the Precambrian period, this era of rock formation probably lasted more than a billion years.[3]

The second was a period of **deformation** or mountain building, known to geologists as the Rocky Mountain revolution.[4] It began not less than 60,000,000 years ago, and witnessed the uplifting of the great slab of sedimentary rock which is now the Park thousands of feet in the air, followed by its eastward movement some thirty miles or more to a resting place upon much younger Cretaceous rocks similar to those underlying the plains east of the Park.[5]

The third period, which might be referred to as one of **delineation,** comprised an era of erosion and glaciation, beginning perhaps 50 million years ago, during which the sculpturing of the raw rock into the present region of living beauty has taken place.[6] Let us glance back for a moment at the geological record of Glacier Park.

The First Stage

At the dawn of earth's history, well over a billion years ago, the site of Glacier Park rested upon the bottom of a shallow sea. It is believed to have been one of several huge depositional basins which then co-existed, although not necessarily interconnected, in Canada, Montana, Utah and Arizona.[7] In these sea-filled troughs, through eons of time, thousands of feet of sediments were deposited and gradually became compacted into shales, sandstones or limestones. The ripple marks and mudcracks still plainly visible on some of these rocks bear witness to this origin.[8] Several hundred million years were required for completion of this process, and there were probably several submersions.

In the Glacier Park of today, these thousands of feet of sedimentary rock have been classified by geologists as falling into several formations. Because each has a characteristic color, these formations can easily be identified, often from a distance of several miles. A single mountain may be comprised of from two to four of these formations, the oldest ordinarily at the base and the youngest on top, these having been their relative positions when deposited in sedimentary form.[9] The four principal formations are the Altyn, the Appekunny, the Grinnell and the Siyeh. The lesser ones are known as the Shepard and Kintla Formations.[10]

Altyn Formation

This is the oldest of the several formations, and is composed mainly of limestones and sandy dolomites that weather to a light buff color. Its average thickness is about 2,500 feet. It outcrops all along the east side of the Lewis Range and comprises the upper section of Chief Mountain. It forms the natural dam at the lower end of Swiftcurrent Lake and creates Swiftcurrent Falls. The rock of this formation can most easily be examined on the low ridge immediately to the east of the Many Glacier Hotel, and above Swiftcurrent Falls.[11]

Appekunny Formation

Three thousand feet of this rock, mostly greenish shales and argillites, are prominent along the eastern side of the Lewis Range, everywhere immediately overlying the lighter-hued Altyn. The lower walls of Appekunny Basin are comprised of this material, and it is readily visible along the lower part of the Grinnell Glacier trail as well as on the side of Singleshot Mountain near the St. Mary entrance to the Park.[12]

Grinnell Formation

Next above the Appekunny rocks are the argillites composing most of the Grinnell Formation, with a thickness averaging 3,000 feet. This conspicuous red rock, the most colorful and prominent in the Park, derives its color from the abundant iron oxide that occurs mainly as a cement between the sand and mud grains. In the Many Glacier area, it makes up the bulk of Mt. Allen, Grinnell Point and the base of Mt. Wilbur. It is readily seen at Red Rock Falls on the trail to Swiftcurrent Pass, the Ptarmigan Tunnel is drilled through it, and it is crossed by the trails to Grinnell Glacier, Cracker Lake and Iceberg Lake.[13]

Elsewhere in the Park it is found in the formation which caps the summits of Rising Wolf and Sinopah Mountains in the valley of the Two Medicine; while on the Going-To-The-Sun Highway the great red rocks of the Grinnell Formation are seen in Goat Mountain on the north side of Lake St. Mary, and in Red Eagle and Mahtotopa on the south side. It is prominent in the mountains surrounding the Sperry basin, as well as on the trail from Sperry Chalet to the Glacier.[14]

Siyeh Formation

Lying next above the Grinnell is a massive limestone formation, the Siyeh, with a thickness of up to 4,000 feet. Since it is younger than the three preceding formations, it is confined mainly to the higher elevations, capping many of the loftier peaks in both the Lewis and Livingston Ranges. In the Many Glacier area, these include Mts. Gould, Siyeh, Grinnell, Wilbur and Henkel, as well as the Garden Wall and Pinnacle Wall. In the Lake St. Mary area, the list includes Little Chief, Jackson, Gunsight, Fusillade, Piegan and Going-To-The-Sun. In the northern region of the Park, the formation is prominent in Rainbow and Carter Peaks, as well as Mts. Kintla, Kinnerly and Cleveland.[14]

Other Formations

While the formations described comprise the great bulk of the Park's rocks, there are others of lesser importance which are seldom encountered. These lie above the Siyeh and are sometimes referred to as the Missoula Group; however, over most of the Park they have been removed by erosion and are visible only on the upper portions of certain peaks.[16] One of this group is the Shepard Formation which weathers a yellow-brown. It is exposed near the summit of Swiftcurrent Mountain and at various points in the vicinity of Logan Pass, including the Hanging Gardens and Mt. Clements. From Going-To-The-Sun Highway it is visible on Almost-A-Dog and Citadel Mountains in the St. Mary Valley.[17]

Still rarer is the Kintla Formation which is found principally on a few summits in the northwestern part of the Park, including the mountains around colorful Boulder Pass and the Hole-in-the-Wall Basin. These argillite rocks are the youngest in the Park, and have the same bright red coloring as those of the Grinnell Formation.[18]

Diorite Intrusion

Running horizontally through the upper part of the Siyeh Formation is a distinctive black band, approximately 100 feet in thickness, known as the Purcell Sill. From Many Glacier Hotel it is readily seen near the summits of Mt. Gould and Mt. Wilbur, as well as on the Pinnacle Wall and the Garden Wall. In the Waterton Lake area, it is plainly visible on the stupendous north face of Mt. Cleveland. From Going-To-The-Sun Highway, it can be seen on Little Chief, Citadel, Piegan and Going-To-The-Sun Mountains, as well as on the west side of the Garden Wall, where it also forms the cap of Haystack Butte.[19]

Dated radiometrically at about 1.1 billion years, this imposing layer of black rock, known to geologists as diorite, diabase or metagabbro, was forcefully intruded, while in a molten state, between beds of sedimentary rocks. Technically referred to as a "sill," it is bordered at top and bottom, wherever it occurs in the Siyeh Formation, by thinner gray-white layers of limestone which were converted into marble by the tremendous heat of the diorite during its intrusion.[20] It represents one of the most characteristic and readily identifiable landmarks of the Rockies of northwestern Montana.

Flows of molten rock have occurred at several times during the region's geologic history. In addition to being responsible for the diorite intrusion in the Siyeh Formation, similar eruptions at one time or another broke through the layers of sedimentary rocks to form massive lava flows which are conspicuous at various places in the Park.[21] These are called the Purcell Flows[22] or Purcell Lava, and have been mistakenly referred to as granite.[23] This basalt type of rock is most readily seen around the Granite Park Chalet, and in the vicinity of Boulder Pass where the trail follows its distinctive surface for a distance of several hundred yards.[24]

The Vertical Dikes

Fascinating features of the Park's topography are its dikes, a dike being similar to a sill except that the latter runs horizontally through a cliff, while the dike runs upward through the sedimentary formations that constitute the face of the cliff. Undoubtedly, these dikes provided vertical channels for the flow of molten rock in early geologic times.[25] Since they have less resistance to erosion than surrounding rock, they have sometimes given way to narrow vertical chimneys which appear as snow-filled chutes on the mountainsides in spring and early summer. From Many Glacier Hotel one of these can be seen on the smaller mountain, now called Bullhead Point or Bullhead Peak, which stands in front of Mt. Wilbur; and a continuation of it can be seen transecting the Pinnacle Wall to the north of Wilbur.[26]

These dikes are of interest because they contain various minerals, including copper and silver, which in the days of the area's mining boom, attracted the attention of prospectors. The old Cracker Mine, situated on the east shore of Cracker Lake, was driven along a dike with a width of over one hundred feet. The Josephine Mine, the ore dump of which is still visible from the boat landing at the head of Lake Josephine, was dug along the edge of a similar but smaller dike. Never productive because the ore taken out of these excavations was lacking in commercial value, both of these ancient mines have been abandoned.[27]

Special Marks Of Ancient Origin

At many places within the Park it is possible to view plain evidence of the origin of its rocks. The surfaces of many of the sandstone layers are covered with ripple marks which could only have been made by wave and current action in shallow water. Mudcracks on some of the former shale beds indicate that the sediments, in their depositional environment, were exposed to the air long enough to dry out. Great thicknesses of limestone and numerous fossils of the communities of primitive algae, called stromatolites, show that the body of water was a sea.[28] These stromatolites are calcareous, mound-shaped structures which range from less than one inch to more than five feet in diameter, and resemble a head of cabbage. Each colony was produced by the activities of millions of microscopic blue-green algae, at a time in the earth's history when animals and more advanced plants had not yet evolved.[29]

Within the Siyeh Formation is a bed of these fossil algae, averaging 60 feet in thickness, which apparently formed an extensive reef on the floor of the ancient sea. This bed appears as a distinct light gray horizontal band on the east face of Mt. Wilbur several hundred feet below the black diorite band, where it can readily be seen from the vicinity of the Many Glacier Hotel. It is also discernible on the Pinnacle Wall, above Iceberg Lake, as well as on Mt. Grinnell. The Swiftcurrent trail crosses it just east of the Pass, and it is also exposed along Going-To-The-Sun Highway below the big switchback on the west side of Logan Pass, where attention is directed to it by a sign. Unweathered portions of the reef are light blue.[30]

A similar but thinner reef outcrops at Logan Pass near the beginning of the Hidden Lake trail. Although most of the fossil algae occur in the Siyeh, they are also present in the younger formations and in the Altyn. Because of the rounded surfaces of some of these colonies, mountain climbers sometimes find the reef difficult to cross.

The Era Of Deformation

The second phase of this earlier part of the Park's creation began after the sea had permanently withdrawn, toward the end of what geologists call the Cretaceous Period, possibly 60,000,000 years ago.[32] This change involved what was undoubtedly an almost imperceptible and long-drawn-out contraction of the earth which caused its outer crust to bulge and wrinkle in places. One row of these tremendous wrinkles was the Rocky Mountains.[33]

In the course of this contracting process, an even greater miracle was wrought at certain points. In what is now Glacier Park, and for distances of about 100 miles to the north and to the south, the mighty wrinkle of the Lewis Range cracked along its crest.[34] As processes deep within the earth continued slowly to raise the western side of this great fracture thousands of feet in the air, it began to slant eastward. Whether the elevated section was then crowded over upon the plains country to the east,[35] or whether it simply slid downhill under the pull of gravity, the result was that it moved eastward in a rolling or folding fashion[36] Thus the billion-year-old slab of Precambrian sedimentary rock which is now Glacier Park came to rest upon the much younger Cretaceous rocks underlying the plains to the east, a process which geologists call an "overthrust fault."[37] The distance covered in this massive movement is unknown, but has been variously estimated at from 15 to 35 miles, its terminus being in rough correspondence with the eastern boundary of the Park.[38] Since it affected the Lewis Range, the phenomenon was called the "Lewis Overthrust."

The entire process consumed a period of time too long for the human mind to comprehend. Such stupendous movements require an unbelievable number of eons for completion and Nature has never hurried. Because of the inconceivable lapse of time during which these titanic earth movements took place, they are divested of much of their excitement. Imagine the spectacle of a mile-high wall of rock suddenly advancing twenty miles or more along a 250-mile front. If this colossal overthrust could have happened in the twinkling of an eye, the resulting cataclysm would have afforded a dramatic tumult too terrible for contemplation.

The Mountains That Moved

Within the Park, the Lewis Overthrust is visible at a number of points along the eastern side of the great front range of the Rockies. Perhaps the most spectacular is the view to the north from the Theodore Roosevelt Memorial at Marias Pass, showing Precambrian rocks lying upon younger Cretaceous rocks for a distance of several miles.[39] Another classic example is Chief Mountain at the Park's northeast corner, although the overthrust fault line is actually somewhat below the lower line of the talus slopes that surround the peak.[40] A good place to view the overthrust at close range is at Trick Falls, where the Cretaceous rocks and the fault are well exposed.[41]

First to study the great overthrust was Professor Bailey Willis, the eminent geologist, who also gave it its name. Having accompanied the Pumpelly Expedition through a part of the future park in 1882-1883, he returned in 1901 to serve as geologist with the United States Geological Survey team which was engaged in the mapping of the region during that period. Since that time, other overthrusts have been discovered or become recognized on various continents; yet it is interesting to learn that nowhere else is there a fault so easily traceable for such a substantial distance, or one so readily evident to the untrained eye.[42]

Third Stage Of The Park's Creation

Even before the internal forces of the earth had completed the stupendous movement of the Lewis Overthrust, the external forces had taken up their never-ending work. The gargantuan block of shale and limestone had been quarried and was ready for the sculptor. The agencies used by Nature in carving her masterpiece were three in number — weathering, erosion by running water, and erosion by glacial ice.[43] As a result of their unceasing activities, Glacier Park has assumed an aspect materially different from its appearance at the conclusion of the overthrust.

Weathering, the slow action of wind, rain and frost, is constantly at work, doing its bit to wear down the rocks wherever exposed. Water is a potent factor in this process. In combination with oxygen, it causes oxidation of rock surfaces; in combination with sub-freezing temperatures, it seeps into crevices, freezes and expands, thereby cracking off small fragments. Even above-freezing temperatures, aided by penetration of moisture, will cause thin layers of rock to flake off through making its surface expand and contract more than its interior. Other disintegrative agents are lichens secreting acids that affect rock surfaces, and roots that creep into small crevices and eventually pry the adjacent rock segments apart. A gradual disintegration of even the staunchest and most massive rocks is thus carried on is an imperceptible way by the elements.[44]

The Shaping Of The Valleys

A much more powerful sculptor of mountainous terrain is running water, which has been more than ordinarily busy in Glacier Park. It has taken an energetic hand in sharpening the relief of the region, and every valley in the Park is in large part the handiwork of some industriously eroding stream.[45]

The successive invasions of the Ice Age completed the task. Repeatedly, vast ice masses buried the region for untold eons, carving and grinding their way down the slopes, enlarging adolescent river valleys, exposing the brilliant hues of the softer shales, but deviating to avoid the firm resistance of the immovable limestones. These rivers of ice smoothly gouged out the once V-shaped stream ravines into their present U-shaped bottoms. They excavated the colossal cirques which have made Glacier famous; they scooped out the basins that cradle scores of lakes. They were responsible for the rugged cliffs and aretes that form such a spectacular part of the Glacier scenery.[46]

Revelation In Rock

Although it still cannot be regarded as a final result, Nature's handiwork in the Park represents a scenic masterpiece. It offers the sensational in its enormous cirques and sawtoothed crests, and presents a phenomenal spectacle in its brilliantly painted shales and tinted limestones. Looking downward, the beds of the swift flowing brooks are bottomed with pebbles of red, green and yellow, and even the macadamized roadways of some of the interior valleys will be found, upon closer inspection, to contain the same colorful rock fragmentation.

Looking upward, unbelievably beautiful vistas of rock coloring lie in every direction. Strata of pink argillite, weathered to madder, mauve and crimson border on grey-green shales. Great mountains of yellow rock, weathered every ochre shade from pale buff to sienna, rival even the glistening glaciers as dazzling spectacles. Titanic masses of grey limestone bear across their bosoms the searing scar of the jet black diorite ribbon. A thousand views of garnet, amber and sea-green meet the eye, harmonizing with the blue of sky and lake, and the deep greens of forested valleys and slopes.

Today the product of earth's great forces is ready for our inspection. Ocean, ice, wind and water have wrought and carved in strange fancy; even mountains have been moved. With the passing of the centuries, many of the birthmarks have been covered over by the luxuriant garb of pines, flowers and kindred vegetation that flourishes up to timberline. An added meaning awaits those who hold the key to Glacier's revelation in rock, for every glimpse of pinnacle wall or sculptured cirque recalls the glaciers of old, and every view of perpendicular precipice or fantastically colored mountain walls brings to mind the miracle of the Lewis Overthrust.

Notes for Chapter 2

[1]For a complete and authentic story of the Park's creation, see "Rocks, Ice And Water, The Geology of Waterton-Glacier Park," by David D. Alt and Donald W. Hyndman, published in 1973 by Mountain Press Publishing Company in cooperation with the Glacier Natural History Association; also "The Geologic Story Of Glacier National Park," by James L. Dyson, published by the Glacier Natural History Association.

[2]"The Geologic Story," supra, at page 2.

[3]Idem, at page 3.

[4]Idem, at page 14.

[5]"Rocks, Ice And Water," supra, at pages 22-23,

[6]Idem, at page 25.

[7]"The Geologic Story," supra, at page 4.

[8]Idem, at page 5.

[9]Idem, at page 5. These relative positions may be reversed wherever the Lewis Overthrust, discussed at pages 21-22 of this chapter, has forced older rocks to override younger ones.

[10]These formations (referred to in geological terminology as "stratigraphic units") were named by Bailey Willis, then geologist for the United States Geological Survey, in an article entitled "Stratigraphy And Structure, Lewis And Livingston Ranges, Montana," published on November 15, 1902 in the Bulletin of the Geological Society of America, Vol. 13, pages 305-352. He had incorporated the same material in an address delivered before the Society on January 1, 1902.

In following this procedure, Willis was conforming to geological protocol (according to a letter dated August 16, 1973 from Robert Horodyski, Professor of Geology at the University of California at Los Angeles), under which the geologist who first works on the geology of a region chooses the names of formations from among those of nearby geographic features, and formalizes them by publication in an appropriate journal, book or report. Name derivations for the formations in Glacier were as follows:

Altyn—from the old mining town at the foot of Canyon Creek.

Appekunny—from Appekunny Mountain.

Grinnell—from Mt. Grinnell.

Siyeh—from Mt. Siyeh.

Shepard—from Shepard Glacier.

Kintla—from the Kintla Lakes.

[11]"The Geologic Story," supra, at page 7.

[12]Idem, at page 7.

[13]Idem, at pages 7 and 8.

[14]Idem, at page 8.

[15]Idem, at page 9.

[16]Idem, at page 10.

[17]Idem, at page 10.

[18]Idem, at page 10.

[19]The Purcell Sill is described at pages 15-16 of "Rocks, Ice And Water," supra. See, also, "The Geologic Story," supra, at pages 11 and 12.

[20]"The Geologic Story," supra, at page 12. In reference to the radiometric dating, see "Rocks, Ice And Water," supra, at page 16. Since approximately 9,000 feet of sedimentary rock had already been deposited prior to the diorite intrusion of 1,080,000,000 years ago, it would appear that some of these rocks may well be two billion years old or older.

[21]"Rocks, Ice And Water," supra, at page 15.

[22]Idem, at page 15.

[23]"The Geologic Story," supra, at page 11.

[24]Idem, at page 11.

[25]Idem, at page 13.

[26]Idem, at page 13. See, also, "Rocks, Ice And Water," supra, at page 14.

[27]Idem. For more about these mines, see Chapter 11, infra, entitled "Advent Of The White Man," at page 96, Chapter 20, infra, entitled " 'Ankle Excursions' Out Of Many Glacier," at pages 163-164, and Chapter 23, infra, entitled "People Problems," at pages 184-185.

[28]"Rocks, Ice And Water," supra, at pages 7 and 8. See, also, "The Geologic Story," supra, at page 9.

[29]This information supplied by Robert Horodyski, Professor of Geology at the University of California at Los Angeles by letter of August 16, 1973. See, also, "The Geologic Story," supra, at page 9.

[30]"The Geologic Story," supra, at pages 9-10.

[31]Idem, at page 9.

[32]Idem, at pages 3 and 14.

[33]Idem, at page 14.

[34]Idem, at page 14.

[35]Idem, at page 14.

[36]"Rocks, Ice And Water," supra, at page 23.

[37]Idem, at pages 21-23. See, also, "The Geologic Story," supra, at page 14.

[38]"The Geologic Story," supra, at page 16. Marius Campbell, at page 30 of his treatise on "Origin Of the Scenic Features Of Glacier National Park," estimated that the extent of the movement was "at least 15 miles." Dyson, in "The Geologic Story," estimates it to have been "at least 20 miles," while Alt and Hyndman, in "Rocks, Ice And Water," at page 23, place it at "probably more than 30 miles." At page 94 they suggest that it was "perhaps as many as 35 miles."

[39]"The Geologic Story," supra, at page 18 (illustration at page 19).

[40]Idem, at page 18. See, also, "Rocks, Ice And Water," supra, at pages 83-84.

[41]Letter of Robert Horodyski, Professor of Geology at the University of California at Los Angeles, dated August 16, 1973.

[42]"Origin Of The Scenic Features Of Glacier National Park," supra, at pages 30-31.

[43]Idem, at pages 31-41. See, also, "Rocks, Ice And Water," supra, at pages 39-61.

[44]"Rocks, Ice And Water," supra, at pages 46-47.

[45]Idem, at pages 55-58.

[46]Idem, at pages 27-38.

Falls near Avalanche Lake
Photo by Hedrich-Blessing, courtesy of Burlington Northern

Mt. Cleveland above Cosley (Crossley) Lake
Photo by Walt Dyke, courtesy of the Burlington Northern

Chapter 3
PEAKS AND PINNACLES

Few of us are immune to the mysterious call of the mountains, a magnet that draws tens of thousands annually to Glacier National Park. However great their appreciation and enjoyment of its mountain architecture, their reactions and impressions tend to reflect rather characteristically their individual backgrounds and interests. For the day-to-day sightseer, for example, it is spectacular and awe-inspiring. The geologist may call it unusual and fascinating. From the standpoint of the mountaineer, the key adjectives are "distinctive," "massive," and "great;"[1] while the poet or connoisseur of alpine scenery may resort to such terms as "infinite variety" or "personality."

Not unexpectedly, of course, it is the impressions and descriptions of those in the "connoisseur category" that usually prove to be the most colorful and interesting, not to say the most vivid and picturesque. Earliest scenic authority to visit this rugged area was George Bird Grinnell, whose love affair with the region, begun in 1885, drew him back to it summer after summer for many years, and who wrote:

"Here are mountains higher than those of the Yosemite. Some are rounded, and some are square-topped, some are slender pinnacles, and others knife-edged and with jagged crests, each a true sierra."[2]

Variety of form and contour is indeed a major source of the eye appeal of Glacier's peaks. Irregular in outline, fantastic in shape, they present a magnificent skyline from almost any point in the Park. They also have two other characteristics in common — the abruptness with which they rise from plains or valley floor below, and the elusive fascination of their unusual coloration. Never does one see them twice the same. Under constantly changing atmospheric conditions they vary their hues from light blue to deep purple, from brilliant red to faint rose, softened by the rich green foliage of the lower levels.

Why The Mountains Are Different

The mountains of Glacier are peculiarly precipitous. They have been produced by a different kind of geology than others with which they may be compared, such as the broad-based mountains of Colorado, the narrow desert ranges of Utah, whose slopes are scored by hundreds of ravines, or the single-crested Sierra. On each of these, Nature, the great sculptress, working with her tools, the elements, has with light touch engraved to the music of brooks or cut boldly to the tumult of a torrent.

In Glacier, on the other hand, as in the Selkirks, the Cascade Range and the Yosemite, glaciers have sunk their icy fingers deeply into the mountains' heart. Rarely are the forms carved by river and rivulet brought into such striking contrast with those sculptured by ice as in the mountains of northwestern Montana. Westward from the North Fork of the Flathead River (Glacier's western boundary), the valleys lie open to the sun, which early slants down the slopes and lingers on them until the shadows are long.

Eastward from the North Fork profound canyons lead into the mountains, and others equally deep lead out to the great plains. Their summit is double, parted by a high valley from which deeply sunken glacial channels lead northward through Waterton Lakes and southwestward through Lake McDonald. Precipices Yosemite can scarcely rival close the heads of these canyons and tower above laticlets lying where only the sunlight of summer noon may reach the snows that chill them. Back to back, each curving about its amphitheatre, the great cliffs rise, while between them run the goathaunted ledges and crags of such aretes as the Garden Wall and the Pinnacle Wall, with their deep, sun-protected recesses serving as vast receptacles for inevitable masses of winter-accumulated snow.

The Ranges And The Divide

Nature's prodigality in the area being what it is, Glacier's mountains are a part of, not one, but two massive ranges. From boundary to boundary, along the eastern side, towers the great front range, with such giants as Jackson, Stimson, Siyeh, Going-To-The-Sun, Gould, Wilbur and Cleveland. This is the Lewis Range, so named for the intrepid Lewis and Clark captain who was among the earliest visitors to the region.[3] On the west side, rising full-blown in majestic Heaven's Peak, is a second range, the Livingston, that climaxes en route to Canada in the fantastic horns of Kintla and Kinnerly and the breath-taking Hole-in-the-Wall country. Both ranges were given their names by Bailey Willis, geologist for the United States Geological Survey, following his study of the area in 1901.[4]

The natural barrier of the continental divide separates the Park into roughly equal parts, with the eastern side presenting the more dramatic effects. There the summits rise steeply from the plains like a fortress of the gods complete with battlements, salients and prominent outposts. At sunset, from the plains, each sharp-cut peak lifts its craggy summit, "a looming bastion fringed with fire," against the evening sky.[5] As the continental divide passes over the bridge of Flattop Mountain to the Livingston Range and moves, by a series of spectacular peaks and passes, into Canada, it there serves also as the dividing line between Alberta and British Columbia.

Mountains With Personality

Those who write about Glacier are sometimes hard put for words to describe the unique quality of its alpine country. The term "personality" may never before have been applied to such inanimate objects as mountains, but it has more than once been pressed into service by writers trying to convey adequately their impressions of the Glacier Park Rockies. As one author put it, their personality is attributable to "the different genius of Glacier's mountains, and the unusual geology that creates the impression of mountains that seem to be marching; or rather seem to have been checked and frozen in the midst of a lateral movement."[6]

Actually the charisma of Glacier's alpine landscape is to be ascribed to a number of distinctive features. The impression of "marching" mountains is attributable to the tilting at an angle of layers of shale and limestone — a tilting which, in some cases, has been carried to the point where the strata are virtually standing on end in colossal and graceful curves. Equally prominent are the horizontal bands, both dark and light, that move symmetrically across the faces of so many of the cliffs and peaks at an elevation of about 7500 feet. Another striking and characteristic feature is the pyramidal or Mayan-temple shape into which the ancient glaciers have carved a number of the region's more spectacular peaks and horns.

Glamorous Going-To-The-Sun

The matter of "personality" extends, also, to some of the Park's individual peaks. Many of them possess outstanding charm and individuality, such as Sinopah in the Two Medicine Valley, Gould and Wilbur in the Many Glacier area, and Heaven's Peak in the McDonald Valley. But if Glacier has one mountain which, more than any other, may be said to be endowed with personality, it is Going-To-The-Sun, overwhelming in its magnificence. From its 9,594-foot summit one may look almost straight down, nearly a mile, into Lake St. Mary. Its impressiveness stems from its massive and cathedral-like symmetry, and the man who named it says he did so "because of its imposing uplift into the blue."[7]

The beauty of this majestic peak has inspired more than one writer to lyric expression. The poet, Vachel Lindsay, who spent part of a summer tramping through the Park, told of his experiences in a little book he called "Going-To-The-Sun."[8] In it he wrote:

"The mountain peak called 'Going-To-The-Sun'
   In Glacier Park
Is the most gorgeous one,
   And when the sun comes down to it, it glows
With emerald and rose."

Its splendor a few years later reminded Margaret Thompson[9] of Byron's song of Mont Blanc:

"Monarch of mountains;
   They crowned him long ago
On a throne of rocks, in a robe of clouds,
   With a diadem of snow."

Lewis Range Landmark

Perhaps the most unusual of Glacier's many peaks is the celebrated Chief Mountain situated on the eastern side of the Lewis Range, only a few miles south of the Canadian border. Its more than 9000-foot bulk looms high above the plains to the east, a landmark known all over the Northwest. Standing alone before the main line of peaks, the Chief looks like a warrior leading his hosts into battle.

Geologically, Chief Mountain is unique and has been described as a "mountain without roots." It is composed of a single block of limestone, known to geologists as the Altyn Formation. It reached its present eastward position by reason of the great Lewis Overthrust. Standing on a foundation of much newer rock, it is the oldest of the several geological formations to be found in the Park and one of the most durable, hence its sturdy resistance to weathering and erosion.

The plains Indians called it "The Chief" and all of them used it as a guide in their travels back and forth from what is now Canada. To white men, it was originally known as "King Mountain," and it was shown by that name on the earliest map of the region, published in London in 1795.[10] It appeared as "The King" on a map forwarded by Captain Meriwether Lewis to President Jefferson from Fort Mandan on April 7, 1805.[11]

The mountain was sacred to the Blackfeet, as well as the Kootenais and Flatheads. According to James Willard Schultz, youths of the Blackfeet tribes frequently climbed to its summit, there to fast and pray and, by a vision or dream, to obtain a sacred helper, a protector along the dangerous trail of life.[12]. On the other hand, when the first ascent of the mountain by a white man was made in 1892 by Henry L. Stimson, later a noted American statesman, one of his two companions was Billy Fox, a full-blooded member of the Piegan branch of the Blackfeet Nation. According to Stimson, Fox became the first of his tribe ever to make the ascent. His conclusion was based upon Fox's story that only one Piegan had attempted to climb the mountain, this happening years before when one of the youngest of a tribal hunting party declared that he would go to the summit. His companions watched him as he disappeared from sight on the ledges high above, but he was never seen again; and thereafter the superstitious Piegans avoided any close acquaintance with the Chief.[13]

Legend has it, however, that a young Flathead warrior who later became a great chief, did climb to the summit of the peak to fast and pray, lugging with him a buffalo skull for use as a headrest, hoping that it might help with the "vision" he sought. When he departed, he left the skull on the mountain.[14] Authenticity was given to this legend by Stimson who reported the finding of an ancient, almost decomposed bison skull on the summit.[15]

Interesting Sequel

Twenty-one years after his 1892 visit, Stimson returned to what had become Glacier Park and resolved to climb Chief Mountain again. At an off-the-trail spot not far from the base of the peak, he chanced to meet two campers who had just returned from its summit. With them, as he learned in conversation, they had brought an ancient buffalo skull—the same one he had seen in 1892. When he told them the legend of how the skull had been brought to the mountain by a Flathead warrior, they turned it over to him for replacement on the peak. When he had climbed the Chief by its western approach the next day, he took care to place it in an obscure spot among the rocks on the summit, and recent climbers do not report having seen it.[16]

Most remarkable of the Park's mountains from a topographical standpoint, although unknown to Blackfeet legend or history is Triple Divide Peak, located on the continental divide about seven airline miles south of Upper Lake St. Mary. While not particularly lofty, at 8,000 feet above sea level, it has the distinction, unique in the United States,[17] of channeling the precipitation which it receives to three different and distant oceans. The melting snows of its western slope drain into the Pacific branch of Nyack Creek, the Middle Fork of the Flathead River, and ultimately into the Pacific by way of the Columbia. The drainage from its northeastern slopes is taken by Hudson Bay and Red Eagle Creeks to the St. Mary Lakes and River, and ultimately to Hudson Bay. The rains that fall on its southeastern side form Atlantic Creek, one of the headwaters of Cut Bank Creek, and through Marias River and the Missouri, reach the Gulf of Mexico weeks or months later. It has fittingly been called a three-ocean peak.

Outlook From Above

Going-To-The-Sun, Chief and Triple Divide are but three of the 185 named peaks within the 1500 square miles of Glacier National Park. Six of the latter rise more than 10,000 feet above sea level, these being Cleveland, 10,448; Stimson, 10,165; Kintla, 10,110; Jackson, 10,033; Siyeh, 10,014 and Merritt, 10,004. There are nine additional peaks between the heights of 9,800 and 10,000; 34 peaks in the 9,000-9,800 category; 89 between 8,000 and 9,000; 37 between 7,000 and 8,000; and 10 between 6,000 and 7,000 feet. These are only the peaks with names, and the list does not include the high ridges, escarpments and connecting rock walls between the taller peaks that in some cases exceed 8,000 feet above sea level.

The views from many of the summits are breath-taking. Extremely rewarding are those from Mts. Jackson, Siyeh, Clements, Gould and especially Cleveland. From the vantage point of the latter's 10,448-foot summit there is visible on a clear day nearly every peak in the Park. To the east the view extends to the Sweetgrass Hills, 100 miles away. To the immediate north, some 6,000 feet below, lies beautiful Waterton Lake, with the town of Waterton and the Prince of Wales Hotel visible at its Canadian end. Far to the northwest are the peaks of the Canadian rockies, including the spire-like horn of Mt. Assiniboine, west of Calgary.[18]

Glacial Architecture

In describing Glacier's peaks, Grinnell used the work "sierra' which, in the parlance of the mountaineering world, refers to mountains with serrated or sawtooth summits. Mountaineering and geological jargon also includes such other terms as "massif," "gendarme," "cirque," "arete" and "horn," each used to denote an unusual rock formation or type of mountain configuration, and each useful in undertaking any description of the Park's peaks, cliffs and rocky eminences.

In reference to Glacier, horns, aretes and cirques are of particular interest, not only because they make a unique contribution to the spectacular quality of its mountain scenery, but also because each has been the handiwork of ancient glacial action. A working glacier, given sufficient time, gouges out a part of the rock wall behind it, thereby creating a cirque, or natural amphitheater. Where two glaciers work toward each other from opposite sides of a range or ridge, their counter-activity produces an arete, or sharp-crested ridge; if continued to the point where the ridge has been worn through, the result is a col, or saddle, between the adjacent higher elevations. When ancient glaciers have been in action on three or more sides of a peak, their combined erosion eventually produces a sharp-pointed, pyramidal-type shape, appropriately referred to as an horn.

All of these products of prehistoric glacial activity are on display in the Park, combining to create a distinctive type of montane environment. Among the classic cirques are those at Iceberg Lake and the Grinnell Glacier, as well as those at Avalanche Lake and in the area of Sperry Glacier. Typical horns are Mts. St. Nicholas, Clements, Kinnerly and Reynolds. Characteristic aretes are the ruggedly serrated Garden Wall and Pinnacle Wall, both visible from the Many Glacier Hotel. Prime examples of massifs are Mts. Gould, Siyeh and Cleveland.

Conquest Of The Peaks

While the popularity of mountain climbing has been on the rise throughout the country in recent years, Glacier Park has a special allure for those with interest in this thrilling sport. Its mountains are massive, many of the climbs are difficult and challenging, and there are a number of spires and horns that were at one time considered unclimbable. Moreover, it presents a somewhat different type of climbing problems, because of the species of rock in-

Mt. Wilbur from the Ptarmigan Tunnel
Photo by Walt Dyke, courtesy of Burlington Northern

Going-To-The-Sun Mountain above Upper Lake St. Mary

Photo by Kabel

volved, than are to be encountered in the Tetons of Wyoming, the North Cascades of Washington, or the Swiss Alps.[19]

Among the earliest climbers were James Willard Schultz, Raphael Pumpelly, Henry L. Stimson, Lyman B. Sperry and George Bird Grinnell, all destined to make their marks in other fields. Schultz climbed and named Flattop Mountain (East) in 1882.[20] Pumpelly climbed a mountain in 1883 which he believed to have been Mt. Stimson.[21] Stimson himself made the first ascents of Blackfoot and Chief Mountains in 1892, and Little Chief Mountain in 1894. Sperry climbed Gunsight Mountain in 1895 or 1806 and placed a register there.[22] Grinnell, accompanied by J. B. Monroe, climbed Mt. Jackson in 1897, and ascended nearby Blackfoot Mountain in 1898.[23]

Many peaks were scaled by members of the United State Geological Survey teams in connection with official mapping of the area that

is now the Park. Among these were Francois E. Matthes, whose ascents, among others in the years 1900-1901, included Chief, Little Chief, Red Eagle, Pinchot and Blackfoot. A later survey crew member, Robert H. Chapman, in the years preceding 1919, climbed Mt. Carter and several other peaks, including Vulture, Kintla and Rainbow.[24]

During the summers of 1923 and 1924, Norman Clyde, the well-known mountaineer, climbed some 60 peaks, at least ten of these being first ascents (the latter including Sinopah, Norris, Logan, Clements, Cannon and Wilbur.) His 1924 conquests included Merritt, Guardhouse, Sentinel, Cleveland, Allen, Red Eagle, Going-To-The-Sun, Gould and Siyeh.[25]

Visits By Mountaineering Organizations

On a number of occasions the Park has received group visitations by climbing organizations, including the Seattle Mountaineers in 1914, 1934 and 1952, the Nature Study Club of Indiana on at least two occasions during the 1920's, the Mazamas from Portland, Oregon in 1936 and again in the early 1950's, and the Colorado Mountain Club in 1958. The many visits of the Sierra Club of California began in 1924 (210 in the group) and were repeated in 1937, 1954, 1955, 1957 and 1968. On all of these occasions, scores of ascents were made, including a number by women.[26]

During the visits of the Nature Study Club of Indiana, they left registers in flat boxes on a number of peaks, including Mt. Gould, Mt. Reynolds, Mt. Jackson, Edwards Mountain, Chief Mountain and Mt. Grinnell. The president of the Club, Dr. Frank B. Wynn, died in an attempt to climb Mt. Siyeh on July 27, 1922. Subsequently, in his honor, a peak in the Many Glacier area which had originally been given the name of Point Mountain by George Bird Grinnell in the early 1890's was renamed Mt. Wynn.[27]

Dean Of Glacier Park Climbers

Without any question the man who knows more than any other about the mountains of Glacier Park, and how they should be climbed, is J. Gordon Edwards, professor of entomology at the California State University, San Jose. Edwards gained most of his intimate knowledge of the Park's high country during the nine years which he spent there as a seasonal ranger and park naturalist. His ascents have comprised eighty or more of the Park's 185 named peaks, some of which he has climbed by varying routes. On many of his ascents he has been accompanied by his wife Alice who has climbed all of the 10,000-foot mountains in the Park, as well as many of the lesser ones.

It is the great good fortune of all mountaineers that Edwards has taken the time and trouble to put much of his valuable information concerning the mountains of Glacier into the form of a book entitled "A Climber's Guide To Glacier National Park." Published by the Sierra Club of California, with a helpful foreword by the Club's executive director, it contains not only climbing route diagrams, general and area maps, skyline drawings of all the major summit views, and nearly 50 pages of photographs of the mountains in Glacier by renowned photographers, but it has been prefaced by the author with a history of climbing in the Park, as well as a description of the rock formations, a classification of the

climbs, and instructions in reference to every phase of safety, all with special reference to the mountains of Glacier Park.[28]

Suitability For Climbing

Glacier Park is one of the mountain areas profoundly affected by the craze for climbing which has been sweeping the country.[29] It used to be considered that these mountains were not entirely suitable for climbing because their sedimentary rocks were too ancient to be safe; that their **sheer** cliffs could rarely be climbed with safety because pitons would be of relatively little value and rappels not often practicable.[30] This idea is no longer regarded as valid, since it has been found that the sheer cliffs do take certain kinds of pitons well, and even the great faces of Gould and Cleveland have thus been scaled.[31] Such sheer walls do, however, demand greater caution and much more skill than the more solid rock faces of Yosemite or the Grand Tetons.

The rock is not always firm, but unsound cliffs can usually be avoided and the ascent continued by way of interesting chimneys, couloirs or more solid rock cliffs nearby.[32] Moreover, the records indicate that where normal safety precautions have been observed, climbing in Glacier is no more hazardous than in other western mountains.[33] On the other hand, the magnificent panoramas and awesome precipices of these rugged Rockies easily surpass those elsewhere in the United States, thereby compensating for any scarcity of uninterrupted faces of "solid" rock.[34]

As for the quality of the challenge posed by the peaks of Glacier, the Sierra Club climbers who conquered Mt. Cleveland in 1924 wrote in the register which they placed upon its summit: "The consensus of opinion was that the ascent of Mt. Cleveland involves all the difficulties of the Red Kaweah, Mt. Whitney and Mt. Shasta combined."[35]

Hazards And Rewards

That the peaks of Glacier can be places of great danger when climbing is undertaken under unfavorable conditions and in the face of sound advice to the contrary was underscored by the catastrophe which befell five young climbers who undertook to scale Mt. Cleveland during Christmas week of 1969.[36] The exact cause of the tragedy will never be known, since the bodies were not recovered until the following summer; but it lends new emphasis to the respect with which these mountains should be regarded, and the vital need for equating mountaineering experience and skills with the hazards of weather and climbing conditions peculiar to this region.

For those prepared to cope with mountaineering problems, and willing to proceed with all due care, the rewards are extraordinary. In addition to the spectacular and beautiful views from the summit, there is a special allure for those who would seek out the trail-less routes to the high cirques, the rugged aretes and the magnificent peaks where time seems to stand still. And finally, there is the challenge to pit one's skill and endurance on dizzy heights where few have stood before.

Notes For Chapter 3

[1]"A Climber's Guide to Glacier National Park," By J. Gordon Edwards, at page 8.

[2]Article entitled "The Crown Of The Continent" by George Bird Grinnell, appearing in the Century Magazine for Sept. 1901, at page 660.

[3]Article by Bailey Willis entitled "Stratigraphy And Structure, Lewis And Livingston Ranges," published in 1902 in Volume 13 of the Geological Society of American Bulletin, at pages 311-313.

[4]Willis indicated in the article cited in the previous note that he was naming the western range "Livingston," since he understood that this was the name given to its continuation on the Canadian side of the line. It bore this name until 1933 when the United States Board On Geographis Names changed it to "Livingstone," presumably because that was the spelling used by Lt. Blakiston of the Palliser Expedition when he named a Canadian range in that area in 1858. However, it has since been determined that the southern end of the Canadian "Livingstone" range lies more than 27 miles north of the international boundary (see page 7 of article by Clyde P. Ross entitled "Geology of Glacier National Park and the Flathead Region Northwestern Montana," published in 1959 by the U.S. Government Printing Office). Based upon this information and the facts that "Livingston" was the name actually conferred by Willis and in general use for more than 30 years thereafter, this author recommended deletion of the terminal "e"; and on February 12, 1974 the Board reversed its prior ruling and restored the name to "Livingston."

[5]Article entitled "Along The Northwest Boundary" by Bailey Willis, appearing in "World's Work" for July, 1902, at page 2336.

[6]From "The National Parks," by Freeman Tilden, at pages 281-282.

[7]In a letter dated May 20, 1929 to the Glacier National Park Naturalist, James Willard Schultz wrote: "I myself named Going-To-The-Sun Mountain; simply because of its imposing uplift into the blue."

[8]Published by C. D. Appleton & Company, **circa** 1923.

[9]From "High Trails Of Glacier National Park," by Margaret Thompson, at page 148. The quotation is from Byron's dramatic poem entitled "Manfred," being the opening lines from the "Voice Of The Second Spirit."

[10]This was Arrowsmith's "Map of all the New Discoveries in North America," based upon information supplied by Peter Fidler, a Northwest Company employee, who had wintered with the Piegans, just east of the Rockies in 1792. See "Oregon and California," by Robert Greenhow, published in 1845, at page 265; also "Through The Years in Glacier National Park," by Donald H. Robinson, at page 7.

[11]A copy of the Lewis map of 1805 is included as an appendix to the modern edition of Elliott Coues' 3-volume "History of the Expedition Under the Command of Lewis and Clark." Lewis is known to have had a copy of the Arrowsmith map, and undoubtedly borrowed from it extensively, since his 1805 map, prepared before he reached Montana, included such features as "The King." As pointed out by several authors, Fidler's information was later discovered to be inaccurate in various respects. See "Oregon And California," supra, at page 265 (footnote), and "The Lewis And Clark Expedition," by Grace Flandrau, at page 29. This accounts for the fact that "The King" is shown on Lewis' map as being north of the 49th parallel, rather than south of it.

[12]See "Signposts Of Adventure," by James Willard Schultz, at page 181. In "Blackfeet And Buffalo," at pages 320-337, Schultz has related a tale of bison skulls on Chief Mountain told him by Ahko Pitsu, a notable historian of the three Blackfeet tribes, about a warrior named Miah who climbed the Chief in quest of a vision, taking a buffalo skull with him for a pillow and finding two other skulls there when he arrived. Schultz's preface to the tale refers to Stimson's ascent of the peak, but errs as to the date, which he thought to be 1902, instead of 1892, as to Stimson's companions whom he stated were William H. Seward III and an Indian guide named Paioto Satsiko (instead of Dr. W. B. James and an Indian named Billy Fox), and as to their having found three skulls there (rather than one). For Stimson's own story, see note 13, immediately following.

[13]"The Ascent Of Chief Mountain," by Henry L. Stimson, first appeared in "Hunting In Many Lands," published in

Mt. Kinnerly above Kintla Lake—highest peak in the park from water's edge

Photo by Hileman

1895 by Forest And Stream Publishing Company, New York. The article was reprinted in the 1948 edition of the "Drivers" Manual (see note 15, Chapter 6, infra).

[14]For a later and more complete report, see pages 53-69 of Stimson's privately printed book entitled "My Vacations."

[15]Idem, at pages 63-65.

[16]Idem, at pages 66-69; see, also, "A Climber's Guide," supra, at page 76

[17]There is actually another triple divide in North America, located in Jasper National Park in Canada, and called Snow Dome. Its shining crown of ice, part of the 130 square miles of the Columbia Icefield, sends melt not only to the Atlantic and Pacific, but also to the Arctic Ocean. See article entitled "From Sun-Clad Sea To Shining Mountains," by Ralph Gray, published in the National Geographic Magazine for April, 1964, at page 586.

[18]"A Climber's Guide," supra, at page 76.

[19]Idem, at page 8.

[20]Idem, at page 30.

[21]In Volume II of "My Reminscences," by Raphael Pumpelly, at pages 638-646, the author describes his expeditions of 1882 and 1883 to Cut Bank Pass, and on page 642 tells of climbing a peak in the Nyack Valley which he believes to have been Mt. Stimson.

[22]"A Climber's Guide," supra, at page 30.

[23]Article by George Bird Grinnell in the Scientific American Supplement for September 23, 1899. See, also, "Glaciers Of Glacier National Park," by William C. Alden, published in 1914 by the Department of the Interior, footnote at page 4.

[24]"A Climber's Guide," supra, at page 31.

[25]Idem, at pages 31 and 32.

[26]Idem, at pages 33-35.

[27]Strangely, both the time and the place of Dr. Wynn's death have been the subject of misunderstanding. "Through The Years," supra, at page 121, gives the date as July 27, 1927, while "A Climber's Guide," supra, states that the tragedy took place on Point Mountain. Thorough research by John Mauff, of Chicago (letter of 4/12/74) establishes beyond peradventure of a doubt that the mountain was Siyeh and the date was July 27, 1922.

[28]The Sierra Club edition of 1966 is out of print; however, Edwards himself brought out a limited edition in 1975.

[29]Article entitled "Climbing Glacier's Massive Peaks," by J. Gordon Edwards, appearing in the Naturalist," Vol. 9, No. 2. at page 45.

[30]Idem.

[31]According to J. Gordon Edwards, author of "A Climber's Guide," supra, the former belief that Glacier's **sheer** cliffs could not be climbed with safety has been disproven. He reports that Helmuth Matdies, formerly a climbing guide in the Austrian Alps, has found cliff climbing in Glacier to be quite similar to the ascent of sheer faces in the Alps. Matdies made many such ascents in Glacier during the 1960's, most of his routes being Class 5 or Class 6 climbs, with the use of large numbers of pitons and 200 or 300 feet of rope.

[32]Article entitled "Climbing Glacier's Massive Peaks," supra, at page 45.

[33]Idem.

[34]Idem.

[35]Idem.

[36]For a more detailed story of the Mt. Cleveland tragedy, see page 181 of Chapter 23, infra, entitled "People Problems." The climb was made against the advice of Park officials.

Chief Mountain

Photo by Walt Dyke, courtesy of Burlington Northern

Chapter 4
THE MOUNTAIN PASSES

No small part of the charm of Glacier National Park is to be found in the variety, the fascination and the relative accessibility of its many mountain passes. These are features which make Glacier unique among our national parks and, perhaps, in all the world. Among the score or more saddles situated within its borders are the only triple divide pass on the continent,[1] and the only pass with a saddle horse tunnel for its "summit,"[2] not to mention the continental divide pass with the most gorgeous transmountain highway in North America.[3] Astride its southern boundary is another pass so unique in character as to require a separate chapter properly to tell its story.[4]

From the days when Alexander marched through the Khyber Pass into India,[5] and when Hannibal with his elephants surged over the Alps into Italy,[6] mountain passes have made history. In our own country they played a prominent role in the winning of the West, as adventurous pioneers surmounted every obstacle from Cumberland Gap[7] to Chilkoot Pass[8] in their eager pursuit of the American dream. Even the forbidding barriers of the Rockies and the Sierra did not stem the persistent tide; and their passes, often lofty and sometimes elusive, were located and put to use.

Eventually some of these great passes became a kind of symbol of the indomitable pioneer spirit. Tinged with an aura of adventure, romance, and occasionally tragedy,[9] they were interwoven into fiction and history alike, and became a part of local folklore as well as the westerns of the cinema. But nowhere, it would seem have they contributed more of interest and pleasure than in Glacier National Park.

Definition And Discovery

A pass is a narrow route across a mountain barrier by way of a relatively low notch or depression.[10] The terms "col" and "pass" have at times been used interchangeably to describe the notch or depression itself, sometimes called a "saddle." They are not entirely synonymous, however, since the term "pass," in its broader significance, refers not only to the saddle as such, but also to the trail or road which runs over it, usually providing a convenient connection between two valleys or key points on opposite sides of the range or ridge.

Some cols or saddles have been the result of long continued erosion by two ancient glaciers working back to back on opposite sides of a ridge or range.[11] Passes in Glacier Park that have been produced in this fashion include Logan, Piegan, Gunsight, Red Eagle and Stoney Indian. Others, such as Marias, simply lead over the broad headland that separates two valleys with rivers flowing in opposite directions.

Among mountain men there is an old saying, tinged with truth and humor, that —

> "The deer made the first trails; the elk followed the deer, the buffalo the elk, and the Indians the buffalo; after the Indians came the trapper, then an army officer came along and discovered a pass."[12]

In reference to Glacier Park, the saying calls for some amendment and comment. The first trailmakers in its valleys were probably the deer, the elk, and to a limited extent, the buffalo; but the pioneering of its early game trails above timberline was unquestionably the work of Rocky Mountain sheep and goats. And although, in fact, some of its passes were "discovered" by army officers,[13] it is certain that several of them had been in use by local tribes for centuries before the advent of the white man.

Crossing The Divide

The journey by trail over one of Glacier's high mountain passes can be a fascinating experience, expecially if it be over the continental divide. For the traveler of today, no matter how seasoned or inured to mountain grandeur, the crossing of such a pass on foot or by horseback rarely fails to product a reaction of awe or ecstasy, or a thrilling combination of both, the degree depending, of course, upon each individual's background and experience. For the tenderfoot, a mountain pass may be, as it was for Mary Roberts Rinehart on her first visit to the Park in 1915,

"... the highest place between two peaks ... a barrier which you climb with chills and descend with prayer ... a thing which you try to forget at the time and which you boast about when you get home."[14]

From mountain authority John Muir, on the other hand, comes the following advice:

"Few places in the world are more dangerous than home. Fear not, therefore, to try the mountain passes. They kill care, save you from deadly apathy, and call forth every faculty into vigorous, enthusiastic action."

The Passes Of Glacier Park Generally

With 185 named peaks in the Park, plus other lesser ones, it might seem that there could be nearly that many saddles between them. Actually, however, the number of named passes within Park boundaries does not exceed 25, ranging geographically from Firebrand and Dawson on the south to Brown and Boulder in the Park's northwesterly sector. Of these, the best known are Logan, Swiftcurrent, Gunsight and Piegan, all but the latter located on the continental divide. At 7186 feet above sea level, Swiftcurrent is the loftiest of these three divide saddles; yet, interestingly, all three are exceeded in elevation by most of the non-divide passes in the Park.

Several of the Park's passes have been in use from prehistoric times as transmountain routes in the form of ancient Indian or game trails. This was the case with Swiftcurrent, Marias, Brown and Logan, as well as Stoney Indian, Ahern, Red Eagle and the original Cut Bank Pass. As the Indians ceased to make use of the future Park region in the waning years of the 19th century, most of their old routes fell into disuse; and by the time the Park was created in 1910, the only passes that could be crossed by serviceable trails were Swiftcurrent and Gunsight.[15]

Swiftcurrent Pass

The Pass was given its name by George Bird Grinnell when he first visited that area in 1887.[16] Long before that, however, an Indian trail had connected the upper McDonald Valley with Swiftcurrent Valley on the eastern side of the Lewis Range. It first became an artery of travel for the paleface in 1883 when Mrs. Nat Collins, operator of a mine on Cattle Queen Creek west of the continental divide, had a crew work over the old Indian trail across the pass to make it possible for supplies to reach her claim.[17] The trail again saw service in the early 1890's when supplies for the prospectors on Mineral Creek on the west side of the future park went over it by pack train.

The Pass continued to be used during the first decade of the twentieth century by Forest Reserve rangers; and a projected trip over the pass in the late fall of 1907 by a party headed by Gifford Pinchot, then Chief Forester of the United States, had to be abandoned when a heavy blizzard hit them at the foot of the pass.[18] It was crossed in May, 1910 by an official of the Department of the Interior in the course of an inspection trip.[19] After the region became a national park, the trail was one of the first to be rebuilt under park appropriations. This was in 1913 when the 3½ miles of spectacular switchbacks on the east side of the pass, sometimes called the "glory trail," were constructed. It was partially relocated later, making three somewhat different routes in all.[20]

This much traveled pass connects Many Glacier Hotel and Granite Park Chalet, lying just west of the divide. It is noted for the magnificent views which it provides of the lake-studded Swiftcurrent Valley and of the erstwhile Swiftcurrent Glacier. Looming a thousand feet above its summit is Swiftcurrent Peak, easily reached by a foot trail, and affording from the fire lookout station atop the crest a magnificent panorama ranging from Mt. Jackson, Sperry Glacier, the Garden Wall and the McDonald Valley to the south and southwest, to Mt. Wilbur and Mt. Allen on the east, and Mt. Cleveland and Mt. Merritt to the north.

Gunsight Pass

Among the major passes of Glacier Park, only Gunsight was not in use as a transmountain route prior to the white man's entry into the region. With its V-shaped notch in the divide between Gunsight Mountain and Mt. Jackson, this saddle presents the classic profile of a col. It was discovered in 1891 by George Bird Grinnell who named it for its resemblance to the rear sight of a rifle.[21]

No trail crossed its summit, however, until 1903 when one was completed from Lake McDonald to the east side of the Pass, the work being done by University of Minnesota students during the summers of 1902 and 1903 under the supervision of Professor Lyman B. Sperry with Great Northern Railway cooperation.[22] As of today, Going-To-The-Sun Road over Logan Pass carries most of the

Lone Horseman on Siyeh Pass

Photo by Hileman

traffic between Lakes St. Mary and McDonald, but Gunsight Pass is still the only practicable route for those who prefer to travel by trail.

Situated on the continental divide at 7010 feet of elevation, Gunsight Pass is considered by many to be the Park's most attractive because of the incomparable view in either direction. To the east lie the shining waters of Gunsight Lake; to the west, the equally beautiful Lake Ellen Wilson. To the south the sheer walls of Mt. Jackson rise 3,000 feet, the glaciers on its southern and southeasterly flanks being invisible from the Pass. For hikers, the stone shelter cabin and cold spring on the very summit of the Pass make an especially attractive place for lunch or overnight stops.

Passes Of The Northwest

Tucked away in the remote northern and northwestern sectors of the Park are a number of passes of beauty and historic interest. Some 14 miles nearly due west of the American end of Waterton Lake is Brown Pass, flanked by Mt. Chapman on the north and Thunderbird

Mountain to the south. It is located on the continental divide at an elevation of 6510 feet, and provides a relatively low-level, yet spectacular, trail connection to Bowman Lake, as well as to the Kintla Lakes on the western slopes of the rugged Livingston Range. As a matter of fact, the trails divide on the summit of the Pass, with that to Upper Kintla Lake heading for Boulder Pass (7910 feet) less than six miles to the northwest, via the great basin of the Hole-in-the-Wall Cirque. To the west of Brown Pass are the amazingly wild and beautiful cirques at the head of Bowman Lake, while to the south lies the Thunderbird Glacier, easily reached from the Pass itself.

Brown Pass was named for John George "Kootenai" Brown, a legendary character who served as the first forest ranger in charge of Canada's Kootenay Lakes Forest Reserve in 1910, as well as acting superintendent when it became Waterton Lakes National Park in 1911. A world-traveled soldier of fortune, Brown had first glimpsed the Waterton area in 1865,[23] reaching it from what is today Fort Steele,

British Columbia, by way of the South Kootenay Pass.[24] He became a permanent resident of the Waterton valley in 1877[25] and in the course of his nearly 40 years in the area spent much time as a trapper and hunter on the United States side of the border.[26] He may well have been the first white man to cross the pass which bears his name.

Stoney Indian Pass

As in the case of Brown Pass, Stoney Indian is too remote to be readily accessible to the traveling public generally; nevertheless, it is regarded by many of those who have seen it as the Park's most beautiful col. Although not on the continental divide, Stoney Indian is situated on the Lewis Range at an elevation of 7310 feet. Separating the headwaters of the Mokowanis River to the southeast from the Waterton valley, it is flanked on the south by Cathedral Peak and on the north by Stoney Indian Peaks. Beyond the latter, not more than five miles from the Pass, as the crow flies, is massive Mt. Cleveland, at 10,448 feet in elevation the Park's loftiest peak.

The pass derives its name from the tribe of Stoney Indians that once inhabited an area to the west and north of this part of the mountains, and were accustomed to follow this route in the course of their occasional visits to the northeastern section of what is now the Park. It provided a back door, so to speak, by which it was possible for them to reach the Belly River country without fear of encountering their enemies, the war-like Blackfeet, who preferred to avoid the more mountainous regions. It was not until 1921 that the ancient trail of the Stonies over the Pass was replaced by a somewhat better one constructed by Park authorities.[27]

Ahern Pass

Less than five airline miles north of Swiftcurrent Pass is a saddle in the continental divide called Ahern Pass. With an elevation of 7000 feet, it stands between the head of the Belly River Valley to the north and the Upper McDonald Valley to the south and west. No trail connects these two areas by way of the Pass, but the latter can be reached by a short sidetrip off the main Granite Park to Waterton Lake trail. The trail does not continue beyond the summit because the route is always blocked by huge, steep snowfields east or northeast of the Pass. Well worth the short sidetrip to the

summit, however, is the enchanting view of Lakes Helen and Elizabeth in the foreground, and of the Belly River Valley and Canada in the distance.

A strenuous scramble up 500 feet of loose scree east of the Pass will take hikers to one of the most startling views in the Park—the spectacle of Iceberg Lake as seen from the "Iceberg Notch." From this vantage point one also sees the Many Glacier area, including the Sherburne Lakes, the Swiftcurrent Lakes, and the Many Glacier Hotel itself.

The Pass was named after the man who is believed to have first crossed it, George P. Ahern. In the year 1890, Lieutenant Ahern, then stationed at Fort Shaw on Sun River, was ordered to explore northern sections of what is now the Park. He did so, with a party that included a detachment of soldiers, packers, guides and Professor G. E. Culver of the University of Wisconsin. After marching up the Belly River Valley to Lake Helen, the entire party spent two days in clearing a trail from the foot of the talus slope to the summit, and on August 22nd successfully crossed the Pass with horses and men. The feat is said to have been repeated with horses on only one other occasion, this being by R. H. Sargent of the United States Geological Survey in 1913.[28]

Many Glacier-Belly River Routes

Some six airline miles north and slightly west of the Many Glacier Hotel lies Red Gap, a non-divide pass at an elevation of 7600 feet, named for the bright color of its shales. Following its discovery about 1920 by Louis Hill and H. A. Noble of the Great Northern Railway, engineers reported the route feasible and a trail was constructed which, for the next decade, became the regular way of getting to the Belly River.[29] The Pass is rocky and windswept, and its vicinity is the abode of the mountain goat and sheep. The view from its open shale summit is inspiring, with Old Sun Glacier perching in a lofty cirque on the great mass of Mt. Merritt. With the completion in 1931 of the much shorter route via the Ptarmigan tunnel, Red Gap Pass fell into disuse and the trail itself is no longer maintained in a condition suitable for saddlehorse travel.

Less than three miles south of Red Gap Pass, as the eagle flies, is the celebrated Ptarmigan Wall, a 7600-foot barrier of reddish Grinnell argillite separating the upper reaches of the Swiftcurrent Valley from the south end of the

Swift Current Lake and 9,243 ft. Mt. Wilbur
Photo by Bob & Ira Spring

Fossil Algae
Photo by Frances R. Hanna

Belly River region. Some 120 feet below its summit, this typical arete has been pierced with a 183-foot tunnel of dimensions sufficient to permit its use by horseback riders as well as hikers. Beyond the tunnel, the trail has been carried down the steep north face of the wall, with its almost vertical drop of 1000 feet, by means of a half-tunnel protected by a masonry guardrail two feet in height.[30] Not only has this engineering feat shortened the trip by ten miles, but it has also provided a variety of sensational views, particularly those from its south portal of Mts. Wilbur, Grinnell and Gould. The tunnel is situated about 850 feet above Ptarmigan Lake and is readily reached from Many Glacier Hotel via the Iceberg-Ptarmigan trail.

Many Glacier-Lake St. Mary Routes

Piegan Pass is located on one of the two trail routes connecting Many Glacier Hotel and the Swiftcurrent Valley with the Lake St. Mary region, the other route being over Swiftcurrent and Logan Passes. Piegan is a non-divide pass in the Lewis Range with an elevation of 7600 feet, taking its name from the Piegan, or Pikuni, tribe of the Blackfeet Nation. From its summit there are striking views in both directions. To the south rise the jagged peaks of Almost-A-Dog, Citadel, Blackfoot and Jackson. Northward are the picturesque Grinnell Valley, Mt. Gould and the Garden Wall. Piegan was one of the three Park passes on the summits of which locomotive bells were placed in 1926 by the Great Northern Railway, and where they remained to be rung and enjoyed by those crossing the passes until they were removed in the fall of 1943 and turned in on a World War II scrap metal drive.[31]

Siyeh Pass lies approximately two miles to the east of Piegan. Like the latter, it is not on the continental divide, but its summit at 8100 feet is the highest of any Park pass. It was named by George Bird Grinnell for a well-known Blackfeet chief, the meaning of the word being Crazy Dog or Mad Wolf.[32] On leaving the Piegan summit, there are two routes available, one leading directly down the west side of the Going-to-the-Sun Mountain and Siyeh Creek to the Going-to-the-Sun Highway. The other and more spectacular leads through Preston Park, a beautiful alpine meadow, to Siyeh Pass, lying between Goat Mountain and Mahtahpi Peak. The Pass owes its origin to ancient glaciers that eroded the headwall in Boulder and Baring canyons. The views from the summit are awe-inspiring, with the precipitous face of Going-to-the-Sun Mountain to the west and exquisite Lake St. Mary shimmering 4000 feet below.

Passes To the South Of Lake St. Mary

Red Eagle, a continental divide pass 6800 feet above sea level, lies about eight airline miles south of the western end of upper Lake St. Mary. It was one of the principal transmountain routes of the Indians, but the trail beyond Red Eagle Lake is now rather primitive and rarely used. The pass, as well as the lake and glacier, takes its name, according to James Willard Schultz, from one of the most noted medicine men of the Pikuni tribe.[33] In the year 1858, William T. Hamilton was sent by the government as an emissary to the Indians and unintentionally became involved in a battle that took place between the Pikunis and the Kootenais at the head of Red Eagle Valley, just below the pass itself. The attacking Pikunis were repulsed and the Kootenais, together with Hamilton's party, fled to safety over the pass and down Nyack Creek to the Flathead region.[34] The pass was created by glacial action through the headward cutting of ancient opposing glaciers. Views from its summit are superb, especially those of Mt. Stimson, of Pumpelly Glacier on nearby Blackfoot Mountain, and down the Red Eagle Valley.

Triple Divide Pass with an elevation of 7400 feet lies just to the east of the continental

Logan Pass on the Going-to-the-Sun Highway
Photo by Walt Dyke, courtesy of Burlington Northern

divide, and approximately four airline miles due east of Red Eagle Pass. It is situated between Mt. James and Triple Divide Mountain, and its bottom is formed by the black diorite band seen elsewhere in the Park. It divides the headwaters of Hudson Bay Creek, flowing north, from those of Atlantic Creek, flowing southeast. To its immediate west is three-sided Triple Divide Mountain, only 600 feet higher than the pass itself. Yet it is really the culmination of the continent, so far as drainage is concerned, since the waters from its apex flow not only to Hudson Bay and Atlantic Creeks, but also to Pacific Creek on the west.

Cut Bank And Pitamakan Passes

For much of the 19th century, Indian travel across the mountains of the present park went over Cut Bank Pass, located on the continental divide at an elevation of 7861 feet. This was perhaps the most historic pass of the period, since it was over its summit that Pitamakan, or Running Eagle, the Blackfeet warrior maiden, led many forays into the Flathead country.[35] This was the route followed by Lieutenant Tinkham in 1853,[36] by Lieutenants Woodruff and Van Orsdale in 1873,[37] and by the Pumpelly Expedition in 1883.[38] Curiously, all three of these parties made the crossing from southwest to northeast.

Cut Bank Pass, with its magnificent view of the Nyack Valley, lies immediately north of Mt. Morgan. It provides access to both the Cut Bank and Two Medicine Valleys, the trail dividing just east of the pass to follow Cut Bank Creek northward past Morning Star Lake, while the southward branch leads shortly to Pitamakan Pass, a non-divide saddle at an elevation of 7500 feet. From its summit, the trail runs past Oldman Lake and down Dry Fork Creek to the valley of the Two Medicine.

The story of how Cut Bank Pass lost its name for several decades is interesting. After the Indians ceased to make use of "the old war-trail" in the latter years of the 19th century, the route over the pass fell into disuse. Much later, after the Park had been established, a trail was built from East Glacier to St. Mary, and the segment of it between the Two Medicine and Cut Bank Valleys led over a non-divide 7500-foot pass located near the original Cut Bank Pass. People began calling the new summit

View from Ahern Pass looking toward Helen Lake with Lake Elizabeth in the distance.
Courtesy Burlington Northern

"Cut Bank," and it became necessary to re-christen the original pass "Pitamakan." After years of trying to straighten the situation out, Park authorities were finally successful in restoring the name of "Cut Bank" to the original pass, and the non-divide summit separating the Cut Bank and Two Medicine valleys will henceforth carry the name of "Pitamakan."

Other passes in the southerly section of the Park are Surprise, Firebrand, Two Medicine and Dawson, the last three of these leading to the continental divide from the Two Medicine area. These are little traveled routes, except for the six-mile trail from the outlet of Two Medicine Lake to Dawson Pass,[39] to the summit of which ranger-guided hikes are made regularly during the season. Other passes in the northerly section include trail-less Jefferson Pass between Mt. Carter and Porcupine

Ridge, Gable Pass out of the Belly River Valley, and Kootenai Pass at the south end of the Fifty Mountain meadows.

Logan Pass

Although relatively unknown when the Park was first established, today the most familiar of all Glacier passes is undoubtedly Logan. Situated at an elevation of 6664 feet, it serves as a natural divide between one arm of the McDonald Valley to the west and the valley of Upper St. Mary Lake to the east. It is the site of an attractive visitors' center and parking area, from which a short foot trail leads to the Hanging Gardens and delightful Hidden Lake. Surrounding the pass are several of the Park's most spectacular peaks, including Clements, Reynolds and Going-To-The-Sun.

The pass was named after Major William R. Logan, the Park's first superintendent, who seems not to have had any other or special connection with the pass. However, he had been a member of the Pumpelly expedition that crossed the original Cut Bank Pass in 1883,[40] and in still earlier years had served with Custer as a scout. While there is said to have been an ancient Indian trail over the pass,[41] its first crossing by white men took place about 1876 when a group of Texas prospectors, headed by one Emerson Brown, utilized it to travel from Lake St. Mary to Lake McDonald.[42]

The Pass was without an official trail prior to the completion in 1918 of that which ran from Upper Lake St. Mary to Granite Park by way of the pass and the west side of the Garden Wall. Of course, Logan is now accessible by automobile as well as by trail and owes much of its distinction to the fact that it provides the summit for the scenically sumptuous Going-To-The-Sun highway connecting Lake St. Mary with Lake McDonald. This extraordinary road, begun in the early 1920's and completed in 1935, ranks as one of the great scenic highways of North America, and it merits a special story of its own in a later chapter of this book.[43]

Notes For Chapter 4

[1]Triple Divide Pass.
[2]The Ptarmigan Wall.
[3]Logan Pass, with its Going-To-The Sun Highway.
[4]See Chapter 5, infra, for "The Story Of The 'Lost' Pass."
[5]Alexander the Great invaded India in the summer of 327 B.C.
[6]Hannibal crossed the Alps in 218 B.C., probably by the Pass of Mont-Genevre or the Col de la Traversette.

[7]The Cumberland Gap is a notch in the eastern escarpment of the Cumberland Mountains at the junction of the states of Virginia, Tennessee and Kentucky. In 1775, Daniel Boone blazed a trail through the pass, following an old Indian trail; and it became famous as the Wilderness Road over which thousands trekked on their way west to Tennessee and Kentucky.
[8]Chilkoot Pass, 20 miles north of Skagway, is situated on the border between Alaska and northwestern British Columbia. It acquired fame as one of the principal routes used by prospectors after the discovery of gold in the Yukon in the 1890's.
[9]The Donner Pass over the Sierra into California recalls the tragedy of the Donner Party at the foot of the pass in gold-rush days.
[10]Definition from the Random House Dictionary (1966 edition).
[11]This process is more fully explained in Chapter 3, at page 26.
[12]Quoted by George Bird Grinnell in his article entitled "The Crown Of The Continent" appearing in Century Magazine for September, 1901, at pages 663-664.

Switchbacks on Swiftcurrent Pass
Photo by Hileman

[13]The original Cut Bank Pass was "discovered" by Lieutenant Tinkham and his party in 1853, and Ahern Pass was "discovered" by Lieutenant Ahern in 1890. However, both were the sites of ancient Indian trails.

[14]From "Through Glacier Park" by Mary Roberts Rinehart, at page 16.

[15]"Through The Years In Glacier National Park," by Donald H. Robinson, at page 56.

[16]Idem, at page 120. According to the "Early History of Glacier National Park" by Madison Grant, at page 10, it had earlier been called Horse Thief Pass by reason of a band of horses stolen on the Blackfeet Reservation having been driven over it.

[17]"Through The Years," supra, by Donald H. Robinson, at page 94.

[18]Article entitled "The Old Ranger" by Frank S. Liebig, early Forest Service ranger in the region which is now Glacier Park, published in Volume I of "Early Days In The Forest Service" compiled by the United States Forest Service, Region I Missoula, Montana.

[19]This was Chief Clerk Ucker of the Department of the Interior, making an inspection trip through the new park in the same month during which it had been created as such by Congress. Packtrip facilities were furnished by one Josiah Rogers, and the party is said to have crossed Swiftcurrent Pass uneventfully. See "Through The Years," supra, at page 94.

[20]"Through The Years," supra, at page 94.

[21]Idem, at page 112. See, also, "Signposts Of Adventure" by James Willard Schultz, at page 108.

[22]Idem, at page 25.

[23]See "Kootenai Brown, His Life And Times," by William Rodney, published in 1969 by Gray's Publishing Ltd., Sidney, British Columbia, at pages 61-62.

[24]Idem, at pages 59-61. South Kootenay Pass is on the continental divide between British Columbia and the Waterton Park. Its elevation is 6903 feet and it is approximately eight miles north of the international border.

[25]Idem, at page 125.

[26]"A Short Story Of Kootenai Brown," by Joseph E. Cosley, at pages 6-7. In this 12-page article or pamphlet, Cosley tells of his pleasant contacts with Brown in the year 1894. Particularly, he describes having spent the night, when seeking refuge from an October blizzard, in the trapper's cabin which Brown for some years had maintained on the Little Kootenai Creek several miles south of the international boundary. For more information on this cabin, see Chapter 11, infra, entitled "Advent Of The White Man," at page 94.

[27]See information pamphlet on Glacier National Park issued in 1924 by the Department of the Interior, at page 14.

[28]"Through The Years," supra, at pages 17-19. According to Schultz, in "Signposts Of Adventure," supra, at page 155, the Blood tribe of the Blackfeet Confederacy used this pass when going on raids on the west-side tribes. This seems doubtful, however.

[29]"Elrod's Guide And Book Of Information," (1924 edition) by Morton J. Elrod, at pages 156-157.

[30]So far as known, the Ptarmigan tunnel is the only one ever constructed for the use of horseback riders as well as hikers. The bore is six feet wide, nine feet in height, with an arched ceiling and a gradient of 3.75 per cent toward the north portal. Construction was by jackhammers and compressed air, and while under way there was speculation on two points: (a) Whether the tunnel would prove to be particularly windy because of the strong winds prevailing along the north face of the wall, and (b) Whether horses could be induced to travel through the tunnel. Neither concern turned out to be well-founded, and when Park Engineer Charles E. Randels rode a saddle horse through the tunnel on its completion, there was no unusual reaction from the animal. Nor has there been any such in the ensuing 40 years. See article entitled "A Tunnel For Saddle Horses" appearing in the Scientific American Magazine for June 1932.

[31]"Through The Years," supra, at pages 69-70. These bells were placed upon the summits of Swiftcurrent, Piegan and Siyeh Passes, with a fourth one on the East Glacier-Two Medicine trail over Mt. Henry.

[32]"Through The Years," supra, at page 119.

[33]"Signposts Of Adventure," supra, at pages 79-80.

[34]"Through The Years," supra, at page 30. A somewhat different version of the encounter is to be found in Hamilton's own story "A Trading Expedition Among The Indians in 1858," an extract from which appeared in "Montana: Its Story And Biography" by Tom Stout, 1921. According to this report, the retreat from Lake St. Mary across the mountains was probably by way of Logan Pass, then across the North Fork of the Flathead River and through Grave Creek Canyon to the Kootenai River where, several days later, another Blackfeet assault was repulsed with heavy losses to the attackers. See, also, article entitled "Over Red Eagle Pass," by M. N. D'Evelyn, at page 17 of Volume VII of "Glacial Drift" for April, 1934.

[35]"Through The Years," supra, at page 117. According to Schultz in "Signposts Of Adventure," supra, at page 120, the name Pitamakan Oksokwi, or Running Eagle's Trail, referred to Marias Pass, because the latter was her favorite trail to the country of the west-side tribes. But see "The Old North Trail," by Walter McClintock, at page 59.

[36]See Chapter 5, infra, entitled "The Story Of The 'Lost' Pass," at page 41.

[37]See Chapter 11, infra, entitled "Advent Of The White Man," at page 92.

[38]Idem, at page 93.

[39]Dawson Pass, at an elevation of 7500 feet, was named for Thomas Dawson, an old-time guide of the area and son of Andrew Dawson, last factor of the American Fur Company at Fort Benton. See "Through The Years," supra, at page 111.

[41]"Signposts Of Adventure," supra, at page 117, states that this pass was traversed from earliest times by the west-side tribes, first by the Snakes, and later by the Salish and Kootenai tribes. See, also, note 34, supra, this chapter.

[42]See pages 11-13 of Volume VIII of "Glacial Drift" for April, 1935, for story by William Veach, Sr., entitled "An Early Trip Into Glacier Park."

[43]See Chapter 15, infra, entitled "Roads And Highways," at pages 126-128.

View near Lincoln Pass
Photo by Walt Dyke, courtesy of Burlington Northern

Chapter 5
THE STORY OF
THE "LOST" PASS

Not within Glacier Park itself, but rather athwart its southern boundary, is a break in the Lewis Range so unusual in character and in its history, so vital to the winning of the West, and so closely related to development of the region that came to be Glacier, that it has acquired the romantic aura of a near legend. This is Marias Pass, which enjoys the distinction, unique in national park annals, of providing the continental divide crossing for the main line of a major railroad,[1] as well as for a transcontinental highway.[2] In the course of its stranger-than-fiction history, it became "lost" for much of the nineteenth century, managing to elude the efforts of various expeditions seeking its whereabouts over a period of more than thirty years.

Although more travelers cross Marias Pass each year than over any pass within the Park itself, many of them are not aware that they have been over the continental divide. With an elevation of only 5213 feet, Marias is the lowest continental divide pass in this country north of Lordsburg, New Mexico;[3] hence the approach by train or automobile is so gradual that there is little to impress upon the traveler's consciousness the fact that a summit has been reached. It really represents the point where two broad valleys meet, and is thus the antithesis of the popular concept of a mountain pass, such as Gunsight. For these reasons it has provided an ideal route over the Rockies for both railway and highway purposes. On the other hand, the view to the north of the Pass has been called a "geologic spectacular," embracing, as it does, several miles of the Lewis Overthrust with its ancient Precambrian rocks overlying layers of much younger plains rocks.[4]

Fortunately, there are a few physical objects in the vicinity of the summit to remind those who are interested in such things that this is indeed the celebrated Marias Pass. One is the tall granite obelisk that stands in the center of the highway at the summit as a memorial to Theodore Roosevelt, after whom the route has

been named. Another is the statue of John F. Stevens, "discoverer" of the pass, standing on an eminence located near the summit and a few rods to the north of the railroad right-of-way.[5]

Meriwether Lewis Almost Discovers The Pass

Perhaps the most fascinating bit of lore connected with the Park is the story of how its presently most used pass escaped official discovery for the greater part of the nineteenth century. Its name was derived from the river by the same name, one branch of which originates near the Pass; and the river in turn was given the title of "Maria's River" by Captain Meriwether Lewis in honor of a cousin named Maria Wood.[6] The name has stuck, but the apostrophe has disappeared.

During the Lewis and Clark expedition of 1805-1806, Captain Lewis made exploratory sidetrips up the Marias River in both years, perhaps recognizing it as a possible future trade route. In July, 1806 he reached a point within 25 miles of present Park boundaries and close enough, weather permitting, to have looked into what we now know to have been Marias Pass.[7] Had he continued westward at that point, he might have been the first white man to set foot in the pass, but the time was not propitious.

From time immemorial, Marias had provided a convenient trans-mountain route for the tribes on both sides of the divide, and particularly for the west-side dwellers, the Flatheads and Kootenais, who felt the need, from time to time, to travel to the buffalo hunting grounds on the eastern side of the range. Toward the end of the eighteenth century, however, as the Blackfeet, moving down from Canada, began to tighten their grip on the buffalo plains, these journeys by the western tribes became fraught with increasing danger from ambush and attack.

It was about this time that the existence and location of Marias Pass became known to at least some of the few white men in the area.

David Thompson, early trader, reported in his journals that a band of 150 Flathead Indians, accompanied by Finan McDonald and two other white men, crossed the mountains in the year 1810 by a route corresponding in description to Marias Pass. They were attacked by an even larger band of Blackfeet at a point believed to have been near Bear Creek, but after a furious battle succeeded in repelling their attackers.[8]

Never-Never Land

Following this and other efforts by the western tribes to mount hunting expeditions into what the Blackfeet regarded as their private domain, the latter became more belligerent and set sentries at high points to watch over the approaches to the passes, particularly Marias. Relentlessly, over a period of years, they ambushed and killed any small bands of invaders that tried to come through.[9]

As a result of this intense hostility, Marias Pass became a area of danger to be shunned by the west-side tribes and even by trappers and traders. Almost concurrently with this turn of events, the Blackfeet themselves came to regard Marias as the abode of evil spirits and religiously to be avoided.[10] This strange combination of fears on the part of all concerned brought about a shift of transmountain trail traffic to Cut Bank Pass, and use of the one easy route from the Flathead Valley to the plains country was, in effect, abandoned for many decades. With such protracted disuse, the once well-worn trail became overgrown with grass and blocked by fallen timber.[11]

Its location, however, seems not to have been entirely forgotten during this period. The "Memoir Historical and Political of the North West Coast of North America," published by Robert Greenhow in 1840, contained a map that included what is now the southern boundary of Glacier Park and marked "Route Across the Mts."[12] This was probably the earliest published map of what is today known as Marias Pass.

Search For A Railroad Pass

At about this same time the pressures of westward expansion began to generate demands for a railroad to the Pacific. Surveys were authorized by Congress in 1853, and Major Isaac I. Stevens, of the United States Army Engineering Corps, succeeded in getting himself appointed governor of the newly created Washington Territory and leader of an expedition to survey the northern route from

the Mississippi to the Pacific. One of its most important responsibilities was the location of a northern pass over the Rockies suitable for railroad use.[13]

It is probable that Stevens was aware of the route indicated by Greenhow's map. At all events, when he reached Fort Benton in Montana, he was visited by Little Dog, a chief of the Pikuni tribe of the Blackfeet, who gave him a fairly accurate description of the pass. In his subsequent report on the survey, Stevens wrote:

"From the Little Dog, a prominent chief of the Piegan tribe and a man of character and probity, I got a very particular description of the Marias Pass we were in search of. From some superstition of the Blackfeet, it has not been used for many years, but formerly it was almost the only thoroughfare made use of by the Indians in passing from one side of the mountains to the other. It is a broad, wide, open valley, with scarcely a hill or obstruction on the road, excepting here and there some fallen timber."[14]

Unsuccessful Reconnaissance

With a view to ascertaining the exact location of the pass so graphically described by Little Dog, Stevens ordered A. W. Tinkham, an army engineer on his staff, to undertake a reconnaissance of the Flathead-Marias region from a western approach. After Tinkham had arranged with a Flathead Indian to act as a guide, the latter declined to go, alarmed by remarks of Hugh Monroe, the redoubtable white Blackfoot, who "told them that he was afraid they would fall in with parties of Blackfeet young men."[15]

Despite this sabotage, Tinkham set forth with a small party in October, 1853, traveling up Flathead Lake and the Middle Fork of the Flathead River to Nyack Creek. There the presence of a prominent Indian trail and the size of the creek deceived them into taking that route over Cut Bank Pass. They crossed this steep col on October 20, 1853 and returned to the winter camp at Fort Benton, reporting the route (which they thought to be Marias Pass) impracticable for railroad purposes.[16] Tinkham thus became the first white man to make an accurately recorded journey through what is now Glacier National Park, although Hugh Monroe and other earlier white trappers and hunters had undoubtedly been over the same pass.

Marias Continues To Be Elusive

Still unconvinced, Governor Stevens in the spring of 1854 sent another of his lieutenants,

James R. Doty, to continue the search. Setting forth in May of that year, with three men and an Indian boy for a guide, Doty explored the east side of the range as far north as Lake St. Mary, returning by the same route in early June, and both times noted the broad opening to the pass. Each time, however, he was misled by the fact that the topography he was seeing did not match the information previously supplied by Tinkham as to his route over Cut Bank Pass; and a shortage of time precluded further investigation.[17] As Stevens wrote later: "It is to be regretted that Mr. Doty did not continue on, and ascertain where the trail issued on the western side of the mountains."[18]

Plans to continue the survey at a later date were unfortunately cancelled by Jefferson Davis, then Secretary of War, on the ground that enough money had been wasted on this protracted search for a mythical mountain pass.[19] However, Stevens' report indicates that in 1856 an Indian agent named Lansdale had traversed a route "much used by the Upper Pend d'Oreille Indians in going to hunt buffalo east of the mountains," giving a description of the route.[20] Stevens was convinced, although never quite able to prove it, that—

"This is the true Marias Pass, described by the Little Dog to me at Fort Benton in September, 1853, and formerly used by the Indians in crossing the mountains."[21]

The 1860's And 1870's

Despite the repeated failures of the Stevens expedition to locate the pass in 1853 and 1854, its existence and whereabouts seem to have been no mystery to many of those who came to the region in the next few years. Montana's first territorial legislature passed an Act, signed into law on February 2, 1865, to authorize the building of a toll road from Fort Benton over the mountains by way of Marias Pass to connect with a road leading to British Columbia. The toll gate was to be located at the Pass, with charges from 50¢ to $8.00[22] The road was never built and the project was abandoned, probably because of the collapse of the Kootenai mines in British Columbia.

By 1870, "Indian troubles" had been brought under control, and the way was opened for safer access into the area now included in the Park, and for an influx of prospectors and miners. The first of such parties, headed by one Frank Lehman, made its way over Marias Pass from the west in 1870, the venture coming to an unsuccessful conclusion in what is now Alberta after prospecting along the eastern side of the Lewis Range. False rumors of a gold strike soon brought other prospectors to Marias Pass and sent them back disappointed.[23]

In 1874 Duncan McDonald, then in charge of the Hudson's Bay Trading Post south of Flathead Lake, and said to have been the discoverer of Lake McDonald in what is now the Park, made his first trip through Marias Pass, accompanied by several Pend d'Oreille Indians. They traveled on snowshoes and chose this as the most direct route from their camp on the Marias River to the trading post. McDonald subsequently crossed the pass on a number of occasions but, like so many before him, left no record of his trips or routes.

Rail Route Search Renewed

Following termination of explorations by the Stevens expedition in 1854, nearly three decades were to elapse before the formal search for a transcontinental rail route was resumed. This time the quest was under the auspices of the Northern Pacific Railroad and the Oregon Railway and Navigation Company, with the eminent geologist, Professor Raphael Pumpelly, as chief of survey. Their 1882 expedition approached Cut Bank Pass from the east in the early summer, but was turned back by the tremendous snowbanks encountered near the summit. Returning in 1883 to undertake a western approach, they duplicated the route followed by Tinkham in 1853 and by Woodruff and Van Orsdale, of the United States Army, in 1873.[25] They were successful, since it was late in summer, in crossing the pass but, of course, did not find it suitable for railroad construction purposes.[26]

Eventually, the time came when something more than "near misses" was necessary. The construction crews of the Great Northern Railway, then called the St. Paul, Minneapolis and Manitoba, had been creeping northwestward across Minnesota and North Dakota. When they reached Havre, Montana, without having located a suitable pass over the northern Rockies, the situation took on an aspect of urgency. So imperative became the need for early location of a northerly transmountain route that James J. Hill, presiding genius of the railroad, decreed that the search must be undertaken at once although the time was then the early winter of 1889.[27]

The man selected to make the reconnaissance was John F. Stevens, no relation to Governor Isaac I. Stevens but, by coincidence, born in 1853, the first of the two years when the latter's expedition conducted a search for the pass from both east and west. Young Stevens (then 36) was principal assistant engineer of the St. Paul, Minneapolis and Manitoba (now part of the Burlington Northern), and before long was to become chief engineer and general manager of the railroad. Ultimately, he would become chief engineer and, to all intents and purposes, chief executive of the Panama Canal.[28]

Stevens Finds The Pass

It was from Fort Assiniboine, some seven miles south of the town of Havre in north central Montana, that Stevens set forth in the early part of December, 1889. Heading west with a wagon, a mule, a saddle horse and a driver, he covered the more than 160 miles to the Blackfeet Indian Agency on Badger Creek within a few days.[29]

On reaching the Agency at Badger Creek, Stevens tried to engage a Blackfeet guide for the final leg of his trip, but none would accept the assignment—whether because of the weather, the evil spirits of the pass, or both, is not clear. However, he finally succeeded in persuading a Flathead Indian named Coonsah to accompany him.[30] Stevens had undoubtedly been furnished with all of the information available to the railroad company at that time, including the stories of both Finan and Duncan McDonald, the report of Governor Stevens concerning the 1853-1854 explorations, and subsequent information from a Major Marcus D. Baldwin, who claimed to have entered and explored Marias Pass from both sides.[31]

It was well into the bitter Montana winter and the snow was deep. Stevens and his guide set forth on snowshoes which they themselves had strung with raw-hide. The rugged travel conditions were such that when they reached what is now known as False Summit, a few miles east of the Pass, Coonsah was unable to proceed and Stevens continued alone. It was a cold 11th of December when he attained the summit and, continuing through the low, wide valley, reached westward flowing water. He had rediscovered the legendary Marias Pass![32]

The "Discovery" Put To Use

Having assured himself that he was really in westward drainage, and that the pass was usable for railroad purposes, Stevens turned back. It was too late in the day to return to camp where Coonsah was waiting; however, he reached the true summit and made a bivouac for the night, tramping a runway in the snow to keep from falling asleep and freezing in the 40° below zero weather. When he returned to camp in the morning, he found that Coonsah had allowed the fire to go out and was almost frozen to death. After reviving the Indian, they returned to Badger Creek,[33] from which point Stevens retraced his steps to Havre where he could wire the great news to St. Paul.

Less than 18 months later, grading and tracklaying crews set forth from the town of Cut Bank, about 50 miles east of the present Park boundary.[34] The rails reached the summit of Marias Pass on September 14, 1891, arrived at Kalispell, well to the west of the present Park, on December 31, 1891, and by 1893 through trains were running regularly between St. Paul and Seattle.[35] While Stevens' "discovery," like that of Columbus of the continent itself, may not have been the first in point of time, it was the first to receive general and official recognition, and to him, therefore, go the honors of discovery.

Apart from its historic significance, finding of the "lost" pass represented a momentous event from a railroad standpoint. In a single stroke, it afforded not merely a better alignment, less rise and fall, and much easier grades (a modest 1.8% eastbound, and a mere 1% westbound), but it also averted the need for a summit tunnel and shortened the otherwise necessary distance to the Pacific Coast by more than 100 miles.[36] For the Great Northern, over the decades, this has made possible an operational saving that can only be calculated in the tens of millions of dollars.

For all the same reasons, Stevens' discovery was to become a boon of inestimable value to highway travel. Once no more than an unmarked foot trail, Marias Pass is now crossed by a modern all-year thoroughfare over which more people travel in a single day than the pass was wont, in ancient times, to see in a decade. At the summit, commemorating the historic reconnaissance by its one-time employee, a bronze statue of Stevens was erected by a grateful Great Northern in 1925.[37] There, at the crest of the continent his heroic likeness still stands, looking silently but prophetically toward the Pacific, with the vast stretches of the Great Plains behind, and the "shining mountains" of Glacier looming magnificently to the right.

Notes for Chapter 5

[1]The St. Paul, Minneapolis & Manitoba became the Great Northern Railway, now a part of the Burlington Northern System.

[2]For a description of the highway over Marias Pass, see Chapter 15, infra, entitled "Roads And Highways," at pages 125-126.

[3]This information comes from "Continental Divide Trail Study Report," a 76-page document prepared and issued in 1971 by the Bureau of Outdoor Recreation, 1000 Second Ave., Seattle, Washington 98104.

[4]"Rock, Ice And Water," by Alt and Hyndman, published in 1973, at page 94.

[5]See infra, this chapter, at page 43. The sculptor was a man named Cecere, and the architect was Electus D. Litchfield, both of New York City. The statue, eight feet in height, is located on a special triangle of Glacier Park land comprising 2.70 acres where, presumably, Stevens spent the night of December 11, 1889. The acreage was granted to the Great Northern Ry. for this purpose by Secretary of the Interior Work, despite strong objections thereto by Stephen Mather, then Director of the National Park Service. The statue was dedicated on July 21, 1925 with a number of distinguished people present, including Associate Justice Pierce Butler of the United States Supreme Court, Governor Erickson of Montana and John F. Stevens himself. (These facts were gleaned from documents in the Park Service records at West Glacier).

[6]Miss Maria Wood was a cousin of Captain Lewis. See pages 353-354 of Volume II of the modern edition of Elliott Coues' "History Of The Expedition Under The Command Of Lewis And Clark." For an interesting conflict on whether she was a cousin of Lewis or Clark, see "Through The Years In Glacier National Park," by Donald H. Robinson, at pages 7 and 116.

[7]See "History Of The Expedition," supra, Volume III, at pages 1093-1101, describing the stay of Captain Lewis and his companions from July 22nd through July 26th, 1806 at what he called Camp Disappointment because overcast weather prevented a taking of solar observations.

[8]"Narrative," by David Thompson, at page 425.

[9]"Through The Years In Glacier National Park," by Donald H. Robinson, at page 9.

[10]"Surveys For A Railroad Route," by Isaac I. Stevens, Volume XII, Book 1, at page 106.

[11]"Through The Years," supra, at page 9.

[12]Greenhow was "Translator and Librarian to the Department of State." His book was printed by Blair & Rives, of Washington. The route shown is amazingly accurate, both as to geographical location and configuration, although presumably based upon information obtained from Indians of the area.

[13]"The Story Of Marias Pass," by Grace Flandrau, at pages 6-7.

[14]"Surveys For A Railroad Route," supra, at page 106.

[15]Idem, at page 128.

[16]"Through The Years," supra, at page 27.

[17]"Official Explorations For Pacific Railroads, 1853-1855," by G. Albright, U. C. Press, 1921, at page 81. See, also, "Through The Years," supra, at pages 27-28.

[18]"Surveys For A Railroad Route," supra, at page 186.

[19]"Through The Years," supra, at page 28.

[20]"Surveys For A Railroad Route," supra, at page 128.

[21]Idem, at page 186.

[22]"Through The Years," supra, at page 30.

[23]Idem, at page 35.

[24]Idem, at page 15.

[25]See Chapter 11, infra, entitled "Advent Of The White Man," at page 92.

[26]"Through The Years," supra, at page 31.

[27]Article entitled "John F. Stevens, Pathfinder For Western Railroads," by Earl F. Clark, appearing in the American West Magazine for May, 1971.

[28]"The Story of Marias Pass," supra, at page 19.

[29]Idem, at page 20.

[30]Idem, at page 20.

[31]"Through The Years," supra, at page 32. The Great Falls Tribune for October 26, 1889, less than six weeks before Stevens' reconnaissance in the Rockies, reported that Major Marcus Baldwin, formerly agent of the Blackfeet Agency, had recently explored Marias Pass from both sides and found it to be the easiest pass in the Rockies for railroad purposes. He planned to talk it over with Mr. Hill at the Great Northern in a few days.

[32]"The Story Of Marias Pass," supra, at page 21.

[33]Idem, at page 21.

[34]"Through The Years," supra, at page 33.

[35]Idem, at page 33.

[36]"James J. Hill," by Stewart H. Holbrook, published in 1955 by Alfred A. Knopf, at page 117, quoting the words of Ralph Budd, who had succeeded Louis Hill as president of the Great Northern Railway.

[37]"The Story Of Marias Pass," supra, at page 22.

John F. Stevens Monument with author
Photo by Frances R. Hanna

Railroad depot at summit of Marias Pass
Photo by Frances R. Hanna

Memorial to Theodore Roosevelt at Marias Pass showing the Lewis Overthrust in the background.

Photo by Mel Ruder

Chapter 6
THE FASCINATING GLACIERS

Much of the story of Glacier National Park has been written in ice. A major share of the sculpturing of its massive shales and limestones was the work of ancient icefields grinding away through countless eons. In a far more modest way, its present glaciers still carve and grind while serving, more importantly, as the primary source of the abundance of water that constantly freshens its beauty. Hence it is altogether fitting that from them—those of long ago, as well as those of today—the Park should take its name.

Glaciers are among the most intriguing phenomena of our natural environment, covering ten per cent of the world's land surface and containing about three per cent of its water.[1] Three features distinguish a glacier from other frozen masses, to wit, color, density and movement. Glacial ice is blue, although when covered with snow or viewed from a distance its blueness may not be apparent. Glacial ice also has a high degree of densification as a result of the compaction of the new snows by which it is replenished each winter. And finally, every glacier is really a moving river of ice. There is no period in the year when a glacier is motionless, although movement is much slower in winter than in summer.

The glaciers of the Park are only a few of the thousands throughout the world, located in every latitude and on every continent except Australia.[2] Not only do they cover almost entirely the sub-continents of Greenland and Antarctica, but they are found on some of the higher peaks near the equator in Africa, in South America, and even on such tropical islands as New Guinea.[3] In North America the most impressive icefields are in Alaska, Canada and the state of Washington. Though small by comparison with the great glaciers of Alaska, those of the Park are nevertheless among the largest and best examples of this interesting phenomenon to be found in the Rocky Mountains south of the Canadian border.[4]

Discovery Of The Montana Glaciers

First white man to visit a glacier in what is the Park of today is reported to have been Hugh Monroe, who had come to live with the Blackfeet early in the 19th century. With his son, Lone Wolf, he is said to have reached the vicinity of Iceberg Lake and its glacier in the 1850's[5] In 1873, Lieutenants Woodruff and Van Orsdale, in the course of an Army reconnaissance, crossed over Cut Bank Pass from the west and thus became the first white men to take note of the nearby glacier that was later seen by, and named for, Professor Raphael Pumpelly.[6]

The name of George Bird Grinnell looms large in the annals of glacier discovery in the region. In 1891 he explored the headwaters of Lake St. Mary and was probably the first to see the then large Blackfoot Glacier.[7] In 1887 he had discovered in the Swiftcurrent Valley the glacier that bears his name, making an examination of the icefield and shooting a bighorn ram sighted on a nearby eminence.[8] During the course of this trip he also visited Iceberg Lake and its glacier.[9] In 1898 he climbed Blackfoot Mountain, from the summit of which he beheld to the south the glacier discovered by Woodruff and Van Orsdale twenty-five years before.[10]

The Sperry Glacier, located on the western side of the continental divide near Gunsight Pass, derived its name from Dr. Lyman B. Sperry, erstwhile professor of geology and zoology at Carleton College in Minnesota, who made it his special project in the years beginning with 1895.[11] Through his efforts a trail was cut from the head of Lake McDonald to Avalanche Lake and ultimately to the glacier itself, then the second largest in what is now the Park, although he did not actually set foot upon it until 1896.[12] In August, 1895, however, he headed a party that traveled from Lake McDonald to the Garden Wall, from the top of which the Grinnell Glacier was viewed; and upon continuing northward beyond the present location of Granite Park, the Chaney Glacier was discovered and named for Professor L. W. Chaney, a member of the party.[13]

The Park's Glaciers in 1911-1913

William C. Alden, of the United States Geological Survey, spent the summers of 1911, 1912 and 1913 in and adjacent to the Park, studying its glacial phenomena, and in 1914 published his classic treatise entitled "Glaciers Of Glacier National Park."[14] While it was intended as a popular, rather than a technical, discussion, it still remains one of the most comprehensive and useful pieces of literature on the subject. Particularly is his monograph valuable for the accurate and intimate picture which it presents of the Park's glaciers as they were in the early years of the century.

From that report we learn that during the period of Alden's study there were 90 glaciers in the Park, ranging from Blackfoot with its then more than three square miles of ice down to masses but a few acres in extent, yet exhibiting the characteristics of true glaciers. It contained an excellent explanation of the origin and history of the Park's glaciers, both ancient and present. It commented in detail upon the characteristics, appearance and behavior of the principal icefields, including approximate dimensions and, in some instances, measurements of forward movement. It paid special attention to Blackfoot and Sperry, but covered all the Park's more important glaciers, including Grinnell, Harrison, Iceberg, Siyeh (referred to as Canyon Creek), Ahern and Chaney, as well as several located in the northwestern area of the Park.

Interestingly, the Alden report contained an important revelation to which little, if any, significance was seemingly attached at the time. This was the fact that the Park was already well into the throes of deglaciation, i.e., of glacial shrinkage. In reference to the Blackfoot Glacier, he noted that its marginal lobes were "somewhat shrunken from their moraines, an indication that some time ago the ice had a greater extension." In similar observations with respect to a number of other Park glaciers, including Sperry, Iceberg, Vulture Peak and Carter, he cited the physical evidence pointing to the fact that each had been of a greater extent in the recent past. He offered no estimate of the period of time that his shrinkage had been in progress, nor any comment as to its probable rate per annum or decade, undoubtedly for lack of earlier data

that could provide an adequate basis for comparison and future prediction.

The Park's Glaciers In The 1970's

There is no accurate census of ice-masses in the Park as it enters its seventh decade as a member of the national park system. While Alden reported a total of 90 glaciers in 1913, it seems unlikely that more than half that number remain as active glaciers today. An accurate count is virtually impossible because many of the glaciers within the Park are near the difficult borderline between small glaciers and large snowpatches. There can be no question, however, as to the fact of a drastic shrinkage in size among those that have survived. For a while it was feared that all of the Park's precious glaciers were destined to vanish before the end of the century, but with the apparent stabilization of climatic conditions since 1950, that downward trend seems to have been checked.

Largest glacier in the Park is now Grinnell in the Swiftcurrent Valley.[15] In 1901 it had an acreage of 525, a figure which shrank to 384 by 1937, to 328 by 1950, to 315 by 1960 and to approximately 300 in 1970.[16] The maximum depth of its ice is estimated at 400 to 500 feet.[17] Its ice-front underwent a steady recession in the first half of this century, showing an average retreat of 34 feet per year.[18] However, this rate of recession began to slow down materially about 1950, with the average for the 1950-1960 decade being only 8 feet, and that for the 1960-1970 decade being approximately 2 feet.[19]

The Grinnell Glacier originally was composed of upper and lower portions connected at the southeasterly end of the former by an ice tongue. This connecting link disappeared in 1926, since which time the two sections have been separate. The area of the upper part continues to be slightly over 50 acres, its length being much greater than its breadth. Because of its shape, as viewed from a distance, it is called the Salamander Glacier.

Sperry Glacier

Situated on the west side of the continental divide, but only nine airline miles from Grinnell, the equally well-known Sperry Glacier has suffered an even more drastic reduction in size. From a 1901 acreage of 810, more than 50% above that of Grinnell, in the same year, Sperry's measurements showed a decrease to 390 in 1938, 305 by 1950, 287 by

1960, and an estimated 275 by 1970.[20] The recession of its ice-front has also proceeded at a faster pace than that at Grinnell, the annual average being 50 feet during the 1938-1945 period, 35 feet during 1945-1950, and 24 feet during the 1950-1960 decade. Shrinkage has continued at a substantial rate during the ten years ending in 1970, but it has been so irregular as to have little value for comparative purposes.[21]

In view of the relative proximity of the two ice-fields, it is natural to wonder why there should be a differential of that kind, i.e., a more rapid shrinkage at Sperry. Experts point out that glaciers are a progeny of climate, with accumulation as their life blood and wastage determining the amount and rate at which their resources are spent. Melting is primarily due to solar radiation, and this in turn varies with such factors as cloud cover, humidity, wind, time of day, altitude and the direction of exposure.[22] The fact that Sperry is located on the western side of the continental divide, with its milder climate, may play a part in its greater wastage.

It is interesting to hear, however, that Glacier Park is not alone in the diminution of its ice masses during the twentieth century. The same trend has affected most of the world's glaciers during the same period, with shrinkage accelerating up to 1945,[23] i.e., considerably less ice was added each winter than was dissipated by melting and evaporation during the remainder of the year. This trend has been attributed to subtle climatic changes, with some scientists being concerned that the increase of carbon dioxide in the atmosphere arising from industrial activity might be causing a warming of the climate. Fortunately, since 1945 the shrinkage has come to a virtual halt, and it would appear that the budget of accumulation and wastage of the Park's glaciers may have reached a state of substantial balance.

Other Park Glaciers

While Grinnell and Sperry now rank one and two, respectively, in size among the Park's glaciers, there are several other important, although less extensive ones. These include, Blackfoot, Harrison, Chaney, Sexton, Jackson, Siyeh, Ahern, Old Sun and a few others nearly as large, but in less accessible locations. Among those named, the major change since 1910 has been in the Blackfoot Glacier, then the largest in the Park and probably the

largest in the Rockies south of Canada. It has now melted back so much that it has broken up into several small glaciers, one of which is Jackson.

One of the most delightful of all Park glaciers was that which once reposed in the great cirque at Iceberg Lake, above which the Pinnacle Wall towers a sheer 3000 feet. Before 1920, the front of the glacier rose perpendicularly nearly 100 feet above the level of the lake, on the surface of which sizable bergs would float all summer long. Rapid shrinkage caused its disappearance by 1940,[24] and only deep snow and non-glacial ice now occupy the glacier's former bed.

Another interesting glacier is the tiny Gem, lying high on the Garden Wall, above and to the southeast of Grinnell. Highly inaccessible, but extremely visible, the Gem is scarcely a quarter of a mile in length and breadth, yet perched so close to the top of the continental divide that it may be seen, not only from the Swiftcurrent side, but also from the westerly side as descent is being made along the Going-To-The-Sun Highway from Logan Pass toward Lake McDonald. Actually, there is doubt as to whether the Gem is still a true glacier or has become merely a deep snowbank, since J. Gordon Edwards, who has explored it thoroughly, reports that it has no crevasses. If it be a glacier, it is one of the few in the Park that have held their own in recent decades.

Park Glaciers In 70,000 B.C.

The so-called Ice Age or Pleistocene Period began more than a million years ago. Much of North America was covered by a continental ice sheet, and all of the valleys in the Park of today were then filled with ice to a depth, in some cases, of 3000 feet, with only the highest parts of the ranges protruding above the glacial surface.[25] Evidence of the height of the ice in the eastern valleys is still visible in the shape of lateral moraines as much as 1200 feet above valley floor level, and of signs of the polishing and striation of rock ledges at the 1600-foot level.[26]

As these great glaciers moved eastward out of their respective valleys, they spread out over the adjacent plains country. Geologic data indicate that the ancient icefield emerging from the Two Medicine Valley attained a maximum length of 48 miles and a breadth of 30 miles.[27] The rivers of ice from the St. Mary and Swiftcurrent Valleys, as well as those from the Belly River and Waterton Lake areas, flowed many miles northward and eastward to points of contact with the colossal Keewatin Ice Sheet pushing westward from the Hudson Bay region.[28] Some idea of the immensity of these pre-historic glacial streams may be gained by comparing them to the huge icefields that today fill some of the mountain valleys in the Alaska-Yukon area.

Repeat Visits

While there is no exact knowledge of the number of times that great masses of ice moved down the valleys of the future park, disappeared, and returned again during the million or more years of the Pleistocene Period, there is geologic evidence of its having taken place in eight different stages.[29] Between each stage was an interval of warmer or drier climate lasting from 2,000 to tens of thousands of years, during which the icefields greatly diminished or disappeared entirely. Most of these eight invasions are believed to have occurred during what is referred to as the Wisconsin stage of the Ice Age, comprising the last 70,000 years, with a good probability that the final incursion was no more than 7,000 years ago, or approximately 5,000 B.C.[30]

Following this final advance during the Wisconsin period, the geologists believe that the glacial ice disappeared from the mountains until about 4,000 years ago when the present relatively small glaciers were born.[31] Even during the period of their existence there have undoubtedly been eras of increase and recession, depending upon climatic conditions, with maximum size probably having been attained around the middle of the nineteenth century.[32]

Accomplishments Of The Ancient Glaciers

In the course of repeated runs by successive ice streams down the valleys of the future park, the contours of the region were substantially altered. The valleys were deepened and reshaped by erosive glacial action. Originally these were V-shaped stream-cut valleys, because a river can cut only in the valley bottom. The glaciers converted them to a characteristic U-shaped cross-section, with steep sides and broad bottom,[33] since the ice filled each valley from wall to wall and abraded the sides as well as the floor. Typical of this kind of glacial handiwork are the Swiftcurrent Valley, viewed from Swiftcurrent Pass; the St. Mary Valley, viewed from Logan Pass; and the Belly River Valley, viewed from the Ptarmigan Wall.

Not only did these ancient rivers of slowly moving ice scour out and reshape all of the region's valleys, but they also accomplished certain other miracles. They created Glacier's sensational aretes, such as the Garden Wall, one of the finest masterpieces of glacial sculpture in America, with its seven-mile knife-edge wall separating two deep, glacier-gouged valleys.[34]. They eroded the huge cirques, or horseshoe-shaped amphitheaters, at the head of each valley.[35] They hollowed out the rocky beds where many of the lakes now repose.[36] They carved the spectacular horns for which the Park is noted, and in many instances created the cols or passes, as has been explained in an earlier chapter,[37] through the interaction of glaciers on opposite sides of a ridge.

What Is A Glacier?

According to the dictionary, a glacier is an extended mass of ice formed from snow falling and accumulating over the years and moving very slowly outward or downward.[38] Such a phenomenon can occur in any part of the world where climatic conditions are favorable, i.e., where the volume of snowfall is great enough and the temperature is cold enough to permit it to accumulate. As of today, the conditions favorable to the formation of a glacier exist only in cold climates, such as polar regions, and above or near the permanent snowline in mountain regions.

Glaciers are made from snow, and each crystal of glacial ice represents hundreds to thousands of tiny snowflakes that have been welded together into a single homogeneous crystal structure.[39] This change from snow to ice by sublimation, crushing and compaction begins within a few days after each flake comes to rest on the glacier's surface and, as the process continues, it produces larger grains, closer packing and increased density.[40] Eventually all pore surfaces are sealed off, the mass becomes impermeable,[41] and the great weight of millions of such crystals forces them to follow the line of least resistance, either outward or downward, or both.

There are different kinds of glaciers. The continental variety covered much of North America and Europe during the Ice Age, but are presently found only in the arctic regions. The ancient ice masses that once filled from wall to wall the valleys of what is now the Park are described as valley glaciers, the name changing to piedmont glaciers when they flowed out of the valleys on to the eastern plains.

Most of the present modestly-sized Park specimens may be described as cliff glaciers, or as hanging glaciers,[42] since they are nearly always found in the high cirques or upon mountain shelves, with their backs against a rock wall.

Glacial Terminology

Like the mountaineering world, that of the glacier has its own parlance, and an explanation of the more common terms will help to provide an understanding of physical characteristics and behavior.

Cirque—a glacial amphitheater quarried out of a mountain wall by ice action.

Neve or *firn*—The field of granular snow at the head of a glacier.

Bergschrund—the deep crevice or opening between the head of the glacier and the rock wall behind it, made as the glacier gradually breaks away on its downward course. In the Park glaciers, these are usually 10 to 20 feet wide at the top, and as much as 50 feet deep.[43]

Crevasse—an open linear crack in the glacial surface resulting from movement of inflexible ice over an uneven bed, or from more rapid movement by some parts of the glacier.

Moraine—rock debris quarried out of its setting by a glacier and piled along its lateral or terminal edge.

Moulin—a vertical hole in the glacial surface. It may be from one to six feet in diameter, sometimes extending to the bottom of the ice, the shallower ones filled with sparkling ice water, others partially filled with snow.

Bagnoires—larger holes in the glacial surface, up to 15 feet long, often shaped like a bathtub, sometimes containing water.[44]

Dust wells—small vertical holes in the surface of the ice, a few inches in depth and diameter, with a little dirt at the bottom.

Glacier table—a mound or pillar of ice capped by a mass of rock debris which protects its underlying stem from solar radiation and prevents it from melting as rapidly as the surrounding ice. Alden reports having seen one more than 15 feet high on the Chaney Glacier in 1913, apparently the same one reported by Chaney himself in 1895.[45]

Striae—glacial scratchings on rocks situated beneath or adjacent to a glacier, resulting from abrasion of material carried by the ice, and always in a line with the direction of its flow.

Rock flour—silt or powdered rock produced by the grinding of glacial ice upon the bed over which it travels, giving a milky appearance to glacier melt-water streams.[46]

Gletschermilch—water that looks milky because it contains glacial rock flour.

The Work of A Glacier

Glaciers are among Earth's greatest face-lifters,[47] and those of the Park carry on a number of functions. They create the amphitheaters in which they lie by separating and ingesting rocky material from the headwall behind them; they abrade the rock floor over which they move; and they make deposits along their routes of the materials which they produce and transport. In the course of these activities, they deepen and widen their beds through the grinding of in-frozen debris upon the surfaces encountered.

Glaciers erode mainly by two processes: plucking and abrasion.[48] The first occurs with greatest frequency near the head of the glacier when it quarries out masses of rock, incorporates them within itself, and carries them along. This is accomplished largely by a process of alternate freezing and thawing, when water percolates into crevices, expands upon freezing, and forces the pieces apart. The fragments thus dislodged then fall or are swept down from the cliffs by avalanches of snow. A glacier may thus be said to gnaw continually at the headwall and to eat its way back into the mountain, ultimately producing, as we have noted before, a multiplicity of cirques, aretes, horns and cols.

The process of abrasion never ceases so long as glacial motion continues. Relatively little erosion is accomplished by the movement of pure ice over bed rock. It is the boulders and rock fragments embedded in the glacier's sides and bottom that give it the effect of an enormous rasp serving to striate, grind and polish;[49] and it is this grinding action that ultimately reduces some of the rocky material to a powdery substance which, in turn, imparts to lakes and streams below the color of the rock formations over which the glacier has moved.

How To Appreciate A Glacier

Glaciers are sensitive and dynamic.[50] They are constantly on the move, and respond in many different and subtle ways to changes in their environment. Standing before, or upon, such a glacier as Grinnell, one senses that it is alive, like a great animal. In warm weather it perspires and becomes noisy, its surface being seamed with brooks that pour into deep wells with loud roarings. The tinkle of these streams, the echoing fall of plunging torrents, and the hiss of confined water rushing along beneath the ice all contribute to a volume of sound above which, at times, it is difficult to hear ordinary conversation.[51]

Glaciers are places of danger, and the answer to the question of how to behave on a glacier is the same as how to romance a porcupine—very carefully. Inexperienced hikers should never venture onto glacial surfaces without a guide. Snow which fills crevasses and wells during the winter often melts out from below, leaving thin snow bridges in the early part of the summer. These constitute real hazards to travel on a glacier because the thinner ones are incapable of sustaining a person's weight.

Glaciers are also beautiful and mysterious.[52] In the Park, they are invariably situated in cirques or upon rugged ledges of unsurpassed grandeur, and they contort their pale blue ice into a million irregular shapes, forms and caves, never repetitive in character. By their actions they have helped to create some of the world's most spectacular scenery. The story of their origin and their many appearances and disappearances is fascinating. They have been larger and more numerous in the past, and there is scant reason to believe that they will not repeat this performance in the future.[53]

Notes For Chapter 6

[1]"Glaciers," by Robert P. Sharp, at page 3.
[2]"The World Of Ice," by James L. Dyson, at page 55.
[3]Idem, at page 61. Also, see "Glaciers And Glaciation In Glacier National Park," by James L. Dyson, at page 3.
[4]"Glaciers Of Glacier National Park," by William C. Alden, at page 4. See, also "The World Of Ice," supra, at pages 60-61.
[5]"Signposts Of Adventure," by James Willard Schultz, at page 149.
[6]"Through The Years In Glacier National Park," by Donald H. Robinson, at page 14.
[7]Article by George Bird Grinnell in Scientific American Supplement for September 23, 1899.
[8]Article entitled "The Crown Of The Continent," by George Bird Grinnell, appearing in Century Magazine for September, 1901, at page 670.
[9]Idem.
[10]Article by George Bird Grinnell in Scientific American Supplement for September 23, 1899. See, also, "Glaciers Of Glacier National Park," supra, published in 1914 by the Department of the Interior, footnote at page 4.
[11]"Through The Years," supra, at page 25.
[12]Idem, at page 24.
[13]Article entitled "In The Montana Rockies," by Lyman B. Sperry, appearing in "Appalachia," Volume VIII, No. 1, January, 1896, at page 68. See, also, "Through The Years," supra, at pages 23-24.
[14]Published by the Department of the Interior in 1914 (48 pages).
[15]According to an article entitled "Glaciers And Glaciation" by James L. Dyson, appearing at page 230 of the "Glacier National Park Drivers' Manual," the Grinnell and Sperry glaciers are the largest in the Rocky Mountains south of the Canadian boundary, with the possible exception of one or more of the Dinwoody glaciers in Wyoming's Wind River Range.

The "Glacier National Park Drivers' Manual" was a mimeographed publication formerly issued by the Glacier Park Transport Company for the information and use of its passenger bus drivers. First published in 1937, its seventh and next-to-last edition appearing in 1948 contained 300 pages of valuable information concerning the Park. For the company's sight-seeing bus drivers, it was required reading but since it was never for sale, it did not become available to the public and now, unfortunately, is likely to be found only in the National Park Service Library at West Glacier. The "Drivers' Manual," as it is referred to hereafter in these notes, contained data and articles seldom available elsewhere, if at all. The articles dealt authoritatively with Glacier's geology, glaciers, fauna, flora, personalities, services and many other features, usually from the pen of the individual best qualified to cover them. This gold mine of information has provided much assistance in the preparation of this volume which also seeks to provide a comprehensive picture of the Park in all its aspects.

[16]"Glaciers And Glaciation," supra, at page 8.
[17]Idem, at page 5.
[18]Idem, at page 8.
[19]Idem, at page 8.
[20]Idem, at page 9.
[21]According to U. S. Geological Survey data available to the National Park Service at West Glacier, the front of the glacier has become so irregular that comparison with prior years is not of much value. The eastern wing seems to have continued to recede, while the other half has apparently made an advance of between 10 and 30 feet in the biennium between 1961 and 1963, although this may well have been due to residual snow from the preceding winter and the fact

Crevasse 50 feet in depth on Grinnell Glacier
Photo by Walt Dyke, courtesy of Burlington Northern

that observations were made two weeks later in 1963 than in 1961. At all events, the degree of recession at Sperry has continued to exceed that of Grinnell.

[22]"Glaciers," supra, at page 21.
[23]Idem, at page 74. Mr. Sharp suggests that the history of glaciers generally during the past 200 years has been principally one of shrinkage and recession, interrupted by minor and local episodes of expansion.
[24]"Glaciers And Glaciation," supra, at page 16.
[25]Idem, at pages 11-12.
[26]"Glaciers Of Glacier National Park," supra, at page 29.
[27]Idem, at page 46.
[28]Idem, at page 46.
[29]"Glaciers And Glaciation," supra, at page 12.
[30]Idem, at page 12.
[31]"The Geologic Story Of Glacier National Park," by James L. Dyson, at pages 21-22.
[32]"Glaciers And Glaciation," supra, at page 15.
[33]"The World Of Ice," supra, at page 43.
[34]Idem, see illustration opposite page 109.
[35]Idem, at page 51.
[36]Idem, at pages 53-54.
[37]See Chapter 3, supra, entitled "Peaks And Pinnacles," at page 26. See, also, "The World Of Ice," supra, at page 52.
[38]Random House Dictionary (1966 edition), at page 599.
[39]"Glaciers," supra, at page 29.
[40]Idem, at page 29.
[41]Idem, at page 31.
[42]"The World Of Ice," supra, at page 49.

A curious ice formation on Blackfeet Glacier
Photo by Hileman

[43]"Glaciers And Glaciation," supra, at pages 15 and 16.
[44]"Glaciers Of Glacier National Park," supra, at page 34.
[45]Idem, at page 34.
[46]"The World Of Ice," supra, at page 43.
[47]Idem, at page 43.
[48]"Glaciers And Glaciation," supra, at pages 15-17.
[49]"The World Of Ice," at page 43.
[50]"Glaciers," supra, at page 3.
[51]Article entitled "The Crown Of The Continent," supra, by George Bird Grinnell, at page 670.
[52]"Glaciers," supra, at page 4.
[53]See discussion in "The World Of Ice," supra, at pages 259-274. See, also, discussion in "Rocks, Ice And Water, The Geology Of Waterton-Glacier Parks," by Alt and Hyndman, at page 28.

Visitors exploring crevasse at Sperry Glacier
Photo by Walt Dyke, courtesy of Burlington Northern

View of Sperry, the Park's second largest glacier
Photo by Walt Dyke, courtesy of Burlington Northern

Hikers with ranger on Sperry Glacier
Photo by Mel Ruder

Grinnell Glacier, largest in the Park
Photo by Walt Dyke, courtesy of Burlington
Northern

Chapter 7
WATER WONDERLAND

The supreme glory of Glacier National Park is in its wealth of water. Fed by its glaciers and the melting snows from a thousand drifts along the continental divide, its swift-flowing streams and sparkling cascades are everywhere, usually leading to or from a vivid tarn or mountain lake. As for the latter, it is impossible adequately to describe the romantic charm, the exquisite beauty and the extraordinary variety of these magnificent lakes.

Collectively, they are even more impressive and comprise a sumptuous lake region that exceeds anything the old world has to offer. Beautiful as the Italian lakes may be, lovely as are the Swiss lakes surrounded by snow-clad Alps, picturesque and charming as are Loch Lomond and Loch Katrine in the Scottish highlands, and delectable as are the English lakes and those of Killarney, they cannot match the numerical profusion, the fantastic coloration and, with certain exceptions, the majestic settings of those tucked away in this remote corner of Montana.

The park's 250 lakes are of many sizes and shapes—long and narrow, round and irregular, little blue ponds in mountain pockets, and long silvery ribbons in slender valleys. Influenced by the continental divide and the direction of the Park's valleys, they generally extend from northeast to southwest, or vice versa.

Along trail and road these glamorous alpine lakes peer at one from all sides. The larger ones lie in the valleys, but dozens are nestled in pockets high up on the mountain slopes. From different viewing points and under different lights, their waters may appear emerald, sapphire or cerulean, while those lying immediately beneath a glacier are often milky-white, turquoise or robin's egg blue. On calm days, they reflect the peaks and walls, but usually the surface sparkles like diamonds as crisp winds agitate the crystal-clear water. At evening, the lakes seem to absorb the glow of the setting sun, as though trying to defy the chilling of the waters as night darkens the valleys.

Glacial Origin

In most instances the lakes of the Park are attributable, directly or indirectly, to glacial action. In general, they may be divided into five main types,[1] depending upon their origin.

(1) *Cirque lakes*—These are frequently circular in shape and occupy the steep-sided basins or amphitheaters scooped out by glacial action after the glaciers themselves have disappeared. One of the most magnificent cirques of this type is at Iceberg Lake, where the former glacier came to an untimely end during the present century. Others in this category are Hidden, Avalanche, Cracker, Gunsight, Ellen Wilson, Ptarmigan and Upper Two Medicine Lakes.

(2) *Other rock-basin lakes*—This type fills basins which have been scoured out by ancient glaciers moving over areas of comparatively soft rock before encountering a more resistant formation. When several of these follow each other down a valley, they are referred to as paternoster lakes because their arrangement resembles that of beads on a rosary. Typical of this type is the chain of four lakes stretching seven miles from the foot of Swiftcurrent Pass to Many Glacier Hotel, last of the four being Swiftcurrent Lake itself.

(3) *Lakes held in by outwash*—These are bodies of water held in by natural dams of stratified gravel washed out from former glaciers when they extended down into the lower parts of the valley. Lake McDonald, as well as most of the large lakes on the western side of the Park, fall into this category.

(4) *Lakes held in by alluvial fans*—These are bodies of water with valleys that have, in their relatively recent history, been blocked with deposits of gravel, thereby either creating a lake or raising the level of one already in existence. Waterton, Lower Two Medicine and the St. Mary Lakes belong to this group. It is believed that the St. Mary Lakes were originally one body of water seventeen miles in length, but that the gravel deposited by Divide Creek at its point of entry built an alluvial fan that

ultimately cut the lake into the two present bodies of water. The St. Mary Entrance Station now stands upon this alluvial fan.

(5) *Moraine lakes* — These are bodies of water the outlets of which are partially blocked by moraines. An excellent example is Josephine Lake near Many Glacier Hotel. Another type is found at Grinnell and Sperry Glaciers, bordered on the rear by the glacial ice and at the front by the moraine. They are interesting because they are ordinarily filled with icebergs throughout the summer.

The St. Mary Lakes

The first bodies of water in the future park to become known to the white man were the St. Mary Lakes on the eastern side of the Lewis Range. They were first glimpsed in 1836[2] by Hugh Monroe, the legendary white Blackfoot, and it was he who christened them before a huge rustic cross in the presence of a group of friendly Kootenai Indians, probably in the autumn of 1845.[3] They were visited in 1854 by Lieutenant Doty, of the Stevens Expedition, while searching for a suitable pass for a transcontinental railroad. In his reports he described the lower one as "the well-known Chief Mountain Lake" and gave the name of "Bow Lake" to the other, because it extended "some nine miles into the mountains in the form of a bow."[4] By the Blackfeet they were known as the "Lakes Inside"[5] or the "Walled-In Lakes."[6]

Of the two, only Upper Lake St. Mary lies within the Park boundaries. Relatively long and narrow, it stretches nearly ten miles toward the continental divide, with a maximum width of one mile and a depth of 300 feet. It was the grandeur and beauty of the lake above the Narrows that caused Colonel Robert Baring, of the distinguished family of English bankers, to exclaim in September, 1889:

> "I have been in the Alps of Switzerland and the Hamalayas in India, but in neither of those ranges have I seen any setting of lake and mountains that can compare with this before us."[7]

This is the same lake that caused the well-known writer, Agnes C. Laut, to rhapsodize:

> "You forget every lake you have ever seen before in all your life. It is giving off diamond flashes where the midday sun strikes the rippling whitecaps; but close ashore are the purple shades and the emerald glints and the peacock blues."[8]

It is difficult to speak of upper Lake St. Mary except in superlatives. It is the Park's largest body of water east of the continental divide. It fills a deep glaciated gorge and is surrounded by some of the noblest peaks of the Rockies. It represents a harmonious blend of land, sky and water unequalled in all the western mountains.

Frequently at early morn or in the evening when the sun drops beyond the western peaks in an aura of varying lights and hues, the lake is placid and reflects in its clear blue depths all the indescribable glory of sky, forests and the encircling snow-patched mountains. At other times, when the sun's rays have dispelled the veil of mists that sometimes cling to the surrounding mountain heads, the surface of the lake receives the brilliancy radiated from these shafts of light, and appears a shining mass of ripples.

By Land And By Launch

The St. Mary Lakes are reached by the Blackfeet Highway that winds down to them over the north slopes of the Hudson Bay Divide. Here is the beginning of the Going-To-The-Sun Highway that leads along the north shore of the upper lake toward the summit of Logan Pass. About half-way up the lake are the comfortable Rising Sun Motor Lodge and Campground, and a little further, slightly off the main highway, is the site of the former Going-To-The-Sun chalet group, commonly referred to as Sun Camp.

These chalets, once the largest such group in the Park, were situated a hundred feet above the lake on a promontory at the base of Goat Mountain. They commanded vistas, up and down the lake, that were among the finest in the Park. They had accommodations for 175 guests, and were a trail-riding hub for those coming over Piegan Pass from Many Glacier, and over Gunsight Pass from Lake McDonald. The years brought increasingly difficult maintenance problems, but removal of the chalets during the 1940's came about primarily because the changing needs of Park travel could better be served by relocation to the more spacious Rising Sun site, four miles to the east.

It is the launch ride from Rising Sun that perhaps best enables the traveler to appreciate the extraordinary beauty of Upper Lake St. Mary and its panorama of enchantment. On the south shore of the lake, Red Eagle and Little Chief Mountains project their ship-like prows into the water and lift their hoary crests to the sky. On the opposite shore the buff and green banded walls of Single-shot and colorful

Okotomi Mountains tower above the lake. Far up the valley, through the narrows, the tilted cone of Fusillade Mountain desputes the right of way to Gunsight Pass.

As the launch rounds the projections of the Golden Stairs at the Narrows, you are brought into the very lap of the enfolding peaks—the sharp, tawny pinnacles of Citadel, the red and gray crags of Goat Mountain, the classic outlines of Going-To-The-Sun, monarch of mountains, and all the rest around to Red Eagle on the south. On each is visible the same record of the rocks, the laminated belts of yellow and red and buff and blue and green and gray which mark the layers of prehistoric seas, and which were created before ever the sun penetrated the drench of vapor rising from a primeval world.

Two Medicine Lake

Situated only a few miles above the Park's eastern entrance and easily reached by highway is Two Medicine Lake. Stretching from southwest to northeast down a glacially carved valley, like a great silver ribbon, this exquisite lake is three miles long, with a maximum width of half a mile and depth of 400 feet. It shares the valley with two sister lakes, the lower of which is almost entirely within the Blackfeet Reservation outside the Park.[9]

The lake is framed in a setting of unforgettable grandeur, particularly impressive as the surrounding peaks, in the last crimson blush of day, are reflected in the quiet depths of its waters. The massive rock walls of Rising Wolf Mountain form its north shore, Appistoki looms to the south, while at its head Sinopah Mountain, resembling a pyramid, seems almost to overhang the water. This magnificent panorama of water, forest and mountains draws many to the lake's pleasant campground to enjoy the excellent fishing, to hike along the many nearby trails or simply to contemplate its beauty.

The Grinnell Chain

Uppermost of the mountain tarns draining the southwestern arm of Swiftcurrent Valley is Grinnell Lake, a circular body of water above which rise perpendicularly the red argillite walls of the great cirques behind it. Its opalescent waters, tinged with green, acquire their hues from the "gletschermilch," or pulverized rock flour that is swept down with the meltings of the glacier above. Despite its smaller size, its coloring and setting are very reminiscent of Lake Louise in the Canadian Rockies.

Even more beautiful, if possible, than Grinnell is Josephine, the middle lake of the chain. It is about one and a half miles in length, with a maximum width of half a mile. Like the abandoned mine situated above it on the slopes of Grinnell Point, it was named after a niece of the owner of the mine.[10] In the opinion of many, Josephine presents a symphony of water, rock and foliage that has few, if any, equals in the Park or on the continent.

Swiftcurrent is the key lake in the valley of the same name, a name originally given it by George Bird Grinnell in the late 1880's. A few years later it was changed to McDermott, in honor of a local lumberman, but officially changed back to Swiftcurrent in 1928. The Blackfeet name for it was Jealous Women's Lake, the legend being that two sisters loved the same warrior and decided to settle their dispute by swimming the lake side by side until one of them drowned. It was the elder sister who succumbed to fatigue and the frigidity of the lake's icy waters.

Swiftcurrent Lake is a mile long with a maximum width of half a mile. Like Josephine and Grinnell, it occupies a basin scooped out of the Altyn limestone by ancient glacial action, and into it flows all the drainage from those lakes, as well as from Bullhead, Red Rock, Fishercap, Ptarmigan and Iceberg Lakes. In ancient times it was larger and deeper, but gradual erosion of the outlet barrier lowered its level, ultimately baring the ledge on which Many Glacier Hotel now stands near its lower end. The panoramic view from the shores of the lake toward Mt. Gould, the Grinnell Glacier, the Garden wall, Mt. Wilbur and the Pinnacle Wall is one of the world's great outlooks.

Other Lakes Of The Swiftcurrent Valley

Most spectacular of all the Park's smaller lakes, as well as one of its most popular, is Iceberg Lake. Half a mile across and 146 feet deep, this miniature polar sea lies on the north side of Mt. Wilbur, partially surrounded by walls that rise almost vertically 3000 feet above its surface. Its name is derived from the fact that, during late summer, small bergs of ice would break loose from the tiny glacier that stood at the rear of the lake prior to 1940, and would float serenely about its surface. A large amount of snow and ice still accumulates each winter in the glacier's old pocket, from which, in July and August, ice cakes break away and sail about on this little sapphire sea. The lake is sometimes frozen over until mid-July, and no fish are able to survive in its waters because their surface temperature, even in August, seldom rises above 42°.[11]

Ptarmigan Lake is a small but interesting body of water about four miles to the north of Iceberg Lake. It lies in a glacial cirque at the head of the deep, narrow canyon below the Ptarmigan Wall. Its elevation of 6500 feet is approximately 450 feet above that of Iceberg Lake, but the warmth which its waters gain from its southern exposure is sufficient to support fish life. Consequently, brook trout of moderate size dwell in its waters.[12] Less than 850 feet above the lake lies the celebrated Ptarmigan tunnel, unique gateway to the Belly River country to the north.

A chain of three paternoster lakes is situated along the trail from Many Glacier to Swift-current Pass. Successively, from below, these are Fishercap, Red Rock and Bullhead, the basins of each scooped out by ancient glacial action. The red argillite rock of the Grinnell formation is very much in evidence along the trail, particularly at Red Rock Falls. Above the falls is Bullhead Lake, a slender body of water over a mile in length. High above its upper reaches lies the snow-filled cirque in which the Swiftcurrent Glacier formerly reposed.

In a different direction from Many Glacier Hotel, and approximately seven miles by trail, lies stunning Cracker Lake. This turquoise gem at the head of Canyon Creek is about half a mile in length, and has a elevation of 5800 feet. Above the head of the lake are the Siyeh Glacier and its moraine, as well as the perpendicular north face of Mt. Siyeh, rising more than 10,000 feet above sea level. On the east side of the lake will be found the abandoned shaft of the old Cracker Mine, to which, in the early years of the century, a road was built and a large ore concentrator was brought in with extreme difficulty from the railroad at Browning.

Reclamation Reservoir

Sherburne Lake is situated at the lower end of the Swiftcurrent Valley. In size, it is among the half-dozen largest bodies of water in the Park, with a length of six miles and maximum width of ⅝ of a mile. It is actually a reservoir with its water backed up by a dam lying just outside the Park boundary, constituting a part of the Milk River Irrigation Project conceived in pre-Park days, although the project was not completed until about 1920. Before construc-

tion, the valley contained two natural lakes and was heavily timbered.

Water from the reservoir flows through Swiftcurrent Creek to the St. Mary River from which, at a point near Babb, a part of it is diverted into a canal. From the latter it is then taken over the ridge of the Hudson Bay Divide in a huge pipe that operates on a siphon principle; ultimately it is delivered into the Milk River for irrigational use in central Montana. The reservoir and dam, as well as the lakes which preceded them, derived their name from J. J. Sherburne, an official of the Swift-current Oil, Land and Power Company which drilled for oil in 1904 near the site of the present dam.

Northbound Lakes

In the Belly River country there are a number of lakes of great beauty. Among the largest of these are Glenn's Lake and Cosley (Crossley) Lake[13] on the Mokowanis branch of the Belly River. Glenn's Lake is nearly four miles long, but very narrow. At its upper end, the water is opaque with gletschermilch, but it becomes a clear sapphire hue at the outlet. It is separated from Cosley Lake, two miles long, by an alluvial fan.

Above Glenn's Lake is a chain of tarns, with a huge waterfall leaping down the cliff from Margaret Lake in the very shadow of milehigh Mt. Merritt. Below Mokowanis Lake, the stream forms a silver apron as it dashes down the rapids called "White Quiver Falls." Near the southeasterly headwaters of the Belly River are attractive Lakes Helen and Elizabeth.

The Park's one international lake[14] is Waterton, seven miles in length and up to 450 feet in depth, with more than half of it south of the border. It lies in a region in which the handiwork of ancient glaciers, i.e., cirques, hanging valleys and waterfalls, is everywhere, and owes the special shape of its own valley to glacial action. Hemming in the lake around the American end are Cleveland, Goathaunt, Porcupine Ridge, Olson and Campbell Mountains. Lakes Francis and Janet, in the great valley leading west toward Brown Pass, are lovely mountain tarns that contribute their respective bits to the volume of water headed for Waterton Lake and Hudson Bay.

Lakes On The Park's Pacific Slope

The story of the lakes on the west side of the Park begins with beautiful Lake McDonald, called Sacred Dancing Lake by the Indians because the tribes of that region would gather there every summer for their annual religious ceremonies. It gained its present name from Duncan McDonald who, in the early 1870's, had been in charge of the Hudson's Bay trading post south of Flathead Lake. About 1878, while engaged in freighting supplies to Canada, he came upon this body of water and camped there overnight, carving his name upon the bark of a birch tree near what is now Apgar. From this, people began to call it McDonald's Lake.[15]

Someone has said that the lakes of Glacier Park really should be divided into two categories. The first, those too small for navigation, but too large to be mounted and carried away as jewelry; the second, the larger, or "sea-going" type. Lake McDonald belongs in the latter classification, being nearly ten miles in length, with a maximum width of one and a half miles. In size and setting, it resembles the Italian lakes more than any other in the Park. Unlike most of the other lakes, it is not walled in, except for its ancient lateral moraines. From its shores gradually rise wonderfully wooded hills which sweep on and up until lost in a silent group of mountains, looming high against the blue sky and guarding the upper end of the lake. Among these attractive sentinels are Mounts Edwards, Brown, Cannon, Vaught and Stanton.

The chief charm of matchless Lake McDonald lies in the clarity of its azure depths fed by silvery threads of melted snow descending to it from several directions. The lake is very deep, and its blue is an ocean blue, its green a peacock's tail green.

"No glacial breath that stirs McDonald's wave
But finds some coupling with the spinning stars;
No pebble on her shore but proves a sphere;
Her crystal surface set with gems from heaven,
She is a page from God's eternal book."[16]

Other West Side Lakes

Avalanche Lake, approximately one mile in length, lies in a basin by the same name located some seven or eight miles above the head of Lake McDonald. This scenic gem is enclosed by mountain walls on all sides except at the outlet. Near the head of its high-walled, U-shaped canyon is a huge, glacially carved cirque. Tumbling some 2,500 feet over the purple-red walls of this cirque are half-a-dozen silvery waterfalls carrying meltwater from Sperry Glacier above. Most of it reaches the lake, but much is dissipated in mist as it strikes the rocks in its downward plunge.

From the water's edge dark green forests of pine and spruce clothe portions of the steep slopes until they give way to showy fields and colored strata of bare rock. On the shelf above, almost in the shadow of Gunsight Mountain, lies the white expanse of Sperry Glacier, carrying on in much the same fashion as did its ancient predecessors. Glacially fed, and with its surface enlivened with countless bubbles, Avalanche Lake looks like nothing so much as a huge pearl in a rugged setting of cirque and cliff.

Highest in altitude among the Park's good-sized bodies of water is Hidden Lake. Located just west of Mt. Reynolds and the continental divide, its elevation is 6,375 feet and its length is in excess of three miles. A point from which it can be viewed to advantage is reached from Logan Pass by a self-guided, two-mile trail that leads through gardens of wild flowers and overledges that contain outcroppings of fossil algae. The trail ends on a bench between Mts. Clements and Reynolds with a breath-taking view of Hidden Lake and the country west of the divide. A footpath, used primarily by fishermen, continues on to the shores of the lake below.

The Flathead country north of Lake McDonald features long, densely forested valleys and slender blue lakes that nose up almost to the glacier-spattered peaks of the continental divide. The longest of these is Bowman, seven miles in length and 250 feet deep, from the upper end of which the trail rises approximately 2,500 feet to the grassy summit of Brown Pass. Trout, Logging, Quartz and the incredibly beautiful Kintla Lakes are, for the most part, wilderness country, although the lower ends of some of them are reachable by car. Accommodations for visitors are limited to campgrounds, and this area of several hundred square miles is largely a hikers' and anglers' paradise.

Waterfalls

The most spectacular features of the Park's tremendous water show are, of course, its hundreds of falls and cascades. They are almost everywhere throughout the Park, especially in the higher reaches, and vary from half a yard to half a mile in height, as well as from ordinary to unusual. As with the lakes, they owe much to the glaciers, not only for a substantial contribution of water itself, but also for the ancient glacial action that had so much to do with determining their location and even, to some extent, their size.

Glacier's waterfalls are of two principal types, one occurring in the bottom of the main valleys and the other at the mouth of the hanging tributary valleys.[17] The former are located where streams drop over the "risers" on what is sometimes called the "glacial staircase," i.e., where a valley floor descends in a series of steps, rather than by a gradual slope, each step ending in a sharp drop to the next level, these steps having been caused by differences in the resistance to erosion of the rock over which the ancient glaciers flowed.[18] Examples of this type of cascade are Swiftcurrent, Red Rock, Dawn Mist, Trick and Morning Eagle, among others.

The second type of falls occurs at the point where a hanging valley enters the main valley high above the latter's floor, necessitating a sudden and often extraordinary drop by the stream draining the hanging valley. The explanation of this phenomenon lies in the fact that the main valleys, with their much greater streams of ancient glacial ice, were deepened at a more rapid rate than that accomplished by smaller glaciers in the tributary valleys, resulting in the latter being left hanging high above the floor of the major valleys.[19] An example of this type is Florence Falls, with its cascades of extraordinary beauty, down which tumble the waters that drain the valley of Florence Creek into the much deeper St. Mary Valley. Others are Virginia, Bird Woman, Grinnell, Lincoln and Appekunny Falls.

Swiftcurrent And Trick Falls

Among the most interesting and accessible of the waterfalls in the Park is Swiftcurrent Falls, over which pass all of the waters from the upper Swiftcurrent Valley. Actually, there are a series of cascades within a short distance of each other, the upper one being only a few feet below the bridge by which the highway leading to Many Glacier Hotel crosses the outlet of Swiftcurrent Lake. The ledge over which the falls plunge is composed of the extremely resistant rock of the Altyn formation, lowest and oldest in the Park; and down the gorge are visible the twisted strata of the Lewis Overthrust. Comfortably situated in a cave below the upper section of the Falls is the nest of a woodrat family, while many generations of water ouzels have made their homes at the foot of the Falls.

Perhaps the most popular of the Park's many cascades is Trick Falls, located in the valley of the Two Medicine, and reached from the highway by a short, self-guided walk. This geological oddity is composed of Altyn limestone through which, some distance back of the falls, stream pressures have excavated an underground channel. It is down this subterranean passage, in times of low water, that the creek flows entirely, emerging somewhat more than halfway down from the upper level of the falls to plunge thirty feet into the pool below. When stream flow is heavier, the water also comes over the top of the falls some fifty feet higher in good volume, thus creating a unique combination of two falls in one. The Blackfeet called it Running Eagle Falls and, because of its mysterious nature, regarded it with great awe.

An even eerier cascade, plainly visible from Logan Pass, is formed by a torrent of water that gushes forth at a point high on the rocky southern slope of Piegan Mountain to the northeast of the Pass. This is apparently meltwater from Piegan Glacier on the opposite side of the peak that has found a means of escape through the layers of shale or other depositional rock that compose the mountain.

Rivers And Rivulets

The streams of the Park are a source of special delight, with their multiple appeal to the senses. The babble of the brooks and the muffled roar of small torrents are wilderness music; the dash and verve of eddies and rapids, and the limpid creeks hurrying over their beds of colorful pebbles are a visual joy; while the pleasure of the thirsty hiker is enhanced by the plentiful supply of pure, clear ice-water rushing by at almost every turn of the trail.

As in every mountain range, the streams of Glacier have their origins near its summits. Unnumbered banks of melting snow and ice release hundreds of rills and rivulets, most of them nameless, being only a few inches in depth and width. As enough of them flow together to reach brook size, they develop a volume and velocity that really entitle them to be called torrents—torrents white as snow with a succession of falls, then blue as the sea where the falls create deep pools. Dancing along, they sing and chant their processional to the cathedral orchestra of the pines and the deep organ boom of the big firs and spruces. They rush along, as they have for centuries, until they merge in a larger stream or lake and move toward the sea.

While countless brooks and creeks deliver substantial quantities of water to the bodies of water into which they eventually empty, the greatest length of any of the small west side waterways is less than twenty miles, McDonald Creek and Nyack Creek being two of the longest. On the east side, no stream attains a length of more than twelve miles within Park boundaries, and only three have been dignified with the name of river by the mapmakers. These are the St. Mary, the Belly, and the Waterton Rivers, all of which flow into and out of lakes on their northward journeys into Canada.

Water To Three Oceans

On the other hand, Glacier's many streams make important contributions to great rivers of the continent. Chief among the latter is the Flathead, the north and middle forks of which carry to Flathead Lake, and ultimately to the Pacific, all of the run-off from the Park's western and southwestern summits and slopes. To the south and east of the Hudson Bay Divide, the Two Medicine and Cut Bank Creeks deliver their water into the Marias River, a tributary of the Missouri. The drainage of the valleys north of the Divide moves through the Waterton, Belly and St. Mary Rivers to junctions with the great Saskatchewan River in Canada; at least this is the destination of all the St. Mary water that is not diverted to the Milk River Irrigation Project in north central Montana.

There are few, if any, other areas of similar size in the "lower forty-eight" states that generate a volume of water equal to that flowing out of the Park each year. Its glaciers and great snowbanks constitute natural reservoirs that store up moisture throughout most of the year, then release it, with solar assistance, during the summer months at a rate with which its streams can conveniently cope. Only once has Nature's timetable been seriously disrupted, this occurring when extraordinary weather conditions produced the disastrous flood of 1964[20] Glacier is obviously a builder of important streams beyond its borders, and were it possible for all of the water originating within the Park to be carried away by a single stream, that stream would be one of the great rivers of the Northwest.

Trick Falls

Photo by Mel Ruder

Avalanche Gorge

Photo by Mel Ruder

Notes For Chapter 7

[1]"Glaciers And Glaciation In Glacier National Park," by James L. Dyson, at pages 20-22.

[2]Monroe himself asserted that he had discovered the lakes in 1836, supplying that information in interviews which were printed in the Fort Benton River Press on February 19, 1890 and in the Chinook Opinion on October 29, 1892. In the course of his life in the early Northwest, Monroe visited the lakes from time to time after 1836, even residing on the shores of the lower lake periodically. See the story of Monroe on pages 91-92 of Chapter 11, infra, entitled "Advent Of The White Man."

[3]For information concerning the christening of the lakes, see notes 26 and 27 of Chapter 11, infra, entitled "Advent Of The White Man."

[4]Doty's visit to the lakes took place in the latter part of May and the early part of June, 1854, according to the report of his reconnaissance in Volume I, Pacific Railroad Reports, at pages 548-549. An earlier reconnaissance had been made in October, 1853 by Lieutenant Tinkham which resulted in a crossing over Cut Bank, rather than Marias Pass.

[5]"Signposts Of Adventure," by James Willard Schultz, at page 122.

[6]See article by George Bird Grinnell, under the pseudonym of "Yo," entitled "To The Walled-In Lakes," originally published in 1885 in Forest and Stream Magazine, and reprinted at page 29 of the 1948 edition of "Drivers' Manual" (see note 15, Chapter 6, supra).

[7]See "Blackfeet And Buffalo," by James Willard Schultz, at page 114. For more information about the Barings, see page 149 of Chapter 18, infra, entitled "Visitors: Distinguished And Otherwise."

[8]"Enchanted Trails Of Glacier National Park," by Agnes C. Laut, at page 74.

[9]The three lakes in this chain are the Lower Two Medicine, the Two Medicine, and the Upper Two Medicine, the first of which lies almost entirely within the Blackfeet Reservation. The lake described here is the Two Medicine.

[10]In the early days of the Park this beautiful lake was called "Altyn," and the origin of its present name of "Josephine" has been somewhat obscure. According to information received by J. Gordon Edwards in the early 1950's from a man representing himself to be Parley Stark, both the lake and the mine above it were named for his niece, Josephine Stark.

[11]See article entitled "Fish And Fishing Waters In Glacier National Park," by A. S. Hazzard, Ph.D., Michigan Institute For Fisheries Research, appearing at page 163 of the 1948 edition of the "Drivers' Manual" (see note 15, Chapter 6, supra).

[12]Idem.

[13]For most of the Park's existence as such, the name for this lake and the nearby ridge has been "Crossley." Recently, because of the belief that this may have been a corruption of the name of Joe Cosley, the names have been changed accordingly. Cosley, an early Park ranger at Belly River, was also a hunter, trapper, guide and, in his later years, a poacher. For a story of his poaching activities, see Chapter 22, infra, entitled "The Guardians Of Glacier," at pages 177-178.

[14]Actually, the southernmost 200 yards of Cameron Lake also lie south of the international boundary.

[15]"Through The Years In Glacier National Park," by Donald H. Robinson, at pages 14 and 15.

[16]From the prologue to the poem "Lake McDonald," written and published in 1914 by J. W. Dowler of Troy, Ohio.

[17]"Glaciers And Glaciation," supra, at page 19.

[18]Idem, at page 16.

[19]Idem, at page 17.

[20]For the story of this great flood, see Chapter 24, infra, entitled "Environmental Problems," at page 190.

Iceberg Lake

Photo by Mel Ruder

St. Mary Falls

Photo by Mel Ruder

Chapter 8
MILLION-ACRE
FLOWER GARDEN

Glacier National Park is truly a vast garden in which flowers of wondrous hues and infinite variety carpet the earth with loveliness for a few weeks in summer wherever the soil is bared of snow by the sun. The Rocky Mountains, as a whole, are blessed with a profusion of wild flowers, but nowhere else, perhaps, are conditions so favorable to their growth as in Glacier. There they bloom in glorious abundance — myriads of varieties and masses of color — and the gorgeousness of their variegated hues is one of the Park's outstanding features.

All this floral beauty heightens the rich color pageant of Glacier Park's mountains. The flowers carpet soft meadows beside waterfall pools; they form festive fringes for glaciers, and shine against the brilliant reds, greens, yellows and purples of the rocks that make these mountains. No more ideal setting could have been chosen for the vivid colorings of alpine vegetation that challenge every traveler's attention.

A technical knowledge of botany is not necessary to an appreciation of the matchlessness of Glacier's floral display. No particular familiarity with genera and species of plant life is needed to enjoy the beauty of sunlit mountain meadow awash with a riot of color — purple, indigo, crimson, pink and milk-white. In fact, the delight of standing knee-deep in the fragrance of countless blossoms is likely to be more profoundly felt by the ordinary flower-lover than by the plant specialist or professional gardener.

Conditions Affecting
Glacier's Vegetation

Alpine flora is the general classification under which flowers that grow in mountain country are grouped. It includes roughly every species of plant growing between plains level and mountain summit, and is a reflection of the basic role played by altitude in determining the character of the vegetation of a region.

In addition to altitude, the conditions under which plants thrive depend upon a number of related factors, such as temperature, moisture, soil conditions and length of growing season. In Glacier Park, the continental divide has created differing conditions of soil, moisture and temperature at similar elevations on opposite sides of the mountains. The climate on the west side tends to be rainier and milder than on the eastern slopes with their drier, windier conditions. As a result, some of the Park's flowers flourish on that side of the Park offering growing conditions to which they have been able to adjust, although most species are found on both sides.

The luxuriance of Glacier's vegetation must be attributed, in large part, to the abundance of moisture which the glaciers and melting snows provide — a supply of life-giving water evenly distributed over the growing season. Perhaps the plenitude of moisture also accounts to some extent for the richness of flower coloring so attractive to the eye.

One of the most important factors influencing the character of alpine flora generally and that in Glacier, in particular, is the abbreviated growing season. The lower mountain slopes of Glacier are garbed in snow for over six months of the year, while the peaks and some of the passes are revealed for scarcely three months. Much of the higher vegetation therefore lies dormant under a blanket of snow for three-fourths of the year at such an elevation that there is barely time for the plants to bloom before they are again buried under the snow.

Classification Of Areas

Because altitude is the primary factor in determining the vegetative cover of any region, science has divided growth levels into seven fairly well-defined belts called "life zones." In Glacier Park, where elevations range from less than 3,200 feet above sea level to nearly 10,500 feet above, the upper four[1] of these seven zones are to be found; in fact, one may pass through three of them in less than an hour by driving over Logan Pass. To some extent, these four zones tend to overlap, but some knowledge of them is essential to anyone who wishes to appreciate and fully enjoy the Park's flowers.

The Transition Zone, sometimes called the Prairie Zone, bridges the gap between plains and lower mountain areas. Largely treeless, most of it lies below the 4,000-foot level, although tongues of it may reach 4,500 feet on the eastern side of the Park as, for example, along Lower St. Mary and Sherburne Lakes. On the west side, because of the heavy snowfall and dense timber, there is really no considerable area that can be called a part of this zone.

The Canadian Zone, also called the Forest Zone, comprises the well-timbered areas of the Park and extends roughly from 4,000 to 6,000 feet above sea level, although it may run higher on southwest slopes. The greater part of the Park lies within this zone, typical of which are the McDonald Valley on the west side, and the Many Glacier area on the east.

The Hudsonian Zone, sometimes called the Timberline Zone, is a narrow belt around the peaks extending generally from about 6,000 feet in elevation up to 7,000 feet on the cold northeast exposures and to 7,000 or 8,000 on the warmer southwest exposures. It is characterized by open alpine meadows, gnarled trees and dwarf plants. In midsummer, however, it becomes one of the Park's most attractive zones, with its brilliant flower gardens carpeting the open slopes and grassy meadows, its miniature forests and scattered groves of stunted and wind-beaten timber, and its numerous snow banks, tiny lakes and roaring rivulets. Typical of this zone is the summit of Logan Pass with its elevation of more than 6,600 feet above sea level.

The Arctic-Alpine Zone extends from peak tops down to the 7,000 to 8,000-foot level, depending on the climatic variations in particular locations. It lies entirely above the last trace of timber and dwarfed trees, and includes most of the glaciers and large snow fields and great expanses of barren cliff and rock. For the greater part of each year it is buried in snow, but during the short summer becomes bright with alpine flowers. Even the cracks and niches in the rocks shelter hardy plants that defy wind and storm and frosty nights.

Floral Varieties And Their Timetables

A wealth of information concerning the plant life of the region is available from a number of sources which not only identify the principal flowers and plants, but also provide excellent pictures of them in color.[2] An exhaustive treatise on Park plants is contained in Paul Standley's "Flora Of Glacier National Park,"[3] Of the 950 species which he enumerates, the flowers of common interest comprise about 100. The remainder consists of trees, ferns, grasses and other non-flowering plants, as well as close variations of some of the familiar flowering species.

During whatever part of the summer the visitor chooses to come, he will find a glorious array of color in Glacier Park. Some of the early flowers may already have ended their brief existence before the travel season opens in June; a few will still be in bloom when it closes in September. As a rule, the month of July is the period of greatest luxuriance, as it is also the time of the melting of the upland snows. The more brilliant blooms then appear and hold forth until the middle of August; thenceforward the display of floral beauty is on the wane, and heavy September frosts fold the flowers away until the sun of another spring shall smile.

Unofficial flower of the Park is the showy bloom of the beargrass, sometimes called "Glacier's crowning glory." It grows about three feet high on a heavy, waxen stalk. Surmounting this stem is an enormous, pear-shaped blossom that somewhat resembles a large tuft of cotton. Often the tiny flowers composing this great white plume feather the stalk half-way down. This flower grows in profusion throughout the Park, and follows the seasonal changes from lower levels in early summer to high mountain passes in July and August. Its name, however, is something of a misnomer, since it is a lily, not a grass, and it is not a particular favorite with the bears.

Flowers Of The Transition Zone

Like the animals, the flowers have their favorite zones. Along the Blackfeet Highway, the first spring flowers are usually the glacier lily and the buttercup. Then come the shootingstars, the larkspur and the blue beard-tongue. In grassy meadows in the St. Mary and Sherburne Lakes areas, the blue camas grows so thick it is as though dark blue patches had been painted on the landscape.

Later in the season the prairie zone exhibits areas of wild geranium, wild onion, lupine, wild rose, cinquefoil, paintbrush and many others. Throughout the summer are to be found quantities of harebells, the bluebell of

Scotland. In swampy places grow the irises. Late summer displays include fleabanes, asters, brown-eyed susans and goldenrod.

Flowers Of The Canadian Zone

One of the earliest and most conspicuous flowers of this zone is the glacier lily, or dogtooth violet. Then there are the yellow arnicas, purple phacelia, the mariposa or mountain lily, the columbine, wild clematis, anemone, forget-me-not, fireweed, wild hollyhock and the many-hued Indian paintbrush. In damp places grow fringed parnassia and lady's tresses, and where woods are thickest, queencup beadlily, prince's pine and pink pyrola are common. An abundance of silky lupine and bunchberry are to be found in northern valleys of the Park.

Waxing enthusiastic, an early visitor to the Park wrote: "There is the windflower or spring anemone with her woolly hair to protect her seedling from neuralgia in the chill of the mountain snows. There is the edelweiss or liveforever, for its bristly florets survive winter cold and summer heat. There is the Jacob's Ladder with the lovely legend of a path to the stars flowering in the sky. There are daisies and asters and sunflowers of every hue. There are purple fire-flowers, growing, as the Indians say, where fires have run, but I suspect the squirrels and birds and winds have seeded the fire-flowers where no fire but the sun's ever ran; for you find it in the depths of the forests and on the edges of lakes. There are azaleas, spireas and roses. There are fringed gentians of deep blue velvet with an embroidery to make my lady swoon with envy. There is that waxen beauty, the mountain laurel, in great banks. There are buttercups holding up a chalice of dew to the sun. There are purple and white heathers to tear at the heart of a Scotchman. There are shy snowdrops just peeping at you. There are bluebells graceful of stem as a girl's throat, ringing a music only the birds hear. There are columbines trembling to the touch of every breeze, and forget-me-nots—believe me, you couldn't forget them if you tried."[4]

Flowers Of The Hudsonian Zone

It is on upland meadows and on the shores of mountain lakes that one is apt to find the most brilliant exhibits of color. The banks of Iceberg and Cracker Lakes are aglow with gorgeous tints much of the summer. Many blooms are found on the alpine uplands near Granite Park and on the trail to Grinnell Glacier, while the floral display along the Indian Pass trail has been likened to a "miniature Garden of Eden."[5]

The Logan Pass area, including the trail to Hidden Lake and the Hanging Gardens, blossoms out with a myriad of colors, some not appearing, however, until late July or August. Among these are the reds of the monkeyflower (Lewis Mimulus) and the mountainheath, the pinks of the fireweed and shootingstar, the purple of the showy fleabane, and the wonderful blue of the gentian. White varieties include the spring beauty, mountain heather, globeflower, parnassia and pasqueflower. Most numerous of all are the yellows of the alpine buttercup, goldenrod, monkey flower and blueleaf cinquefoil and, late in the season, the bright blossoms of the St. John's wort. Most common of all flowers at this level is the delicate glacier lily, for the succulent bulbs of which the bears are wont to dig. A few of the slopes near the Pass and above Hidden Lake have great stands of beargrass.

The Flower Pass

The undoubted climax of Glacier's prodigious garden of flowers is to be found in a Hudsonian locale along the trail to Piegan Pass. For most of the summer whole meadows are there aflame with the vivid crimsons and pinks of the Indian paintbrush and its kin, the painted cup. The gamut of blue, from azure to indigo, is run by the harebell, the vetch family, the forget-me-nots and the blue phacelia; while a note of purple is added by the blossoms of the butterwort and thickly matted beardtongue. All shades of yellow are found in the profusion of glacier lilies and columbines, while banks of red and white heather add their notes of color to that of the wild heliotrope.

One visitor described the vista "in the valley at the foot of that huge escarpment and bleak precipice that forms the majestic Garden Wall as a glorious 'Field of the Cloth of Gold,' spread out as by enchantment. High upon the trail were yellow carpets of arnica flowers, gaillardias and lilies, followed in turn by great banks of flaming Indian paintbrush and painted cup, and vetches in shades of blue, mauve, lilac, purple, violet and heliotrope, hardly to be distinguished from the gentians."[6]

Flowers Of The Arctic-Alpine Zone

There are always a few courageous plants flaunting their blossoms to the breeze above timberline. Wherever a cranny permits the lodgment of a mite of soil, there grows a handful of tiny alpine flowerlets. Their pathetic struggle against overwhelming odds cannot but excite admiration, although their less ostentatious, even inconspicuous, blossoms cannot compare with those of lower elevations.

Sometimes these hardy pioneers of the bleak summits are dwarf lowland species which have adapted themselves to the changed conditions. Mostly, however, they are alpine or subalpine flowers, such as the true forget-me-not with its lovely blue flowers, the tiny blossoms of the shooting star, the dwarf lupine, the alpine bistort, and whole upland meadows gleaming white with the flowers of the mountain dryad. But with all of them, there is only a brief month or so of life; then the frosts of more than seven thousand feet of elevation take their toll.

Patterns Of Growth

All the brilliant-hued, more attractive flower varieties are not, of course, to be found blooming together at any one time or place. Some peep forth in late spring only, while others blossom until the snow flies in autumn. A few follow the course of spring up the mountainside, blooming in the valleys in May and on the uplands in August. As the snow recedes, they come to life, some even protruding through an inch or more of snow.

Some of the most interesting species frequent the high places and hug the fringes of the snow. Others haunt the upland meadows, while many grow only in the valleys and along the lake shores. Many plants that make their late-season appearance in Hudsonian or Arctic-Alpine zones are not confined to such inaccessible spots. They may also be found at lower elevations where the rays of the sun have power to lay bare in spring the vast meadows of rich grass set with countless flowers that appear almost as soon as the snow has receded. For instance, the far-famed flower of heaven-reflected blue, the gentian, blooms abundantly in late spring and early summer in the lower meadows while sister plants are still sleeping under a deep snow shroud on high slopes of the Hudsonian Zone for another two months or more.

Fruits And Forests

In addition to its plethora of flowers, Glacier Park offers a variety of attractive and edible berries. These include the huckleberry, black currant and wild strawberry, all of which make marvelous jams, jellies and pies, as well as the western serviceberry, the bearberry and the black elderberry. All hold a strong attraction for the animals of the Park, particularly the bears; and some of them were used by the Indians to make a pemmican, a mixture of dried berries and buffalo meat. They are most frequently found along the trails to Iceberg Lake, Grinnell Glacier and Piegan Pass.

The forests of the Park present an interesting contrast between the trees growing on opposite sides of the continental divide.[7] Those west of the divide are typical of the forests of the Pacific Coast, although somewhat smaller. Those on the east side more generally resemble the forests of the southern Rocky Mountains. Practically all of the trees of the Park, other than the ponderosa pine and a few subalpine species, will be found in its Canadian, or Forest, Zone.

In the valleys and on the slopes of the east side of the Park are stands of Engelmann spruce, lodgepole pine, limber pine, black cottonwood and quaking aspen, together with whitebark pine and subalpine fir at or near timberline. On the western slopes, where there is a heavier rainfall and milder climate, nearly all of the eastern slope varieties are found as well as ponderosa pine (beautiful parklike stands along the North Fork of the Flathead River), western white pine (sometimes called the aristocrat of pines), Grand and Douglas firs, western and subalpine larches and Rocky Mountain juniper.[8] Growing in the McDonald Valley only are the western hemlock and the magnificent redcedar, the latter attaining heights of up to one hundred feet and diameters of up to seven feet.[9]

Notes For Chapter 8

[1]These life zones are based upon the "life zone theory" of C. Hart Merriam. For a detailed explanation of these zones as they affect Glacier National Park, see "Wild Animals of Glacier National Park," by Vernon Bailey and Florence Merriam Bailey, at pages 18-24.

[2]The illustrated pamphlets include "101 Wildflowers Of Glacier National Park" by Grant W. Sharpe, "Flowering Beauty of Glacier National Park and the Majestic High Rockies" by Ralph E. Reiner, and "Wild Flowers of Glacier National Park" by Alan G. Nelson. The first two are published by the Glacier Natural History Association, Inc., a non-profit organization pledged to aid in the preservation and interpretation of the scenic and scientific features of the Park. Also published by this organization is "Trees and Forests of Glacier National Park" by Donald H. Robinson. Unfortunately, both "101 Wildflowers" and "Trees And Forests" are no longer in print.

[3]Paul Standley's monumental work is out of print, but may be found in many libraries.

[4]From "The Enchanted Trails of Glacier National Park" by Agnes C. Laut, at pages 165-166.

[5]From "A Vacation Trip Through Glacier National Park" by E. I. Lawrence, appearing in the Sierra Club Bulletin, Volume XII, at page 116.

[6]"Glacier National Park, Its Trails And Treasures" by Holtz and Bemis, at pages 108-110.

[7]Trees And Forests of Glacier National Park" by Donald H. Robinson, at page 5.

[8]John Muir, at page 18 of his 1901 book entitled "Our National Parks," had the following to say of the Lake McDonald forests: ". . . You will find the king of the larches, one of the best of the western giants, beautiful, picturesque and regal, easily the grandest of all the larches in the world. It grows to a height of 150 to 200 feet, with a diameter at the ground of five to eight feet, throwing out its branches into the light as no other tree does . . . Associated with this grand tree in the making of the Flathead forests is the large and beautiful mountain pine, or Western white pine (Pinus monticola), the invincible contorta or lodgepole pine, and spruce and cedar. The forest floor is covered with the richest beds of Linnaea borealis I ever saw, thick fragrant carpets, enriched with shining mosses here and there, and with Clintonia, pyrola, moneses, and vaccinium, weaving hundred-mile blooms that would have made blessed old Linnaeus weep for joy."

[9]"Trees And Forests Of Glacier National Park," supra, at page 25.

Chapter 9
THE WORLD OF
WILD LIFE

Glacier National Park is one of the great game preserves of the North American continent. Among national parks of the United States, its only peers in this respect are Yellowstone and Mt. McKinley. While smaller in size than either of these, Glacier compares favorably with them in variety and numbers of the wild creatures within its boundaries. In addition to being one of the last strongholds of the magnificent grizzly, it is the home of that unique animal, the Rocky Mountain goat, a distinction shared with but two of our other national parks.

As game sanctuaries, our national parks seek to preserve, for the pleasure and edification of their visitors, the wild life as it was when our pioneering ancestors first saw it. The parks are not intended as zoos or menageries, and the animals are not on display or available for viewing at the visitor's whim or request. However, the mammals and birds of the Park are an important part of its natural picture, and it is a special thrill for most of us when we happen to stumble unexpectedly upon members of the great wild population as they go about their daily affairs.

Since the Park's fauna live in their natural environment and seek their sustenance as they always have, the primitive rule of tooth and claw still prevails. The injured fawn falls prey to the foraging coyote, the mountain sheep is fair game for the wolves of the area, and the deer furnish a part of the food supply for the mountain lion. The ancient law of the wilderness governs the abundance or scarcity of a particular species, and somehow over the years, Nature maintains her balance between the strong and the weak.

Slaughter Of Species

The one predator that the wildlife of the future Park and nearby areas could not withstand was man, and the protecting hand of the national park organization arrived none too soon to save the larger animals. While the plains were black with easily slaughtered buffalo, they continued to be the targets of the hunters, both red and white, since their robes brought good prices at the trading posts. With the disappearance of the buffalo in the early 1880's, attention began to be turned to the mountain regions where game was still plentiful. Hunters and trappers took a devastating toll of the fur-bearing animals during the final decades of the nineteenth century. During the same period eastern sportsmen, such as George Bird Grinnell, came to the St. Mary region to stalk and shoot the Rocky Mountain sheep and goats.

The grizzly came to be the principal target, most of the trapping being done in the spring when, following hibernation, their skins were in prime condition. Traps were usually baited with the carcasses of mountain sheep, goats and deer, as well as elk and moose. It was estimated that in the year 1895 approximately 500 elk and moose were killed in what is now Glacier Park to provide the bait used in the trapping of 100 grizzlies. One trapper and his partner alone killed 70 elk and moose for this purpose in connection with a single spring's trapping.[1]

Benefits Of A Game Preserve

A policy of protecting the game in the region that is now Glacier National Park actually dates back to the time when it became a part of the Lewis and Clark Forest Reserve created in 1897. An active program of protection against game poachers was undertaken in 1902, and by 1925 was paying substantial dividends. The intervening years had done wonders toward increasing the numbers of wild animals within the Park, as well as toward stocking the adjacent districts with game for the benefit of hunters.

The protection provided by national park status also accomplished another result. After years of freedom from being hunted, Glacier's wild animals began to lose some of their fear of man. Of course, their natural shyness will in most cases prove a barrier to any intimate acquaintance with them and their way of living. Nevertheless, there are always a

Bear grass and Heaven's Peak

Photo by Mel Ruder

Hikers on Grinnell Glacier Trail

Rocky Mountain goats near Sperry Glacier

Photo by Mel Ruder

number of the less shy creatures that are seen by nearly everyone. Some of the larger game are not frequently encountered by visitors, but their trails, tracks and traces are continually in evidence. In fact, if we are but clever enough to recognize the signs, we might see the beaten paths over which nearly all the animals travel.

The "Park Mammal"

The Rocky Mountain goat, sometimes called the Montana mountain goat, is the most distinctly representative animal of Glacier National Park.[2] It is really one of a small group of mountain-frequenting antelopes, of which the European chamois is a member. This eccentric animal is one of the Park's most popular attractions because of its distinctive appearance, its remarkable alpine prowess, the ease with which it can usually be seen, and the relative rarity with which it is found in our national parks.[3] Accordingly, it has come to be regarded as the "Park mammal."

For these same reasons it has long served as a symbol for Park-related enterprises, including the Glacier Park Transport Company and the Arizona-based company which presently operates the hotels, motor inns and chalets of Glacier. For decades its likeness has been familiar to all who have ever seen the box cars or publicity of the Great Northern Railway,[4] the story of which is so interwoven with the history of the Park itself.

The goats of the Park are the only large white animals among its 57 species,[5] and therefore cannot be confused with any other. They are about the size and shape of an ordinary goat, but have humps on their shoulders like a buffalo. They stand from three to three-and-a-half feet high at the shoulder and weigh from 150 to 300 pounds. They are well covered with a shaggy coat of warm, silky-white wool, tinged with pale yellow; and their chin beards and pantalettes give them a grotesque appearance. The sexes resemble each other closely and are not distinguishable at a distance. Both have slender, black, spike-like horns, 8 to 10 inches in length. Males are usually larger than females and have slightly longer horns.

Goat Viewing

Mountain goats are active during the winter as well as in the summer and may remain high on the peaks even in the most severe weather. Their shaggy coats are shed during the summer, this change usually being completed by August. Their compact, square hoofs have soft, adhesive pads bordered by sharp, knife-edged ridges that enable them to grip with ease surfaces on which other species would not dare to venture. They are the most daring, yet nonchalant, of all rock climbers; and even the more precipitous areas are crossed without apparent difficulty, including cliffs that appear to present only the slightest ledges for toeholds.

The number of goats in the Park is estimated to be about 800. Their trails are everywhere above timberline, particularly in the vicinity of the Garden, Pinnacle and Ptarmigan Walls in the Swiftcurrent Valley, They can usually be seen from the trails over most of the high passes, and particularly Logan, Gunsight, Piegan and Boulder. They are often glimpsed from the shores of Iceberg Lake and regularly haunt the vicinity of the Sperry Chalets.

It is sometimes possible to descry a goat or two even while merely driving through the Park by automobile. Near Walton, on Highway No. 2 over Marias Pass, there is a roadside exhibit overlooking a large mass of bluish rock that has been exposed by erosive action of the Middle Fork of the Flathead River. This rather steep rock area contains a natural salt lick which is extremely attractive to members of the goat family; and they come to it from considerable distances, even creating an occasional traffic problem by crossing the highway. They are at the lick more frequently in early morning or late evening hours. This is perhaps the only place in the world where it is possible to sit in one's car and look **down** on mountain goats.

Bighorn Sheep

Also abundant throughout the more rugged sections of the Park are the Rocky Mountain bighorn sheep. The ram is built like a large domestic sheep, but is clothed with fur like that of a deer. His horns are curled and massive. He may stand up to three-and-a-half feet high at the shoulder and weigh up to 300 pounds. The female is distinctly different in appearance, with a slender body, small, spike-like horns, and a weight of up to 175 pounds. Both male and female have a creamy-white rump patch surrounding the short, brown tail.

The bighorns are expert mountain climbers and seem to be able to traverse steep slopes with a nimbleness almost equal to that of the goat, but tending to frequent less lofty elevations. In summer, the rams roam in bands

Rocky Mountain sheep near Swiftcurrent Lake with Mt. Gould in the distance
Photo by Mel Ruder

Ranger-Naturalist guiding hikers past crevasse in Grinnell Glacier
Photo by Bob & Ira Spring

by themselves well above the timberline, while the ewes and lambs are to be found in their own groups in the upland valleys. With autumn comes the mating season, at which time the rams join the bands of lambs and ewes, and compete for the favors of the latter. Fierce duels are fought between the more aggressive males, which charge at each other and meet head-on, the impact of their huge horns creating a resounding crash. These combats continue until supremacy among them has been established, and mating with the ewes is able to proceed.

The number of sheep in the Park is estimated at about 200, a major reduction from the 2,000 estimated by an expert in 1917.[6] They are common in the Two Medicine and Swiftcurrent Valleys. At Many Glacier Hotel, they occasionally venture down to secure a taste of a salt lick, braving rather nervously the gaze of camera-clicking tourists. They are also encountered along the trail from Granite Park to Logan Pass, often showing surprisingly little fear of hikers or saddlehorse riders.

The severity of the upland winters drives the mountain sheep to lower feeding grounds and the wolves and coyotes, which are their greatest enemies, then take a heavy toll of their numbers. They respond well to kindly treatment and have been known to become almost tame under it. The winter custodian of Many Glacier Hotel gained the friendship of a flock during the winter of 1919-1920 and before long was on familiar terms with 25 or 30 of them. They even became so bold as to eat from his hand, and he took many pictures of them feeding and standing on the roof of his chalet, onto which the great depth of snow had permitted them to clamber.

The Black Bear

On a substantial par with the mountain goat and the bighorn sheep, so far as public interest is concerned, are the Park's bears. Of course, Bruin is a general favorite everywhere. At the zoo, he leads all rivals in point of popularity, and he plays a leading role among the fauna of all of our national parks where his species is to be found. In Glacier Park there are bears of all kinds — big ones and little ones, black, cinnamon and blond ones, and the king of them all, the silvertip grizzly.

Black bears, this term including the cinnamons and blonds, are found in all regions of the Park, usually ranging through the areas below timberline. Their number in the Park is estimated at 400, and at one time they were more frequently seen than any other large mammal. They are essentially scavengers by nature and it was this tendency, combined with their boldness, that led them to become well publicized visitors at the garbage dumps of the principal hotels in Yellowstone Park as well as in Glacier. In recent years a different method of garbage disposal has been instituted, but in the half century before that, the huge beasts were regular evening callers at the Lewis Hotel on Lake McDonald and, to a lesser degree, at the Many Glacier Hotel.

In spite of present strict rules against feeding, teasing or molesting the large mammals of the Park, visitors are not always content merely to observe or photograph the bears. The latter soon learned that begging for food on the highway from passing cars could produce good results, particularly along Going-To-The-Sun Highway. One of these "bum" bears, as the beggars came to be known, was "Gertie," a blond with winning ways.[7] Summer after summer she would take her stand along the highway, beneath the Garden Wall, obviously soliciting handouts. When motorists took her picture without payment in food, she indicated her resentment on more than one occasion by thrusting a paw in the car and scratching them. Rangers trapped Gertie and released her in a remote area, but within a few weeks she was back at her old beat.

Other Bear Escapades

Many years ago there was a black bear that frequented the neighborhood of the St. Mary Chalets. In the course of his investigation of the interior of a large but empty molasses pail, it became firmly fastened over his head, and all his efforts to dislodge it were in vain. The sense of sight and smell having thus suddenly been cut off, the bear panicked and ran pell mell toward the lake, whither his unguided footsteps chanced to lead him. He floundered into deep water and, in spite of an attempt at rescue by the ranger, the unfortunate beast drowned.

Bears have always been plentiful in the vicinity of the Granite Park Chalet. All of the window sills as well as the roof of the kitchen had to be densely covered with sharp spikes to keep bears from making an entry in and out of season. Various past experiences with burglarious bears rendered this step necessary. On one occasion a black bear broke into the storeroom and consumed a pail of tomato preserves before he could be frightened away. At times, half-grown black bears would hang around the chalet, sometimes in the backyard, sometimes on the front porch. They were not mean, but one chap who tried to play with them received a good cuff for his pains. The cub intended no harm but did not realize that he was able to do so much damage with one playful slap.

Although many minor injuries have been inflicted by black bears upon Park visitors and employees, no death or major injury has ever been attributed to these animals during the 65 years of the Park's existence as such. In most instances, the injuries resulted from a disregard of Park regulations forbidding the feeding or teasing of bears. Because of their boldness, black bears have a penchant for becoming nuisances, encumbered with few, if any, inhibitions about breaking and entering in search of sweets or meats. It is advisable for campers in the Park, even those in regularly established campgrounds, to avoid placing food in any container or location where it could be attractive to the sensitive nose of a passing bear, for they are rummagers by nature and will tear apart flimsy structures or containers to get at the food they hold.

Ursus horribilis

The grizzly is a large bear with a massive head, a profile that seems to be "dished in," and eyes that are small and set wide apart. It has a robust body and stout legs, and weighs up to 900 pounds. The shoulder area is higher than the rump, the fur is dense and coarse, and the color is usually a light brown. Because the ends of the longer hairs on head, shoulders and back are of a silvery hue, the animal is sometimes called a "silvertip grizzly." It is the largest of the Park's carnivores; however, like the black bears, it is omnivorous and will eat a variety of food, including berries, bulbs and other vegetable matter.

In summer, the grizzly is often found above timberline, as well as on the lower forested slopes. One may occasionally see places in the alpine meadows where, with their long, powerful claws, they have turned over the soil in search of lily bulbs, meadow mice, ground squirrels or marmots. They cannot climb trees as do the black bears. Once the commonest species of bear in certain parts of what is now the Park, their numbers were greatly decimated by hunting and over-trapping in the latter part of the nineteenth century. Today it is believed that their numbers in Glacier approximate 200.

Grizzlies And People

Until 1967 no human had ever been killed by a Glacier Park grizzly. Since then there have been two fatalities, thereby arousing intense public interest as well as a storm of condemnation of the grizzly's presence in the national parks. The subject has been given detailed study by Park authorities who reached the conclusion that the problem was primarily the result of man's attracting bears by "people food," i.e., through the hotel garbage dumps and by feeding from cars, thereby causing the animals so enticed to lose their natural fear of man.

New regulations and procedures have been adopted to correct this situation, removing by various means the availability of man food to Park bears, and thereby reducing their opportunities to become over-familiar with human beings. Also, under this program, any bear that becomes a serious nuisance or menace to life or property in the Park is trapped and transported to a distant part of the Park for release. If the culprit returns and proves to be incorrigible, then as a last resort, he or she is destroyed. The story of the problem bears and the program designed for their control is the subject of another chapter.[8]

The Park's Big Cats

Several members of the feline family are inhabitants of Glacier Park, including the Rocky Mountain cougar, the Canada lynx and the bobcat. The cougar is known by a variety of names, including mountain lion, puma, panther, painter and catamount. On the western slopes where dense forests and plentiful game offer an abundance of shelter and food, these animals are numerous. The cougar is large, with a tawny brown color and long cylindrical tail. The lynx is small, its fur is long and silky, and its tail is bobbed. Its weight seldom runs above 25 pounds, while that of the cougar may reach 200 pounds.

Although cougars themselves are rarely seen, their tracks are regularly noted throughout the Park, so it is believed that they exist in the area in substantial numbers. In territory adjacent to the Park they are relentlessly hunted because of their reported depredations on livestock. The cougar preys upon almost any of the animals found within its range. Deer are probably preferred, but the menu has been known to include moose, elk, porcupines, marmots, rabbits and even mice.

74

The animal is so shy that it avoids man whenever possible; as a matter of fact, the big cats fear man and will fight him only with their backs to the wall. They kill mainly by stealth and carry on much of their activity at night, hence the infrequency with which they are encountered or seen by Park visitors.[9]

Other Predators

There is but one other important class of carnivorous animal in the Park, namely, the wolves and coyotes. The Rocky Mountain wolf is a large, powerful dog-like animal weighing up to 200 pounds. Though once common throughout the country, wolves have become a rare and endangered species, and Glacier Park is one of the few areas where they can still be found. A 1974 study in the Park's remote North Fork Flathead and boundary region indicated their continued presence in that wilderness area, but in rather small numbers.[10]

The coyote is a slender animal resembling a small wolf, and weighing about 35 pounds. Coyotes are the arch enemies of the sheep and goats which they pursue to timberline and beyond. They are also accountable for the destruction of numerous deer. Their numbers in the Park are estimated at about 400. It was once the policy of the National Park Service, in order to protect the gentler animals in the Park, to reduce the numbers of such predators as coyotes. Today Nature is permitted to maintain her own balance among the Park's animals, and the coyotes' distinctive yapping or barking may be heard throughout the Park. While seldom seen by visitors to the Park, coyotes may be found in almost all habitats from the plains and valleys of the east side up to the tops of the ranges and down into the deep forest of the western slopes.

Among smaller species of carnivores found in the Park are the wolverine, badger, marten, otter, mink, skunk and two or three kinds of weasels. They are rarely seen by visitors, although martens, minks and short tailed weasels occur in abundance. The powerful wolverine and badger are not common in the Park, the latter being more apt to be found in the west side valleys. The mink and otter find most of their food along water courses. The otter is not frequently found within the Park, but the mink appears to be equally at home in the dense forests of the west side and the willow bottoms of the prairie meadows.

The Deer Family

Members of the deer family include some of the most conspicuous and colorful of our North American fauna. As found in the Park, the family comprises the moose, the elk, and both the mule and white-tailed varieties of deer. All adult members of this family possess antlers which are shed each year and subsequently regrown.

No visit to the Park is complete without a view of the moose, huge lord of its streams and marshes. Ungainly and grotesque in appearance, this out-sized member of the deer family has the dignity of one accustomed to having his own way, particularly the bull moose with his broad palmated antlers and characteristic growth of hair-covered skin, called the "bell," dangling from the throat. The males are larger, standing up to 7½ feet in height at the shoulder and weighing up to 1200 pounds. Moose population in the Park is estimated at 115, with most of that number located along the North Fork of the Flathead River and its tributaries, and a few in the Moose Flat area along the Going-To-The-Sun Highway.

The elk, or wapiti, is a deer-like animal, somewhat smaller than a moose. They have pale-colored bodies, with dark head, neck and legs, and a light rump patch. Their numbers in the Park are estimated to exceed 3,000, most of which range during the winter along the Middle Fork of the Flathead River and along the lower ridges of the eastern side of the Park, scattering into the higher backcountry during the summer.

Mule deer are commonly found at higher elevations on the eastern side of the Park, and only occasionally west of the continental divide. During the summer months they browse on the new growth at the tips of various shrubs in the open areas of the middle and higher elevations. In spite of the attacks by mountain lions, bears and coyotes, the numbers of these attractive animals in the Park are estimated to be around 800.

The white-tailed deer are mainly denizens of the bottom lands and valley floors of the western slopes. The latest census of Park animals places their number at about 500, and they appear to have been decreasing in recent years. They may often be seen at or near Park headquarters at West Glacier, along the North Fork of the Flathead River, and in the Swiftcurrent Valley.

The Smaller Animals

Another interesting Park creature is the porcupine. It never fails to excite curiosity, chiefly because of the unusual protection provided by its quills. It is not able, as some have believed, to throw its quills, but its uncanny power of wielding its heavily barbed tail upon the enemy compels respect among other inhabitants of the wilderness. Dogs, practically the only beasts that will attack a porcupine, are barred from the Park, except on leash, so it is seldom disturbed. The "claws" in its tail are an unique type of protection, but it needs some drastic form of defense since it is practically powerless to flee when danger approaches.

When the Granite Park Chalet was being built in 1916, the workmen's camp was overrun by an army of porcupines. They did real damage, gnawing at anything which the hand of man had touched. This perverted appetite is said to be due to a craving for things with a salty flavor, such as might be produced by perspiration of the hand. Nightly raids on the cook's supplies continued until that worthy at last took his axe in hand and set about to gain retribution. After the slaughter of several dozen porcupines, the remainder "made themselves scarce" in that neighborhood.[11]

Porcupines still inhabit the Park in goodly numbers, and their bizarre appetites remain unchanged. They seem to be particularly fond of rubber, and will chew on the tires of any vehicles left along the road at higher elevations, including those of the Park's road graders and snow plows. They have even been known to gain entry to the engine compartment and to gnaw enthusiastically on hoses and ignition wiring. Their liking for salt-flavored items such as axe handles, saddles and doorsteps has often resulted in the damaging or destruction of such property.[12]

Attractive Rodents

The hoary marmot of Glacier Park is a cousin of the more familiar woodchuck or groundhog commonly found in our eastern states. It is much larger than the woodchuck and emits a shrill, bird-like whistle. It burrows into the ground and under rocks, usually at or near timberline. It leads a life of eternal vigilance since, like the porcupine, it is unable to make much speed toward escaping danger but, unlike the porcupine, has no armor for defense. One member of the colony mounts a rock and signals the approach of anything strange by sounding the high-pitched warning whistle. Thus all are able to scurry to safety. Marmots flourish at the higher elevations throughout the Park, often being seen near

Logan Pass and along the Going-To-The-Sun Highway.

Many other small rodents abound within the Park. There are several varieties of chipmunks and ground squirrels, all with very similar habits. The commonest of these are the fat Columbia ground squirrels, the burrows of which are found nearly everywhere in the Park uplands. They can be seen in greatest numbers at Piegan Pass and on the grassy slopes of the creek south of the Pass, where nooning hikers and riders often share their lunches with the little creatures. Some of them become bold enough to snatch morsels from the extended hand.

Anglers' Paradise

Of all the wildlife found in Glacier Park, the one legitimate prey of the sportsman is the fish. In season, and except in certain closed areas, all members of the finny tribe may be caught with hook and line, subject to reasonable restrictions as to equipment and bait, and in reference to the size and number of fish taken. Fish are more abundant in the nutrient-rich lakes during the summer, and more common in streams during spring and fall spawning.[13] The Park's many lakes are famed for the quality of piscatorial opportunities which they afford. Swiftcurrent, Josephine, Grinnell, Sherburne, St. Mary, Waterton, Red Eagle, Two Medicine,

Landing a big one at Two Medicine Lake
Photo by Walt Dyke, courtesy of Burlington Northern

Trout laden Swiftcurrent Creek

Great Northern photo

Avalanche and McDonald head the list, while Logging, Bowman and Kintla Lakes on the western slopes are well stocked.

Twenty-two species of fish, all but six of them native, inhabit the Park. The principal fish is the trout, and the rainbow, cutthroat, eastern brook and Dolly Varden, all patrician members of the trout family, are the chief varieties. The larger mackinaw or lake trout, weighing up to thirty pounds, are found in Lake St. Mary, Lake McDonald, Waterton Lake,[14] and to some extent in Cosley and Kintla Lakes. Sherburne Lake is the home of the northern pike, the lake whitefish and the Rocky Mountain whitefish, while the latter two species are also found in Lake St. Mary. Arctic grayling abound in most of the lakes located in Hudson Bay and Flathead River drainages.

Kokanee salmon were introduced into the waters of the Flathead River system in the 1920's, and have flourished. They spawn each year, usually in November, in a five-square-mile area between the foot of Lake McDonald and the Middle Fork of the Flathead River, just within the Park's southwest boundary. As the salmon spawn and die in the Apgar region along McDonald Creek, the feast attracts many of the Park's fish loving creatures, including coyotes and an occasional bear. This is a rather dramatic spectacle that attracts annual attention and local headlines.

The Birds Of Glacier

A spectacular feature of the salmon spawning on McDonald Creek is the year's most unusual convention, a gathering of bald eagles. Counts of their numbers are made each year, with a record high of 373 reported on November 20, 1969. How they know about the salmon feast and where they come from is a mystery. Since the total number of these magnificent birds, some with a wing spread of six feet, is believed to be in the neighborhood of 200 for the entire state of Montana, it seems likely that many of them fly in for this special event from Idaho, Washington and perhaps even from British Columbia. Assisting them with their orgy are ospreys, snowy owls and golden eagles, the latter the king of birds in Glacier Park.

A total of 210 species of birds spend all or a part of their time in the Park.[15] This rich variety of birdlife has attracted many skilled observers, some of whom have produced a wealth of descriptive literature, much of it splendidly illustrated.[16] These treatises make it clear that, since birds depend upon plant life

for food, shelter and nesting sites, the kind of birds found in each of the Park's life zones varies with the climatic conditions, the soil and the available water.

The round-bodied, white-tailed ptarmigan has been chosen by Glacier Park visitors as the "park bird."[17] It is often seen in the Arctic-Alpine area, while the blue grouse and Clark's nutcracker frequent the timberline areas of the Hudsonian zone. In the Canadian, or Forest, zone the list is long, including hawks, jays, owls, thrushes, woodpeckers, wrens, waxwings, and hummingbirds. The Park's mountain lakes are the habitat of eagles, ospreys and spotted sandpipers, while the water ouzel nests near waterfalls and the harlequin duck prefers to live near stream rapids or the nearby lakes. Birds living near marshes and wet meadows include the redwinged blackbird, the yellow warbler, the marsh hawk and the common snipe, In prairie grassland areas of the Park will be found magpies, hawks, larks, and swallows. Detailed accounts of the interesting habits, life histories and typical habitats of the more commonly observed birds are readily available from a number of sources.[18]

The Glacier Park Wimpus

No resume of the wildlife of Glacier National Park would be complete without a few words about a quaint creature which, in times past, was indigenous to the Park, but is now extinct. This is the far-famed wimpus, a species which has defied classification as mammal, bird or fish, but seemed to partake of the characteristics of all three. From an examination of the specimens once on display at the larger hotels, it was apparently part fish and part bird, with an odd little cranium like that of a monkey surmounting its body.

No explanation ever accompanied these former exhibitions of this bizarre beastie, its impossible get-up apparently being considered sufficient. Nevertheless, as a means of preserving for posterity the salient facts about the grotesque little creature and its incredible habits, I pass along the tongue-in-cheek observations of one who studied the wimpus in its native habitat.[19]

"The Park is just naturally alive with wimpuses. A wimpus grows about as big as a hooglebug, but it has a long tail like a collywop and wings like a bearcat. It lives in the top of high trees, whence it flies down to attack the defenseless travelers. No harm is to be feared from a wimpus if you know what to do when you see one coming. It is folly to shoot at them for a wimpus catches bullets in its teeth and eats them. The only way to do when a wimpus comes at you is to take a piece of cheese, either Edam or Swiss, and tack it securely on a waterfall. The wimpus makes a swoop at the cheese and gets mixed up with the waterfall and gets his feet wet.

"It makes a wimpus mad as all-get-out when he get his feet wet and so he hunts around for a nice piece of grass to dry them on. The minute the wimpus lights on the grass, the hunter rushes at him and ties his tail in a double bow-knot. When a wimpus has his tail tied in a double bow-knot he is gone, because when he flies he always ducks his head under his body to see who is following him and in doing this he gets his head caught in the double bow-knot and chokes himself to death.

"The young wimpus is very good eating in season, but it must be cooked with strips of bloop. You first parboil the bloop and remove the pinfeathers and fins. Then you cut off the tender part and lay in the frying pan, first a strip of bloop, then a strip of wimpus, than a strip of bloop and so on until the pan is full. Now put on the fire and boil twenty-four hours and serve with frapped chow-chow."

The Fabled Trout Of Iceberg Lake

A legend that became even better known in Park annals than that about the wimpus was the story of the fur-bearing trout. It was about 1915 that a photograph of such a fish was received by the publicity department of the Great Northern Railway which then operated the Park's hostelries. With it was the information that it had been taken from Iceberg Lake in the then new Glacier National Park. Recognizing its publicity value, the Great Northern sent prints to hundreds of newspapers throughout the country, and the story became a sensation. Soon postcard reproductions of the picture became a best-selling souvenir in the hotel and chalet gift shops, and continued to be so for years.

Research subsequently disclosed the fact that the subject of the picture was a trout caught in Whitefish Lake (west of the Park), to which a coat of fur had been added in a local taxidermy shop. The hoax had been "dreamed up" on a Sunday fishing trip by a group of anglers from Whitefish, Montana with an inspired sense of humor, but with no idea, of course, that their "gag" would attract nation-wide attention or come to find a place in Montana history.[20]

Notes For Chapter 9

[1] "Wild Animals Of Glacier National Park," by Vernon Bailey, published in 1918 by the Department of the Interior, at page 97.

[2] Article by Park Ranger L. Floyd Keller, at pages 147-149 of the 1948 edition of the "Drivers' Manual" (see note 15, Chapter 6, supra), describing the mountain goat as "an imperturbable, daring ungulate; a mountaineer possessing unexcelled qualities for alpine climbing."

[3] The goat is indigenous to Mt. Rainier National Park. It has also been introduced into the Olympia National Park where its numbers, since 1920, have increased to about 400, according to the National Geographic Magazine for February, 1974, at page 193.

[4] In recent years the Great Northern Railway has become a part of the Burlington Northern System, but many of its box cars still carry the goat as a part of their insignia.

[5] "Mammals Of Glacier National Park," by R. R. Lechleitner, published by Glacier Natural History Association in 1955, at page 3.

[6] "Wild Animals Of Glacier National Park," supra, at page 27.

[7] "Many-Splendored Glacierland," by George W. Long, appearing in the National Geographic Magazine for May, 1956, at pages 598 and 622.

[8] See Chapter 25, infra, at page 192, entitled "Bear Problems."

[9] A cougar was observed eating a bighorn sheep on the slopes of Mt. Altyn in the latter part of March, 1973 by Don Hall, caretaker-engineer at the nearby Many Glacier Hotel. While the cougar was enjoying his meal, three lynxes watched from a respectful distance. Later a wolverine was seen feeding at the carcass, and still later a golden eagle. Reported by the Hungry Horse News for March 30, 1973.

[10] "History And Status of Wolves in Northern Glacier National Park, Montana," a study done by Francis J. Singer during the months of October to December, 1974 under the supervision of Clifford J. Martinka, the Park's research biologist. Estimates ranged between five and ten animals, with little, if any, pack organization. An earlier article entitled "Wolves In Glacier Park" by Ranger Naturalist M. N. D'Evelyn was published in Volume VII of "Glacial Drift" for June, 1934, at page 24.

[11] "Wild Animals Of Glacier National Park," supra, at page 67.

[12] "Mammals of Glacier National Park," supra, at page 60.

[13] See booklet on "Fish And Fishing In Glacier National Park" published in 1973 by the Glacier Natural History Association in cooperation with the National Park Service. See, also, article entitled "Fish And Fishing In Glacier National Park," by A. S. Hazzard, Ph.D., Michigan Institute for Fisheries Research, appearing at pages 162-163 of the 1948 edition of "Drivers' Manual" (see note 15, Chapter 6, supra). Dr. Hazzard explains that conditions conducive to the flourishing of fish in the smaller streams are seldom present, despite their great attractiveness, because the water is usually too cold, too rapid and too pure (or roily with rock flour from the glaciers) to contain much of the mineral and organic matter essential to the growth of fish food organisms.

[14] A specimen weighing 30 pounds and 8 ounces was landed in May, 1971 at Waterton Lake by Albert Webster of Lundbreck, Alberta, according to the Hungry Horse News for June 4, 1971. It is interesting to learn through William Rodney's book entitled "Kootenai Brown, His Life And Times," at page 130, that Brown had caught a trout in Waterton Lake in the spring of 1883 weighing 30 pounds, so the big ones have been in residence there for close to a century, at least.

[15] "Birds Of Glacier National Park," by Lloyd P. Parratt, at page 9.

[16] The literature dealing with the birds of the Glacier Park region began with the publication in 1888 by George Bird Grinnell in Forest and Stream Magazine of an article entitled "Some Autumn Birds of the St. Mary Lakes Region." Later publications and articles on this subject have been collected and listed by Lloyd P. Parratt at pages

vii and viii of his authoritative work entitled "Birds Of Glacier National Park," supra.

[17]The ptarmigan is the only permanent bird in the alpine sector of the Park. In 1929, by popular vote, visitors chose it as the Glacier National Park bird because it symbolizes the high mountain pass regions of the Park. See "Birds of Glacier National Park," supra, at page 22.

[18]See notes 15 and 16, supra, this chapter.

[19]Courtesy of Richard Henry Little, in whose column "A Little About Everything," from the Chicago Tribune, this sketch originally appeared in August, 1911.

[20]See article entitled "Origin Of Fur Bearing Trout" appearing in the Hungry Horse News for August 25, 1972 by C. W. "Dinty" Moore, retired chief of public relations for the Great Northern Railway, now the Burlington Northern System.

Doe near Granite Park chalet
Photo by Mel Ruder

A small visitor along the Going-to-the-Sun Highway
Photo by Walt Dyke, courtesy of Burlington Northern

Bull moose coming out of water at Moose Flats
Photo by Mel Ruder

PART II
WHAT MAN HATH
WROUGHT
Chapter 10
THE ORIGINAL OWNERS

No attempt to describe fully the charm and fascination of Glacier National Park would be complete without the story of those picturesque and authentic Americans who were its original proprietors, and whose descendants are still its next-door neighbors. The Blackfeet people live and have long lived, in the very shadow of the nearby mountains and their tribal life pattern has become intertwined with that of the area, particularly with that part of the Park lying east of the continental divide.

Many of the region's outstanding scenic features—peaks, passes, lakes and streams—carry Indian names. Indeed, in no other national park are the native nomenclature, lore and legends so frequently encountered; and no other has been so happily enriched by the traditions and history of its earlier inhabitants. This colorful background stems not so much from the fact that this has been "Indian country" for unnumbered centuries, but rather from its close association with the Blackfeet people during the nineteenth century when the white man was in the process of "discovering" it.

To the Blackfeet, the continental divide was the "backbone of the world." Many of the names that they conferred upon the future Park's peaks had a picturesque flavor, such as Almost-A-Dog, Appistoki, Calf Robe, Heavy Runner, Lone Walker, Red Eagle, Rising Wolf and Siyeh (Mad Wolf). Others possessed something of a poetic quality, such as Morning Star Lake, Running Eagle Falls, Old Sun Glacier and Sinopah (Fox woman) Mountain. Several volumes of delightful legends, dealing mostly with the area east of the continental divide, have fortunately been preserved for us by adopted sons of the tribe.[1]

In Earlier Times

Not always, however, had the Blackfeet been the overlords of the future Park region. Prior to the nineteenth century an entirely different group of aborigines enjoyed the glorious hunting ground that extended from the forested areas at the feet of the Lewis Range, with their abundance of elk, deer and bear, across the rolling plains to the east and southeast, teeming with buffalo. Among the tribes that roamed through this vast territory were the Snakes, Stonies, Kootenais, Nez Perces and Flatheads. The Blackfeet were still far to the northeast on the prairies of what is now Alberta.

In the latter part of the 1700's, the Blackfeet, acquiring horses and modern weapons, began to move toward the Rockies, driving all that opposed them westward and southward, and eventually forcing them into the Yellowstone country or over the continental divide. Only rarely thereafter did the Flatheads and other tribes that had taken refuge west of the mountains dare to return to their former territory to hunt the buffalo. The Kootenais and Stonies contented themselves for the most part with summer visits to the northwestern sections of the future park to camp, fish and hunt. The Gros Ventres spent much time in the Belly River area and it took its name from that tribe.

It is because of these events that a number of tribes are represented in the annals of Glacier Park. However, from 1800 onward, the aggressive Blackfeet so dominated the region that they have been the tribe most closely identified with the Park in nomenclature and legend. The so-called western tribes, despite their early and continued association with various parts of the area, have failed to leave a major impact upon the Park of today. That of the Blackfeet, on the other hand, has been substantial, enduring and materially enhanced by their continuing presence near the Park's eastern portals.

The Blackfeet In War

When the white man began to arrive upon the upper reaches of the Missouri during the early decades of the 19th century, he found the Blackfeet in control of all the vast region from the North Saskatchewan River in Alberta to the Yellowstone country[2]—an empire more than twice the size of New England.[3] They were comprised of three tribes—the Siksika, or Blackfeet proper, the Pikuni, sometimes called the Piegans, and the Kai'na (incorrectly named the Bloods by the white man).[4] Sometimes called the Blackfeet Confederacy, their name carried an awesome impact throughout the regions which are now southern Alberta and western Montana. It meant danger and possibly death to adventurous white trappers and traders,[5] as well as to their traditional foes of the Indian world—the Crows, Assiniboine and Cree, Flatheads, Shoshonis and Kutenais.[6]

The Blackfeet were primarily a plains people. Even at the zenith of their power they did not spend much of their time in the mountainous areas of their domain now embraced within the present-day park. But they did not hesitate, when it suited their purposes, to make predatory excursions into and over the Rockies in order to harass their west-side enemies. Some of these raids were against the Flathead tribe, with history recording a bitter battle near Marias Pass in 1810.[7] Others were fought against the Kutenais in 1858 just below Red Eagle Pass, and in 1810 at a point between Kutenai and Citadel Peaks.[8]

The Blackfeet In Peace

There is reason to believe, also, that the Blackfeet made use of some of the eastern valleys of the future Park for peaceful purposes. When George Bird Grinnell first visited the Swiftcurrent Valley in 1887, he found much evidence of old Indian camps in the vicinity of Swiftcurrent Falls, together with trails into the Grinnell Valley, all suggestive of long usage by Blackfeet hunting parties.[9] To some extent, also, the tribes hunted in the St. Mary and Cut Bank Valleys, and there was a well-worn trail into the latter.[10] They preferred, however, to avoid the Belly River Valley, as well as the regions which are now the northwestern section of the Park.

The valley of the Two Medicine was the place where the Pikuni tribe held one of its religious ceremonies, called the Okan', at which it was customary to construct a medicine lodge. One year, only a few days after they had put up their lodge, the Blood tribe came to the same spot and erected theirs nearby. From this circumstance came the name of the area, Two Medicine Lodges, but this happening or legend, as the case may be, suggests that the Pikunis, as well as the Bloods, were regular visitors to this section of what is now the Park.[11]

On the other hand, there is evidence that at least one of the region's peaks, although regarded as sacred, was also feared by all of the tribes. This was Chief Mountain, 9000-foot outpost of the Lewis Range. Close contact with it was avoided by the Blackfeet after one of their young hunters, venturing to conquer its heights, was never seen again. The Blackfeet, however, were aware, of a legend among the Flatheads to the effect that one of their great chiefs, as a youth, had dared to climb the mountain, carrying the usual sacred bison skull for his pillow, and had spent four days and nights on the summit, praying and fasting. Since none of the younger Flathead braves had the courage to emulate this example, the Chief thereafter remained unclimbed by the red man.[12]

The End Of Blackfeet Supremacy

The decline of Blackfeet power had its beginning in 1855 when, through a treaty with the government, they were obliged to renounce their rights to the territory south of the Musselshell River in central Montana.[13] Further reductions in their homeland were imposed upon them in 1873, 1874, 1888 and 1896, leaving them with essentially what is contained in the Blackfeet Reservation of today. Coincidentally, the vast herds of buffalo that had long roamed the Montana plains were being slaughtered in wholesale numbers, especially during the 1870's, and by 1884 they had disappeared altogether.[14] Their extermination represented the coup de grace for the Blackfeet.[15] In less than 35 years they had lost their position as the most powerful people on the northwestern plains, as well as their means of livelihood and the greater part of their land.[16] They had no choice but to become dependent upon the government for even the bare necessitites of life — food, shelter and clothing.[17]

The Blackfeet In Today's World

Today the Pikuni Blackfeet occupy a reservation containing what is left of their originally immense territory. This land, lying immediately to the east of the Park, shares a common boundary with it. It is known as the Blackfeet Reservation, and its capital is the town of Browning. Its million and a half acres represent no small area, actually larger than the state of Delaware,[18] yet less than five per cent of the pre-1855 Blackfeet domain.[19] The greater part of it is still owned by individual Pikunis,[20] who valiantly struggle, after four successive generations, to adjust to the white man's way of life.

The town of Browning is located on the main line of the Burlington Northern Railroad, only 13 miles east of the Park boundary. Its streets are paved and its buildings look much like those of any other small western town, but its citizens are mostly Indians. Here is located the Museum of The Plains Indian, operated by the Department of the Interior, with an impressive collection of artifacts, specimens of native arts and crafts, diorama and murals, principally by Blackfeet artists. Here also is Bob Scriver's Museum of Montana Wildlife, together with an art gallery and diorama room, all seriously damaged by fire in 1975. Over a four-day period in July of each year is presented the festival known as North American Indian Days, which draws to Browning the Blackfeet, young and old, from every corner of the Reservation.

Blackfeet Religion And Mythology

The Indians of the Blackfeet Reservation are today mostly members of the Catholic Church.[21] In more primitive times they were essentially sun worshippers; however, they ascribed both human and supernatural attributes and magical power to many animals and inanimate things. Individual acts were influenced largely by dreams, and each Indian had his personal "medicine" bundle through which he hoped to ward off the ill will of the spirit world and to invoke the aid of magic powers. The tribe also had many sacred bundles by means of which they sought to heal their sick, bring success in war, and insure tribal welfare.[22]

In the minds of the Blackfeet, all things emanated from the sun, to them the visible source of light and life, and a symbol of the invisible Great Spirit. Central figure in their mythology was Napi, or "Old Man," who was believed to have created man in the beginning out of the earth and to have given him dominion over the animals and the grasses, herbs and trees. Napi was a strange composite of both wisdom and passion, of power and weakness, of benevolence and malevolence. He was the personification, in human form, of strength and supernatural power — a power, however, that was not always controlled by reason. Sometimes he assumed the cleverness of a demon in working mischievous pranks; at others he served as a butt for the sly humor of some irreverent Blackfeet mortal. The tribal

myths and legends about his exploits and misadventures were many.[23]

At sun dance time, all of the scattered bands of the tribe came together in one great encampment, each band having its assigned location in the camp circle.[24] The encampment also had important social value, providing opportunity for the renewal of old friendships, for competition in games and races, for the bartering of horses and other possessions, and for council meetings to discuss tribal plans and problems. Yet, important as these social functions were to the welfare of the tribe, they were always secondary to the observance of the prolonged and earnest religious ceremony dedicated to the worship of the sun.[25]

The Blackfeet And Glacier Park

In the Park's earlier years as such, tepees of the Blackfeet tribe were pitched on the grounds of the Glacier Park Hotel and occupied by members of the tribe who usually met arriving passenger trains and sometimes staged tribal dances for the benefit of the admiring visitors. For many years Blackfeet pictographs, or picture writing upon skins, were on display in the larger hotels; and at the Glacier Park Hotel, pitched on the gallery of the second floor, was a tepee of buffalo skins which had once been the great Council Lodge of the Blackfeet. For the most part, these colorful reminders of former tribal glory have vanished.

There still remain, nevertheless, a few tangible reminders of the Indian world. At the St. Mary junction are located two excellent shops operated by people of Blackfeet descent, and featuring Blackfeet arts and crafts. One of these is under the aegis of the Blackfeet Tribal Arts and Crafts Association, and markets the products of modern Blackfeet craftsmen living on their Montana Reservation. The other is the Blackfeet Indian and Western Art Gallery, formerly operated by Albert Racine and located in a building said to have been Grinnell's original hunting lodge.

Of French, German and Blackfeet extraction, Albert Racine studied under a number of artists and sculptors, including attendance at the summer art school conducted in 1934 by the great German-born artist, Winold Reiss, on the south shore of Upper Lake St. Mary. Racine's principal works are wood carvings, usually dipicting Indian themes, painstakingly etched in relief. An outstanding piece of his work is "The Lord's Last Supper," now in the Methodist Church at Browning. Other examples may be seen at the Museum of the

Plains Indian.[26] Following in his father's footsteps is Frank "Smokey" Racine, already a woodcarver of exceptional talent.

Other Blackfeet students of Reiss have achieved success in the field of graphic art. Perhaps the best known of these was Victor Pepion (1908-1956), who learned to do Indian portraits in much the same style as the master. The best known of his works is a series of four murals in the lobby of the Museum of the Plains Indian at Browning, executed shortly after the Museum opened in 1941. They show four stages of a buffalo hunt as it might have taken place on the Museum site a century earlier.[27]

Portrait Painter To The Blackfeet

Though not of Indian descent, Winold Reiss himself was closely associated with the Blackfeet for much of his life. He attained distinction, both here and abroad, as a portrayer of Indians, mainly members of the Blackfeet Nation. For more than 30 years, beginning in 1920, he spent many summers in and about Browning doing portraits of the Canadian and Montana tribal members. When, in 1928, he exhibited fifty of these pictures at a one-man show entitled "American Indian Portraits" at the Belmaison Galleries in New York City, H. V. Kaltenborn, in his introduction to the catalog for that exhibition, wrote in part:

> In selecting his subjects among the three branches of the Siksika or Blackfeet tribe he has chosen Indians renowned for form and feature. Kindly and simple in character, stern and rugged in physical appearance, they present a rare challenge to an artist . . . To say that Winold Reiss has done his Indian friends no injustice in translating them to canvas is to give him high praise."[28]

For three decades, beginning in 1933, the Great Northern Railway published a large, full-color reproduction of one of Reiss's Indians at the top of its annual art calendar. These reproductions are now collectors' items. His portraits are rare combinations of realism and decorativeness, with appeal to young and old, to those with little knowledge of Indians, as well as to those having made them a lifetime study. The Blackfeet themselves enjoyed his pictures, and Reiss was immensely popular with the people of the tribes whose portraits he painted. The Blackfeet named him Beaver Child because he worked so persistently and intensely.[29] This friendship was mutual. Winold Reiss was proud of his long and close association with the Blackfeet. When he passed away in 1953, his ashes were scattered over the Blackfeet Reservation by his Indian friends.[30]

Master Woodcarver

Another great artist among the Blackfeet people was John Clarke, deaf-mute woodcarver, whose tumbledown studio stood for more than 50 years up the road a few rods from the Glacier Park Hotel. It was in the summer of 1918, when he had a small workshop near the Many Glacier Hotel, that I first met John and purchased some of his exquisite carvings.

Clarke was no ordinary Indian. His grandfather, Malcolm Clarke, was an army captain who had married a Blackfoot woman and settled down to the life of a fur trader in the latter part of the 19th century in western Montana. Their children included, among other other outstanding citizens, Helen P. Clarke, who acted in Shakespearean drama with Sarah Bernhardt and, subsequently, became the first territorial superintendent of schools for Montana.[31] In later years, she returned to the Reservation and engaged in ranching with her brother Horace (John's father), to whom there had been allotted by the government the property on which the Glacier Park Hotel was later built.

Almost a legend in his own time, John Clarke has been one of the most talented artists on the American woodcarving scene, and his reproductions of various Glacier Park animals were triumphs of realism. His favorite subjects were bears and mountain goats, small carvings of which proved popular with Park visitors. Among his larger pieces, one of the classics was his representation of a grizzly bear caught in a trap. Into a mere block of wood, the artist all but breathed the precious spark of life—the quiet anguish on the grizzly's face, the mangled paw, and the blood-spattered, unrelenting trap. It brought a fancy price from a discerning eastern collector, and Clarke's artistic talent has won for him a richly deserved recognition in the pages of Who's Who In Art.[32]

Other Artistic Endeavors

Blackfeet talents have also extended to other fields of art. In the milieu of motion pictures, Martin Pepion, a thirteen-year-old full blood, played opposite Shirley Temple in the 1939 film called *Susannah Of The Mounties*. Martin took the name Goodrider for the movie, and quite a few other Blackfeet were recruited by Twentieth Century Fox to serve as extras.[33]

The Blackfeet were a musical people, and a number of their songs have been preserved for posterity by Walter McClintock, who lived among them for several years. It was his feeling that the beautiful motifs of their sacred hymns, war-songs, love and night songs, springing from aboriginal sources "like pure water from a mountain spring, were so entirely original and so thoroughly American that they ought to be rescued from oblivion and permanently preserved."[34]

In 1905, McClintock persuaded the American composer, Arthur Nevin, to visit the camps of the Blackfeet with him, and there suggested the composition of an opera founded on the ancient Blackfeet legend of Poia, using an Indian environment and Indian musical themes. Nevin completed the opera, called "Poia," in the spring of 1906, using a libretto by Randolph Hartley of New York City. Premier performance of the opera took place on April 23, 1910 at the Berlin Royal Opera House, followed by three other performances, one of which was attended by the Crown Prince and Princess and other members of the royal family.[35]

Blackfeet Names For Park Places

In the summer of 1915, according to James Willard Schultz, a number of Pikuni families set up their lodges in the Two Medicine Valley, just outside the east line of the Park.[36] While the women gathered berries to dry, the hunters rode out through the timbered foothills of their Reservation in quest of game. As some of the hunters were successful, Schultz and his friends feasted around the evening lodge-fires upon fat roasted ribs and talked of many things, and particularly of the days when the buffalo were everywhere on the plains.[37]

As they were thus visiting, Schultz's old friend, Tail-Feathers-Coming-Over-The-Hill, complained that while the tribe had sold to the whites in 1896 "this Backbone-of-the-World portion of our Reservation," the sale did not include the Indian names for the Park's mountains, lakes and streams, some of which had been replaced by white man names, "foolish names of no meaning whatever."[38] The speaker proposed a restoration of the Blackfeet names, and those around the lodge-fire were in agreement. They urged Schultz to take on this important assignment and he promised to do so.[39]

Not until 1925, however, was he able to get around to the task, in collaboration with Takes-Gun-First and Curly Bear.[40] With great

care, the restoration of Indian names was undertaken, and other new Blackfeet and Kutenai names were conferred. The whole story has been chronicled by Schultz in his book of 1926 entitled "Signposts Of Adventure," in which he explains the reason for, or the story behind, the name of each of the Park's topographical features covered therein.

Story Of Going-To-The-Sun Mountain

The Blackfeet people regarded Going-To-The-Sun Mountain as the most beautiful of all their peaks, next to Chief Mountain. According to Schultz, its original Indian name had been Lone High Mountain; however, when hunting along the base of the peak in 1885 with Tail-Feathers-Coming-Over-The-Hill, they decided that it deserved a more sacred name, and forthwith christened it "Natos' Ai'tupo Istuki," meaning Sun Going-To-Mountain, or Going-To-The-Sun Mountain.[41]

Schultz subsequently denied categorically that there had ever been a Blackfeet legend in connection with this magnificent peak,[42] but the Messiah-like story is encountered so often and is so delightful that it will bear recounting once more.[43]

The legend begins at a time many, many years ago when the people of the Blackfeet were in sore distress. A long era of plenty had accustomed them to living without worry over the tomorrow. The arts of the home became neglected. The women lost the knack of preserving meat and berries; they forgot how to dry and tan the hides and how to fashion them into useful and enduring garments. The warriors, too, had forgotten the art of making the implements of the chase, and no longer knew the finer points of hunting for game. The people were indeed in a sorry state of affairs when the moon of starvation set in.

It was at this critical juncture that a stranger appeared among the people—Sour Spirit, the representative of the Sun Father. He was well versed in all the arts of the tepee and the chase, and he taught the women once more how to lay away stores of jerked venison and dried berries. He showed them how to tan the skins and how to make warm clothing. He also revealed to the men the secret of making the best of weapons and the proper way to employ them in obtaining food. Thus equipped, the people were enabled successfully to weather the hard times.

When Sour Spirit had imparted this knowledge to the Blackfeet, he departed from their midst. Those who watched saw him ascend the slopes of a great mountain, from which they concluded that he was about to return to his father in the sun. As he reached the summit, a great storm suddenly raged about him and when it cleared away, he was gone. But in order that his teachings might not be forgotten, he caused the likeness of his face to be outlined in ice and snow upon the side of this mountain. Ever since then the Indians have called the great peak "Mah-tah-pee-o-stook-sis-meh-stuk," which means "The mountain with the face of Sour Spirit who has gone back to the Sun."

Still visible on the east side of the mountain near its summit is the "face" of Sour Spirit in the form of a huge snowbank resembling the profile of a warrior looking south, with the feathers of his war bonnet trailing behind to the north.

Notes For Chapter 10

[1]"The Old North Trail," by Walter McClintock, University of Nebraska Press, Lincoln, Nebraska, 1968 (reprint of original 1910 edition).
"Blackfeet Lodge Tales," by George Bird Grinnell, Charles Scribner's Sons, New York, 1892.
"Blackfeet Tales Of Glacier National Park," by James Willard Schultz.

[2]"The Story Of The Blackfeet," published by the Bureau of Indian Affairs (latest edition issued by the Haskell Press, 1966) at pages 7, 30 and 51.

[3]Idem, at page 30.

[4]"Signposts Of Adventure," by James Willard Schultz, Houghton Mifflin Company, 1926, at page 15.

[5]"The Story Of The Blackfeet," supra, at page 7. According to "North American Indians," by George Catlin, Volume 1, at page 59, the Blackfeet were "perhaps the most powerful tribe of Indians on the Continent." Membership of the Blackfeet confederacy in the 1830's was estimated at close to 30,000, with the numbers being placed by a former agent for these tribes at "not far from 60,000."

[6]"The Story Of The Blackfeet," supra, at page 30.

[7]Idem, at page 30. In his book "The Old North Trail," supra, at page 39, Walter McClintock describes a hunting expedition in the late 1890's with William Jackson as follows: "Passing through the foothills, and riding along the Cut Bank River, we entered the mountains, Siksikakoan (Jackson) followed the old Blackfoot war trail, used by them in the early days, when they crossed the Rockies on war expeditions against the Pend d'Oreille, Kutenai and Flathead tribes." In reference to the 1810 encounter, see "Through The Years In Glacier National Park," by Donald H. Robinson, at page 8.

[8]See "Signposts Of Adventure," supra, at page 186, which describes the latter battle as a "hard fight." With reference to the Red Eagle encounter, see Chapter 4, supra, entitled "The Mountain Passes," at page 49.

[9]Article entitled "The Crown Of The Continent," by George Bird Grinnell, published in Century Magazine for September, 1901, at page 669.

[10]See Note 7, supra, for McClintock's description of the trail.

[11]"Signposts Of Adventure," supra, at page 43.

[12]Idem, at page 181. See, also, Henry L. Stimson's story of "The Ascent Of Chief Mountain," appearing in "Hunting In Many Lands," published in 1895 by Forest And Stream Publishing Co., New York.

[13]"The Story Of The Blackfeet," supra, at page 48. For the story of the purchase of the "ceded strip" in 1806, see "Through The Years," supra, at pages 36-37.

[14]"The Story Of The Blackfeet," supra, at pages 50-51.

[15]Idem, at page 51.

[16]Idem, at page 51.

[17]Idem, at page 52.

[18]Idem, at page 7.

[19]Idem, at page 7.

[20]Idem, at page 7.

[21]Idem, at page 66.

[22]Idem, at page 44.

[23]"The Old North Trail," supra, at pages 337-338.

[24]"The Story Of The Blackfeet," supra, at page 44.

[25]Idem, at page 44.

[26]Article by John C. Ewers entitled "Winold Reiss; His Portraits And Proteges," at page 53 of Montana Western History, Volume XII, Number Three, Summer of 1971.

[27]Idem, at pages 52-53.

[28]Idem, at page 51.

[29]Idem, at page 52.

[30]Idem, at page 52.

[31]"High Trails Of Glacier National Park," by Margaret Thompson, at pages 40-41. See, also, "Signposts Of Adventure," supra, at page 155. Clarke died in November, 1970.

[32]"High Trails Of Glacier National Park," supra, at page 41.

[33]"Mission Among The Blackfeet," by Howard L. Harrod, published by University of Oklahoma Press, 1971, at pages 85-86.

[34]"The Old North Trail," supra, at page 283.

[35]Idem, at pages 518-519. According to an article on Walter McClintock by Howard H. Hays, appearing on page 69 of the 1948 edition of the "Drivers' Manual" (see note 15, chapter 6), the opera "Poia," meaning "Scarface," received enthusiastic praise from scholars as well as high officials of the German court.

[36]"Signposts Of Adventure," supra, at page 3.

[37]Idem, at pages 3 and 4.

[38]Idem, at page 4.

[39]Idem, at pages 4 and 5. It was also in 1915, according to Horace M. Albright and Frank J. Taylor, authors of "Oh, Ranger," at pages 87 and 88, that "three distinguished Blackfeet, Bird Rattlers, Curly Bear and Wolf Plume, came to Washington to protest to the Secretary of the Interior against the use of white men's names in Glacier Park. They were promised that henceforth only Indian names or their translations would be used in Glacier National Park."

[40]"Signposts Of Adventure," supra, at pages 5-8.

[41]Idem, at page 118.

[42]In a letter ot the Glacier National Park Naturalist dated May 20, 1929, Schultz wrote: "I myself named 'Going-To-The-Sun Mountain;' simply because of its imposing uplift into the blue. There is no Indian legend in connection with the name."

[43]See, for example, the National Geographic Magazine for June, 1950, at page 719 of an article by Leo A. Borah entitled "Montana: Shining Mountain Treasureland;" also the National Geographic Magazine for May, 1956, at pages 598 and 621 of an article by George W. Long entitled "Many-Splendored Glacierland." Earlier and longer versions will be found at pages 103-104 of "High Trails Of Glacier National Park," supra, and at pages 193-194 of "Glacier National Park, Its Trails And Treasures," by Holtz and Bemis, published by George H. Doran Co., 1917. In his book entitled "Friends Of My Life As An Indian," published in 1923, at pages 274-277, Schultz not only recited the legend in its entirety, but rejected it as being of non-Indian origin and stated that he himself had named the mountain in 1884.

Blackfeet Indians displaying their handicraft
Photo by Walt Dyke, courtesy of Burlington Northern

Native dances of the Blackfeet never fail to interest Park visitors
Photo by Walt Dyke, courtesy of Burlington Northern

John Clarke ready to hit the trail

Rough pen sketches of Indian types which Clarke loved to depict

A visitor receives archery instruction at Glacier Park Lodge from a young brave of the Blackfeet Tribe

Photo by Hedrick-Blessing, courtesy of Burlington Northern

Chapter 11
ADVENT OF THE WHITE MAN

More fascinating than most fiction is the story of how the white man came to the region that is now Glacier Park. Like a pageant of pioneer progress, each successive event in its early history coincided with a new phase in the development of the west. First came the trader after fur, then a priest on behalf of the church, an explorer searching for a transcontinental route, surveyors to fix the international boundary, professors interested in scientific data, prospectors probing for treasures of the earth, sportsmen on the trail of game, and finally the American people, in quest of wilderness and mountain magnificence.

But long before anyone with European blood in his veins had even glimpsed the future Park or its red overlords, the fateful shadow of the white world had been cast upon it. As a matter of fact, because of the natural basis which its triple watershed afforded for generalized territorial claims predicated upon areas of water drainage, it was destined to figure in the political machinations and territorial maneuvering of the great powers of the old world as far back as the seventeenth century.

Region East Of The Continental Divide

The original charter of the great Hudson's Bay Company, signed on May 16, 1669 by Charles II, King of England, gave or purported to give the Company virtually sovereign powers over the vast portion of North America drained by streams entering Hudson Bay.[1] Included was a specific grant of all trading, fishery, navigation and mineral rights in Rupert's Land, as the territory thus granted was referred to by the charter. So more than 300 years ago, with a stroke of the pen, a dissolute English monarch gave the Company possession of an empire that not only included most of the present Dominion of Canada but also a substantial part of what is today Glacier National Park, since all of the streams in its northeastern section, i.e., east of the continental divide and north of the Hudson Bay divide, drain into Canadian rivers, the waters of which ultimately reach Hudson Bay.

Only thirteen years later, in 1682, the French explorer, LaSalle, traveled down the Mississippi River to its mouth and laid claim, in the name of Louis XIV, to all of the territory lying within the drainage basin of the Mississippi and its tributaries.[2] Of course, never having explored the Missouri, he had no conception of the vast territory he was claiming. Nevertheless, such a claim embraced the southeastern part of what is now the Park, since all of its streams east of the continental divide and south of the Hudson Bay divide flow into the Missouri and their waters eventually reach the Mississippi itself.

This southeastern section also had a colorful subsequent history, with several changes of European ownership. The title acquired by France in 1682 through LaSalle's exploration of the Mississippi was transferred to Spain in the 1760's, but was returned to France in 1800 by the secret treaty of San Ildefonso. Napoleon did not keep it long, however, selling it to the United States as a part of the Louisiana Purchase in 1803.[3] Thereafter, it passed through a series of territorial changes, being successively a part of the territories of Louisiana, Missouri, Nebraska, Dakota, Idaho and Montana, prior to the attainment of statehood by Montana in 1889.[4]

Region West Of The Continental Divide

By reason of its more remote location and watershed of its own, the western side of the present day Park escaped international attention during all of the seventeenth and most of the eighteenth centuries. It became controversial, however, about 1790 with beginnings of the conflict in interest between Great Britain and the United States in the "Oregon Country," the name then given to a vaguely defined section of the Northwest extending from the Rocky Mountains to the Pacific Ocean including, of course, that part of the present Park lying west of the continental divide.

In 1818, after a period of wrangling, the two nations agreed to joint usage of the territory for a ten-year period, a pact that was extended indefinitely in 1828.[5] By an 1846 treaty, however, the continuing stalemate was resolved by making everything south of the 49th parallel United States property, thus including the western part of the Park of today, as well as all of Montana west of the continental divide.

Thereafter, in quick succession, the area became a part of the territories of Oregon, Washington, Idaho and Montana, and finally a part of the state of Montana when the latter was admitted to the Union in 1889.[7]

The International Boundary

It is delightfully unimportant, yet intriguing, to contemplate the fact that the Glacier Park of today was once the "end of the line" for the United States-Canadian boundary, as well as for the survey of that boundary made some decades later. During the nineteenth century, it became necessary for the nations involved to determine the physical location of their mutual boundary west of the Lake of the Woods (in present day Minnesota), and subsequently to fix it with precision by actual survey. When for political or other reasons, neither of these troublesome and monumental projects could be more than partially completed at one time, it was the continental divide in the northwest section of the future Park that provided a convenient temporary terminus for many years and eventually, in each case, the concluding or junction point.

This 1500-mile boundary is undoubtedly the world's longest international border without a turn, as well as without a fortification; hence, on the basis of sheer length alone, it is not surprising that both its fixing and its survey had to be accomplished in sections. The following chart may assist in an understanding of the actions taken:

Actions In Reference To United States-Canada Boundary Along The 49th Parallel

Segment of Boundary Involved	Date of Fixing Boundary	Date of Completing Survey of Boundary
Westward from Lake of the Woods in Minnesota to Continental Divide in future Park	1818	1874
Eastward from Pacific Coast to Continental Divide in future Park	1846	1861

Fixing The Boundary

On the eastern side of the divide, the northern boundary of the Park-to-be had been settled in 1818 when Great Britain and the United States entered into the agreement that first dealt with the status of the "Oregon Country." Under this agreement, the international line was to follow the 49th parallel westward from the Lake of the Woods to the Stony (Rocky) Mountains, i.e., to the continental divide in what is now Glacier Park, a distance of more than 850 miles.[8] This agreement served, incidentally, to wipe out any further claim which the Hudson's Bay Company may have had to the northeastern section of the future Park.

On the western side of the divide, there was no boundary for the next 28 years, since both nations claimed all of the area. However, this territorial controversy was settled in 1846, as previously noted, by again utilizing the 49th parallel as the dividing line running eastward from the Pacific Coast.[9] In that year, accordingly, the two ends of the boundary were enabled to meet at the continental divide in what is now Glacier Park.

Conducting The Survey

Although the final boundary agreement was reached in 1846, the tedious task of confirming it by physical survey was not undertaken until 1857 when a party of the Northwestern Boundary Commission, in collaboration with a corresponding British party, headed eastward from the Pacific Coast. After four difficult years, they completed the work as far as the summit of the continental divide where, in 1861, they erected a suitable stone monument.[10]

Nothing was done on the eastern side of the divide until 1872 when Congress appropriated the necessary funds and a party under Commissioner Archibald Campbell, again working in conjunction with a British party, headed west from Minnesota. In August, 1874, despite the perils of a trackless wilderness and of frequently unfriendly natives, they reached the crest of the Montana Rockies, located the 1861 monument, and thus closed the boundary survey gap upon the soil of what, 36 years later, was to become a national park.[11]

Fur Traders And Early Explorers

History does not record any visit by the white man to the vicinity of what is now Glacier Park prior to 1790. The first of such visits was probably that of Peter Fidler, a young surveyor in the employ of the North

West Company. In 1792 he traveled from Fort Buckingham on the Saskatchewan River to the foot of the Rocky Mountains where he wintered with a band of Piegan Indians and where, near the end of December of that year, he caught his first glimpse of Chief Mountain.[12] Some of the information thus acquired was reflected in the famed Arrowsmith Map of 1795,[13] showing the Old Man River and "King Mountain" (as the Indian name for Chief Mountain came through in translation). However, Fidler's description of his 1792-93 adventure contained nothing to indicate that it took him into the future Park.[14]

A more familiar record of an early approach to the Glacier Park area is to be found in the journals of the Lewis and Clark expedition of 1804-1806. On the return trip from the Pacific Coast, Captain Meriwether Lewis and three of his men made a side-trip up the Marias River in an attempt to locate its source. On July 22, 1806 they reached a point about 25 miles east of present Park boundaries, where they remained for four days hoping to make astronomical observations. When overcast weather prevented, they named the place "Camp Disappointment," and turned back to rejoin the main part of the expedition.[15] At this point, weather permitting, Lewis could have had a good view of the Glacier Park peaks, but was considerably north of the eastern approach to Marias Pass itself.[16]

Records indicate that by the early 1800's there were fur traders in and about the Park of today. In the year 1810 three white traders, Finan McDonald, Michel Bordeaux and Baptiste Bouche, in company with a band of Flathead Indians, headed across an early Indian pass (probably Marias) to hunt on the eastern side of the mountains. En route they were ambushed, although unsuccessfully, by a larger party of Blackfeet.[17] A similar expedition in August, 1812, accompanied by two French traders, was less fortunate in undertaking an eastward crossing of Cut Bank Pass, with heavy casualties on both sides, including one or possibly both of the Frenchmen.[18]

First White Resident

Without question the first white man to make his home in the area bordering on what is now Glacier National Park was Hugh Monroe. While not the first of his race to gaze upon the shimmering beauty of Glacier's great Lewis Range, he spent much of his time near the Park's eastern border and lived, from time to time, during the middle years of the nineteenth century, in the St. Mary region.

Monroe had come from eastern Canada as a youth in his teens and entered the employ of the Hudson's Bay Company in 1815.[19] He was assigned to live for a year with the Piegan Blackfeet under the wing of their chief, Lone Walker, in the hope that his contacts with the Indians, their language, customs and mode of life might produce benefits and future business for the Company.[20]

The plan had an unexpected denouement. Young Monroe's sojourn with the Blackfeet proved to be so enjoyable that on his return to the Hudson's Bay post a year later, he had resolved to cast his lot with his new-found people permanently,[21] and thus embarked upon a unique career as the "white Blackfoot." One can only surmise that he succumbed to a variety of attractions—the freedom and pleasures of a nomadic existence, the charm of an Indian maiden, and perhaps the magic allure of the buffalo plains and the great front range of the Rockies. The girl that became his mate was Sinopah, the daughter of Chief Lone Walker.[22] His new life pattern included every responsibility of a young brave. He was given the name of Rising Wolf and fought along with his adopted people in many battles. In later years he became a respected member of the tribal councils.[23]

Life In The St. Mary Country

There are no records to indicate that Monroe had ever set foot on the soil of what is now Glacier Park prior to 1836 when he discovered the St. Mary Lakes.[24] Still more years were to elapse before he gave the lakes their present name in a formal ceremony that is believed to have occurred in 1845.[25] This christening took place in the presence of a group of friendly Kootenai Indians, and before a rude cross of logs which had been reared on the shore of the lower lake.[26] According to some writers, a noted Catholic priest was present and participated in the ceremony, but this story does not agree with Monroe's version of the event and now seems to be without support.[27]

Be that as it may, from the date of discovery onward Monroe and his family were frequent visitors to the St. Mary region because of its abundance of fish and game, including moose, his favorite meat. Sometimes a whole winter would be spent at the foot of the lower lake, trapping great numbers of wolves and other fur animals for the good prices their pelts would bring at Fort Benton.[28] To this day some of his descendants are to be found on the Montana plains, not too far away from the lakes their ancestor named.[29]

During his seventy-five or more years of association with the region, Monroe undoubtedly spent much time on the fringe or within the boundaries of what is Glacier Park today. The great Rising Wolf Mountain near Two Medicine Lake bears his Blackfeet name, while nearby Sinopah is named for his wife. When he died in December, 1892, he was buried at the Holy Family Mission on the Two Medicine River, not many miles from the "shining mountains" he loved so well.[30]

An Early Missionary Happens Along

Whether Father Pierre De Smet, famed Jesuit priest of early Montana, ever visited the future Park or its vicinity has long been debated.[31] However, a careful study of his 1845 itinerary on the eastern side of the Rockies points to the probability that he did so. On October 31st of that year he had headed south from Rocky Mountain House, a trading post northeast of Lake Louise, traveling with a small band of Blackfeet Indians, a young Cree half-breed, and an unreliable interpreter.[32] When the latter unexpectedly deserted on the twelfth day of travel, it became necessary for the priest to seek a replacement. Having heard that Hugh Monroe lived some distance to the south,[33] he continued on until he came upon what he recognized as Monroe's camp, but found that Hugh was away.[34] Pressing on south for several days with only the young Cree as a companion, he wandered through a "labyrinth of valleys" until unfavorable weather and diminishing supplies forced him to turn back.[35] Since Monroe's only "hang-out" in that region was at Lower Lake St. Mary, and the valleys immediately to the south included Cut Bank and Two Medicine, it is reasonable to believe that these valleys, now parts of the Park, were visited in November, 1845 by Father De Smet in the course of his unsuccessful search for Hugh Monroe.

The Quest For A Railroad Route

In the middle of the nineteenth century, the people of the United States were agog with dreams of a transcontinental railroad. The discovery of gold in faraway California had greatly increased the pressures for the location of feasible routes and for early construction of one or more roads to the Pacific. The key to every route lay in the discovery of a mountain pass suitable for railroad use; and in the case of northern Montana, the search, begun in 1853, did not reach its conclusion until within a few days of the 1890's.[36]

The heroes of the quest for a feasible route through northern Montana were both named Stevens, although unrelated. The active search was begun in 1853 under the personal direction of Isaac I. Stevens, newly appointed governor of the Territory of Washington. His efforts were thwarted by indifferent or pretended cooperation on the part of the Blackfeet, and it was not until December, 1889 that the "discovery" of a suitable route was ultimately achieved by John F. Stevens of the Great Northern Railway. His task was made difficult by a total lack of cooperation by the Blackfeet, and by rather feeble assistance from a member of the Flathead tribe. In a sense, this was really the "break-through" that was to provide the white man with effective control of the northwest, and the fascinating details of search and "discovery" have been set forth in an earlier chapter on the "lost" pass.[37]

Early Expeditions By The Military

Beginning with the memorable expedition of Captains Lewis and Clark in 1804-1806, the United States Army played a substantial role in exploration of the region in which Glacier Park is situated today. Both Tinkham and Doty, who carried out important assignments in connection with the Stevens expedition of 1853-1854, were army officers. Likewise, the military leader of the boundary survey party that reached the continental divide in the future park in 1874 was Captain Ames of the Sixth Infantry.[38]

In the year 1873, Lieutenants Charles A. Woodruff and John T. Van Orsdale, with a small detachment of troops from the Seventh United States Infantry, then stationed at Fort Shaw, Montana, on the Sun River, were ordered to make a reconnaissance to Fort Colville in Washington Territory. On the return trip, they proceeded up the Middle Fork of the Flathead River To Nyack Creek, thence up that stream, through what is now the Park, over Cut Bank Pass and down the eastern side of the continental divide. On this trek they discovered the glacier later seen by Raphael Pumpelly in 1883 and named for him.[39]

In the summer of 1886, Lieutenant S. R. Robertson was dispatched on a reconnaissance from Fort Assiniboine on the Milk River to the Lake St. Mary area. In proceeding as far as the head of lower Lake St. Mary, he mapped the country along the eastern face of the mountains, showing many of the peaks and rivers with the names they still bear.[40] In August, 1890, Lieutenant George P. Ahern, then stationed at Fort Shaw, was ordered to explore the mountains of what is now Glacier Park. His party skirted the Lewis Range from the Cut Bank valley to a point north of Chief Mountain, then entered the Belly River valley and, with no little difficulty, crossed the pass which now bears his name. Continuing down through the McDonald Creek and Lake areas, they exited by way of the Flathead Lake region.[41]

Explorations by Professors And Writers

The final two decades of the nineteenth century were notable in Glacier Park annals for the number of college professors, editors and writers who visited and explored its inner fastnesses. These were scholars who became fascinated by the variety of attractions which the region had to offer and who, in some cases, returned summer after summer at their own expense to pursue further studies and explorations.

Professor Raphael Pumpelly, on behalf of the Northern Transportation Railway Survey, spent parts of the summers of 1882 and 1883 in the Nyack-Cut Bank corridor. With him were such eminent scientists as Professor Bailey Willis, geologist, Professor Charles Sargent, forester, and Professor W. W. Hilgard, soil specialist. In 1883 they climbed the peak later named Mt. Stimson, and visited and named Pumpelly Glacier, verifying its prior discovery by Woodruff and Van Orsdale in 1873.[42]

The Grinnell Expeditions

In 1885 George Bird Grinnell made the first of many visits to the future park area, inspired by articles written by James Willard Schultz for "Forest And Stream," a popular outdoor magazine of which Grinnell was editor. He had traveled to Helena by railroad, thence by stage to Fort Benton, by wagon to the Blackfeet Agency at Badger Creek, and by saddlehorse and duffel wagon to the St. Mary Lakes.[43] Here he was joined by Schultz and they hunted and explored, but did not go beyond Upper Lake St. Mary.

Grinnell returned in 1887 and annually for many years thereafter, spending much time in the eastern valleys of the future park, usually in company with Schultz. Among their companions on various trips were George H. Gould, J. H. Beacom, William H. Seward, Jr., grandson of Lincoln's Secretary of State, Henry L. Stimson, William Jackson (Siksikakoan), J. B.

Monroe and Charles Rose (Yellow Fish).[44]

In the Swiftcurrent area, Grinnell Glacier, Lake and Mountain were named after the head of the party, and Mt. Gould after one of its members. When the headwaters of Lake St. Mary were visited on another occasion, Mts. Stimson, Seward and Jackson were named after members of the expedition. Fusillade Mountain was given its title when two of the party, on the trail of a band of goats, fired shot after shot without causing their quarry to do more than slowly clamber up the mountainside and move out of sight.[45]

In one of his many visits, Grinnell was adopted into the Blackfeet tribe and given an Indian name—Fisher Cap. He became an authority on the Blackfeet and, at their request, was appointed to negotiate with them concerning government acquisition of the future Park area east of the continental divide which, up to that time, had been a part of their Reservation.[46] In 1901, after the land had been purchased, thrown open to prospectors, and the ensuing mining excitement had subsided, Grinnell pointed out the great value of the area as a reservoir for the storage of water and the importance of preserving its forests in order to protect the water supply.[47]

One of Grinnell's companions on his trips to what is now Glacier Park was Henry L. Stimson. The latter's first visit was in 1891, and in the course of his various trips to the region's eastern slopes, he climbed a number of peaks, including first ascents of Chief in 1892 and Little Chief in 1894. Stimson was later to serve as Secretary of War under two presidents and as Secretary of State under still a third.[48]

Visits Of Sperry And Schultz

Dr. Lyman B. Sperry, erstwhile Carleton College faculty member, first visited the future Park in 1895 and, in June of that year, accompanied by Professor J. Paul Goode and others, made his way to Avalanche Lake and gave it its name.[49] In the course of a second trip to the lake in August of the same year, in company with his nephew and Professor L. W. Chaney, also of Carleton College, the party continued up the McDonald Valley to the Granite Park area, where they viewed the Grinnell Glacier from the Garden Wall, and discovered and named Chaney Glacier.[50]

In 1896 Dr. Sperry was able to reach the glacier which is named after him and saw the possibilities of a well constructed trail to it. With such a project in mind, he recruited University of Minnesota students and Great

Northern Railway assistance and succeeded, during the summers of 1902 and 1903, in completing a trail to the east side of Gunsight Pass, with a side trail to the headwall below Sperry Glacier.[51] Although later rebuilt by the National Park Service, the present trail varies but little from that built more than 70 years ago.[52]

Friend and advisor to Grinnell and other eminent visitors to the future Park area, beginning with the early 1880's, was James Willard Schultz, author and authority on the region itself as well as its people. Schultz came to Montana in 1878 and, like Hugh Monroe, became a member of the Blackfeet tribe, married an Indian girl, and spent much of his life on the Blackfeet reservation and in the nearby valleys on the eastern side of the Rockies. He wrote extensively for outdoor magazines, and was the author of such classics as "Signposts Of Adventure" and "Blackfeet Tales of Glacier National Park." His Indian name, Apikuni, as he spelled it, meaning Scabby Robe or Spotted Robe, is borne by Appekunny Peak and Basin in the Swiftcurrent area, as well as by one of the Park's principal rock formations.

Pioneers Of The Park's Northern Sector

Perhaps the first white men to set foot on the northern part of what is now Glacier Park were members of the British-sponsored Palliser Expedition, which trekked over much of southwestern Canada seeking a suitable rail route across the Rockies. In the summer of 1858, a section of it commanded by Lieutenant Blakiston, after exploring the country to a point near what is now Eureka, Montana, turned eastward to the North Fork of the Flathead River. From the latter's junction with Kishenehn Creek, they followed a trail along the latter across the northwestern corner of the future Park, and thence over South Kootenay Pass to the lush Waterton Valley, which was discovered and named by Blakiston.[53]

In this same time bracket were members of the United States and British crews engaged in a survey of the international boundary from the Pacific Coast to the continental divide.[54] This was a task which they completed in 1861 with the erection of a rock cairn at the crest of the Livingston Range,[55] but the sojourn there was brief and contact of the parties with the area south of the border was little more than visual.

The original pioneer in the northern reaches of the Park-to-be was John George "Kootenai" Brown, who came from British Columbia to the Waterton Valley in 1865,[56] not by way of Brown Pass, as some have surmised, but rather over the more convenient South Kootenay Pass.[57] In 1877 he became the first permanent resident of the Kootenai Lakes country,[58] as the Waterton Lakes area was known until 1911,[59] and his activities thereafter as hunter, trapper and guide frequently took him south of the border. He may, indeed, have been the first white man to traverse the pass which bears his name.

As a matter of fact, Brown became a part-time resident of Glacier's upper Waterton Valley during the 1880's and 1890's, and the trapper's cabin that he maintained on the edge of a meadow near Little Kootenai Creek, now called the Waterton River, was undoubtedly one of the earliest structures of its kind in the future Park.[60] This cabin, situated some 7 or 8 miles south of the border, was kept well stocked with traps, snares and provisions, as well as a goodly supply of reading matter, since it was here that Brown and his Cree wife, Isabella, spent much time.[61]

After becoming a ranger and acting superintendent of the Canadian park in 1910 and 1911, respectively, Brown continued his friendship with such Glacier Park rangers as Joe Cosley[62] and Dan Doody;[63] and it was in September, 1913 that he hosted Louis W. Hill, then board chairman of the Great Northern Railway and early benefactor of Glacier Park.[64]

Early Belly River Resident

Another pioneer in the northern valleys of Glacier Park was the Joe Cosley just referred to as a contemporary of Brown. Joe first visited the future park region early in September, 1894 when, with a companion known as Porcupine Jim, he spent several weeks doing excavation work on five mining claims owned by Joe Kipp and others on the summit of Flattop Mountain.[65] After one trip to Lake McDonald for supplies, a late October blizzard made further work impossible, and they headed north. Floundering desperately for a few miles through the snow, they came to a trapper's cabin, within which they found a note, signed by "J. G. Brown," giving permission to use the cabin.[66]

After gratefully availing themselves of the owner's hospitality, they resumed their northward journey the next morning, crossed the international border and, on the second day, came upon another cabin situated on

Blakiston Brook, then called Pass Creek. Here they were greeted by Kootenai Brown himself and were royally entertained by Brown and his wife.[67] In the years that followed, Joe Cosley was to become an habitue of the Belly River region, pursuing a career as trapper, guide, park ranger and trapper again, until discovery in 1929 of his illicit activities as a poacher drove him out of Glacier forever.[68]

Early West Side Settlers

The Great Northern Railway reached Belton, on the west side of the future park, in the latter part of 1891, bringing rail transportation to that area for the first time; and it was this side of the divide that first began to attract homesteaders and summer visitors. Among the early arrivals were Milo B. Apgar and Charles Howe, the former reportedly having come over Marias Pass with his belongings in a two-wheeled cart and settled on the spot that was later to bear his name, the present village of Apgar at the foot of Lake McDonald. Apgar and Howe soon began to build cabins on the site of the present Village Inn as a means of offering overnight accommodations for visitors to the area.[69]

The number of people coming into the attractive McDonald Lake region increased rapidly. Some residents of nearby communities built themselves summer cottages at the lake; others acquired strategic sites and erected guest facilities, camping accommodations, and eventually even dude ranches. In 1895, George Snyder built a two-story frame hotel near the head of the lake and the site of the present McDonald Lake Lodge. In order to get visitors to his hotel, he purchased a 40-foot steamboat from the Flathead Lake area, built a narrow wagon road from Belton to Apgar, and succeeded in hauling the craft to the lake and getting it launched. This was the first power boat to haul passengers and freight on any of the lakes of the future park.[70] Soon a stage line over the new road was started by Ed Dow, who had built a small hotel in Belton, and public transportation all the way from the railroad to the upper end of the lake thus became available.[71]

Sometime during these early years Charles M. "Charlie" Russell, well-known cowboy artist, bought lake-shore property near Apgar and built himself a summer home which he called Bull Head Lodge, after the buffalo skull that was his trademark. Here it was that he spent the summers of many of his later years.[72]

Mineral Explorations

Prospectors and miners were said to have made an occasional appearance in the area of the future park in the 1870's. Undoubtedly, however, the earliest authenticated record of a prospecting expedition in or near the park-to-be had to do with a trip made in 1867 by Joseph Kipp, John Wren, Charles Thomas and several other erstwhile employees of the American Fur Company. With a team of eight bulls and wagon, and a number of saddle horses, they skirted the feet of the Rockies from the Teton River north to the Saskatchewan, prospecting every stream for placer gold but finding none.[73] Presumably, although it is not clear, they may have set foot on portions of what is now Glacier Park.

In 1876 a party of 5 Texans entered the future park region on a prospecting trip, crossing the area by way of Logan Pass and arriving at Quartz Lake late in August. After finding a 30-ounce gold nugget at the waterfall directly northeast of the lake, they built a one-room cabin at the lake's northeast corner. As winter was setting in, 3 of the party left for California and there is no record of what became of those who remained at the lake.[74]

In the 1880's Mrs. Nat Collins, popularly known as the "Cattle Queen Of Montana," undertook to operate a supposedly promising copper mine in the upper McDonald Valley. While she acted as both foreman and cook, her crew worked the mine for three summers and a winter with little success. Finally she consulted a mining engineer who checked the mine over and advised her to drop the venture. She did so and returned to her ranch at Choteau, Montana, but the stream on which the mine was located is still known as "Cattle Queen Creek."[75]

Until about 1890 prospecting on the west side of the future park was rather aimless and sporadic. In the early years of the 1890's, rumors began to circulate in the mining centers of Butte and Anaconda to the effect that there were rich veins of copper ore in these mountains.[76] As a result, many prospectors flocked to the area and spent whatever time was necessary to satisfy each that the reports had been without foundation.

The Swiftcurrent Boom

All of the prospecting activity of the eighties and early nineties had to be confined to the west side of the park-to-be, because the area east of the continental divide, being a part of the Blackfeet Indian Reservation, was "off limits" to mining activity. Some of the bolder prospectors would nevertheless sneak into the area and bring out stories tending to fire the imagination of others. Finally, the pressures on Congress were such that something had to be done, and a commission was appointed to negotiate with the Blackfeet for purchase of the strip of land between the continental divide and the plains, i.e., the eastern part of the present Park. A purchase price of $1,500,000 was agreed upon, leaving the Indians, however, with fishing, hunting and timberland rights in the "ceded strip," as the section was called. Congress confirmed the purchase in 1896, and the "ceded strip" was thrown open to miners and settlers on April 15, 1898.[77]

There was a tremendous stampede of miners and prospectors on horses, in wagons and on foot. Within a matter of hours, hundreds of claims had been staked in the Swiftcurrent and St. Mary valleys.[78] A small boom town sprang up at the mouth of Canyon Creek near the head of Sherburne Lake. This town, called Altyn, continued to be the center of Swiftcurrent activity as long as mining activity itself continued. It was at its height in 1899 and 1900 when it boasted a postoffice and a newspaper, in addition to stores, saloons and other facilities appropriate to a western mining camp. Before long, however, it had become a ghost town, and by 1918 its once lively buildings were but a shambles, its deserted streets visited only by an occasional coyote.

The Cracker And Josephine Mines

The mines themselves never produced any ore of importance, copper being the principal mineral sought. Most prominent of these was the Cracker Mine located on the shores of Cracker Lake.[79] Its main shaft was driven 1,300 feet into the mountainside and a 100-ton concentrator was brought in from the Coeur d'Alenes and hauled up from Browning by mule team. The 16,000-pound machine required 29 days to reach Cracker Lake where it was installed and made two short runs for test purposes.[80] For many years its remains could still be seen near the old mine entrance.

The Cracker Mine, along with 12½ other claims, was controlled by the Michigan and Montana Copper Mining & Smelting Company, organized in September, 1898 with a capital stock of 8,000 shares of the par value of one dollar. By September, 1900, $97.50 each was reportedly being offered and refused for some of its shares. The owners of the Josephine Mine, above the lake of the same name, incorporated it under the name of the Josephine Copper Mining Company, with a capital stock of 100,000 shares of a par value of one dollar each.[81]

Nearly all of the turn of the century mining activity was centered in the Swiftcurrent area. As with the west-side flurry and influx of prospectors in the early 1890's, nothing of importance was ever found. In this same era, efforts to make coal deposits on the North Fork of the Flathead River commercially profitable failed, at first because no practicable means of getting the coal to the railroad could be devised, and subsequently because the coal itself was found to be of too low a grade to be worth excavating.[82]

The Oil And Gas Boom

Following the discovery of the presence of gas and oil on both sides of the future park, considerable drilling activity developed. A minor oil and gas boom more or less paralleled the mining mania and ran a similar course. Oil seepages were found at the head of Kintla Lake in 1901, and during the same year in the lower Swiftcurrent Valley, near the site of the present Sherburne Dam.[83] Companies were formed, men and equipment were procured, and drilling continued intermittently for several years. Two wells in the Kintla area were begun but soon abandoned when they failed to produce.[84]

In the Sherburne area, eight or ten wells in all were drilled. One of these was put down to a depth of 1500 feet, and actually received an award at the 1905 State Fair as the "first producing oil well in the State of Montana."[85] However, neither oil or gas was ever recovered in commercial quantities, and the boom died almost completely after 1907. Most of the drilling sites are now covered by the waters of the Sherburne Reservoir.[86]

One of the oil prospectors, Mike Cassidy, did find gas in quantities sufficient to enable him, in 1907, to pipe it to his home and to use it until 1914 for heating and lighting purposes. In 1920, in connection with the construction of the Sherburne Dam, his claim was condemned by the federal government and he was paid $7,675 in settlement for that part of it lying below the flow line, which included the gas well. Later he exchanged his remaining acreage for lands outside the Park.[87]

Mapping Of The Area

The earliest map of the future Park region was prepared by George Bird Grinnell and is now in the National Park Service archives at Park Headquarters in West Glacier. It is entitled "Sketch Map of the St. Mary's Lake Region, Montana" and is dated 1885-1892. It shows that part of the future Park lying between the international boundary and the Blackfoot Glacier, and between the Hudson Bay Divide (which he called the Milk River Ridge) and the continental divide. It shows many of the present names of lakes, streams and mountains and is surprisingly true to scale and topographical features.[88]

As the oil and mineral activity burgeoned in the Park-to-be, a need developed for accurate maps of the entire region. The United States Geological Survey sent crews into the area, commencing in 1900, to map the area and the adjacent mountains.[89] The original project covered the years 1900-1904, followed by additional work during the period 1907-1912. So accurate was the survey that the basic map completed in those years, but updated to reflect subsequently added features, such as roads, trails, hotels, campgrounds and ranger stations, as well as added nomenclature, remained in use until 1972 when a completely revised version first became available.

Administration Of The Pre-Park Era

With the creation of the Lewis and Clark Forest Reserve in 1897, administration and protection of the area became necessary. In 1900, President Theodore Roosevelt appointed one of his former "Rough Riders," Frank Herrig, as forest ranger to patrol the country drained by the North Fork of the Flathead River.[90] Herrig was the first federal officer to be placed in charge of any part of the area included in the present Park. He was an imposing figure, usually mounted on a big bay horse, decked out with a silver-mounted bridle and martingale. He wore high-topped boots, a big "44" strapped on his belt, and a 45-70 in a scabbard on his saddle. He always wore his ranger's badge in plain sight, and his constant companion was a large Russian wolfhound.[91]

Next forest ranger to serve the future Park region was Frank Liebig, appointed on June 1, 1902 to cover all of what is now Glacier National Park.[92] His duties were to "look for fires, timber thieves, squatters and game violaters."[93] Operating out of a ranger station at the head of Lake McDonald, Liebig continued to be in full charge of the entire area until it became a national park in 1910.[94] His hobby was bird taxidermy, and the best of his work, long on display at Park headquarters at

West Glacier, became a part of the Glacier Park Information Center opened at Apgar in July, 1973.

Notes For Chapter 11
[1]"Oregon and California," by Robert Greenhow, published in 1845, at Pages 97-98, 465-466.
[2]"Oregon Territory," by Travers Twiss, published in 1846, at page 154. LaSalle had laid claim to all "of the country of Louisiana, from the mouth of the great river St. Louis, otherwise called Ohio, on the eastern side, and also above the River Colbert or Mississippi, and the rivers which discharge themselves into it from its source in the country of Kious or Nadioussious, as far as its mouth at the sea, or Gulf of Mexico."
[3]"Oregon Territory," supra, at page 157, states that "By a secret treaty with Spain, made in 1762, but not signed until 1764, France ceded to her all the country known under the name of Louisiana. This transfer, however, was not promulgated until 1765, two years after the treaty of Paris had been signed by France, Spain and Great Britain; nor did the Spaniards obtain possession of the country until 1769." After retaining it until 1800, Spain retroceded it to France which, in turn sold it to the United States for 60,000 francs.
[4]"Through The Years In Glacier National Park," by Donald H. Robinson, at pages 2-4.
[5]"Oregon Territory," supra, at pages 145, 223. See, also, "Oregon And California," supra, at page 477.
[6]"Through The Years," supra, at page 3.
[7]Idem, at pages 3-4.
[8]"Oregon And California," supra, at page 477.
[9]"Through The Years," supra, at page 3.
[10]"West On The 49th Parallel," by John E. Parsons, published in 1963 by William Morrow and Company, at pages 7-11. See, also, "Survey of Northern Boundary of the United States, 1878," by Commissioner Archibald Campbell and Captain W. J. Twining, at pages 365-366.
[11]"West On The 49th Parallel," supra, at pages 117-119. Subsequent detailed surveys have established a precise 49th parallel which is sometimes north and sometimes south of the agreed boundary. It is interesting to note that at the crest of the continental divide in Glacier, the agreed boundary runs nearly a tenth of a mile (500 feet) south of the true parallel. See page 150 and map on the rear jacket of "West On The 49th Parallel."
[12]"Peter Fidler: Canada's Forgotten Surveyor," by I. G. MacGregor, published in 1966 by McClelland & Stewart, Ltd., of Toronto, at page 75. See, also, "Oregon And California," supra, at page 265.
[13]Arrowsmith's "Map Of All The New Discoveries In North America," published in London in 1795, has served as the basis for many later maps, including that projected for the northwestern Montana area by the Lewis and Clark expedition in 1805.
[14]"Peter Fidler," supra, at pages 74-75.
[15]"Journals Of The Lewis And Clark Expedition," by Meriwether Lewis (1814 Unabridged Edition), published in 1961 by J. B. Lippincott Company, Volume III, at pages 724-726.
[16]While "Through The Years," supra, at page 7, suggests that Lewis would have been able to look into Marias Pass but for the overcast, a footnote to the "History Of The Lewis And Clark Expedition," published in 1961 by Dover Publications (edited by Elliott Coues), at page 1094 places the location of Camp Disappointment at a point considerably north of Marias Pass.
[17]"Narrative," by David Thompson, at page 425.
[18]"Through The Years," supra, at pages 8-9.
[19]Letter from Hudson's Bay Company, London, dated 5/8/73, with respect to Monroe's employment, states in part: "In the earliest list of servants in which he appears, i.e., for trading season 1815-16, he is listed as an 'apprentice' . . . the usual age for an apprentice was a lad in his teens." A later communication dated 8/8/73 stated in part:

"Monroe's first year with the Company, 1815-16, was spent at Edmonton House, North Saskatchewan River."

Until recently, the date of Monroe's birth was controversial. He himself asserted repeatedly that he was born on May 4, 1784, while James Willard Schultz, his long-time friend, stated in at least two of his books that Monroe was born at Three Rivers, Quebec, on July 0, 1799. Recently it was learned from the birth records of the parish church at L'Assomption, Quebec, that he was born there on August 25, 1799 and baptized the following day. Consequently, he died at the age of 93, not 108.

[20]"My Life As An Indian," by James Willard Schultz, at page 176. See, also, "Signposts Of Adventure," by James Willard Schultz, at page 49, and "Blackfeet Tales Of Glacier National Park," supra, at page 4.

[21]"Signposts Of Adventure," supra, at page 50; "Blackfeet Tales," supra, at page 4.

[22]The story of his romance with the daughter of Chief Lone Walker is related to Schultz at pages 180-183 of his book "My Life As An Indian." See, also, "Through The Years," supra, at page 10.

[23]"Through The Years," supra, at page 10.

[24]In the interviews that Monroe gave to Montana newspapers near the end of his life, he stated that he had discovered the St. Mary Lakes in 1836, more than 20 years after he came to the Northwest.

[25]See "Friends Of My Life As An Indian," at pages 65-66, and see note 27, infra, as to the probable date.

[26]It was Monroe who stated that the christening took place in the presence of a group of friendly Kootenai Indians, this information having been given in the course of the interviews mentioned in note 24, supra. The same story was contained in George Bird Grinnell's "The Crown Of The Continent," appearing in Century Magazine for September, 1901, at page 661.

[27]There seems to be little disagreement as to the fact that the lakes were christened by, or in the presence of, Hugh Monroe before a huge cross of logs. There has been much disagreement among writers as to whether a priest was present at the ceremony and officiating; as to his identity, if present, and as to the year in which the incident occurred. James Willard Schultz has named two different priests and several different dates in discussing the matter in four of his books. Another writer named two different priests and two different dates in different parts of the same book, Monroe himself made no mention of the presence of a priest at the christening ceremony.

It now appears from a study of all available evidence, including Father Pierre J. De Smet's book entitled "Oregon Missions And Travels Over The Rocky Mountains In 1845-1846" and a letter written by him to Monroe in 1850, that De Smet had nothing to do, at least directly, with the christening ceremony. On the other hand, it also appears that De Smet, seeking Monroe's services as a guide and interpreter, came to the latter's St. Mary camp site in November, 1845. Although he didn't find Monroe there, he did take note of certain "signs evidently left for my benefit," one of which there is good reason to believe was the still standing rude cross of pine logs which had been used for the christening ceremony some weeks earlier, after it had been erected by Monroe's Kootenai friends.

[28]For the story of Monroe's activities at St. Mary Lakes, according to Schultz, see pages 147-149 of "Blackfeet Tales Of Glacier National Park," and page 185 of "My Life As An Indian."

[29]Still living on the Blackfeet Reservation only a few miles from the old stamping ground of Hugh Monroe is one of his grandsons, Angus Monroe who, with his wife, celebrated their 60th wedding anniversary on January 4, 1973. Angus was born on May 27, 1887 at Old Agency on Badger Creek between Browning and Heart Butte, and says he remembers his grandfather Hugh. His father, John Monroe, died in 1908. Angus helped pack building materials over Swiftcurrent Pass for the construction of Granite Park Chalet about 1915 or 1916, and also served as a saddlehorse guide in the Park for many years. The Angus Monroes live in a comfortable home near the Canadian border some 35 miles, as the crow files, from the St. Mary Lakes. See the Hungry Horse News for March 23, 1973.

[30]Schultz mistakenly reported in two of his books that Monroe died in his 98th year which, to correspond to Schultz's statements about his birth, would have had to be in 1896. See "Signposts Of Adventure," supra, at page 51, and "Blackfeet Tales Of Glacier National Park," supra, at page 6. The correct date of Monroe's death was December 8, 1892.

[31]"Through The Years," supra, at page 118, also page 12.

[32]"Oregon Missions, And Travels Over The Rocky Mountains In 1845-1846," by Father Pierre De Smet, at pages 180-182.

[33]Idem, at page 182.

[34]In a letter written by Father De Smet to Hugh Monroe under date of June 12, 1850, De Smet relates how he had tried to find Monroe, traveling through a "a labyrinth of narrow valleys . . . always searching for you." He told how he had found Monroe's encampment and of the signs that Monroe had left there "evidently for my benefit . . . I took up your trail with fresh courage, believing you to be very near . . . Then snow began to fall in great flakes . . . and with it vanished my hope of finding you that season in some Blackfoot camp." This letter was published as a footnote to page 527 of volume II of "The Life, Letters And Travels of Father Pierre-Jean De Smet," compiled by Chittenden and Richardson, and published in 1905.

[35]Idem.

[36]See discussion of the search for a suitable railroad pass in Chapter 5, supra, entitled "The Story Of The 'Lost' Pass," at pages 55 et seq.

[37]Idem.

[38]"Through The Years," supra, at page 13.

[39]Idem, at page 14. Van Orsdale returned to the Park with his wife more than 40 years later as a visitor, according to an interview with Mrs. Cora Hutchings appearing in the Hungry Horse News for May 12, 1972. Mrs. Van Orsdale was a sister of Major Logan, the Park's first superintendent, according to the Hungry Horse News for July 10, 1975.

[40]"Through The Years," supra, at page 17.

[41]Idem, at pages 17-18.

[42]Idem, at page 31.

[43]"Early History Of Glacier National Park," by Madison Grant, at page 5. See, also, article entitled "The Crown Of The Continent," by George Bird Grinnell, appearing in the Century Magazine for September, 1901, at pages 660-672.

[44]"Early History Of Glacier National Park," supra, at pages 6-11. According to Schultz in "Signposts Of Adventure," supra, at page 138, he and J. B. Monroe (no relation to Hugh) were Grinnell's companions in his 1887 visit to the Swiftcurrent Valley. Both Jackson and Rose were of partial Blackfeet descent.

[45]Article entitled "The Crown Of The Continent," supra, at pages 667-668.

[46]"Through The Years," supra, at page 17.

[47]Article entitled "The Crown Of The Continent," supra, at page 672.

[48]Stimson (1867-1950) served as Secretary of War for Taft (1911-1913) and for Franklin Roosevelt (1940-1945). He served as Secretary of State for Hoover (1929-1933).

[49]Article entitled "In The Montana Rockies," by Lyman B. Sperry, appearing in "Appalachia," Vol. VIII, No. 1, January, 1896, at page 58.

[50]"Avalanche," by Alfred L. Sperry, at page 55.

[51]"Through The Years," supra, at pages 24-25.

[52]Idem, at page 25.

[53]For a description of Blakiston's trek across the corner of the present Park, see "The Papers Of The Palliser Expedition," edited by Irene Spry, at pages 576 and 577, and map attached to "Further Papers Relative to the Exploration of British North America," showing Blakiston's route from the North Fork of the Flathead River in early September, 1858 to the Canadian border, and the fact that he spent one night in the future Park area.

It is interesting to note Blakiston's description at page 75 of "Further Papers Relative To The Exploration," supra, of a "Flathead Pass" reachable via the west shore of Waterton Lake and then to the Flathead River (presumably over Flattop Mountain) to the "Flathead (St. Mary) Mission."

[54]As described at page 90, supra.

[55]"Through The Years," supra, at page 12.

[56]"Kootenai Brown, His Life And Times," by William Rodney, at page 61.

[57]Idem. At one time it was thought that Brown had "used this (Brown) pass on his first trip into the Waterton Lakes area from California." See "Through The Years," supra, at page 108.

[58]"Kootenai Brown," supra, at page 125.

[59]Idem, at pages 196-198. While the name of "Waterton" was originally conferred upon the lakes by Lieutenant Thomas Blakiston in 1858, it did not become their official name until 1911. In the meantime, they were commonly referred to as the Kootenay Lakes.

[60]"A Short Story Of Kootenai Brown," by Joseph E. Cosley, at pages 6-7.

[61]Idem.

[62]"Kootenai Brown," supra, at page 207.

[63]Idem, at pages 206 and 211.

[64]Idem, at pages 199-200.

[65]"A Short Story Of Kootenai Brown," supra, at pages 1 and 2.

[66]Idem, at pages 6-7.

[67]Idem, at pages 10-11. "Nechemous" was Kootenai's pet name for his Cree wife, Isabella.

[68]For a more complete story of Cosley, see Chapter 22, infra, entitled "The Guardians Of Glacier," at pages 177-178, and particularly notes 21-26, inclusive, for that chapter.

[69]"Through The Years," supra, at page 23.

[70]Idem, at pages 61-62.

[71]Idem, at page 62.

[72]Idem, at page 62.

[73]"Signposts Of Adventure," supra, at page 108.

[74]A story of this trip was prepared by William Veach, Sr., who was a member of the party and who, at age 16, acted as its cook and killer of game. The story appears at pages 11-13 of Volume VIII of "Glacial Drift" for April, 1935.

[75]"Through The Years," supra, at page 36.

[76]Idem, at page 36.

[77]Idem, at pages 36-37.

[78]Idem, at page 37.

[79]Idem, at page 39.

[80]Idem, at page 38.

[81]As reported in the columns of Altyn's newspaper, the "Swiftcurrent Courier," edition of September 1, 1900. For more information concerning this publication, see Chapter 20, infra, entitled "'Ankle Excursions' Out of Many Glacier," at page 164, and footnotes 10 and 11 for that chapter.

[82]"Through The Years," supra, at page 50.

[83]Idem, at page 40.

[84]Idem, at page 40.

[85]Idem, at page 42.

[86]Idem, at page 43.

[87]Idem, at pages 41-42.

[88]Idem, at page 18.

[89]Idem, at page 43.

[90]Idem, at page 51-52.

[91]Idem, at page 52.

[92]Idem, at page 52. See, also, "Early Days In The Glacier Park Country," by Frank S. Liebig, printed at page 7 of the Spring Edition of "Montana West" for the year 1970. The story originally appeared under the title of "Early Days In The Forest Service," in Volume I, compiled by the United States Forest Service, Region I, at page 52.

[93]"Early Days In The Glacier Park Country," supra, at page 7.

[94]"Through The Years," supra, at page 52. According to "Early Days In the Glacier Park Country," supra, at page 8, Liebig came to have a number of assistant rangers during the later years of his service, including a man named Daughs, who helped him on trail work.

Swiftcurrent Lake and Mt. Grinnell in foreground

Courtesy Burlington Northern

Twilight campfire at Swiftcurrent Lake

Courtesy Burlington Northern

View of Lake St. Mary and the Continental Divide

Photo by Mel Ruder

Chapter 12
ATTAINMENT OF
NATIONAL PARKHOOD

The idea of national parks was a novel concept a century ago. Perhaps the first man ever to advocate this type of governmental preserve, and certainly the first to propose the establishment of such a park for the Rocky Mountain region, was George Catlin, noted painter and friend of the American Indian.[1] It was he who, circa 1840, suggested that a strip of country just to the east of the Rockies and extending from Mexico to Canada be set aside as

> ". . . a **magnificent park** where the world could see for ages to come the native Indian in his classic attire, galloping his wild horse, with sinewy bow, and shield and lance, amid the fleeting herds of elks and buffaloes. . . . A **nation's park,** containing man and beast, in all the wild and freshness of their nature's beauty!"[2]

It was more than 30 years after the publication of Catlin's extraordinary proposal that the first[3] and still the largest of our 28 national parks was created. This was the fabulous Yellowstone country on the southern border of Montana, set aside by Congress in 1872 as a "pleasuring-ground for the benefit and enjoyment of the people."[4] Thirty-eight years later Montana found itself honored again when Glacier Park (5th in size, 9th in seniority) was established on its northern border. The people and events that brought Montana's second great scenic area to the status of national parkhood make a seldom-told story of more than passing interest.

The idea for a park in the region that is now Glacier may be said to have had its genesis in 1873, the year after Yellowstone had been created by Congress. At least it was during 1873 that the area was visited by the man who first proposed that it be "set aside as a national park," although he did not make his idea known to the world until a decade later. The man in question was Lieutenant John T. Van Orsdale who, with Lieutenant Charles A. Woodruff and a detachment of troops, passed through the future park while returning from a reconnaissance in the Territory of Washington. Their route took them up the Nyack Valley and over Cut Bank Pass to the eastern side of the continental divide.[5] Both officers were profoundly impressed with the scenery, and particularly by the glacier which they had seen to the north of the headwaters of Nyack Creek.[6]

Publication of First Proposal
For A National Park

Van Orsdale was still in Montana when those in charge of the Pumpelly expedition of 1882-1883 were laying plans for further exploration of the transmountain route over which he had earlier traveled; and they very understandably asked him to join the group. He accepted the invitation, and repeated the earlier trek with much interest. As the expedition proceeded up the Nyack Valley at a leisurely pace and crossed the Cut Bank summit in early August of 1883, its distinguished scientists marveled at the rugged beauty of the region on both sides of the continental divide, and were amazed to discover that there were glaciers in the Rockies south of the international border. In Montana, the Pumpelly expedition became the big news of the day, fully covered by every one of its newspapers.[7]

It was to correct certain inaccurate statements which had appeared in the Fort Benton River Press of August 29, 1883, that Van Orsdale sent a communication which shortly thereafter was published by that paper. His closing paragraph read, in part, as follows:

> "I sincerely hope that publicity now being given to that portion of Montana will result in drawing attention to the scenery which surpasses anything in Montana or adjacent territories A great benefit could result to Montana if this section could be set aside as a national park."[8]

This appears to have been the first public presentation of the idea of Glacier National Park, and the lieutenant was well ahead of the times, for neither the East nor the West was then giving a great deal of thought to the conservation of natural resources, not to mention additional national parks.

An Unpublished Thought

George Bird Grinnell, owner and publisher of the popular and influential magazine "Forest and Stream," first visited the future park area in 1885, returning frequently in subsequent years. It was in 1891, while revisiting the St. Mary region, that he made an entry in his notebook that it would be—

> ". . . a good idea for the government to buy the mountains about the St. Mary Lake and turn the region into a national park."[9]

However, according to James Willard Schultz, serving as guide on the 1885 visit of Grinnell to the area, the latter had at that time remarked—

> ". . . how fine it would be if that part of the Rockies could some day be set aside as a national park and kept intact as a refuge for big game, a pleasure ground for all the people for all time to come."[10]

In any event, whatever thoughts Grinnell may then have had along these lines were not brought to public attention at the time. Even his celebrated article appearing in the Century Magazine for September, 1901,[11] while sometime hailed as the opening gun in support of a campaign to establish the future park, was simply a popular travelogue on the parts of the region which had been explored by him, together with praise for its inclusion as a part of the Forest Reserve created by the United States Forest Commission in 1897. It made no mention of the possibility of converting the area into a national park.[12]

Grinnell nevertheless did a great deal, both before and after publication of his Century Magazine article, to publicize his favorite stretch of mountains. In 1885 and 1886 he had written and published in "Forest And Stream" a series of letters about the St. Mary region,[13] and had published other articles on the same subject from the pen of Schultz.[14] At Grinnell's request, Emerson Hough, well-known writer on outdoor topics, made two visits to the area in 1902, which he followed with articles "in favor of making a national park of the Rockies from the Canadian line south to Marias Pass."[15]

Other Early Recommendations
For Park Status

In the year 1897, Dr. Lyman B. Sperry, the discoverer of Sperry Glacier, prior to his trip of that summer to the Lake McDonald region, wrote to F. I. Whitney, General Passenger Agent for the Great Northern Railway, that the woods of that country were full of hard-to-reach glaciers; and that good times and good trails would make the area a popular resort for campers, climbers and lovers of science and scenery. He closed by saying: "The region ought to become a national park."[16] Again, as in the case of Grinnell's notebook entry, this was not a document intended for general public attention or consideration.

In the summer of 1901, the United States Geological Survey began a study of portions of what is now the Park. The survey party included F. Matthes, who mapped the area, Stuart Weller, paleontologist, Dr. Bailey Willis, eminent geologist who described and named the Lewis Overthrust, and George I. Findlay, his assistant. Both Matthes and Willis, in their official reports, suggested the establishment of the region as a national park.[17]

Another proponent of national park status for the area, although somewhat belated, was Walter McClintock, a Yale graduate who had lived among the Blackfeet in the late 1890's. In his authoritative book entitled "The Old North Trail," published in June, 1910, McClintock urged that "the region should be preserved by the Government as a national park and game preserve."[18] However, by the time his book was off the press, his recommendation had already been accomplished.[19]

The Region Becomes Better Known

In the meantime, during the final decades of the nineteenth century, the area of the future park had been receiving increased attention on a national level. The Pumpelly expedition of 1882-83 had been staffed by several highly connected scientists from the eastern part of the country, including Professors Sargent and Canby of Harvard University, the former subsequently to become the first chairman of the United States Forest Commission.[20] It also included two young newspaper men, one of whom was W. A. Stiles, later a well known writer. All were instrumental in disseminating authentic information about the fascinating Montana mountains through which they had marched.

The region had also been attracting attention in other ways, It had been the subject of congressional enactments, including the 1891 forest reserve act, and the 1896 act authorizing purchase from the Blackfeet Indians of that part of their reservation lying between the continental divide and the plains on the eastern side of what is now the Park. It had been arousing increasing interest among hunters and trappers, as well as prospectors in search of minerals and oil. It had received a substantial influx of permanent settlers and summer visitors to the Lake McDonald area following arrival of the railroad at what is now West Glacier (Belton) late in 1891.

Early Legislative Activity

It was really the national conservation movement, as it gathered momentum in the latter part of the nineteenth century, that led indirectly to the establishment of Glacier National Park. A few of its far-sighted leaders, aware of how the forests were being stripped from one region after another and wondering what would happen when all of these areas were denuded, began to publicize the situation. The ultimate result was a demand for withdrawal of certain forested areas from un-regulated public entry and wholesale cutting of timber.

The first legislative effort toward conservation of lands included in the present park occurred in 1885 when a bill was introduced in the United States Senate "To establish a Forest Reservation on the Headwaters of the Missouri River and Headwaters of the Clark's Fork of the Columbia River." Although not enacted, the measure evidently acted as a forerunner of the 1891 act authorizing the president to set aside forest reserves in the forested lands of the nation, to be administered by the Department of the Interior. Under the provisions of this Act, a part of northwestern Montana which included the present park was designated as a forest reserve.[21]

It was not until 1897, however, that activity with respect to the area became more specific. On February 22nd of that year, largely through the initiative of the United States Forest Commission, of which Charles S. Sargent was chairman, the Lewis and Clark Forest Reserve was formed. This reserve included all of what is now Glacier National Park, together with the Kootenai, Blackfeet, Flathead and Lewis and Clark National Forests, that portion which lay north of the Great Northern right-of-way being called the North Division and that south of the rail line the South Division.[22] Administration of the Forest Reserves continued under the Department of the Interior until 1905 when the Forest Service was set up under the Department of Agriculture, and they were transferred thereto.[23]

The Plot Thickens

In retrospect, of course, it is possible to perceive that the interests of most of the early invaders of the region, being selfish in character, were not calculated to enhance its standing as a candidate for national park status. But none of these activities seemed to pose any special threat to the natural attractiveness of the region, or to arouse local or national concern as to its future, until representatives of the lumbering industry appeared after the turn of the century and began casting covetous eyes at the virgin timber on the west side of the divide—timber that, by contract with officials of the Forest Reserve, could be easily and inexpensively logged off.

In the summer of 1906 the report became current in the town of Browning that steps were being taken by prominent Montanans to urge the government to convert into a national park that part of the Lewis and Clark Forest Reserve extending from the main line of the Great Northern Railway to the international boundary; and this rumor was reported in the Kalispell Inter Lake of September 7, 1906.[24] This evidently spurred some of the lumbermen of the Flathead into activity, and before many months had passed it was noised about that lumber interests were moving to purchase the timber along the shores of Lake McDonald. Citizens of the Flathead area, on learning of this movement, became highly concerned and formed a strong opposition to it under the leadership of W. C. Whipps, former mayor of Kalispell.[25]

It was on April 18, 1907 that Whipps learned of the timber-buying plan, and he immediately prepared extensive letters to President Roosevelt, and to Montana senators Thomas H. Carter and Joseph M. Dixon, emphasizing the devastation which would befall the Lake McDonald area with the despoliation of its timber and urging prompt steps to prevent the "irretrievable ruin of this magnificent region . . . with the view and ultimate object of having the whole region made into a national park, after proper investigation by the government." In the letter to the president, a suspension of timber sales was requested, pending investigation of the situation. The letters were co-signed by other prominent Kalispell citizens and mailed on April 19, 1907. Within a few days, telegraphic instructions were received by the Supervisor of the Forest Reserve to make no contracts for the sale of timber at Lake McDonald until further notice.[26]

The Scene Shifts To Washington

Within a few months after this flurry of activity at Kalispell, congressional wheels began to turn on the project of a national park. A bill to set the area aside for park purposes was introduced into the Senate on December

11, 1907 by United States Senator Thomas H. Carter, a prominent member of Congress and well-known throughout the country.[27] Presumably this action was in response to the pressures generated by Whipps and his associates; however, a vigorous part in the movement was undoubtedly played by George Bird Grinnell, who has written:

"After the mines were all abandoned, I took my old project up with Senator Carter of Montana and with Congressman Pray, and also brought the matter to the attention of Mr. L. W. Hill of the Great Northern Railroad. These men were active and interested . . . "[28]

Grinnell was a member of the small inner circle of conservationists which President Theodore Roosevelt had gathered about him,[29] and deserves the title sometimes given him of "father of the Park,"[30] since he may have been more responsible, directly and indirectly, than any other man, for its creation. The Great Northern Railway was unquestionably a positive force. Its hustling officials, led by their new president, Louis W. Hill, perceived that the creation of a public recreational area in northwestern Montana would attract tourists and provide a lucrative source of passenger and freight traffic. Consequently they took an active part in the fight to establish the proposed park.[31]

Strategy Of Proponents

Opposition to the measure was largely based upon its projected removal of the area's economic resources from reach by the people, i.e., the closure of its valleys and lakes to unrestricted private ownership and utilization, and the end of possible exploitation of its timber and mineral resources.[32] These objections were beamed at a Congress which, like its predecessors, was willing to preserve scenery only if it was clearly without commercial value.[33] Because of this traditional attitude, it was necessary for the sponsors of Glacier to show that the region would be virtually useless to the economic interests of the country and, in effect, to urge its preservation for what it was not, as well as for what it was.[34]

In the course of rather strenuous debate before the Senate, Senator Penrose of Pennsylvania, who had hunted throughout the future park region, asserted that it was without mineral resources and "absolutely unfit for cultivation or habitation."[35] On this basis, and

because he believed it to be "one of the grandest scenic sections in the United States," he opined that it was "admirably suited for a park."[36] Senator Dixon of Montana described the area as "fourteen hundred square miles of mountains piled on top of each other" and containing "no agricultural land whatever."[37]

Congressional Action

Because of various objections to the Carter bill, it had to be rewritten and, in its revised form, it was re-introduced on February 24, 1908. After an early hearing by the Committee on Public Lands, it was approved with minor amendments, and was passed by the Senate. On May 16, 1908, it was sent to the House of Representatives and referred to its Committee on Public Lands. There it received favorable consideration through the skillful guidance of Congressman Charles N. Pray, Montana's only member of the House, who happened also to be a member of the committee. However, the House itself failed to act on the measure with the result that it was dead for that session of Congress.[38]

On June 26, 1909, Senator Carter introduced the bill for the third time. For undisclosed reasons, it lay in the Public Lands Committee until January 25, 1910, when it was reported out and approved by the Senate on February 9th. Shortly thereafter, the measure was agreed to by the House, although with minor amendments which required Senate concurrence. After differences were ironed out by a conference committee, the resulting compromise was approved by both House and Senate on the same day. President Taft affixed his signature on May 11, 1910,[39] and thus Glacier National Park was born.[40]

The measure signed into law in 1910 was a substantially different bill from that introduced by Senator Carter in 1907. It had been necessary, in order to obviate various objections to its enactment, to accept amendments which would permit those owning property in the prospective park to retain it with rights of "full use and enjoyment." In addition to this protection for property owners, the bill, as amended, provided that railroad rights of way through the valleys of the north and middle forks of the Flathead River might be acquired, and reserved to the government the right "to utilize for flowage or other purposes any area within the park which may be necessary for development and maintenance of a government reclamation project."[41]

Lake Josephine and Mt. Gould near Many Glacier Hotel
Photo by Bob & Ira Spring

Glacier Lily
Photo by Danny On

Concurrent Publicity

Strangely enough, the indecision of Congress in arriving at final action on Senator Carter's bill was not reflected by the periodicals of the day. World's Work Magazine for May, 1908, the same month in which Carter's revised bill became dormant in the House, carried an article entitled "Glacier National Park: Crown Of The Continent."[42] In June, 1909, at a time when the second bill was still moribund in the House, the Overland Monthly printed an article entitled "Glacier Park."[43] Even as late as March, 1910, while a successor measure was still under consideration by Congress, the National Geographic Magazine was telling its readers about Glacier under the title "A New National Park."[44]

The name "Glacier National Park" first appeared in Senator Carter's bill. There is no definite evidence that the name was conceived by him, but this is believed to have been the case; and it was quickly borrowed by Alfred W. Greeley for use in his 1908 World's Work article referred to above. The name reflected the tremendous interest in the region's glaciers evinced by such prominent early explorers as Pumpelly, Grinnell and Sperry.[45]

A legislative postscript remained to be added in order to make establishment of the Park complete. The Montana legislature on February 11, 1911 enacted a statute ceding to the federal government all jurisdiction over the region, saving only the right of taxation and the right to serve criminal process within the ceded area for acts committed outside of it.[46] With characteristic delay, however, it was not until August 22, 1914 that Congress finally got around to giving approval to an Act by which it accepted exclusive jurisdiction of the Park on the terms specified by the Montana legislature.[47]

Notes For Chapter 12

[1] Catlin was born in 1796 and died in 1872.
[2] This is an excerpt from pages 295-296 of Volume 1 of Catlin's book entitled "North American Indians." Published in 1926 by John Grant of Edinburgh, Scotland, it was undoubtedly a reprint of the original work issued *circa* 1840. Lavishly illustrated, it described Catlin's travels among the tribes of North America during the years 1832-1839. The italics shown in the excerpt were those of Catlin, who noted that his idea could only be implemented "by some great protecting policy of government."
[3] The proponents of Yellowstone had something of a precedent for its creation in the fact that the Yosemite Valley had been set aside by Congress in 1864 as an area to be preserved under the protection of the state of California; however, it did not become a part of the national park system until 1891.
[4] The Act of Congress of March 1, 1872 also provided for "the preservation, from injury or despoliation, of all timber,

mineral deposits, natural curiosities or wonders . . . and their retention in their natural condition." Chapter 24, Statutes of 1872.
[5] See description of the Woodruff-Van Orsdale reconnaissance at page 92 of Chapter 11, supra, entitled "Advent Of The White Man."
[6] Letter of L. O. Vaught to M. E. Beatty, Chief Park Naturalist, Belton, Montana, dated February 24, 1948, now preserved in the records of the Park Headquarters at West Glacier, Montana.
[7] Idem.
[8] Idem.
[9] Notes by Grinnell preserved in the records at Park Headquarters at West Glacier indicate that his notation was made on September 17, 1891.
[10] In a section of his book "Blackfeet And Buffalo" entitled "Conception Of Glacier National Park (1885)," at page 123 (reprint of an article appearing in the Great Falls Tribune on November, 1936), Schultz wrote: "George Bird Grinnell, in his influential weekly journal, 'Forest And Stream,' had ever strongly advocated the preservation of Yellowstone National Park as originally defined . . . On his first trip with me into the St. Mary Lakes country in 1885, he had remarked how fine it would be if that part of the Rockies could also some day be set aside as a national park . . . He wrote for Century Magazine an article describing its mountains, glaciers, and its . . . game animals . . . Also he interested his close friend, Theodore Roosevelt, in the proposal and sent his Chicago representative, Emerson Hough, out to see that section of the Rockies and write about it for "Forest And Stream."
[11] Article entitled "The Crown Of The Continent," published in Century Magazine for September, 1901, at pages 660-672.
[12] The article was prepared in 1891 or 1892, at which time it was forwarded to Century Magazine, but remained unpublished for nearly a decade. Concerning its belated appearance, Grinnell later wrote (according to notes by him which are now in Park records at West Glacier) ". . . they wanted it to grow, I suppose, and so held it for nine years."
[13] Grinnell prepared a total of 15 such "letters," which he published under the pseudonym of "Yo." Two of them were reprinted at pages 29-33 of the 1948 edition of the "Drivers' Manual" (see note 15, Chapter 6, supra).
[14] "Blackfeet And Buffalo," supra, at pages 76 and 83.
[15] Idem, at pages 123, 126 and 127. The fact of actual advocacy of national park status by Hough in his articles, as asserted by Schultz, cannot be verified owing to current unavailability of copies of "Forest And Stream" for the period in question.
[16] See letter of L. O. Vaught, described in note 6, supra.
[17] See page 27 of the 1948 edition of the "Drivers' Manual" (see note 15, Chapter 6, supra)
[18] Originally published in June, 1910, and republished by the University of Nebraska Press in 1968. The quotation is from page 15.
[19] The Park was established as such on May 11, 1910, a month prior to publication of McClintock's book.
[20] Letter of L. O. Vaught, described in note 6 supra.
[21] "Through The Years In Glacier National Park," by Donald H. Robinson, at pages 50-51.
[22] Idem, at page 51.
[23] Idem, at page 52. In 1910, with establishment of the Park, control of the area was returned by the Forest Service to the Department of the Interior. Since that time it has been in the hands of the latter, acting through the National Park Service since the latter's inception in 1916.
[24] See letter of L. O. Vaught, described in note 6, supra.
[25] Idem.
[26] Idem.
[27] "Through The Years," supra, at pages 53-54.
[28] Notes by Grinnell now preserved in records at Park headquarters at West Glacier, Montana.
[29] Letter of L. O. Vaught, described in note 6, supra.
[30] "Through The Years," supra, at pages 15 and 53. According to the "introduction" by Dee Brown to "Pawnee,

Blackfoot and Cheyenne," describing the presentation by President Coolidge in 1925 of the Theodore Roosevelt medal for promotion of outdoor life to Grinnell, the president said, *inter alia:* "The Glacier National Park is peculiarly your monument." Final sentence of this "Introduction," in reference to Grinnell's famous article, "The Crown Of The Continent," says that he had written it as "a sort of keynote for his long campaign to create Glacier National Park."

[31]Letter of L. O. Vaught, described in note 6, supra.
[32]See article entitled "'Worthless' Lands—Our National Parks," by Alfred Runte, appearing at pages 5-11 of "The American West" for May. 1973 (Volume X, No. 3).
[33]Idem.
[34]Idem, at page 8.
[35]Idem, at page 8.
[36]Idem, at page 8.
[37]Idem, at page 8.
[38]"Through The Years," supra, at page 54.
[39]Chapter 226, U.S. Statutes, 61st Congress.
[40]Following approval of the bill establishing the Park on May 11, 1910. Congress appropriated the munificent sum of $15,000 "for construction of trails and roads." This was a part of Chapter 384, Statutes of the 61st Congress, which was the "Sundry Civil Appropriations Act" for the fiscal year 1910-1911, approved on June 25, 1910.
[41]Chapter 226, U.S. Statutes, 61st Congress.
[42]By Alfred W. Greeley.
[43]By H. F. Sanders.
[44]By Guy Elliott Mitchell, of the United States Geological Survey
[45]Letter of L. O. Vaught, described in note 6, supra.
[46]"Through The Years," supra, at page 55.
[47]Chapter 264, U.S. Statutes, 63rd Congress.

Spectacular waterfall in northern section of the park
Courtesy Burlington Northern

Boat landing at Two Medicine Lake, Mt. Sinopah in left foreground
Photo by Walt Dyke, courtesy of Burlington Northern

Avalanche Lake

Photo by Lacy

Chapter 13
GODFATHER TO GLACIER

The man who did more than any other to put Glacier Park on the map, to enhance its scenic and recreational appeal, and to make its name a byword with the traveling public was Louis Warren Hill.[1] In depth of devotion to the region and multiplicity of contributions to its development, he had no peer. Yet by all but the Park's history buffs, the record of his amazing accomplishments has been long forgotten, nor is any adequate account of them currently available. Even more incredible is the fact that in all of Glacier's more than 1500 square miles there is no peak, pass, lake, valley or road honoring the name of this remarkable Park pioneer.

Other leading parks have had their outstanding sponsors and benefactors: Nathaniel P. Langford, often called the father of Yellowstone, John Muir for Yosemite, George W. Stewart for Sequoia, Will G. Steel for Crater Lake, and Enos Mills for Rocky Mountain.[2] All were endowed with a superabundance of dedication, determination and imagination, as was Louis Hill. But in his relationship with Glacier, Hill's contributions were unquestionably greater because he was able to command the financial means of converting his dreams into reality. With the power of a great transportation system at his disposal, it was unnecessary for him merely to propose and propagandize. He could and did take steps to initiate many Park projects that would have been delayed for years, if left to governmental inertia. Indeed, one estimate covering the first five years of the Park's existence as such was that Hill had put in nearly ten dollars for every one spent there by the government.[3]

Helping To Get The Park Created

Hill was a son of the famed "Empire Builder," James J. Hill, and succeeded him in the presidency of the Great Northern Railway in 1907, just at the time when a movement to create a national park in northwestern Montana was getting under way. In a matter of months he had put all of the forces of his company into the fight to persuade Congress to

act.[4] His motivation was not entirely altruistic, of course, for passenger traffic was then a major contributor to railroad revenues throughout the country; and the development of an outstanding scenic attraction along the very border of a transcontinental railroad gave promise of a substantial boost to both its freight and passenger traffic.

On this subject, Hill himself had stated frankly, in a speech to the first national parks conference, held in Yellowstone in 1911: "The railroads are greatly interested in the passenger traffic to the parks. Every passenger that goes to the national parks, wherever he may be, represents practically a net earning."[5] This was said, of course, in the full realization that with a new wilderness park, its potential for augmentation of company profits would be virtually nil until such time as attractive and convenient travel facilities within its environs had been created.[6]

Hill Waves A Magic Wand

When Glacier was established in 1910, such facilities were out of the question so far as federal funds were concerned, nor was private capital interested in this kind of pioneer work. But Hill, undaunted by this impasse, acted realistically and promptly to bring his own company into the picture through the medium of a subsidiary organized for that purpose, the Glacier Park Hotel Company.[7] Under Hill's personal direction, bold and imaginative plans were drawn for a chain of "forest" lodges and chalets at strategic points throughout the new park. As a result, the great Glacier Park Hotel was completed in time for the opening of the summer season of 1913,[8] and the Many Glacier for the summer of 1915.[9] Ultimately, also, it was Hill's intense personal interest in the construction of a quality hotel at the neighboring Waterton Lakes National Park in Canada, that made the attractive Prince of Wales hostelry a reality in 1927.[10]

Equally critical to any solution of the travel problem was the need for usable roads in what was then a roadless area. When government agencies failed to meet this need, it was Hill who again stepped into the breach. Using Great Northern funds, under an arrangement with the Department of the Interior for eventual reimbursement, the original road along the eastern border of the Park was built,[11] leading from what is now East Glacier to Swiftcurrent Lake, site of the future Many Glacier Hotel, together with stub roads into the Cut Bank and Two Medicine Valleys.[12]

Hill was likewise a prime mover in getting action on some of the Park's early scenic trail facilities. It was at his bidding, again with Great Northern money, that the trail from the Glacier Park Hotel over Mt. Henry to the Two Medicine Valley was constructed in 1913.[13] His father in 1902, years before creation of the Park, had sponsored construction of a trail from Lake McDonald to Sperry Glacier and Gunsight Pass, making Great Northern funds and materials available to Lyman B. Sperry for that purpose.[14] But it was Louis, many years later, who recognized the possibilities of a route over Red Gap Pass to the Belly River country, and persuaded the National Park Service to construct a trail over it in the early 1920's.[15]

Public Relations Genius

Among the greatest of Hill's accomplishments on behalf of Glacier was the phenomenal publicity which he gave it. It was he who coined the slogan "See America First," so effectively used in promoting passenger travel to Glacier Park. And it was he who conceived the idea of using the Rocky Mountain goat, symbol of the Park, as a part of the famous Great Northern trademark, seen for decades on the company's rolling stock, timetables and advertising brochures. The authenticity of this origin of the slogan was vouched for by Freeman H. Hubbard, editor of Railroad Magazine, who went to some trouble to run down and verify it. As Hubbard observed,

"Few symbols in America are better known than the Great Northern goat. It is generally regarded as a million-dollar idea."[16]

It was also Hill who instituted an advertising campaign featuring the Park's attractions that had few equals in its time. Of this extraordinary publicity drive, a contemporary wrote:

"As a drummer up of trade for Uncle Sam's newest sideshow he was about to make all previous performers on the tautened cowhide sound like guitar thrummers at a sociable for the deaf."[17]

The then incipient motion picture industry was effectively utilized to film the Park's sensational scenery for showing in movie theatre weekly news reels. The Blackfeet Indians were brought into the act to provide colorful backgrounds for these pictures as well as for the edification and entertainment of Park visitors.

Blackfeet chiefs were taken east to Chicago and New York where they proved to be sensational newsmakers. They were taken to the travel show in New York and pitched their tepees on the roof of the McAlpine Hotel. They went to the Land Show in Chicago and stopped the traffic in the streets. They went to the Rose Carnival in Portland, to the Mardi Gras in New Orleans, and to the convention of the Mystic Shrine in Atlanta. Often Hill himself would be on hand to sponsor and protect them. They were photographed visiting the automobile factories, prancing into the Library of Congress, and discussing policies with the president on the steps of the White House. They were even photographed shaking hands with the popular Metropolitan Opera diva, Mary Garden, on her arrival at the Union Depot in Chicago.[18]

Other Promotional Projects

Valuable publicity was gained through bringing well-known organizations to the Park. Invitations were extended to many geographical and mountaineering societies. The members of the Chicago Geographical Society went home and produced an illustrated book. Special safaris were arranged for the Mazama Club of Oregon, the Mountaineers of Washington, and the Sierra Club of California.[19]

Travelogue lecturers visited the Park in order to get the material needed to present their illustrated versions of its attractions. Hill established a lecture bureau of his own, and countless high schools, lodges, Y.M.C.A.s, clubs and commercial organizations heard the Park story and saw the accompanying pictures of its incomparable scenery.[20] Shots of its outstanding peaks, glaciers and lakes were made by an official photographer for wide distribution throughout America,[21] the work being facilitated by a special Great Northern press car equipped with a photographic dark room.

Last Of The Glidden Tours

One of the most spectacular of Hill's ideas for publicizing the Park was that of having it serve as the terminal point for a nationally

Louis W. Hill and party among the peaks in
Glacier Park

Courtesy Burlington Northern

known automobile endurance contest. This was the popular Glidden Tour[22] which had been induced, with strong Hill support, to stage its 1913 competition over a rugged route roughly paralleling the Great Northern right of way between Minneapolis and Glacier.[23]

Hill's enthusiasm did not stop with this, however. He undertook, utilizing Great Northern facilities, to provide food, lodging, repairs and general hospitality along the entire route by running a special "hotel" train. Besides six sleepers, two diners and an observation car, the traveling accommodations included a garage car with equipment for repairing automobiles, and a press car fitted out with a linotype machine, a photoengraving plant, and mailing facilities.

Registered as the first entry and leading off at the starting line was a Packard driven by Hill who covered a part of the first day's run, then quietly returned to St. Paul. On the eighth day of the race, however, as the travelers pulled into Poplar, Montana, they were met by a band of mounted and costumed Blackfeet braves led by none other than their host, Louis Hill. He had bypassed the cavalcade by train and was now prepared to rejoin them for the final days of the trek.

The contest was a great success from every standpoint. Numerous trophies were awarded, and the coveted Glidden cup went to a team of three Model 22 Metz roadsters which had finished with perfect scores. Last and most colorful of all the Glidden tours, it had served to draw the nation's attention to the northern route across the Great Plains and to the as yet little-known beauties of Glacier Park.[24]

Celebrating An Important Birthday

Undoubtedly the greatest of all the publicity stunts concocted by Louis was that staged in June, 1913, to mark the 75th birthday of his famous father, James J. Hill. Plans were made to invite all of the latter's old friends to the party, including every Great Northern engineer, conductor, brakeman and station agent who had served the company for 25 years or more. The problem was to find a dining hall where 600 guests could be comfortably seated for the banquet. As the story was told by Rufus Steel in the March, 1915 issue of Sunset Magazine:

"It was left to Louis. With each engraved invitation that went out, he enclosed a suggestion that the guest bring along an extra shirt. The party was put on a special train. The collation that celebrated James J. Hill's

seventy-fifth anniversary was served in the 'forest' lobby of the Glacier Park Hotel. After the walnuts and the oratory, each guest took his choice of auto, saddle-horse or climbing staff and went for a little exercise in the interests of digestion. Whenever two or three old railroaders are gathered in the state of Minnesota, you will hear them talking about that birthday party yet."[25]

Background And Sidelights

Louis Hill was a man of many talents and interests. Educated at Exeter and Yale, he entered the railroad business in 1893, starting at the bottom of the ladder. After five years of diversified training in some eighteen different jobs, including everything from section hand and shop mechanic to general office clerk, Louis became an assistant to his father, the president of the company. Only nine years later, at age 35, he took over the presidency itself, and in 1912, at the tender age of 40, he became chairman of the board.

Second of three sons, Louis was the only one to achieve outstanding success in the family business. There was always a close relationship between himself and his dynamic father, and the resemblances were rather considerable. He had the same stocky build and red beard, the same enthusiasms, the same vehement loquacity in talking about them, the same instinct for friendship with the common man, and the same talent for anecdote and homely phrase.

Hill was also a man of hobbies and non-business activities.[26] Of these, his family was the most important, but he enjoyed hunting and fishing, as well as his paintbrushes and canvas.[27] He had a great love for the West and concern for its people. During his frequent business trips, he explored it on horseback, by wagon and by automobile, studying the land, talking and listening to the people. It was said that he knew more people of more different kinds west of the Mississippi than any other man.[28]

Few men knew the Indians of northwestern Montana as Hill knew them; they in turn knew him only as "Gray Horse" and loved him. He knew the country through which the Great Northern tracks were laid; had studied its history, its flora and fauna, and especially the Indian lore. In so doing, he became profoundly impressed with the belief that it was here, on the Montana side of the line, rather than in the Canadian Rockies, that Nature had reached her scenic climax.[29]

Accordingly, his interest in the Park was not confined to its business potentialities; and he became accustomed to spending a part of each summer there. Arriving with his family and himself would be a retinue of servants, an automobile or two, and a string of saddlehorses. They usually arrived at Many Glacier in August;[30] and often there would be a packtrip with his sons into the backcountry of the Park's northwestern wilderness area.

Dealings With Park Service Personnel

The anecdotes about Louis Hill and Glacier National Park were many. Some of these had to do with his relationship to the National Park Service and the officials of that agency having supervision over Glacier. In its earlier years, Hill felt that the many things that he had been doing to advance the development of the area had not been adequately appreciated by the government people. Consequently, when Mark Daniels was made general superintendent and lanscape engineer for all of the national parks, Hill promptly invited him on an impressive party which left St. Paul by private railroad car, accompanied by another car carrying an automobile and some fine saddle horses.[31]

Starting north by car from the Glacier Park Hotel along the Lewis Range, Hill pointed to rocky Mt. Henry, remarking to Daniels "That's the baldest mountain top I've ever seen. Why do you suppose nothing grows up there?" Daniels shrugging his shoulders, consulted his notebook to check the Glacier appropriation, which was $30,000. "Tell you what I'll do," he said. "I'll use $5,000 of this to have trees planted up there. Maybe we can find out what's the matter."[32]

Instead of pleasing Hill, as Daniels had intended, this threw him into a towering rage and he abruptly called off the trip. On returning to St. Paul, he lodged a bitter complaint with Daniels' boss, Franklin K. Lane, then Secretary of the Interior, on the ground that anyone willing to use one-sixth of Glacier's entire wretchedly inadequate appropriation to plant trees on bald Mt. Henry would probably end up by wrecking the national park system. Lane took no action since he knew that Daniels had accomplished some valuable, even brilliant things for the parks.[33]

The Saw Mill At Many Glacier

There were other instances where Hill, in spite of his benevolent concern for the Park, did not see eye to eye with its authorities. Following construction of the Many Glacier Hotel, the saw mill used to process most of its

lumber had been left standing along the shore of Swiftcurrent Lake, half a mile south of the hotel. National Park Service Director Stephen Mather let Hill know that he felt that the mill had served its purpose and that the time had come for it to be removed, along with the masses of sawdust surrounding it. When nothing had been done by 1925, Mather reminded Howard Noble, the Great Northern's Park manager, that action should be taken. Noble said he needed a little more lumber, and Mather agreed to his request, but reluctantly, and with pointed warning that one short stay of execution was all that the mill could have.

Mather happened to be in the Park on August 10, 1925, the 19th birthday of his daughter, and it came to his attention that Noble was still seeking delay in removal of the mill. Deciding on immediate action, Mather arranged for trail crews to be transported from St. Mary to Many Glacier and given certain orders. Then he invited the hotel guests to step outside for a demonstration, and personally lighted the fuse of the first of 13 charges of dynamite. With each detonation, his mood seemed to lighten, and when people finally inquired into his motives, he replied: "Celebrating my daughter's birthday."

When the news of this outrage to the corporate property reached Mr. Hill, he was reportedly purple with indignation and ready to take legal steps against Mather. Before the situation could reach a critical stage, however, mutual friends intervened and the impasse was broken.[34] The Great Northern finished the job of removing the mill and surrounding debris,[35] and the incident passed quietly into anecdotage. While Hill and Mather continued to have great respect for each other, subsequent relations between them were said to have been something less than cordial.[36]

Personal Recollections

Hill was exceedingly good-hearted, as well as human and democratic. In the summer of 1918, when he discovered that my post at the Many Glacier transportation desk was not equipped with a geological survey map of the region, he promptly turned over his own copy to me that I might have a better understanding of Park trails and topography.

That same summer a pack trip into the Belly River region had been planned for the Hill family, but had to be cancelled at the last minute because of the illness of one of his boys. This made it necessary for a rancher's wife, who had come from south of the Park to do the cooking on the trip, to return home from Many Glacier where the trip was to have begun. She learned that Hill had ordered his groom to take the saddle horses back to East Glacier, and asked permission to ride back on one of them. Hill asked her which horse she would like to ride, and she expressed a preference for the blue mare, finest of the lot.

"If you like the blue mare," said Hill simply, "I'll make you a present of her."

The good woman was visibly overcome for a moment and, with tears in her eyes, protested that he was much too generous. He overruled her with a princely wave of the hand, explaining:

"When anyone does something for Louie, she gets something of Louie's."

And so the bewildered, but delighted, woman rode home on her own blue mare.[37]

Notes For Chapter 13

[1] Early and justly deserved tribute was paid to Hill's accomplishments by none other than James Willard Schultz who, under date of September 10, 1915, dedicated his book entitled "Blackfeet Tales of Glacier National Park" as follows:

To LOUIS WARREN HILL, Esq.,

True friend of my Blackfeet people and the one who has done more than any other individual, or any organization, to make the wonders of Glacier National Park accessible to the American people.

[2] "Steve Mather Of The National Parks," by Robert Shankland, published by Alfred A. Knopf in 1951, at page 79.

[3] "Louis W. Hill," an article by French Strother in the magazine "World's Work" for September, 1916, at page 552.

[4] "Through The Years In Glacier National Park," by Donald H. Robinson, at page 55, stated: "The truth of the matter was that the late Louis W. Hill, then president of the Great Northern, was foremost among the sponsors of the bill (to create Glacier National Park), hoping with Senator Carter, Congressman Pray, George Bird Grinnell and others to create a public recreational area for Montana which could attract tourists and subsequently be a source of passenger traffic and new income dollars for the state."

[5] "Steve Mather Of The National Parks," supra, at page 145.

[6] During the years 1911 and 1912, prior to completion of travel facilities on the eastern side of the Park, the numbers of visitors, according to "Through The Years," supra, at page 127, were only 4,000 and 6,257 respectively; and practically all of these were in the Lake McDonald area, where there had been a small hotel, plus cottages and limited transportation facilities for many years.

[7] An article by H. R. Wiecking, entitled "The Glacier Park Hotels, Chalets and Cabin Camps," appearing in the 1948 edition of the "Drivers' Manual," at pages 57-58, states: "Mr. Hill, a leader in all matters relating to the Park, was enthusiastic over its possibilities as an outstanding scenic recreational area on the railway's main line. He devoted much time to the planning, building and furnishing of the hotels and chalets and to the construction or roads and trails opening the area to visitors. The Department of the Interior which supervised the national parks (this was before the creation of the National Park Service) could not be expected to supply the initiative, energy and capital needed for quick development of visitor comforts in this great and attractive wilderness. Mr. Hill did all that needed doing. His enthusiasm was contagious and there was

hardly a department of his large railway organization that was not called upon to make a contribution to the work in hand."

[8] "Through The Years," supra, at page 64.

[9] Idem, at page 66.

[10] Idem, at pages 66-67. For a particularly good account of Hill's role in the construction of the "Prince," see "Adventure Among The Glaciers," by Edmund Christopherson, at pages 50-53.

[11] According to Louis W. Hill, Jr., the entire job of laying out the original road to Lake St. Mary, including the stub roads to Two Medicine Lake and the Cutbank Valley, some 50 miles in all, was done by an old timber cruiser named Hildegoss in a period of not more than three days.

[12] "Through The Years," supra, at pages 87-88. In her delightful book entitled "High Trails Of Glacier National Park," published in 1938 by the Caxton Printers, Ltd., Margaret Thompson says at page 34:

"The building program assumed generous proportions largely because Louis W. Hill was, and still is today, one of Glacierland's most enthusiastic lovers. His deep attachment to the region caused to be appropriated funds in unstinted amount to make it available to others—even to the extent of building the first road from Glacier Park station to St. Mary Lake. To Mr. Hill, more than to any other one person, Glacier Park owed all its development during the early years of its existence. He it was who decreed that the Swiss chalet should furnish the inspiration for all all architectural designs. And it was he who invited the Brewster family, who had been so successful in fostering saddlehorse travel in the Canadian Rockies, to come to Glacier and perform the same service for travelers in the American Rockies."

[13] "Through The Years," supra, at page 95.

[14] Idem, at pages 24-25.

[15] "Elrod's Guide and Book of Information," by Morton J. Elrod, at pages 156-157 of the 1924 edition.

[16] "James J. Hill" by Stewart H. Holbrook, published in 1955 by Alfred A. Knopf, at pages 191-192.

[17] "The Man Who Showed His Father," by Rufus Steele, in Sunset Magazine for March, 1915, at page 482.

[18] Idem, at pages 483-484.

[19] Idem, at page 484.

[20] Idem, at page 484.

[21] Kiser Photo Company did most of the photography for the Great Northern Railway, although T. J. Hileman, of Kalispell, also turned out a great many fine pictures of the Park in its early years.

[22] These yearly events began in 1905 when Charles J. Glidden, a retired New England Telephone magnate and an automobile enthusiast, established a trophy to be awarded the winner of an annual long-distance reliability run, open only to stock cars, and conducted by the American Automobile Association. However, the tour scheduled to run from Detroit to New Orleans in 1912 had failed to materialize, and the 1913 tour was put over by the Minnesota automobile clubs mainly with the enthusiastic support of Louis W. Hill.

[23] The 9-day 1245-mile course through the Red River valley and over the plains of North Dakota and Montana was rugged and provided plenty of challenges, especially during the heavy rains of the first two days. After these first miserable days, however, the affair became a gay social event rather than a grueling test of men and machines.

[24] For information about "The Last Of The Glidden Tours," we are indebted to Louis W. Hill, Jr., who furnished us with a copy of an article by that name written by Dr. Alvin W. Waters and published in the March, 1963 issue of "Minnesota History," magazine of the Minnesota Historical Society.

[25] "The Man Who Showed His Father," supra, at page 484. What the author did not explain was why the party was held on June 15, 1913 when the father's 75th birthday actually fell on September 16, 1913.

[26] "Louis W. Hill," supra, at page 551.

[27] A number of Mr. Hill's fine canvasses adorn the walls of the offices of the Northwest Area Foundation (formerly the

Louis W. and Maud Hill Family Foundation) in St. Paul, Minnesota.

[28]See page 10 of the report of the Louis W. and Maud Hill Family Foundation (now the Northwest Area Foundation) for the fiscal year March 1, 1972 to March 1, 1973.

[29]"The Man Who Showed His Father," supra, at page 478.

[30]Mr. Hill had a small chalet or cottage built on the south shore of Upper Lake St. Mary, opposite Going-To-The Sun Chalets, but Louis W. Hill, Jr. states that it was never completed or occupied by the family. It was razed about 1940.

[31]"Steve Mather Of The National Parks," supra, at pages 64-65.

[32]Idem.

[33]Idem.

[34]Letter from Horace M. Albright dated 1/30/75. See, also, "Steve Mather Of The National Parks," supra, at pages 209-210.

[35]There are differing stories about the old mill. In his book "Montana Memories IV," at pages 47-48, Charles K. Green, of Coram, Montana, tells of how, when he was superintendent of a Civilian Conservation Corps camp at Many Glacier in the summer of 1939, he was given the assignment of removing all evidence of the old sawmill. He found its machinery in the lake nearby, but in a condition "just like new," having been coated with black grease before being submerged. He had it pulled out of the lake with tractors and taken to their "tool cache" on Sherburne Lake, from which point it was stolen sometime during the ensuing year. A few years later, during World War II, Green saw it piled in the yard of a machinery company in Kalispell, with a "for sale" sign attached. He is convinced, accordingly, that the reported dynamiting never took place.

Still another version of the end of the old mill has been supplied by Ray Kinley, a Many Glacier Hotel employee since the early 1920's. In a letter dated June 24, 1973, Ray recalls that he was in a boat with a fishing party at a point in Swiftcurrent Lake just west of the sawmill, when he was attracted by shouting on the shore and noticed rangers waving red flags to warn approaching hikers. Next there was an explosion (his recollection is that there was only one) and a black object rose in the air. Soon after this, the Great Northern hired a man (a fireman in the hotel boiler room) to tear down whatever remained of the old mill. He had partially completed the job when a fire broke out that consumed everything else. Despite the suspicion of arson, the fireman succeeded in collecting his full contract price from the company. Ray concludes his letter by saying: "Getting all that machinery out of the lake sounds fishy to me."

[36]According to a letter from Horace M. Albright dated 1/30/75, when legal action was threatened by Hill, Mather retained the services of former Secretary of the Interior Fisher (in Taft's cabinet) to defend him. On hearing of this development, Albright journeyed to St. Paul and, with the assistance of Ralph Budd, then president of the Great Northern, was able to get matters smoother over.

[37]From Louis W. Hill, Jr., it has been learned that the name of the blue mare was "Kentucky," that the name of her new owner was Mrs. Jennings, and that the former outlived the latter.

Louis W. Hill with Blackfeet chieftains
Photo courtesy Burlington Northern

James J. Hill, The "Empire Builder," and his son, Louis W. Hill, taken about 1913
Photo courtesy Burlington Northern

Louis W. Hill near Glacier Park Lodge

Chapter 14
TRAILS AND EARLY ROUTES

Glacier National Park has at various times been called the "saddle-horse park," the "pack-trail park," and the "hikers' paradise," all serving to emphasize that Glacier is the trail park supreme. Other national parks have their unique and delightful trails, such as those of the Grand Tetons, Mt. Rainier and the Grand Canyon; but Glacier is a trail park on a much vaster scale. The fact is that nowhere else on the continent, within an equally compact and accessible region, is there such a variety of intriguing mountain trails. Glacier is literally a land of the great open spaces—an enchanted wilderness.

Many important points in the Park can be reached by automobile, but superficial sight-seers pass up the area's greatest treasures. The best of its scenic displays will never be viewed save by those hardy enough to brave the trails. Glacier is more than Swiss-type scenery, plush hotels and rustic campsites. Off the trail, free for the looking, are to be found what is becoming increasingly rare in our modern world—a million acres of the earth as God made it. Glacier's trails have been called its crowning glory. They carry one, afoot or on horseback to the zenith of outdoor enjoyment.

The Blackfeet used to call these mountains the "backbone of the world," and the name is appropriate as well as picturesque. This "backbone," really the continental divide, meanders back and forth from the Lewis Range to the Livingston Range, with spurs like ribs jutting out from it on both sides, each a segment of the mountain range, each "rib" separated from the others by forest-carpeted, lake-studded valleys. Interlacing this "backbone of the world," as well as many of its "ribs" is a network of trails. Over the ribs as well as the backbone, they lead from valley to valley, threading every pass, ascending and descending seemingly unscalable heights, providing answers to the challenge of the wilderness.

Trail Destinations

In a wilderness area, with road and highway access largely limited to its perimeter, trails serve many purposes. First of all, they are

necessary for efficient administration, to permit proper patrol of the valleys and passes by rangers and other members of the Park Service staff. They are needed for protective purposes, to provide ingress and egress to fire lookout stations; and to facilitate access to potential forest fire zones. And, of course, they make it possible for Park visitors to make closer contact with much of the back country, as well as the more adjacent areas.

While the extent of Park trails is usually spoken of rather loosely as 1,000 miles, the total does not quite reach that figure. National Park Service records show that there are actually a total of 910 miles of trails divided into four categories. Class 1 trails are those primarily for visitor use, that is, those considered to be used by 500 or more visitors each season. These total 324.8 miles. Class 2 trails aggregate 248.2 miles, being those with a seasonal use estimated at 50 to 500 visitors. Class 3 trails, totaling only 31.3 miles, are administrative in character. Class 4 are primarily for fire use and comprise 306.1 miles.[1]

The longest trail in the Park intended principally for visitor use is the 30.9-mile route from the foot of Kintla Lake over Boulder and Brown passes to the head of Waterton Lake. There are, of course, scores of short trails, such as the 8-mile trip from McDonald Lodge to Avalanche Lake, the 7.4 mile hike from Logan Pass to Granite Park, and the 6-mile trail from the Many Glacier Hotel to Grinnell Glacier, these being one-way mileages.

Most popular, among longer hikes, are the "highline trail" from Logan Pass to Granite Park and Waterton Lake, and the "north circle route" from Many Glacier to Granite Park, then back to Many Glacier via Stoney Indian Pass and the Ptarmigan tunnel. The first, of approximately 30 miles, may be interrupted by an overnight sojourn at Granite Park. The second, involving three passes and approximately 54 miles, ordinarily requires three days for those prepared to make use of the excellent camping facilities at Fifty Mountain and at either Glenn's Lake or Cosley (Crossley) Lake.

Game Routes

The earliest of Glacier's trails were created by various members of the animal kingdom, as they traversed its valleys, slopes and passes. The once mighty bison wandered into the lower valleys on the eastern side of what is now Park, and an occasional buffalo skull is yet stumbled upon near the trails. The deer, elk and moose tramped out passages through the forests, while on the higher reaches the sheep and goats blazed their trails over the summits and across the natural passes. All of these game pathways were fashioned according to the habits of their makers and usually according to the line of least resistance.

The original routes across Brown and Marias passes are said to have been game trails that antedated human use. Upland areas of the Park still disclose a multiplicity of goat and sheep trails, as they forage where predators fear to follow. These shy creatures are frequently pursuing routes, to them well-known, on the cliffs of the Pinnacle Wall above Iceberg Lake, near Gunsight and Logan Passes, and in the vicinity of the Sperry Glacier and Chalets. Inevitably, pursuit of the game caused Indian hunters to follow in some of their well-worn tracks.

Trails Of The Tribes

Early Indian trails led into many of the valleys, including particularly those of the Two Medicine, Cut Bank, Swiftcurrent, Belly River and Lake McDonald. The various tribes, especially the Kutenais and Stonies, had many trails across the "backbone of the world," including the following passes: Marias, Cut Bank, Red Eagle, Swiftcurrent, Stoney Indian and Brown. These primitive trails were not much in comparison with what we think of as park trails today, but they did follow well-defined routes and were often deeply worn by heavy use. Without trails of this kind, tribe travel from place to place, and particularly through the mountain passes, would have been extremely difficult.

It was probably an ancient Indian trail that led from Waterton Lake to Lake McDonald, over which trappers and hunters were wont to trek in the 1880's and 1890's, usually on their way to the Flathead country for supplies. Likewise, the dim old trails that once led to the Seward Mountain area, and along Lee Ridge west of Chief Mountain, perhaps long since obliterated, may also have been of Indian origin.

The Grandfather Of All Trails

Most ancient and notable of all the trails in the vicinity of what is now Glacier Park was that known as the Old North Trail.[2] This was the "travois trail" that ran from Athabaska to Aztec Land, perhaps the oldest and longest trail in human history. As it came down from what is now Alberta, it hugged the feet of the peaks along the eastern border of the present park, purposely taking advantage of the protection offered by the lower and less visible country.

Its usage by generations of Indians left such an enduring imprint upon the prairies that, in spite of the fact that the old trail has seen no travel for more than three-quarters of a century, it is still distinguishable at various places. The Blackfeet Highway crosses it at several points en route from East Glacier to St. Mary, and its traces may be discerned along the route by the observant traveler.

This pathway at the feet of the Rockies was a popular trail; in fact, it was undoubtedly the greatest highway in America prior to discovery of the continent and for long afterward. In the days after they came into the possession of horses, the Indians used the "travois," a contrivance formed by two tepee poles serving as shafts and fastened so that they crossed above the horse's withers. These trailed downward and backward, with the large ends dragging on the ground. In the space back of the horse was lashed a skin or blanket, forming a sort of container, into which the Indian loaded his belongings. The rear ends of the "travois" left a double track in their lee, and in the course of centuries of following the same route, a deeply worn set of ruts was gouged out. Though used only in sections by the various tribes, it was one unified trail extending up and down the length of the continent.

Along this trail the Indians moved their possessions as they hied themselves from one hunting ground to another. War parties skulked along its much frequented tracks, hoping to waylay members of some hostile tribe. Oft-times it was traveled by night to avoid the possibilities of a daylight ambush. It was a main artery of Indian communication, with the mountains for a landmark and the lowlands for protection and shelter. As some one has said, "there was a trail there for man and beast when the Romans were building roads to Britain; it was there when the first Hudson Bay hunters peered through the passes, and

118

since then many a hard pressed man has raced with death over it."

Other Pre-Park Pathways

The trails of the region that is now the Park served many purposes. For the Indians, they were paths to the sources of food and clothing, and to the locale of unsuspecting enemies. To the early explorers, they were routes to new areas of scenic delight and scientific interest. To the seekers of precious metals, oil, lumber and furs, they were a necessary means of achieving commercial objectives.

Earliest use by white men of the pre-Park trails was by traders and prospectors. Representatives of the big fur companies were in the region before 1800, and it is known that a group of them, including Finan McDonald, undertook to cross Marias Pass in the year 1810.[3] Sixty-five years later another McDonald (Duncan, no relation to Finan) traversed the same pass in connection with his duties for the Hudson's Bay Company.[4]

Trapping continued to flourish in the area throughout the nineteenth century. Following the trails south of Waterton Lake and throughout the Belly River country during the decade preceding 1895 was "Kootenai" Brown.[5] At about this same time, Donald Stevenson was hunting and trapping on Swiftcurrent Creek, and the trapping of grizzly bears was carried on on a large scale along the middle fork of the Flathead River.[6]

Trails were essential to the operations of the early miners and prospectors. There was a time in the 1880's and again in the 1890's when it seemed to many that both sides of the range were about to prove rich copper country. It was to provide a supply route for these activities that the old Indian trail over Swiftcurrent Pass was rehabilitated by Mrs. Nat Collins, the Montana Cattle Queen, in 1883. It was subsequently utilized for the same purpose by west side prospectors in the nineties.[7]

Trail Building By Explorers

Perhaps the earliest trail constructed solely for scenic reasons was completed in the latter part of July, 1895 between the head of Lake McDonald and the foot of Avalanche Lake. It was described by Dr. Lyman B. Sperry as "a passable saddle and pack trail." With his party, he hiked over it on August 1st, expecting to be the first to use it. They found, however, that they had been preceded by a group of sightseers from Kalispell, consisting of J. E. Edwards, his wife and brother, who had followed immediately upon the heels of the trail-makers and reached Avalanche Lake a few hours ahead of the Sperry party.[8]

Sperry himself became enthusiastic about the area and the glacier above it which later was to bear his name. Envisioning the possibilities of a trail to the glacier and summit of the continental divide east of McDonald Lake, he conferred with James J. Hill, president of the Great Northern Railway, about an idea he had for such a trail. By 1902 he had entered into a unique agreement with Hill whereby the railroad would furnish transportation to and from the area, together with tents, food and supplies, while Sperry would recruit students from the University of Minnesota to do the work without wages for the opportunity of spending a summer in the mountains. The project was started in 1902 and finished by the end of the summer of 1903, the trail being completed to the east side of Gunsight Pass, with a lateral or spur to the headwall below Sperry Glacier.[9]

Other trail building projects during this era were mostly incidental to clearing the way for a particular journey or expedition, The Ahern party of 1890 found it necessary to construct a trail of sorts over the pass by the same name in order to get their packtrain over it.[10] Other early explorers also had to do a certain amount of trail clearing as, for example, when Grinnell made his first visit to the head of Upper Lake St. Mary in 1885, and when Pumpelly made his historic trip up the Nyack Valley in 1883.[11]

Early West Side Wagon Routes

In addition to trail construction and usage, private interests also built a number of primitive wagon roads into the area in pre-Park years, always in the hope of finding a way to exploit its natural resources. It was to create a means of getting from the railroad at Belton to the foot of Lake McDonald in the middle nineties that a narrow, unimproved road was cut through the three miles of redcedar that blocked the route. This made it possible to transport a launch to the lake, to provide a buckboard route to its landing pier, and thus to bring interested tourists to the hotel that George Snyder had built near the upper end of the lake.[12]

When oil seepage was discovered in the year 1901 at the head of Kintla Lake, the Butte Oil Company was formed to undertake drilling. In order to get the necessary equipment to the lake, the company put crews to work building a road from the foot of Lake McDonald to the foot of Kintla Lake. This was merely a route cut through the timber, with corduroy (timbers laid crosswise) over the swampy areas, but without grading or bridges. In spite of this, most of the heavy machinery and supplies were moved to the foot of Kintla Lake before the first snowfall. After the lake froze that winter and the machinery had been hauled over the ice to the head of the lake, drilling began. Ultimately its lack of success was established, and the well was abandoned along with the access road.[13]

Early East Side Wagon Routes

During the same era, similar activities, centering principally in the Swiftcurrent Valley on the east side of the mountains, created the necessity for transporting equipment and supplies to this remote area, and constituted the motivating factor in the development of early routes from Fort Browning on the Great Northern Railway to the mining camps and the boom town of Altyn.[14] Actually, no road, as such, was ever built. The treeless terrain, however, provided relatively few obstacles, compared to the heavily forested west-side valleys; and the freight wagons simply took off over the rolling plains, each following the path of least resistance. Occasional traces of some of these ancient freight roads may still be discerned, usually consisting only of a few week-choked ruts through the area east of the present Blackfeet Highway — mute evidences of the transportation difficulties of those early times.[15]

When the myriad of routes stretching northwest from Browning reached the tiny settlement of Babb, at the north end of lower Lake St. Mary, they converged to follow the course of Swiftcurrent Creek westward, skirting the north shores of the Sherburne Lakes a distance of about 11 miles to the outlet of Canyon Creek, where the boom town of Altyn had sprung up. From that point the promoters of the Cracker Mine found it necessary to clear a route of sufficient breadth to get their equipment from Altyn up Canyon Creek to the site of their mine, a rise of more than 1,200 feet through the canyon's five miles of wooded slopes.

The purpose of this clearance project was to make possible the transportation of a 16,000-pound ore concentrator from Fort Browning to the mine. This task required a large freight wagon, twelve husky mules, and 29 days of time.[16] There was only the most primitive of routes on the way to Altyn and none after

leaving it. The heavy load had to be hauled with block and tackle much of the way up Canyon Creek;[17] and as one looks at this narrow gorge today, it is difficult to believe that the feat was ever accomplished. Since the mine failed to produce, the existence of this remarkable access route was brief; vestiges of it, however, are still visible along the Cracker Lake trail.

Early North Side Wagon Routes

All of the future park's early roads owed their existence to commercial ventures. On the west side it was tourism and oil; on the east side, the needs of prospectors and miners. In the case of the northern sector, the objective was the lumber of the lush forests of the upper Waterton and Belly River valleys.

Constructed around the turn of the century, these ancient roads necessarily gave access to and from Canadian bases. One extended from the south end of upper Waterton Lake to a point near the foot of Kootenai Pass, a distance of several miles, following rather generally the route of the present Granite Park-Waterton Lake trail.[18] Its purpose was to make possible the hauling of logs to the head of the lake for shipment to Canadian points. When a great flood destroyed the company's equipment, both the project and the road were abandoned.

A similar wagon route, also for logging purposes, ran a dozen miles up the valley of the Belly River to the foot of Cosley (Crossley) Lake. Traces of the old road are still visible near the trail leading along the east bank of the river to the Belly River ranger station.

Park-Constructed Trails

When the era of supply roads and trails for the various commercial projects of the region had finally come to an end, few useful routes remained. Much of the west-side road to the Butte well had fallen into disuse, as had the wagon routes on the east side of the mountains. Among regularly used roads, only the three-mile stretch from Belton (West Glacier) to the foot of Lake McDonald continued in fair shape. By the time the region became a national park, the only serviceable trails across the mountains were those over Swiftcurrent and Gunsight passes.[19]

Trail building began in earnest soon after the establishment of the Park, although the congressional appropriation of $15,000 earmarked "for improvement of Glacier National Park, Montana, for construction of trails and roads"[20] for the fiscal year of 1910-1911 did not go very far. Most of the major trails were constructed between 1913 and 1918,[21] the notable exceptions being the routes over Stoney Indian and Red Gap passes in 1921 and the Ptarmigan tunnel route to the Belly River region in 1931.

Among the first to receive attention when adequate funds became available was Swiftcurrent Pass. It so happened that the Park was visited in May, 1910, the same month it was created by Congress, by the chief clerk of the Department of the Interior, a man named Ucker. In order to make an inspection trip through the Department's new facility, he arranged with a packer named Josiah Rogers for a trip through the Park. This was to include Swiftcurrent Pass, at that time the only feasible trail leading across the continental divide within Park boundaries.[22]

Rogers was reluctant to undertake a crossing of the pass so early in the season because of the great amount of snow on the trail and the danger to pack animals. After much haggling, however, an agreement was reached whereby Rogers would take him on condition that Ucker would pay $100 for any animal lost en route. Fortunately, the trip over the pass was uneventfully acccomplished, and undoubtedly for Mr. Ucker the trip was educational as well as impressive. For on his return to Washington, D.C., he set the wheels in motion to secure congressional approval for funds to build and improve the trails of the Park. When, in 1913, work was done on the spectacular 3½ miles of switchbacks on the eastern side of the Pass, they were dubbed "Galen's Ladder," for James Galen, then superintendent of the Park.[22] Although the trail has since been partially relocated, these sensational switchbacks continue to be one of the route's great thrills.

Other Trail Builders

The Great Northern Railway, which played an important role in the early building of Park roads and the construction of its hostelries and chalets, also made a substantial contribution to the trail-building program with the purpose of getting Park facilities of every kind ready for use as early as possible. It contracted for the building in 1913 of the Mt. Henry trail between the Glacier Park Hotel and the Two Medicine Valley.[24]

A substantial amount of trail work was also done by Eagle Scouts under a unique program which, for most of its duration, was funded by the National Park Service. During the years 1925 to 1934, as many as 54 scouts, selected on merit from troops throughout the United States, took part in the encampments each year.[25] Under supervision of Park foremen, they worked five hours a day on the trails, and contributed their labor to parts of the trail from Bowman Lake to Brown Pass, of that leading to Two Medicine Pass, and of that along the south shore of Upper Lake St. Mary.

The Making Of A Trail

The building of a first-class trail is an engineering project. Trails are planned for the safety and comfort of the hiker. Grades on the main trails have been limited to 15%, and alignment has been planned so as to eliminate switchbacks and snowdrifts wherever possible. Particular attention has been given to locating the trails where the most magnificent country can be viewed.[26]

Some of the trails in Glacier Park can be classed as marvels of modern day science. Among the more unusual feats of trail building are the reconstructed trails over Triple Divide Pass and Gunsight Pass, and the route through the Ptarmigan Wall. Obstacles little dreamed of by the layman have fallen before the ingenuity, energy and skill of the engineer and the construction crew. Vertical cliffs have been crossed by half-tunnels with rocks and crags overhanging; trails have been built along narrow ledges, twisting lake shores and shifting talus slides; and sturdy bridges have been reared over swift and icy streams.[27]

As travel through the Park increases each year, so also does the use of its trails. Particularly is this true of the highly popular trails, such as those to Iceberg Lake, Grinnell Glacier and Avalanche Lake.[28] Travel to the backcountry is likewise on the rise. Trail maintenance, unfortunately, has not kept pace with trail use, a situation attributable to an inadequacy of congressional appropriations. Consequently, available funds have had to be devoted to the most used trails, with the result that others receive less attention, and still others none at all. Hopefully, this is a deficiency that will be remedied when Congress can be made to realize the relatively small amount of funds needed to maintain all of the Park's trails at their original level of utility and beauty.

Notes For Chapter 14

[1]Information as of August 1, 1975 from Park Service records.

[2]According to an article by Howard H. Hays appearing at page 69 of the 1948 edition of the "Drivers' Manual" (see note 15, Chapter 6, supra), Walter McClintock, author of "The Old North Trail," while in Glacier Park in the

summer of 1936, identified a part of the old trail in the vicinity of Glacier Park station, indicating that it used to run across what is now the seventh fairway of the Glacier Park golf course. For more detailed information on this trail, see McClintock's book, originally published in 1910, republished in 1968 by the University of Nebraska Press. An excellent chapter on the subject will be found in "Glacier National Park, Its Trails And Treasures," by Holtz and Bemis, at pages 87-99.

[3]"Through The Years In Glacier National Park," by Donald H. Robinson, at page 8.

[4]Idem, at page 15.

[5]See Chapter 4, supra, entitled "The Mountain Passes," describing Brown Pass at pages 33-34.

[6]"Wild Animals Of Glacier National Park," by Vernon Bailey. The footnote on page 96 of that text identifies Stevenson, and the trapping of grizzlies is covered on page 97.

[7]"Through The Years," supra, at pages 36 and 94.

[8]See Dr. Sperry's article entitled "In The Montana Rockes," at page 59, printed in "Appalachia," Volume VIII, No. 1, January, 1896.

[9]"Through The Years," supra, at pages 24-25.

[10]See discussion of the Ahern party in Chapter 4, supra, entitled "The Mountain Passes," at page 46.

[11]Grinnell's trip is described in Madison Grant's "History of Glacier National Park" at page 5. W. R. Logan crossed the Cut Bank Pass with the Pumpelly Expedition in 1883, and in an article entitled "Early Days In Glacier National Park," appearing at page 12 of Volume V of "Glacial Drift" for March/April, 1932 stated that the trip was "a strenuous one, as we had to chop almost our entire way through the mountains, the Indians having abandoned the trail some 25 or 30 years previous."

[12]"Through The Years," supra, at pages 86-87.

[13]Idem, at page 40.

[14]Idem, at pages 39-40.

[15]Idem, at page 87.

[16]Idem, at page 38.

[17]Idem, at page 38.

[18]While Kootenai Brown was quoted as having said, around 1911, that he could drive a team and wagon through the pass to the Flathead in Montana (see "Kootenai Brown, His Life And Times," by William Rodney, at page 196), there is no confirmation from other sources that this early wagon road ever extended beyond the headwaters of the Waterton River.

[19]"Through The Years," supra, at page 56.

[20]Chapter 384, Statutes of 61st Congress, 1910.

[21]"Through The Years," supra, at page 95.

[22]Actually, Gunsight Pass was also usable, though not passable in the month of May because of heavy drifts of snow in the pass and on the trail.

[23]"Through The Years," supra, at page 94.

[24]Idem, at page 94.

[25]Idem, at page 94.

[26]See article on "Roads And Trails In Glacier National Park," by Ira S. Stinson, appearing in the 1948 edition of "Drivers' Manual" (see note 15, Chapter 6, supra), at pages 98-100.

[27]Idem.

[28]Commencing with the season of 1972, saddlehorse trips to Iceberg Lake and Grinnell Glacier were prohibited for the first time in Park history. This may or may not prove to be a permanent restriction.

Heading for Iceberg Lake looking toward Mt. Wilbur
Photo by Walt Dyke, courtesy Burlington Northern

Chapter 15
ROADS AND HIGHWAYS

Because Glacier National Park is a wilderness area, the roads and highways of its more than 1,500 square miles are limited in number and distance to that minimum which is consistent with reasonable use by the public.[1] Of the mileage actually servicing the Park, totaling less than 250 miles in all, more than half are not within Park borders, merely skirting them on the south, the east, and to some extent on the north. Half of the mileage within the Park comprises the east-west roadway that crosses Glacier at approximately its middle. The rest is made up of the perimeter road just within the Park's western boundary, together with short stub roads into a few of the valleys.

The roads that have been given special names are four in number: the Theodore Roosevelt Highway, 58 miles in length; the Blackfeet Highway, 50 miles; the Chief Mountain International Highway, 15 miles in the United States and 20 miles in Canada; and the Going-To-The-Sun Highway, 51 miles. Additionally, there is the road leading up the North Fork of the Flathead River to the Kintla Lakes near the Canadian border, usually referred to as the North Fork Road, approximately 42 miles. With the notable exception of the Going-To-The-Sun transmountain highway, these are all essentially perimeter roads that parallel one or another of the Park's boundaries.

The North Fork Road
There are actually two roads, rather than one, that roughly parallel the Park's western boundary which, of course, is the North Fork of the Flathead River. The more westerly of these is the Flathead National Forest service road, extending from Columbia Falls to Polebridge and on to the town of Flathead in Canada. The other lies entirely within the Park, connecting West Glacier with Kintla Lake. This is the one now known as the North Fork Road, originally built in 1901 in connection with the incipient oil boom of that year.[2]

Modernization of the lower segment of this road became one of the initial projects of Major Logan, the Park's first superintendent. By 1912, the three miles between Belton (West Glacier) and Lake McDonald had been rebuilt and macadamized, and the section from Apgar to Fish Creek was completed the following year. In 1915, the task of improving the rest of the ancient route to Kintla Lake was undertaken and, with its eventual completion, travel to and from the North Fork country was greatly facilitated.

Even today, however, most of the North Fork Road cannot be classified as modern. Although paved for the first five miles or so, it then becomes a rather narrow, gravel-surfaced road winding through the lush forests to the west and northwest of Lake McDonald. About 30 miles north of West Glacier, near the outlet of Bowman Creek, the route is linked with that on the opposite side of the North Fork of the Flathead River by a picturesque old bridge that leads to the tiny settlement of Polebridge situated on the Flathead National Forest Road to Canada.

This lack of modernization is by design, and the road is adequate for the needs of hikers, campers and fishermen who use it. In other words, the North Fork area is purposely without hotels, paved roads and other trappings of civilization in order that this section of the Park may the better maintain its wilderness flavor and primitive appeal.

The Blackfeet Highway
One of the most important of all the roads that provide access to Glacier Park is the 50-mile stretch that runs from the Glacier Park Hotel (East Glacier) northward to the Canadian border, roughly paralleling the Park's eastern boundary. It lies entirely within the Blackfeet Indian Reservation and hence has come to be known as the Blackfeet Highway. Officially, it is Montana State Highway No. 49 and, in part, U. S. Highway No. 89. Its primary route carries it 31 miles to St. Mary, another 9

miles to Babb, and a final 10 miles to the international boundary where it becomes Alberta Province Highway No. 2.

This is an excellent hard-surfaced highway on which work was begun in 1926 and largely finished in 1929. It really had its beginnings in 1911 when the Great Northern Railway, anxious to get under way with its crash program for construction of hotels and chalets, found itself hampered by the lack of adequate roads.[3] Federal appropriations for Park development and administration had been pitifully small, and it became apparent to Louis W. Hill, president of the railroad company, that its building program would be at a virtual standstill if it had to await federal action. Accordingly, under an agreement with the Department of the Interior, the company stepped into the breach and contracted in 1911 for the construction of a road from Midvale (then the name for East Glacier) to the Swift-current Valley.[4]

This pioneer road, forerunner of the present Blackfeet Highway, was two years in building and the first official party to travel over it was that of Louis W. Hill on August 7, 1913.[5] From East Glacier to St. Mary, it had been entirely new construction; from that point on it followed the old Browning-Babb freight road to Many Glacier, with this older section being improved to permit the handling of heavier traffic. During the next few years, reconstruction and improvement of various parts of the St. Mary-Many Glacier segment were completed by the Department of the Interior and by the United States Reclamation Service, the latter in preparation for construction of nearby Sherburne Dam.[6]

This early road, although graded, was unsurfaced. During dry weather, it presented no problems but during a period of heavy rains it would become almost impassable. During the extremely rainy summer of 1915, the Milk River Flats became a veritable quagmire and the passenger buses which plied daily between East Glacier and Many Glacier often spent as much time off the road as on it. Jack Galbreath, who owned an 8-horse team, camped on this flat that summer and pulled many a bus and private car through the ooze.[7] Before long, however, gravel surfacing was added and the effects of bad weather were largely mitigated, although substantial repairs and maintenance continued to be regularly necessary until the hard-surfacing of the road in the 1926-1929 era.[8]

Beauties Of The Route

Paralleling the great front range of the Rockies, the Blackfeet Highway presents the traveler with a constantly changing view of its magnificent peaks. It winds over glaciated hills and across broad valleys that have been scoured out by ancient rivers of ice flowing eastward in Pleistocene times from deep mountain gorges, giant glaciers that gave way to tremendous torrents of meltwater as they slowly receded. Nearby, and visible from time to time, are vestiges of travois tracks of the Old North Trail by which the Indians traveled for centuries back and forth from Mexico to Canada.[9] A myriad of multi-colored flowers carpet the roadsides, and the alert traveler is likely to see many varieties of birds and animal life.

On its way to Divide Mountain, winding over gently rising slopes, the highway crosses the richly flowered valleys of the Two Medicine, the Cut Bank and the Milk Rivers. There are stands of lodgepole pines, as well as spruce and fir. Highest elevation reached is the St. Mary Ridge, at 6067 feet above sea level which, together with Divide Mountain, forms a part of the Hudson Bay Divide. The country south and east of this divide is drained by the Milk River which ultimately empties into streams that reach the Gulf of Mexico. To the north and west, the drainage is through the St. Mary, Saskatchewan and Nelson Rivers to Hudson Bay.

The St. Mary Side Of The Divide

As the traveler continues northward beyond the divide, the great peaks of the St. Mary region begin to loom on the horizon. First to be visible is Siyeh, 10,014 feet in elevation. Presently, to its left, Going-To-The-Sun Mountain can be seen, together with the permanent snowfield near its summit which has the appearance of the head of an Indian looking southward, with the feathers of his headdress trailing back to the north. This is the celebrated profile which supposedly has given rise to an oft-repeated legend. Soon the St. Mary Lakes themselves are visible, the upper lake being to the left; and from the St. Mary Junction looking westward is one of the Park's greatest views — a panorama of peaks that includes, among others, Red Eagle, Mahtotopa, Little Chief, Citadel, Gunsight, Fusillade, Reynolds, Goat, Singleshot and East Flattop.

The highway skirts the lower lake for the full length of its eight miles. Aspen groves alternate with poplars, and the meadows are rife with flowers, the varieties depending upon the season. On this section of the highway are seen the famous profiles of Singleshot Mountain, said by the Blackfeet to be that of Napi, a tribal deity, and of East Flattop, the profile of which, at its north end, is thought to resemble a St. Bernard dog. Presently the summit of Chief Mountain, sacred peak of the Blackfeet, looms to the north with its precipitous eastern face in bold relief.

At the forty-mile mark, the little town of Babb is reached, its name derived from an early superintendent of the nearby Milk River reclamation project. At this point, a branch of the road to the left leads to Many Glacier; while four miles farther north another left fork represents the beginning of the Chief Mountain International Highway. The main highway continues north to the international border, at which point it becomes Alberta Province Road No. 2 and leads to the little town of Cardston with its handsome Mormon temple.

Chief Mountain International Highway

While the Waterton-Glacier International Peace Park was formally created in 1932, still another four years were to elapse before a direct route was available between Glacier National Park and its sister area, Waterton Lakes National Park, immediately to the north in Alberta. This road, originally called the "Kennedy Creek Cutoff," was later renamed the "Chief Mountain International Highway."[10] Major construction on it began in 1934, and it was opened to travel on June 14, 1936, despite the fact that surfacing was not yet completed.[11]

This picturesque highway is less than forty miles in length, including the entire mileage between Babb and Waterton. Until 1936, it had been necessary for those desiring to proceed from one park to the other to drive from Babb to Cardston, and thence to Waterton, a distance of nearly 60 miles. The need for a shorter route became obvious with the creation of the International Peace Park, as well the increase in travel itself. The route has become a popular one, since a substantial percentage of those who arrive by automobile make it a point to visit both parks.[12]

Principal feature of the road after it leaves the Blackfeet Highway, four miles north of Babb, is the great monolith of Chief Mountain, an historic landmark visible for long distances in every direction. Like the "Chief," the nearby Sherburne and Yellow peaks are of unusual geological interest because they represent the plainly visible effects of the extraordinary overthrust that reshaped much of the Lewis Range near the end of Cretaceous times.

A fifteen-mile drive after leaving the Blackfeet Highway takes the traveler across a small corner of the Park, and brings him to the United States Customs and Immigration Office, with the Canadian counterpart a few rods down the road. Between them is the international boundary, plainly marked as such by the twenty-foot swath which has been cut through wooded areas. Some ten miles across the line the highway reaches a well-marked vista point, from which a panorama of several of the peaks of the Waterton Valley are best seen. Some three miles later, it merges with the Cardston-Waterton Highway, Alberta Province No. 5, from which point it is six miles into Waterton Village itself.

Theodore Roosevelt Highway

One of the busiest parts of the Glacier Park road system is that segment of United States Highway Number 2, which runs between East Glacier Park and West Glacier. This stretch of 58 miles is a modern, year-round road called the Theodore Roosevelt Highway.[13] Reconstructed in 1966, it was originally opened to traffic on July 19, 1930 and formally dedicated at Marias Pass on August 23, 1930.[14]

The route of the Roosevelt Highway is shared with the right of way of the Great Northern Railway, and with the southern boundary of Glacier Park. From West Glacier, at an elevation of about 3200 feet, the roadway follows the Middle Fork of the Flathead River and its tributary, Bear Creek, a total of 40 miles to Marias Pass at 5213 feet. Thereafter, by a gradual descent along Summit Creek and Railroad Creek, it reaches East Glacier at 4796 feet. For the most part, it parallels the railroad on its southerly side, but crosses a bridge over the Middle Fork at Walton and runs through the Park itself for nearly three miles before leaving it again near Nimrod.

West of the summit, the highway is located on soil of the Flathead National Forest; east of the pass, the area becomes the Lewis and Clark National Forest. Both are a part of the Bob Marshall Wilderness Area, a 950,000-acre mountain preserve that straddles the continental divide, and almost equals Glacier itself in size. In combination with that part of the Flathead National Forest bordering Glacier on the west, with the Indian Reservation on the east, and Waterton Lakes National Park on the north, the Bob Marshall Wilderness serves pretty well to insulate the Park from the inroads of civilization.

Need For A Transmountain Route

The Roosevelt Highway did not become a reality until the Park had been in existence a full twenty years. Prior to 1930, there had been no transmountain road for more than a hundred miles to the north or south of the present U. S. No. 2. To get an automobile across the divide, it was necessary to have it loaded upon a flatcar at either East Glacier Park or West Glacier, to be ferried across the summit by freight train while its owner made the same trip in a passenger coach. This ferry service was provided by the Great Northern Railway, in proper season, for $12.50 per car.

The Roosevelt Highway is the most northerly of year-round routes over the continental divide in this country. It lacks the elevation and spectacular scenery of its sister highway over Logan Pass, some 20 to 50 miles to the north. It is not without its thrills, however, because of the frequent glimpses of the great Glacier Park peaks to the north, including Jackson, Gunsight, St. Nicholas, Stimson, Pinchot, Summit and Little Dog, the latter named for the Blackfeet chief who first told Governor Stevens in 1853 that a usable pass in this area really existed.[15]

One of the unique sights along the highway is at Walton where the Park Service maintains a large plaque describing the nearby salt lick and the mountain goats that can often be seen from the special vista point created for that purpose. Other sights of special interest include the tall granite obelisk which stands at the center of the highway at the very summit of the pass, a memorial to Theodore Roosevelt;[16] and the heroic statue of John F. Stevens, which is located north of the station and is illuminated at night. It commemorates his 1889 "discovery" of the "lost pass" needed by the Great Northern Railway as a link in its low level route to the Pacific Coast.[17]

Going-To-The-Sun-Highway

Linking the east and west sides of Glacier is the only transmountain route for motor travel within Park boundaries, one which is unique also because the motivation for its construction was almost entirely to provide a means of viewing the Park's great beauty for a few brief months each year, rather than to serve merely as a means of getting from one location to another. It was originally named Going-To-The-Sun Road by the Park's first naturalist, George C. Ruhle,[17] and the Park Service still prefers that it be called a road since it lies entirely within Park boundaries. Notwithstanding these facts, and because of the spectacular scenic splendor of this tremendous transmountain artery of travel, it has been referred to in these pages as GOING-TO-THE-SUN Highway.

Whatever the appellation, the G T S Highway, as it is also sometimes called, is a marvel of engineering accomplishment. Climbing nearly 2500 feet to the 6664-foot summit of Logan pass, it extends 51 miles between the Park's western entrance and St. Mary on the eastern side. Sections of it have literally been carved out of the vertical walls of that great barrier known as the "Garden Wall." From the time of original concept and preliminary survey to the date of putting on the finishing touches in 1935 had required some twenty years of time and the expenditure of $3,000,000 in non-inflated, depression dollars.[18]

In response to administrative recommendations for a trans-mountain road through the Park, engineering surveys had been conducted over a three-year period, beginning in 1916.[19] Based upon their results, the first $100,000 for the beginning of construction were appropriated in 1921, and a few miles of road were built along Lake McDonald that year.[20] Work did not begin on the St. Mary end of the job until 1924 when it was decided that a resurvey would be necessary in order to establish a better gradient for the western approach.[21] Construction moved along at an accelerated pace thereafter, and the road from Lake McDonald to the summit of Logan Pass was opened to the public in June, 1929.[22]

The Twenty-Year Project Is Finished

Further contracts were awarded for the uncompleted sections on the eastern slopes of the mountains, and the last major construction was completed on October 19, 1932 with the holing through of the east side tunnel. In September of that year, an inspection party, headed by National Park Service Director Horace Albright, had driven from Lake McDonald to the Pass and on to the tunnel. There they walked around the unfinished tunnel and took another car to the Glacier Park Hotel.[23] However, grading was not completed until the summer of 1933, and although the road was open for through traffic that summer, the final surfacing, re-grading, guardrail installation, roadside cleaning, etc. was not brought to a conclusion until 1935.[24] The final section of the west side, from Logan Creek to Logan Pass, had been the most difficult part of the entire construction job; and its cost, including surfacing and guardrail work, was close to $80,000 per mile.[25] During the height of this section of the work, an average of 225 men were being employed, operating out of five or six camps; and it was estimated that for every cubic yard of material removed, approximately one pound of dynamite had to be used.[26]

In that section of the road along the west side of the Garden Wall, the roadway had to be literally blasted out of the face of the cliff. To make this possible, workmen had to be lowered by ropes from above to set the original markers, followed by others who risked their lives in precarious positions to place the dynamite where it would do the most good. In early construction, much of the equipment was hauled or skidded in by means of horses. In later stages, dump trucks were utilized, and the cubic yardage of rock debris removed from tunnel and face-wall construction ran into the hundreds of thousands, all of which, for esthetic reasons, had to be carted away.

Difficulties Encountered

The obstacles and hazards presented by this kind of construction were great. Much of the twenty-year period required for the job, has to be attributed to the short work season at high elevations, averaging four months per year. Snowfalls, early and late, created another problem; and it was necessary to clear huge drifts, up to 70 feet in height, with the primitive snow-removal equipment then available, in order to get to work on affected sections of the road by late June. Animals, particularly pillaging bears, added to the difficulties in maintaining a supply of food; and porcupines, with their odd appetites, raised havoc with rubber tires and construction equipment. Even forest fires in nearby areas produced occasional work stoppages.

The highway, as a through road, was opened to the public on July 11, 1933, and official dedication ceremonies were held on July 15th.[27] This was a gala event, staged on the meadows of Logan Pass, and attended by an estimated 5,000 people.[28] Among the distinguished visitors were several Montana officials, including Senators Burton K. Wheeler and W. A. Buchanan, Governor Frank Cooney and Congressman Scott Leavitt.[29]

Indians of the region also turned out in full force, with representatives present from the Blackfeet, Flathead and Kootenai tribes. Among their numbers were the Blackfeet chief, Two Guns White Calf, whose profile graced the

buffalo nickel, and Kustata, ancient chief of the Kootenais. Also on hand was Duncan McDonald, venerable frontiersman and early resident of the Flathead area, after whom Lake McDonald had been named. Following a colorful pageant by the Indians, depicting events leading up to completion of the highway, gifts were exchanged and the pipe of peace was smoked by the tribes, to signify that these long hostile peoples were now at peace forever.[30]

Highway Extraordinary

The Going-To-The-Sun Highway presents a continuing series of spectacular views. Running between Park entrances at West Glacier and St. Mary on the east, it connects the two lakes which are the largest as well as, perhaps, the most beautiful in Glacier Park. From West Glacier it runs along the eastern edge of Lake McDonald, penetrating lush forests of red-cedars, following the McDonald Creek Valley to a point almost directly below Granite Park at the 4000-foot level. There it doubles back sharply to the right, continuing in the lee of the great Garden Wall escarpment, and climbing gradually at about a six per cent grade to the flower-carpeted summit of Logan Pass. En route, across the valley, the tall cataract of Bird Woman Falls is prominent, and the snowy summits of Cannon, Gould and Heaven's Peak loom large.

In June there are still drifts of snow across the highway, through which Park equipment has been busily cutting canyons that will get the road open by the target date of June 10th.[31] These great drifts only disappear, if at all, late in the summer months. Some five miles west of the Pass is the celebrated Weeping Wall, which serves to keep the roadway drenched, especially in the early summer.

The summit of Logan Pass, though on the continental divide, is not the narrow saddle that one might expect; rather a large, more or less flat meadow, a part of which has been macadamized to serve as parking space for the cars of its many visitors. The adjoining area is studded with stunted alpine firs and is usually a mass of color, featuring glacier lilies, heather, heliotrope, blue gentians or parnassias, according to the season. Great peaks surround the Pass, Pollock to the north, Reynolds to the south with Going-To-The-Sun looming toward the east, while dozens of mighty peaks in the northern Lewis and Livingston Ranges are visible. Just to the north of the Pass, the trail to Granite Park takes off along Pollock Mountain and the Garden Wall.

The Pass Itself

An attractive visitor center is located on the summit, featuring informative displays and exhibits. Ranger naturalists are on hand to provide information, and a trail, covered for a part of its length with a controversial boardwalk, leads to a lookout above Hidden Lake and to the Hanging Gardens. Snow often persists in the Pass until the latter part of July or early part of August. Diligent observers are often rewarded with a glimpse of the mountain goats that frequent the upper slopes of Mt. Clements.

Descending eastward along the highway, the views are even more breath-taking than those on the ascent. The road, gently sloping, passes through a tunnel and along snowbanks, with glaciers, peaks and waterfalls constantly in view. Prominent along the route are Pollock, Piegan and Going-To-The-Sun Mountains. High on the face of Piegan, a stream gushes forth from the bare rock, apparently fed from Piegan Glacier on the opposite side of the mountain. Much of the roadway along the mountain has been carved from the rock wall; and views of snow-girdled Blackfoot Mountain with Blackfoot Glacier resting against it are soon succeeded by others of Citadel and Little Chief Mountains across the great valley.

Presently the western end of Upper Lake St. Mary comes into view, with its bluer than azure hue, contrasted against the crimson of Red Eagle Mountain on its south shore. Of special interest, across the Lake, are Virginia Falls and the hanging valley from which this spectacular cataract plunges. The amazing Sunrift Gorge is just above the highway, but invisible until one walks 100 feet uphill and sees the great natural "fault" through which Baring Creek runs at a right angle to the rest of the stream bed, while Baring Falls is a short distance down stream. Approximately half a mile east of the Gorge is a side road leading to Sun Point where, in earlier years, were located the chalets known as Sun Camp. Situated high on a cliff with an unsurpassed overview of the lake, this was a popular stopping place for horseback and hiking parties before World War II.

Geological Footprints

Three miles eastward are the Narrows of Lake St. Mary, with a tiny island nearby that long served as a nesting place for wild geese.

The Narrows are geologically attributable to the resistance presented by rock of the Altyn formation at the face of the Lewis Overthrust. The gray rock seen at Logan Pass is of the Siyeh limestone formation, the most conspicuous of the rock strata found throughout the Park. As the road descends, it passes through maroon colored Grinnell argillite, then through the predominantly green coloring of the Appekunny argillite formation, and finally, along the highway near the Narrows, through the buff coloring of the Altyn limestone, oldest of the Park's rocks.

At the Narrows the Lake is little more than a quarter of a mile in width. About half a mile eastward along the highway are the Rising Sun Motor Inn and Campground by the same name; and from that point it is less than six miles to the St. Mary Entrance and Campground.

Impact Of The Transmountain Road

The original St. Mary Chalets are no longer in existence, but the village of St. Mary, lying just outside the Park boundary, has become an important center of Park activities, with its motor lodge and motels, restaurants, gift shops, Indian craft shops, service stations, horse rental facilities and the like. A mile west of the village, beside the Going-To-The-Sun Highway, is an attractive and well conceived visitor center, featuring slide shows, interpretive displays and naturalist talks.

The impact of the Going-To-The-Sun Highway upon the park has been great. As the only transmountain road within Park boundaries, it gives the visitor who is unable to get into the backcountry by trail a cross section of the beauties and scenic attractions offered by wilderness areas of the Park. As a result, it has completely transformed the pattern of travel for Park visitors, making it possible for them to see as much of the peaks and passes in a few hours as might have been encompassed in a week's time by hikers or saddle horse riders. On the other hand, the heavy volume of daily traffic over the summit during the Park season has caused ecological problems in the form of damage to vegetation along the Logan Pass to Hidden Lake trail, as well as some pollution of the headwaters of St. Mary Lake to the east.[32]

Other Roads

On the west side of the Park, a branch of the North Fork Road leads off from the latter at a point about five miles north of West Glacier. It runs northwesterly past Huckleberry Mountain and crosses the North Fork of the Flathead River into the Flathead National Forest to connect with the road on that side of the river. Its approximate length is ten miles, all of which is paved. The bridge across the river is an attractive span of recent construction.

Also on the west side are spur roads servicing some of the valleys. That along Quartz Creek leads only to a private ranch. That along Bowman Creek takes off just above the Polebridge junction and runs a little over six miles to the excellent campground at the foot of Bowman Lake. The road is narrow and tortuous, but the view of the lake and adjacent peaks is well worth the sidetrip. Perennially proposed is a plan to extend the North Fork Road into Canada, thence eastward over the continental divide to Waterton Lakes National Park—a plan which seemingly has no early prospects of becoming a reality.

From the Blackfeet Highway, spur roads lead into the eastern valleys. That into the Two Medicine Valley is a paved road that takes off at a point four miles north of East Glacier, skirts the north shore of Lower Two Medicine Lake, runs past the beginning of the short trail to Trick Falls, and reaches the shore of gorgeous Two Medicine Lake about seven miles above the junction. Seventeen miles north of East Glacier on the Blackfeet Highway, another spur road takes off to the left. Narrow, winding and unpaved, it runs approximately six miles into primitive Cut Bank Valley, ending at the point where the former chalets were located.

The branch to the Swiftcurrent Valley takes off, as previously indicated, at the little settlement of Babb and runs approximately twelve miles westward into the Many Glacier area. This excellent paved road leads past the Sherburne Dam and Reservoir, and provides attractive views of the Grinnell Glacier, the Garden Wall and Swiftcurrent Falls and Lake, as well as of the encircling peaks in and near the continental divide

Notes For Chapter 15

[1]In an article entitled "Roads And Trails In Glacier National Park," appearing at page 96 of the 1948 edition of "Drivers' Manual" (see note 15, chapter 6, supra), Ira S. Stinson, formerly the Park Engineer, explained why the mileage of roads within a wilderness park should be kept to a minimum: (a) Road building causes permanent scarring of the landscape; (b) It also causes much damage to adjacent trees by reason of rocks thrown by dynamiting, by trampling, by machinery, and by fills which choke out the roots; (c) Unnatural canyons are created, which expose nearby trees to sudden change to which they cannot adjust, and these dead and dying trees are hosts for destructive beetles, are splendid tinder for a forest fire, and are unattractive to users of the highway; and (d) The noise associated with a modern highway, the attendant activity, and the smoke and stench of exhaust fumes are all repellant to many kinds of wild life.

[2]See Chapter 11, supra, entitled "Advent Of The White Man," at page 96, describing the short-lived oil and gas boom at Kintla Lake. See, also, Chapter 14, supra, entitled "Trails And Early Routes," at pages 119-120, describing the original 1901 construction of the route to Kintla Lake.

[3]"Through The Years In Glacier National Park," by Donald H. Robinson, at page 87.

[4]Idem, at pages 87-88.

[5]Idem, at page 88. Mr. Hill had become Chairman of the Board in 1912.

[6]Idem, at page 88.

[7]Idem, at page 88.

[8]Idem, at pages 88-89.

[9]See Chapter 14, supra, entitled "Trails And Early Routes," at page 118.

[10]"Through The Years," supra, at page 89.

[11]Idem, at page 89.

[12]In recent years the number of travelers over this route has been approximately 200,000 per annum.

[13]"Through The Years," supra, at page 90.

[14]Idem, at page 90.

[15]"Surveys for A Railroad Route," Volume XII, Book 1, at page 106.

[16]Construction of a Theodore Roosevelt Memorial was authorized by Chapter 372 (HR 4752, 71st Congress) of the Laws of 1929-1930, approved June 2, 1930. The cost was $50,000.

[17]"Through the Years," supra, at page 90.

[18]Idem, at page 94.

[19]Idem, at page 90.

[20]Idem, at page 90.

[21]Idem, at page 91.

[22]Idem, at page 92.

[23]Idem, at page 92.

[24]Idem, at page 94.

[25]Idem, at page 92.

[26]Idem, at page 92.

[27]Idem, at page 92.

[28]Idem, at page 92.

[29]Idem, at page 92.

[30]Idem, at page 93.

[31]To get the highway cleared for each season, an average of more than 100,000 cubic yards of snow must be removed in May and June.

[32]See Chapter 24, infra, entitled "Environmental Problems," at pages 190-191.

Celebrated Weeping Wall along the Going-to-the-Sun Highway

Photo by Mel Ruder

A section of spectacular Going-to-the-Sun Highway with Mt. Clements in left foreground

Photo by Walt Dyke, courtesy Burlington Northern

Chapter 16
THE GREAT LOG LODGES

Greatly enhancing the delightful charm of Glacier Park are the majestic hostelries that greet the arriving traveler. When it comes to visitor accommodations of a size, style and character to match the magnificence of their surroundings, Glacier has few equals among our national parks. Yet it is seldom realized that creation of some of these great hotels in the remoteness of Montana during early years of the century was an achievement that bordered upon the miraculous.

When the Park was established as such in 1910, its tourist facilities were virtually non-existent;[1] and the task of converting a million-acre mountain land into a travel paradise was a prodigious one. Accomplishment of this feat, largely within three to five years from scratch, was remarkable not only because it produced such attractive and appropriate structures within a limited period, but also because it was achieved under conditions of great difficulty by people without previous experience in this field. Even more amazing, perhaps, is the fact that it was done without federal funds or assistance, and in the face of a certainty that the investment would not become profitable for years to come, if ever.

Early congressional appropriations for Glacier were pitifully meager, and the Department of the Interior, which then supervised the parks, simply did not have the funds or authority, let alone the initiative and energy, needed for quick development of visitor comforts in this great and attractive wilderness. Stepping promptly into the breach were the Great Northern Railway and its capable president, Louis W. Hill. The ink had hardly dried on President Taft's signature on the founding Act before Hill had begun work on a crash program to create visitor facilities. He not only mobilized the forces of his own great organization, but took a personal interest in the planning and location of hotels and chalets, as well as roads and trails.[2]

The area to be provided with facilities was enormous but by 1913 work had been finished on chalets at Two Medicine, at Cut Bank, at St. Mary, at Many Glacier and at Sun Camp (including a dining room and eight dormitory buildings), together with a tent camp, dining room and dormitory at Gunsight Lake.[3] Most important of all, of course, was the completion of the main wing of the principal hotel, including its lobby and dining room, at East Glacier, then called Midvale.

Flagship Of Park Hostelries

This was the "Glacier Park" Hotel, known to the amazed Blackfeet as the "Great Log Lodge" or "Big Trees Lodge."[4] Its spectacular "forest lobby" was patterned, upon the order of Louis W. Hill, after the forestry building at the Portland Exposition of 1912. The sixty immense timbers which support the building were monarchs of the forest, from 500 to 800 years old when cut, and brought in from Oregon and Washington. Fifty-two feet in length, thirty-six to forty-two inches in diameter, and weighing fifteen tons each, they were so huge that often only two could be placed on one flat car. Those in the lobby are of Douglas fir, while those supporting the verandas are of cedar. In every case they retain their original bark.

These massive pillars rise majestically in the lobby from basement to rafters and provide an impressive frame for the central lounge area which is surrounded at each floor level by decorated balconies. From similar logs, brought in by the carload from western Washington, have been fashioned huge beams, girders, counters and even lampstands. Everywhere is the warmth of natural western wood of which the hotel has been so painstakingly wrought.

An Exciting Beginning

The opening of the "Glacier Park", as well as of the Park season, took place on June 15, 1913. Louis Hill, by that time chairman of the Great Northern board, had conjured up a plan for a sensational party, ostensibly to celebrate the 75th birthday of his father, the great James J. Hill. This took the form of a tremendous banquet for 600 of the company's veteran employees, brought in by special trains from all over the system for the event.[5]

This colorful event taxed all of the hotel's facilities. After the birthday party was over, the hotel continued to be overwhelmed with hundreds of visitors from near and far, some arriving in special trains. Scores of Blackfeet had pitched their tepees on the hotel grounds and many of the tribe's famed chiefs were there—Medicine Owl, Curly Bear, Heavy Breast, Two Guns, Stabbed-By-Mistake, Tail Feathers, Mountain Chief, Heavy Runner and others. The Indians staged a great demonstration in honor of the hotel's opening, a celebration marred only by the death of old Chief Heavy Breast. With his fellow celebrants he danced too long and suffered a fatal heart attack.[6]

Environs Of The "Glacier Park"

Eastward from the hotel lies the vast sweep of the rolling plains of the Blackfeet Indian Reservation, on the western edge of which the hotel is situated.[7] Westward from the great veranda, off the main floor of the lobby, is outspread an incomparable panorama of the Rockies—a hundred-mile stretch from Heart Butte on the south to Divide Mountain on the north, with Squaw Mountain and Mt. Henry holding the center of the stage.

To the rear of the hotel is a nine-hole golf course and a large and attractive swimming pool; to its front is a pitch-and-put golf layout. Close at hand is the ranger station, as well as motor transportation headquarters for the Park. Only a few rods up the road from the hotel is the John L. Clarke Western Art Gallery, now under the auspices of the daughter of the great woodcarver. To the south of the railroad track, along Highway No. 2, is a year-round village[8] with postoffice, stores and the usual facilities for travelers. With the closing of the great hotel each September, its satellite facilities go into hibernation for another nine months, while the village continues to carry on during the long winter.

Inland Capital Of The Park

The original plans of President Hill contemplated the early construction of another great hostelry in the heart of the Park. This was to be the "Many Glacier," on which work was begun in the spring of 1914, and which was opened for business on July 4, 1915. With the addition of its south wing in 1917, this

"Showplace of the Rockies," as it is often called, became not only the largest hotel in the Park, but also the largest at that time in the state of Montana.[9] Here in the midst of what is undoubtedly the region's greatest concentration of scenic attractions, visitors tend to linger longer, and the need for housing facilities is correspondingly greater.

Situated 55 miles from the railroad, the site of Many Glacier is reachable only on foot, or horseback or by highway vehicle. Despite completion of a road of sorts in 1913 from what is now East Glacier, the problems connected with its primary construction in the years of 1914-1915 were king-sized. Native stone was quarried nearby for foundations and fireplaces, but all the huge logs required for the lobby had to be hauled or skidded from the railhead; and by this same route came the boilers and heavy equipment of varied types.[10] Moderate-sized lumber was secured through the cutting of logs in the Grinnell valley, floating them down to Swiftcurrent Lake through the chain of waterways lying above it, processing them through a saw and planing mill erected nearby, and seasoning them in temporary kilns. Most of the furniture was made on the site from local lumber, but window sash, door frames and similar items had to be freighted in.[11]

Size And Motif

The Swiss style of architecture is apparent in the hotel's every detail, although it is quite different from its sister structure, the "Glacier Park." A foundation of native red and green rock supports four stories of quaintly carved wooden superstructure. It has been built as a series of connected units, so contrived as to fit the shoreline of Swiftcurrent Lake. Its length of 900 feet places it among the largest of its kind.

Within the Many Glacier, one is at once reminded of its prototype at East Glacier. Monarchs of the forest again serve as pillars rising from basement to skylighted roof, framing a series of balconies or interior galleries. On the east wall stands a tremendous fireplace of native stone while another, copper-hooded, is suspended from the roof into the central lounge area. It is in this area, furnished with a grand piano and many davenports, that the employees stage some of their evening shows. At other times, a college combo may be playing for dancing on the floor below. In addition to featuring a spacious and well patronized gift shop[12] the lobby opens at either end to the broad western veranda with its view of views.

The lobby walls were originally adorned with an historic collection of Indian picture writings (20 in all) by Blackfeet chiefs, consisting of canvas friezes depicting the personal exploits of each artist in his own primitive style. Today's decor is alpine in its motif, with plaques representing each of the Swiss cantons and Swiss crests on guestroom doors. Without doubt, the "forest lobby," with its colorful fireplace, unusual galleries and great west windows has to be one of the most attractive in our national parks.

Scenic Advantages

Draped as it is along the shoreline of Swiftcurrent Lake, the Many Glacier Hotel possesses a location unequalled in the world of American scenery. More than a panorama, it is a cyclorama, a complete scenic circle with Swiftcurrent Lake as its central point.

Directly east is Mt. Wynn with its interesting overthrust formations, and to the south Mt. Allen, huge and impressive. To the southwest rises awe-inspiring Mt. Gould with its great gabled roof, from which stretches northwestward that celebrated section of the continental divide known as the Garden Wall. Looming above Swiftcurrent's western shore, sentry-like are Grinnell Point and Mt. Grinnell itself behind it. Toward the northwest, lofty Mt. Wilbur buries its head in the clouds, while stalwart Mt. Henkel and Mt. Altyn to the north complete the circle of giants.

Across the lake from the hotel is the Swiftcurrent Motor Inn, with its comfortable cabins, restaurant, store and curio shop.[13] This facility lies close to the trails that lead over Swiftcurrent Pass and to Iceberg and Ptarmigan Lakes. Nearby also are the Swiftcurrent Campground and the Many Glacier ranger station. There is no year-round village, and no one spends the winter in the area except the hotel custodian.

Visitor Facilities At Lake McDonald

While the Great Northern was moving with its extensive program of developing suitable hotel accommodations on the eastern side of the Park, there had been similar progress in the Lake McDonald area. The small Snyder hotel built near the head of the lake in the late nineties had been replaced by J. E. Lewis during the winter of 1913-1914 with the Lake McDonald Lodge, long referred to simply as "Lewis's."[14] Originally consisting of 65 rooms and 16 cabins, its facilities have subsequently been expanded to take care of present day requirements.

This alpine-style lodge lies nestled on the eastern shore of Lake McDonald, approximately two miles from its upper end. It is connected with the south end and with Belton (West Glacier) on the railroad, 11 miles away, by excellent highway. It represents the last bastion of hospitality for those travelers headed by automobile over Logan Pass, or by trail over Gunsight Pass. It is likewise the departure point for those who would visit Avalanche Lake or Sperry Glacier.

Development During Pre-Park Period

Lake McDonald is not only the Park's largest lake and one of its most beautiful, but also one of its most accessible. Soon after the arrival, in 1891, of the Great Northern at Belton, only three miles to the south, its development as a resort began at both ends of the lake. The great activity, of course, was concentrated at Apgar, near the lake's lower end, where today there are a number of overnight facilities, including the ultra-modern Village Inn. However, by 1895 the previously mentioned Snyder Hotel had been completed near the lake's upper end, and it became necessary to have transportation facilities by water, as well as by land, including the providing of saddle horses for hire.[15]

Change In Operation

Like the other large hotels of the Park, the Lake McDonald Lodge is operated by Greyhound Food Management Corporation, a subsidiary of the Greyhound Corporation of Phoenix. It was in February, 1930 that the Great Northern Railway, through a subsidiary, the Glacier Park Hotel Company, purchased the property from its original owner, J.E. Lewis, including 285 acres along the lake. It was then sold to the National Park Service for something over $150,000.[16] As a part of the agreement, the latter then leased it back to the Glacier Park Hotel Company, which continued to operate the hotel for the next three decades. In 1961, the operation was taken over by Don Hummel, who in turn was succeeded in 1981 by the present operator.

Like the Park's other major hostelries, Lake McDonald Lodge is distinctively alpine in structure and styling. Above its lobby floor, huge bark-lined logs of redcedar rise three stories to the roof. The lobby itself, though of lesser dimensions than those of the sister hotels, seems to bring the out-of-doors inside. With its huge fireplace[17] and abundance of pelts and mounted heads looking down from every direction, it is strongly reminiscent of a great hunting lodge. The attractive dining hall and veranda overlook the grassy slope leading down to the lake, as well as the lake itself and its pine-clad western shore.

Visitor Accommodations On The Canadian Side

The need for a hotel of quality in the Waterton Lakes area was apparent long before 1926, when the Great Northern Railway began construction of a Swiss-type facility at the north end of the upper lake. This hostelry, the International Park's fourth major one, is called the "Prince Of Wales." Seven stories in height, it is situated upon high ground nearly 100 feet above lake level. From this extraordinary vantage point, the southward vista extends the greater part of the length of the beautiful lake.

Legend has it that the idea for the building of the Prince of Wales Hotel was also a concept of the Great Northern's imaginative board chairman, Louis W. Hill, and came to him in the course of a visit to Waterton Lakes shortly after Glacier became a park.[18] When he viewed the eminence at the north end of the lake and the incomparable vista that it provided, he made up his mind that it deserved a hotel that would compare favorably with those elsewhere in the park.

Difficulties In Building The Prince

Construction did not get under way until 1926 and the hotel was not opened for business until July 25, 1927, a full year after ground was broken. The logistics again were almost insuperable since the railhead at Cardston, Alberta was 33 miles away and the roads were unimproved. Between these basic obstacles and the extraordinary weather conditions during the fall and winter of 1926, it was difficult to get the boilers and other heavy equipment to the building site.[19] Repeated changes of plans during the course of construction, including an increase in height from the originally intended three stories to seven, added to the problems, delayed the completion, and more than tripled the cost.

All of the trouble has proven to be well worthwhile, for the Prince of Wales is not only a hotel worthy to go with the great trio on the American side, but it boasts a site of incredible beauty, second only to that at Many Glacier. To the north, from its windows, can be seen the lower lakes of the Waterton chain, and their connecting waterways, the Bosphorus and the Dardanelles. To the south, the magnificent view extends across the international boundary to Mt. Cleveland and other giants of the American Park's northern sector. Immediately below and to the right lies Waterton Townsite, a comfortable village that has been a part of the Canadian national park for more than the period of its existence as such.

Auxiliary Facilities

Except for the Prince of Wales Hotel, all of Louis Hill's original construction program had been completed by 1917, when the south wing was added at Many Glacier Hotel. As travel patterns began to change in the late 1930's, some of the chalets were phased out and later razed, including those at Cut Bank, St. Mary, Sun Camp, and all but the store at Two Medicine.[20] When the Many Glacier chalets burned in the great fire of 1936, they were not replaced.[21] The tent camp facilities at various points were discontinued at about the same time.

There are, of course, other facilities that more adequately serve today's needs. In addition to the previously mentioned Swiftcurrent Motor Inn near Many Glacier Hotel, a similar installation, the Rising Sun Motor Inn, is located on the north shore of upper Lake St. Mary. Facilities for hikers and horsemen continue to be provided by the mountain chalets at Granite Park and near Sperry Glacier, both of which are reachable only by trail.[22] Dozens of excellent campgrounds for the use of motorists make it easy to spend time in the Park on an economy budget, while the "great log lodges" provide the type of service desired by those with more expensive tastes.

Skyland Camps

Unique in the Park's history of travel accommodations was a group of facilities once located on the upper west side of the continental divide. Called Skyland Camps, they were operated by the Culver Military Academy of Culver, Indiana, with Colonel (later General) L. R. Gignilliat as the moving force. Opened in the summer of 1922, their headquarters were at the foot of Bowman Lake, with auxiliary tent camps at Upper and Lower Kintla Lakes. While they served primarily as a camp for boys, their facilities were available to the public when not in use by the boys. A central chalet of logs, called Rainbow Lodge, served as dining room, recreational hall and winter storehouse. The sleeping quarters were tents with wooden floors. Other facilities included a

Forest Lobby, Glacier Park Lodge
Courtesy Burlington Northern

Sperry Chalet dining room and kitchen with Mrs.
Anderson on the porch
Photo by Mel Ruder

Lake McDonald Lodge
Photo by Walt Dyke, courtesy Burlington
Northern

Spectacular setting of the Prince of Wales Hotel
on Waterton Lake
Courtesy Burlington Northern

store, icehouse, shower room and fleet of row boats. Saddle horses were available for those who wished them.[23]

This was the program during the early years when the project seemed headed for success. After a few seasons, however, insufficient patronage, growing out of poor management and a difficult access road, made the venture unprofitable, and the camps were obliged to close in 1929. Thereafter, except for occasional use by the Park rangers, by a group of Eagle scouts, by members of the Geological Survey, and by a CCC encampment (1934), the facilities remained unused until 1940, when all but Rainbow Lodge were razed. Now serving as the Bowman Lake Ranger Station, the former Lodge is all that remains today of this interesting but ill-fated venture.[24]

Young hikers resting near Granite Park Chalet with Heaven's Peak at the right
Courtesy Burlington Northern

Operation Of The Park Hotels

The lodging facilities of Glacier Park are presently operated by an organization known as Glacier Park, Inc. The principal owner, Don Hummel, once served as a ranger in some of the national parks, thus developing a deep interest in the system. As opportunities presented themselves, through companies under his control, he acquired the primary concessions in various of our western parks, including Yosemite National Park.[25] Control of the Glacier Park operation, including the Prince of Wales Hotel at Waterton Lake, was assumed in 1961. Mr. Hummel has always regarded such a concession as an opportunity to give the traveling public the best possible service, without regard to the amount of profit therefrom.

When the Glacier Park facilities were taken over from the Great Northern Railway, they were a losing operation. To show a profit on a three-months-a-year basis at government-fixed rates is a difficult feat. However, today the company's indebtedness to the Great Northern is nearly paid off and the business is showing a slight profit. Of course, there is long deferred and much needed maintenance for all Park structures, particularly at Many Glacier Hotel. Nevertheless, certain improvements, including a large swimming pool at the Glacier Park Hotel, have been added.

Staffing Of Facilities

Recruitment of seasonal employees is handled by Glacier Park, Inc. from its Tucson, Arizona headquarters during the off-season. While a staff of less than 900 employees is needed, job applications average between 12,000 and 15,000 per annum and many employees, of course, are anxious to return for subsequent seasons. Because of this favorable hiring situation, it is possible for the company to screen carefully all job applicants through the use of questionaires and photographs, thus assuring, so far as possible by such means, high-class as well as talented people. The program has been very successful in the procurement of waiters, waitresses, bellmen, chambermaids and other hotel personnel who also have abilities in the field of entertainment.

The season's schedule at Many Glacier calls for the maintenance crew to move in on the 1st of May to get the plant in physical shape for operation. The first members of the summer hotel crew arrive on June 1st and are engaged in "opening" work through the 8th. On the 9th, the manager holds the first orientation meeting of employees. Official opening day is usually the 13th, although sometimes an early convention is booked prior to that date.

Park Hotel Entertainment

Mr. Ian Tippet, now Executive Director of personnel for the Park's hotels, is responsible for one of the most delightful features of any visit to the Park, including the Prince of Wales Hotel at Waterton Lake. Tippet has been 31 years with the Park's concession operation, most of them as manager at Many Glacier. A musician himself, he early realized the pleasure that could be provided to guests if all, or some of the employees were gifted musically.

About 1960 he began to recruit college students, many of them music majors, who were happy to spend a summer at Many Glacier as waiters, chambermaids, kitchen helpers, etc., with an opportunity to display their musical talents in the lobby during evening hours. Commencing in 1960, they staged for more than twenty summers well-known Broadway/London musicals, including the following:

1961	Oklahoma
1962	The Boy Friend
1963	Brigadoon
1964	Carousel
1965	South Pacific
1966	Guys and Dolls
1967	How to Succeed in Business
1968	Fiorello
1969	Three Penny Opera
1970	Little Mary Sunshine
1971	The Fantastiks and I Do, I Do
1972	Barefoot in the Park and You're A Good Man, Charlie Brown
1973	Fiddler on the Roof
1974	The Music Man
1975	One Hundred and Ten in the Shade
1976	Promises, Promises
1977	Company
1978	You're A Good Man (second time)
1979	Half a Sixpence
1980	The Fantastiks (second time)
1981	Brigadoon (second time)
1982	How to Succeed in Business (second time)
1983	Kiss Me Kate

Musicals were discontinued at Many Glacier in order that more talented employees could be added at all four large hotels with evening entertainment under an entertainment director at each.

Other Programs

Sunday is a day when interdenominational services are held at the hotels and principal campgrounds throughout the Park, under the direction of employees recruited from various seminaries and divinity schools throughout the country.[28] At Many Glacier, on Sunday evenings, commencing with the first Sunday in

July, it has been customary to present a vocal or pianoforte concert, perhaps by one of the waiters or other employee of exceptional ability. It has also long been the custom at the Many Glacier Hotel to have some kind of entertainment nearly every night of the week. It may be a so-called "Hootenanny Night," featuring a variety of vocal and instrumental numbers. Other nights may be devoted to community singing, to the showing of motion pictures or to other programs, with Saturday evening set aside for dancing. Each performer holds down a regular job at the hotel, and must find time on his own for rehearsal of personal numbers or with one or another of the groups.

Notes For Chapter 16

[1]There were no facilities at all on the eastern side of the new park, while on the western side there were only a few rental cabins at the foot of Lake McDonald and the small Snyder hotel at its head. Facilities were needed in most of the eastern valleys as well as near the continental divide.

[2]See article entitled "The Glacier Park Hotels, Chalets and Cabin Camps," by H. R. Wiecking, appearing in the 1948 edition of the "Drivers' Manual" (see note 15, Chapter 6, supra) at pages 57 and 58.

[3]"Through The Years In Glacier National Park," by Donald H. Robinson, at page 64. In reference to the Many Glacier chalets, see article cited in Note 2 above, by H. R. Wiecking at page 59.

[4]The Glacier Park Hotel was built on 160 acres of land which, by a special Act of Congress, Louis W. Hill was authorized to buy from the Blackfeet. This was Chapter 37 (S 4216, 62nd Congress) of the Laws of 1911-1912, approved February 10, 1912. The architects were Thomas D. Mc-Mahon and S. L. Bartlett, of Chicago, and the contractor was E. G. Evensta Construction Company of Minneapolis. The section housing the lobby, dining room, and 61 guest rooms was erected in 1912-1913. The annex with 111 rooms, together with the present kitchen, the employees' quarters, the powerhouse and the laundry were added in the winter of 1913-1914. See page 59 of article entitled "The Glacier Park Hotels, et al," supra.

[5]James J. Hill, the "Empire Builder," was actually born on September 16, 1838. For a more complete description of the great celebration held on June 15, 1913, see chapter 13, supra, entitled "Godfather to Glacier," at page 112.

[6]Article entitled "The Glacier Park Hotels, et al," supra, at page 59.

[7]The hotel site (see note 4 above) was purchased from Horace Clarke, father of John Clarke, the deaf-mute Indian woodcarver.

[8]In 1950 the name of the village near the Glacier Park Hotel was officially changed from "Midvale" to "East Glacier Park,"usually shortened to "East Glacier" or simply "East." However, the railroad declined to concur, and its depot still bears the name of Glacier Park Station. See "Through The Years," supra, at page 79.

[9]According to its manager, the Many Glacier Hotel has a total of 234 rentable rooms, with house counts running as high as 490 guests.

[10]"Through The Years," supra, at page 65.

[11]"The Glacier Park Hotels, et al," supra, at page 59 of the 1948 edition of the "Drivers' Manual" (see note 15, Chapter 6, supra).

[12]As originally constructed, a part of the present gift shop space was occupied by a large conical fountain of stone that rose from its base on the floor below and well into the lobby proper. Captive trout disported in the shadows of the tiny pools surrounding the foot of the fountain, while attractive spiral staircases rose on either side of it. The fountain was removed in 1957 to provide additional space for the gift shop.

[13]The forerunner of the Motor Inn was opened in 1933, and augmented in the next three years. However, the great fire of August 31, 1936 destroyed 31 units. These were replaced in 1937 and the coffee shop was added in 1941.

[14]"Through The Years," supra, at pages 63 and 64. J. E. Lewis, subsequent to building the hotel and cabins in 1914, removed all of the cabins and operated only the hotel until it was sold to the Park Service in 1930. The present cottages and auxiliary quarters have been added since that time.

[15]Idem, at page 62.

[16]Idem, at pages 67 and 68.

[17]Charles Russell, famed Montana cowboy artist, maintained a summer cabin and studio near Lake McDonald in the early years of the Park. He was a friend of J. E. Lewis, and is said to have scratched the pictographs on the base and hearth of the hotel fireplace, according to an article by H. R. Wiecking entitled "The Glacier Park Hotels, Chalets and Cabin Camps," at page 57 of the 1948 edition of the Drivers' Manual" (see page 15, Chapter 6, supra).

[18]According to the diary of Kootenai Brown, Hill's visit occurred on or about September 30, 1913 when he came there "from St. Paul, Minnesota in three days in an automobile." Undoubtedly, Hill brought the automobile with him from St. Paul in his private train, and only drove from East Glacier to Waterton via the new road along the east side of the Lewis range (now the Blackfeet Highway), part of which had just been completed the preceding month. The Hill visit is reported at pages 199-200 of the book entitled "Kootenai Brown, His Life and Times," by William Rodney.

[19]Most of the equipment was made in Canada, but the large two-story window frame in the lobby, permitting an unobstructed southerly view, was fabricated in England. Much of the furniture was constructed on the site from British Columbia cedar. See article by H. R. Wiecking, supra, at page 59 of the 1948 edition of the "Drivers' Manual" (see note 15, Chapter 6, supra).

[20]The smaller cabins of the Two Medicine chalet group were built in 1911, while the large dormitory and dining hall followed in 1914. See article by H. R. Wiecking, supra, at page 59 of the 1948 edition of the "Drivers' Manual" (see note 15, Chapter 6, supra.)

[21]Idem, at page 59. See, also, "Through The Years," supra, at page 85.

[22]The Granite Park Chalet was completed in 1915 or 1916.

[23]See article by Michael J. Ober in MONTANA, the magazine of WESTERN HISTORY, Volume XXIII, Number three, Summer of 1973, at pages 30-39. See also, "Through The Years," supra, at pages 68-69.

[24]Idem.

[25]Mr. Hummel's earlier interests included the primary concessions at Mt. Lassen National Park in California and at Mt. McKinley National Park in Alaska, as well as a controlling interest in the Yosemite Park and Curry Company. His interests in the latter two have been terminated.

[26]The season of 1975 was Mr. Tippet's 23rd in Glacier Park. After graduating in 1950 from the London Hotel School, he was connected for a time with the Hyde Park Hotel and the Grosvenor House in London. In 1953 he became manager of the Lake McDonald Lodge and after serving a few years there, transferred to Many Glacier.

[27]During the school year Mr. Stephens is a member of the faculty of music at the University of Nebraska.

[28]These services are under the auspices of "A Christian Ministry In The National Parks" and there are usually 25 or more student volunteers, recruited from various seminaries and divinity schools, participating in the program in Glacier National Park.

The Glacier Park Lodge

Courtesy Burlington Northern

Many Glacier Hotel looking toward Mt. Wilbur

Courtesy Burlington Northern

Chapter 17
THE "DUDE-WRANGLERS"

With its sensational and far-flung network of mountain trails, Glacier National Park offers visitors a choice of hiking or riding; and because in days gone by so many chose the latter it came to be known as the "saddle-horse park."[1] In some seasons, as many as 10,000 visitors elected to take advantage of this means of sightseeing. To cope with such a peak-load, more than a thousand horses were needed, a business of such dimensions as to make its operator the largest outfit of its kind in the world.[2] For more than a quarter of a century preceding World War II this record-breaking entity monopolized the furnishing of horses and guides in Glacier.[3] Its name was the Park Saddle Horse Company.[4]

Those were the days, of course, when the company was the beneficiary of the extraordinary publicity campaigns mounted on behalf of the park by the Great Northern Railway. All of the literature which it issued between the two world wars featured the delights of trail travel and carried full particulars concerning "saddlehorse, pack horse and guide rates." Among such publications during the 1930's was an attractive 30-page brochure entitled "Trail Riding In Glacier National Park,"[5] illustrated with single and double-page pictures of horses and riders on park trails, replete with descriptions of "The Triangle Trip," the "North Circle Trip," and other similar safaris. It made the saddle horse mode of travel almost an imperative with such lyrical sales pitches as the following:

"The camps and trails in Glacier National Park combine to make a Paradise for those who love the out-of-doors. You can spend a summer here and not see it all. You'll be riding a trail in the shade of silent pines and presently you'll hear a melodic murmur, now rising, now falling with the wind. Your guide will turn off the main trail, leading the way into a canyon between walls that rise like the Empire State Building. It's dark and cool and fresh down there. Then all of a sudden you swing around a bend in full sight of the sun . . . shining down through a notch, spotlighting the foaming torrent at your feet. You see rainbows in the mist. You see green-gold patterns in the pungent gloom. . . . You hate to leave when the guide finally says, 'We've got to get going'."[6]

Promotional Procedures

Those were also the days when the hotels, operated by a Great Northern subsidiary, joined hands with the saddle horse company to promote the horseback operation effectively. Prominently situated in each of the lobbies of the large hotels was a transportation desk or counter manned by a knowledgeable individual whose business it was, not only to dispense general information concerning the park to all and sundry, but especially to arrange saddle horse trips to the surrounding beauty spots. The hotel guests were made to feel that scenery viewing from the top of a horse, under the leadership and watchful care of well-informed guides, was something of a romantic adventure as well as the easiest way to do it.

In those days the most colorful characters in Glacier were undoubtedly the "dude-wranglers," or trail guides for the saddle horse parties. With few exceptions they were of the cowboy type, and natives of the region. The chief requisite of the guide, or self-styled "dude-wrangler," was an intimate knowledge of horses and their handling; and on this score, of course, the cowpuncher was eminently qualified. On other requirements for the job, he could readily adapt himself.

The chief difference between the ordinary cowpoke and the Glacier Park variety of guide lay in their appearance and apparel. The everyday type of cowpunchers wore little or no special regalia; they were hard-working ranch hands and, with the exception of a battered broad-brimmed hat and a pair of boots, their raiment very much resembled that of an ordinary farm hand. Not so the Glacier Park guides, for Solomon in all his glory was not arrayed like these. As with the cowboys of the movies of that era, the Park guide prized decorative finery as an adjunct of his trade, having learned that the customers admired that sort of thing. Also, the special wearing apparel did quite a bit for his sense of vanity.

"Dude-Wrangler" Duds

Scarcely any guide would be without a pair of "chaps," or "woollies" — leather breeches usually faced with wool, and long a sovereign possession of the genus cowboy. Another essential part of the costume was the neckerchief — a silk one at that — gaily colored and clasped about the throat by any means that the wearer's ingenuity might devise. Buckskin and beaded shirts, though well liked, were not numerous, being regarded as something of a luxury. Large leather belts, three to four inches wide and heavily studded with nickel or silver, were highly prized possessions, while leather wristlets of similar adornment were not infrequently worn.

The cowboy guide was usually something of a crank about his hat, boots and spurs. He would order a beaver hat made up by Stetson, wait several weeks or months for delivery, and pay from twenty to forty pre-depression dollars for it. He was equally fussy about his boots, ordering them from his favorite bootmaking firm at a fabulous price. He had small feet, your genuine cowpuncher, and it was not unusual for a strapping six-footer to wear a number five or six boot. A set of spurs would cost anywhere from twelve to twenty-five dollars, their owner insisting that they were silver-mounted and of the finest workmanship. Every genuine cowboy owned his own saddle and outfit, some of them rather ornate. The bridle, for example, might be woven of brilliantly colored horse hair, and the bit might be fashioned of sterling silver.

Although something of a dandy in his own way, the old-time cowboy guide usually possessed a frank, open-hearted, friendly disposition. Generous to a fault, he was often a ne'er-do-well, spending his summers in the Park and then drifting to some other part of the country. His restlessness kept him from settling in a permanent location or steady job; and, of course, there were sometimes other reasons, such as a weakness for poker or a pronounced liking for a wee bit o' scotch. He valued money lightly, and seldom was able to retain much of it.

Super Guide

Never having seen a cowboy of any description before I came to serve on the transportation desk at Many Glacier Hotel in the summer of 1918, I was totally unprepared upon arrival to meet the most colorful guide of them all — Cal Peck. He was the first man I saw on entering the hotel, a huge, bronzed individual that I could only regard with awe and astonishment. A black beaver hat of the ten gallon variety shaded his well tanned face. Round his neck was a bright, pink silk handkerchief, held in place by a contrivance of bone. His broad shoulders and torso were encased in a beaded buckskin shirt, from which emanated a peculiar, leathery fragrance. Black woolly "chaps" and a pair of spurred cowboy boots completed his costume.

Fierce though he looked, Cal's hearty grip and pleasant manner soon filled me with reassurance. In his voice was all the nasal twang of the westerner, with some additional effects which must have been exclusively his own. Before the end of the summer we had become fast friends.

Peck had seen much of the western part of the United States. Over a period of 14 years he had guided at Lake Tahoe and at various national parks, including Yosemite and the Grand Canyon. For a time he had doubled in the movies for William S. Hart, then the idol of the westerns. His participation in rodeo bronc-riding had left him with an injury that forced him to abandon this type of activity. He subsequently became a ranger at the Grand Canyon, where he gained no little notoriety as the first man ever to spend his entire honeymoon at the bottom of the canyon.

"Dude-Wrangler's Diction

Peck's vocabulary was as colorful as his attire. To him, easterners were "tenderfeet," a tourist was a "dude," his wife a "dudess," his daughter a "dudine," and his children "didlets." The horse to be ridden by any of them was a "cayuse," laughingly guaranteed to be all right after the first eight or ten bucks. A horse unsafe for tourists was a "snake." The horse that was kept at the corral at night to be used at dawn in rounding up and driving in the main herd of ponies was the "jingle-horse," and the man who rode him for this purpose was the "jingler."

In Peck's lexicon, an expert horseman and cowhand was a "wrangler," or "horse-wrangler;" hence a guide became a "dude-wrangler." Grasping the pommel to prevent being thrown from the saddle was "pulling leather" — a disgraceful offense, disqualifying the perpetrator, if done in a riding competition.

Red Monkey Flowers near Logan Pass

Photo by Danny On

A Ptarmigan—the "parkbird" in winter garb.

Photo by Danny On

141

For the tenderfoot undertaking his first horseback experience, the pommel, of course, was a source of great comfort and security.

A hiking trip, in Peck's parlance, was an "ankle excursion." Canyon Creek, providing the outlet from Cracker Lake, was facetiously referred to as "Biscuit Creek," while Iceberg Lake was familiarly alluded to as "Icicle Lake." Anyone making the five-day trip to Lake McDonald and return by way of the circle trail was said to be going "around the horn." The figures representing the day's business were the "powder-sheet;" and so far as Cal was concerned, the coolness of the Glacier Park climate was best described as "nine months of winter and three months of damn cold weather."

Indian Guides

Many of the "dude-wranglers" were young Blackfeet from the adjoining reservation. Their familiarity with the park and with horses made them excellent guide-material. One of these was Frank Doney, a fine horseman who twice had won the broncho-riding contest at the Lewiston Round-up. Then there were Big Tom and Little Tom Jackson, full brothers. Their mother had named one of them Thomas and the other Tom, so that in later years people were obliged to distinguish them further according to size. Little Tom won the riding championship at the Browning Fair in 1917, defeating Tom Three-Persons who had previously won the world's championship at the Calgary Round-up of 1912. Big Tom Jackson won the bulldogging title at the same time (1917), downing his steer in fifty-seven seconds.

Memorable guides of the pre-Park era included James Willard Schultz and William Jackson, a grandson of Hugh Monroe, in the St. Mary and Swiftcurrent valleys; and Kootenai Brown and Joe Cosley in the Waterton-Belly River region. Among notables of the Park's early days were Tom Dawson, veteran frontiersman and one-time Royal Canadian Mountie; Jim Whilt, cowboy humorist and writer; and the hoary patriarch, Dad Dunham, often referred to as "the old man of the mountains."

Last of the old-time dude-wranglers was the venerable, bushy-bearded "Blackie" Dillon, veteran of a thousand days and nights on the trails, as well as a witty, charming raconteur. Blackie finally moved on to another job in 1965—that of "holding up" the stage-coaches at Knott's Berry Farm in southern California

Born in 1862, Tom Dawson's long life was both varied and colorful. An explorer of what is now Glacier Park in the latter part of the 19th century, he served a "dudewrangler" in the Park's early years as such.

Courtesy, Burlington Northern and Westward Ho Motel, Grand Forks, North Dakota

every few minutes to amuse the adults and frighten the kiddies. He passed away at Cut Bank, Montana at the age of 68 in August, 1975.

Functions Of The "Dude-Wrangler"

Usually the experienced guide had "wrangled" so many "dudes" that he was somewhat "fed up" with his occupation. The one or two kill-joys in every trail party were sure to wear his patience rather thin. On the other hand, the utter helplessness of the average tenderfoot tended to bring to the guide an awareness of a certain superiority, born of his own capability in the saddle. To his little flock on the trail, however, he was a competent shepherd, tutor, raconteur, comforter, disciplinarian, groom and valet, always prepared for any emergency that might arise.

The functions of Glacier's saddle horse guides were aptly summarized in a Great Northern Railway brochure entitled "Glacier National Park And The New Logan Pass Detour" under the caption "Paradise For Those Who Ride With Guides Who Know The Passwords:"

"The guides add a great deal to your enjoyment of this Land of Shining Mountains. They can answer questions pertaining to the geography, geology, animal life, Indian lore, forests, flowers and fish of Glacier Park. They act as reassurance to any timid member of the

Glacier Park guide and his horse
Courtesy Burlington Northern

party that you won't get lost. Then, too, they work. They build the noonday fire beside the trail, prepare the lunch and cook coffee that smells like manna from heaven. They tell you stories like true sons of Baron Munchausen. They know the passes and the passwords, and the park is an open sesame to you because of their presence."[7]

Unquestionably no one in the Park's history has done more to make sight-seeing exciting than the best of the old-time saddle-horse guides. That we shall ever see their likes again is unlikely, for the hey-day of trail-riding itself has come and gone, never to return. Along with other Glacier Park concessions, the Park Saddle Horse Company closed down its operation after the 1942 season, because of World War II and the financial problems which the resulting decline in business had entailed.[8] Other saddle horse concessionaires took over after the war and carried on at various locations throughout the Park. However, an era had come to an end, and things have never been the same so far as the saddle horse business in Glacier is concerned.

Why Trail Riding Has Diminished

Today, with well over a million annual visitors, travel to and through Glacier has been vastly multiplied. Yet the number of horses needed to meet total trail requirements is down to between 100 and 200, not that the joy of viewing the park on horseback is any less, but that many factors have combined to diminish and deglamorize that mode of travel.

To begin with, times and travelers have changed materially. An increasing percentage of today's Park visitors are youthful, vigorous,

and not too familiar with locomotion by horse. Moreover, hiking has come into vogue and backpacking has become a popular mode of trail travel, not in Glacier alone, but in similar areas all over America.[9] Also, the advent of the modern automobile and camper has brought a different group of visitors to Glacier, making it accessible to hundreds of thousands who never could have afforded it a generation ago. For many of these, an economy budget simply cannot be stretched to cover such unanticipated extras as saddle horse trips.

Other factors have affected the trail-riding picture. The tremendous cooperation and encouragement once accorded to the saddle horse concessionaire by the Great Northern's advertising department have become things of the past. No longer does the railroad publish beautifully illustrated brochures extolling the pleasures of trail-riding in the Park. No longer do those at the hotel information desks sell tickets for saddle horse trips or actively promote this type of sightseeing. Indeed, with the disappearance of the old-time guides and their colorful attire, picturesque speech and sly humor, something of glamour and romantic adventure has also vanished from the trail-riding scene.

Physical Differences

The Park itself has changed in some respects. Completion of the Going-To-The-Sun Highway, together with the improvement of other Park roads and campground facilities, has greatly expanded the areas and views available to the motoring public. At the same time, it has made them so accessible and so enjoyable to those in their own cars that there is a substantial decrease in the incentive or need to make use of saddle horse facilities.

Ascendancy of the automobile as a mode of travel has led to the elimination of many of the chalets originally designed as overnight facilities for trail travel. Meeting this fate were the chalets located at Two Medicine (except for a store), Cut Bank, St. Mary, Going-To-The-Sun (Sun Camp) and Many Glacier, as well as the so-called permanent tent camps at Fifty Mountain, Gunsight Lake, Goathaunt and Cosley (Crossley) Lake. The passing of these facilities has, in turn, had the effect of doing away with the three-day and five-day circle trips that once were popular, and thus of limiting trail riding largely to one-day trips.

Ecology has become more of a factor. Saddle and pack horses not only clutter up trails for those who follow on foot, but also create

A gentleman elk

Photo by Danny On

something of an erosion problem for both trails and camping areas, particularly in wilderness backcountry through which large parties sometimes pass, followed by substantial numbers of pack animals necessary to their support. Consequently, some trails are being closed to horse travel, while limitations are being placed upon the use of others.[10]

Low Profile

Last but not least among the factors which have adversely affected the saddlehorse operation is the fact that its visibility has become minimal. In earlier days at Many Glacier, for example, all saddlehorse trips began and ended immediately in front of the hotel's main entrance, where they attracted much interest and attention. They have since been relegated to a location where they are not visible from the hotel. This low profile is maintained in other ways. Saddlehorse representatives are not permitted to solicit business in the hotels, and the saddlehorse concessionaires lack the facilities for making their services adequately known to the potential customers in the hotels, motor inns and campgrounds. Consequently there are few advance bookings and the business is far less than could be expected from the large numbers of Park visitors.

Still A "Saddle Horse Park"

Although the volume of saddle horse usage is not what it used to be, this method of sight-seeing continues to be an important Park feature and a delightful highlight for those who take advantage of it. Most of the trails over which as many as 10,000 visitors rode each summer prior to World War II still await the rider, as well as the hiker. The horses are just as safe and easy to ride, the rates are reasonable, and the views from the high places provide the same thrills.

In short, the trail-riding scene is still very much there for those who enjoy the equine bit. You may have to ask a ranger or inquire at the hotel information desk for the corral or the location of the local saddle horse concessionaire; but you will find satisfactory mounts and guides, whether you have in mind a two-hour jaunt to a nearby lake, or a two-day Granite Park trip. And you will also find that viewing Glacier's superlative scenery from the vantage point of a saddle, with a breath-taking picture around every turn, is trail travel de luxe.

At all events, whether afoot or on horseback, the trail's the thing. As the superintendent of the Park once told a visiting editor of the National Geographic Magazine:

"You'll have to do plenty of hiking and horseback riding if you want to know Glacier. We've tried to preserve the Park's fragile wilderness beauty; so there are only 70 miles of paved highway compared with more than 1,000 miles of trail.[11] My advice is to get out on the trails—only go easy at first."[12]

Glacier Notes For Chapter 17

[1]See Chapter 14, supra, entitled "Trails And Early Routes," at page 117.
[2]"Through The Years In Glacier National Park," by Donald H. Robinson, at page 70.
[3]Idem, at page 71.
[4]As far back as the turn of the century, saddle horse and pack service had been provided in the Lake McDonald area by various operators. After establishment of the Park as such, service on both sides of the Divide began to be furnished by a number of independent operators under permit from the Department of the Interior. In the year 1915, under the leadership of W. N. Noffsinger, a Kalispell, Montana attorney, a number of these small concessioners were merged into the Park Saddle Horse Company with their base ranch on the St. Mary River east of Babb, Montana. They then became the sole and official purveyor of saddle horse services in the Park. When Noffinger died in 1924, his son, George, took over the business and continued it until 1943, when he requested the National Park Service to terminate the contract because of financial reverses. See "Through The Years," supra, at pages 70-71.
[5]This 1934 publication contained 31 photographs of Glacier Park scenes, 12 of them featuring saddle horse guides. Included was a complete list of all the available saddle horse trips, together with a page of "useful information on trail riding" and a "Trail Rider's Map of Glacier National Park."
[6]This was the commentary below the double-page spread on pages 16-17 of the brochure, showing a guide and party of two at Dawn Mist Falls above a caption reading "Sunlight Weaves A Pattern In the Pungent Green-Gold Gloom."
[7]This was the descriptive comment appearing at page 11 of the brochure under the picture of a typical "dude-wrangler" and his mount, with the Sun Camp chalets and Lake St. Mary in the background, circa 1935.
[8]"Through The Years," supra, at pages 70-71.
[9]See, for example, page 807 of the June, 1973 issue of the National Geographic Magazine, quoting two purveyors of saddle horse service at Mount Assiniboine Park in Canada as saying: "Fifteen years ago hardly anybody walked these trails. Now backpackers, who bring in their own supplies, outnumber mounted travelers."
[10]Commencing with 1972, various restrictions have been placed upon horse utilization in the Park, including a ban on their use on the Iceberg Lake and Grinnell Glacier trails. With respect to backcountry travel, wranglers are now required to carry with them all feed needed for their "string," and they may no longer be tethered near camp at night, or be turned loose to graze in the meadows, thus adding considerably to the cost and inconvenience of such travel.
[11]The comments were only intended as an approximation. Glacier's trail mileage totals 910, of which less than 600 are intended for the use of Park visitors. The paved road mileage mentioned obviously referred only to roads entirely within Park boundaries.
[12]These comments by Superintendent Emmert appeared in an article entitled "Many-Splendored Glacierland," by George W. Long, appearing at page 589 of the May, 1956 issue of the National Geographic Magazine.

Leaving Many Glacier Hotel on Trip to Iceberg Lake

Photo by Kabel

With Pack Horses in Glacier Park

Photo by Walt Dyke

Party on the trail in the scenic Many Glacier area

Courtesy Burlington Northern

Party heading for Iceberg Lake with Swiftcurrent Lake in background

Photo by Kabel

Chapter 18
VISITORS: DISTINGUISHED AND OTHERWISE

Travel figures have shown a steady rise in the number of Glacier Park visitors, the annual total in recent years having exceeded the million mark.[1] They come from near and far, by car, by train and by air. Canadians from all provinces mingle with Americans from every state, not to mention a sprinkling of people from foreign shores. Most of them are on a holiday or recreational tour; a few come on business or official duty.

The visitors to Glacier get what they look for, whether it be scenery, vacation fun, resort luxury, or back-to-nature simplicity. Some view the Park through the windows of automobiles and deluxe hotels; others use the public campgrounds, reveling in the joys of wood smoke and good fellowship. Disciples of Izaak Walton find excellent fishing, free from the need for a license. Hikers take to the hundreds of miles of Park trails, and alpinists find the many peaks a challenge to their climbing skills. For those with geological inclinations, the Park is a living textbook, while animal and bird lovers find scores of interesting species to study. There are horses for the trails and launches for lake travel — the visitor can even bring his own boat, if he wishes.

In the Park's earlier days, nearly all visitors arrived by train and enjoyed the alpine atmosphere of its chalets and great hotels. As time went on, the personal automobile became a common mode of travel, new and improved highways were built to and through the Park, and attractive campgrounds were established throughout its environs. Consequently, the volume of visitors has been multiplied many times over, with most of them traveling in their own vehicles and making use of the excellent camping facilities. The arrivals include a surprising number of cars bearing licenses from Europe, Japan and Hawaii.

Types Of Travelers

The traveling public are pretty much a cross-section of the general public. Doubtless there will always be a certain number of eccentrics, such as the middle-aged couple from Los Angeles who traveled by car so that they could bring along her special pet, a four-foot alligator named Victor. They smuggled Victor up to their third floor room at Many Glacier Hotel where, presumably, he took his meals and slept in one bed while the master and mistress occupied the other.

There are always the "pernickety" folks who find themselves unable to accept some of the conditions that may be imposed by trail travel. For example, one man who was contemplating a horseback trip from Many Glacier to Granite Park and return, involving an overnight stay there, recoiled in horror when he learned that the Chalet, located near the summit of the continental divide, could not provide him with the luxury of his customary morning bath. A woman considering the same trip abandoned the idea when she could not be assured that Heaven's Peak beyond the divide would be snow-capped.

Distinguished Visitors

Visiting celebrities, on the other hand, are rarely the creators of problems. No records of their identities are kept, but unofficial sources disclose a visiting list that through the years has included royalty and presidents, distinguished members of our executive, legislative and judicial branches of government, foreign dignitaries, eminent writers, scholars and actors, as well as others of national and international note.

The first members of a royal family to visit the Park were Queen Marie of Romania and her children, Princess Ileana and Prince Nicholas, who stopped briefly at Glacier Park Station on November 8, 1926, and were welcomed by a committee of Blackfeet Indians. In a circle of tepees on the lawn of the Glacier Park Hotel, the queen and her children were adopted into the Blackfeet tribe, given appropriate Indian names and presented with buckskin garments and war bonnets.[2]

Royalty again visited the Park on June 3-5, 1939 in the persons of Crown Prince Olav and Princess Martha of Norway.[3] It was 18 years tha the prince ascended his country s ... to become King Olav V.

In the late 1880's, many years before Glacier became a park, the region was visited by Thomas Baring, first Earl of Northbrook, and other prominent members of the well-known English banking family by that name. They hunted along the north shore of Upper Lake St. Mary under the guidance of Joseph Kipp and James Willard Schultz, and Baring Creek and Baring Falls, both in that area, were named for them.[4]

Presidential Visitors

Among the nation's chief executives, Franklin Delano Roosevelt passed through the Park with his official party on June 5, 1934. Entering on the west side of the Park, they were driven over Logan Pass to St. Mary and south to the Two Medicine Chalets where the president and Mrs. Roosevelt were inducted into the Blackfeet tribe. He was presented by the Indians with a peace pipe, supposedly the one that had been used to seal the 1855 treaty at Judith Basin, Montana, between the United States and the Blackfeet Nation. He then made one of his celebrated fireside chats from the Two Medicine Chalet, and was driven to Glacier Park Station to board his special train for the return trip to Washington, D.C.[5]

Although no other president has made a trip **through** the Park, there have been several "close calls." Richard Nixon, in the course of a brief visit to the Flathead area in September, 1971, was scheduled to make a helicopter flight over the Park, but lack of visibility due to an extensive overcast necessitated a last-minute cancellation. On his last official trip as president, Harry Truman made a brief railway stop on September 30, 1952, at West Glacier where he made a talk on behalf of Adlai Stevenson, the then Democratic candidate for president.[6] Theodore Roosevelt, whose final term as president ended in 1909, is said to have visited the St. Mary area in 1910, but there is no record of his having entered what is now the Park.

Other National Figures

Among members of the Supreme Court to visit the Park have been Chief Justice Earl Warren and Associate Justice Harlan Stone, who later became Chief Justice. Warren has been a frequent visitor to the St. Mary area and nearby Duck Lake. Stone and his wife spent a two-week vacation in the Park in 1939 and were inducted, like many other notables, into the Blackfeet tribe.[7] An earlier associate justice, Pierce Butler, visited the Park in July, 1925, and attended the dedication of the Stevens Monument at Marias Pass.[8]

Cabinet members visiting the Park included Franklin K. Lane, Harold L. Ickes and Douglas McKay, all of whom were serving as Secretaries of the Interior at the times of their respective visits in 1919, 1934 and 1953.[9] Henry L. Stimson, who had held various cabinet posts during the years 1911 to 1945, was a visitor to the future Park in the 1890's, and one of its principal peaks still bears his name.[10]

Robert A. Taft, future senator from Ohio, was warmly greeted by a Blackfeet welcoming committee when he came to the Park in 1915.[11] Former Senator Burton K. Wheeler, a long-time summer resident at Lake McDonald, was among those who escorted President Roosevelt through Glacier in 1934.[12] With Senator Walsh, also of Montana, Wheeler had the unique experience of seeing a mountain goat swim across Lake Elizabeth in the Belly River Valley.[13] Senator Harry F. Byrd of Virginia visited the Park and hiked over some of its trails in August, 1954.[14] J. Edgar Hoover, FBI chief, was a Park visitor in 1937, and was adopted into the Blackfeet tribe by a group of its chiefs.[15]

Executives And Diplomats

A notable event in Park history was the 52nd annual Governors' Conference held at Many Glacier Hotel on June 26-29, 1960. Except for those from Pennsylvania and Hawaii, all governors were in attendance, including those from Guam, Puerto Rico, American Samoa and the Virgin Islands. The session was monitored by 73 news agencies and representatives, for the convenience of which special telephone facilities had to be installed in the lobby. Principal speaker at the State Dinner on June 27th was John G. Diefenbacker, the prime minister of Canada. During their stay in the Park, the visitors were supplied by General Motors with 60 white Cadillacs and 140 Chevrolets.

During the month of August, 1970, Glacier Park was visited by a party of distinguished foreign diplomats and their families, including several of ambassadorial rank. The tour was sponsored by the nonprofit "Travel Program For Foreign Diplomats, Inc.," which invites members of foreign embassy staffs to visit interesting parts of the United States. The trip was made in 23 deluxe camper trailers, furnished through the courtesy of the manufacturer, as were the pickup trucks that provided the motive power.[16] Similar safaris in subsequent seasons have brought other foreign dignitaries to Glacier as a means of acquainting them with its many attractions.

Savants, Writers And Explorers

Among distinguished scholars to visit the area of the future Park, we have already noted Professors Raphael Pumpelly, Bailey Willis, L. W. Chaney and Lyman B. Sperry, all of whom spent much time there in the last two decades of the nineteenth century.[17] In 1949, James B. Conant, president of Harvard University, spent a month in the Park with his family, enthusiastically tramping over its wilderness trails.[18]

The region that is now the Park has long been a mecca for authors and writers, especially those who liked to write of the outdoors and the western frontier. Among early visitors in this category were George Bird Grinnell, James Willard Schultz, Walter McClintock,[19] John Muir, Emerson Hough, Hamlin Garland and Irvin S. Cobb. The first three named were all adopted Blackfeet and both Schultz and McClintock lived the tribal life for periods of time.

Lincoln Ellsworth, of polar expedition fame, was a Park aficionado. In 1911 he spent a month on Park trails, returning again in 1912 and 1926. On the latter occasion, Captain Roald Amundsen and his crew had just completed the first successful flight over the North Pole in the dirigible "Norge," and were on their way back from Alaska, accompanied by Ellsworth, who had sponsored the flight. The party made a brief stop at Glacier Park station en route to the east.[20]

In September, 1927, Charles A. Lindbergh visited the Park by air, traveling in his celebrated plane, the NX-211, with which he had spanned the Atlantic the preceding April. A part of his Montana itinerary called for him to fly from Butte to Helena, but he was anxious to have a look at Glacier Park. Accordingly, he made an unscheduled detour that took him over many of the peaks and lakes in its southeastern reaches. Having lingered as long as possible, feasting his eyes on the beauty of the Lewis Range, he reluctantly departed for Helena — perhaps the most distinguished visitor ever to do his sightseeing in Glacier exclusively by air.[21]

Visitors From Hollywood

With its spectacular scenery, the Park provides an unending series of superb settings for motion picture purposes and it is not surprising that a number of films have been made there, mainly in the St. Mary region. "Cattle Queen of Montana," featuring Barbara Stanwyck and Ronald Reagan, was shot there in 1953. In the following year, "Dangerous Mission" was filmed with a cast that included Victor Mature, Vincent Price, William Bendix and Piper Laurie. The action included scenes near Trick Falls and along Going-To-The-Sun Highway, with concluding sequences on the crevassed ice of Grinnell Glacier. There, after an exchange of gunfire and deeds of derring-do on the part of Mature, he rescued the heroine from the dastardly clutches of archvillain Price.

"All the Young Men," made by Ingemar Johansen near Lake St. Mary in 1959, starred Allen Ladd and its cast included Bobby Darrin, Sydney Poitier and Mort Sahl. As far back as 1928, westerns were filmed in this area, the stars of two silent pictures made that year, "Sioux Blood" and "Humming Wires," having been Elsie Janis and Tim McCoy.[22]

Gary Cooper, who had been born in Montana as Frank James Cooper, returned to his native state in 1957 and, on September 12th, in company with Governor J. Hugo Aronson, visited Glacier Park where he was inducted into the Blackfeet tribe as Chief Eagle Cloud. Continuing to Lake St. Mary and Logan Pass, he had the pleasure, without the use of field glasses, of seeing five mountain goats on the slopes of Mt. Oberlin.[23]

Dude-Ranch Visitors

One of the outstanding personages of many Glacier Park seasons was Howard Eaton who died in 1922. During several previous summers the arrival of his party was eagerly looked forward to for weeks in advance. It was the event of the season, enjoyed by all the folk of the Park and never, never forgotten by those so fortunate as to be members of one of his expeditions.

Howard Eaton was an unusual individual. In 1881 he had taken up ranch life with his brothers, Alden and Willis, in the Bad Lands of North Dakota,[24] but moved on in 1904 to the wilder and more western plains of Wyoming where their ranch was located near Wolf in the Grand Tetons.[25] There they went into the business of "dude-ranching," a "dude-ranch" being one that professionally demonstrates the life of the wild and woolly west for the edification of those who care to become paying customers.

From among the sojourners at the ranch, Uncle Howard used to rally his cohorts for an invasion of the domains of Glacier Park. Late in July the volunteers, numbering anywhere from fifty to one hundred and twenty-five, would proceed by train to East Glacier where guides and horses were available for the trek by special arrangement with the Park Saddle Horse Company.

Prince Of Guides

Despite his sixty-odd years, Howard Eaton always accompanied the party and personally took charge of its activities. He was more capable and energetic than any of his assistants, and his personality seemed to radiate through the entire caravan. With the pitching of camp, he became the life of the party, witty and refreshing; and with the coming of darkness and the gathering around the campfire, Howard always proved to be the most interesting raconteur of them all.

The Eaton Party came to have a fairly well mapped-out itinerary, from which few deviations were made from year to year. They traveled "on their own" so far as practicable. They were independent of all other parties and, to a large extent, of the hotels. As far as Many Glacier they carried a huge cook tent, as well as their own kitchen equipment and supplies. Simple but appetizing meals were served to a ravenous crowd after they had been summoned by the cook's "come and get it." Each person slept in an individual small tent, of which there were dozens clustered about the camp center. Beyond Many Glacier the party put up at the chalets and hotels.

The Eatonites were always a merry, fun-loving crowd and a hard day on the trail never dampened their ardor. They were a cosmopolitan group, made up of people from all parts of the country and from every stage of life. Howard used to declare that his parties contained folks from seven to seventy-seven years of age, and that frequently the two extremes proved to be the best travelers.

Howard himself was a jovial type, never lacking for a reply. While in conversation with him on his arrival at Many Glacier one summer, we were interrupted by a woman who had accompanied him through the Park in a previous year. She greeted him and commented upon the fact that he looked healthy.

"Oh yes," he replied in a trice, "beastly healthy—disgustingly so, in fact."

Celebrities Among The Eaton Visitors

The best-known member of any of Howard Eaton's parties was probably Mary Roberts Rinehart, the famous author. Mrs. Rinehart has sung the praises of the Eaton pilgrimages in a delightful little volume entitled "Through Glacier Park: Seeing America First with Howard Eaton."[26] Another attractive member of the Party was Martha Hedman, popular stage star. Fresh from a month at the "dude-ranch," she was full of enthusiasm over the wonderful horses, marvelous riders and good times she had enjoyed at the ranch.

With the death of Howard, the annual trips through Glacier Park came to an end. The loss of his personality and leadership proved too great a handicap to surmount, but hundreds of people of that era still carry happy memories of the treks through Glacier and the thrilling days of the Wolf ranch.

Visit From A Treasury Secretary

One of the Park's most notable visitors, from a political standpoint, was William Gibbs McAdoo, later an aspirant for the presidency on the Democratic ticket. At the time of his visit to the Park in August, 1918, he was Secretary of the Treasury and he had been appointed by his father-in-law, Woodrow Wilson, to serve also as Director General of the Railroad Administration, a selection that did not sit too well with many of the nation's railroad executives.

When McAdoo decided to hold a conference of American railroad presidents at the Glacier Park Hotel, the plans made by Great Northern officials included a ceremony by which he would be initiated into the Blackfeet tribe. After dinner, everyone gathered around the hotel's indoor campfire, including many Indian "braves" in war paint, their chief, Two Guns White Calf, who was to speak in his native tongue, and an interpreter named Hamilton. Horace Albright was present as a representative of Franklin K. Lane, Secretary of the Interior.[27]

Presently Two Guns White Calf began to speak eloquently about the exploits of his grandfather, which Hamilton translated as McAdoo's early successes as a lawyer. The chief then continued in a similar vein about his father, which Hamilton translated as a laudatory salute to McAdoo as Secretary of the Treasury. And, finally, the chief spoke with pride of his own achievements, which was translated as McAdoo's brilliant administration of the railroads in war time. Then McAdoo was given the name of "Going-To-The-Sun," roughly translatable as "about to depart this world," all of which greatly thrilled McAdoo and his wife, the former Eleanor Wilson.

While it took place, the truth of what was going on was known only to the Great Northern officials who had devised the elaborate hoax, to the Blackfeet who participated, to Hamilton, the interpreter, and to Horace Albright, who had been clued in to the duplicity. They regarded it as the "great McAdoo hoax."[28] It is not unlikely, of course, that the incident was too amusing to be kept a complete secret, and the story soon "leaked out" to the railroad executives for their private enjoyment.

Temporary Financial Embarrassment

While the McAdoos were sojourning at Many Glacier, the cowboys obligingly staged a riding exhibition at the saddle-horse corral. Most of the hotel guests were on hand, including, in addition to McAdoo and his wife, Louis W. Hill, then board chairman for the Great Northern Railway, and his family. After the horses had bucked their best, and the riders had acquitted themselves creditably, the four-quart hat was passed among the crowd for the benefit of the performers.

When the hat reached McAdoo, he searched through pocket after pocket vainly, finding himself temporarily embarrassed for funds. Mrs. McAdoo saved the day by producing and chucking into the hat a bill of generous size. Mr. Hill was not so fortunate, however for he not only found himself entirely without ready money, but his better half was in a like predicament. It was a rare treat to catch both the Secretary of the Treasury and the railroad king of the northwest in a momentarily penniless condition. However, a friend came to the rescue with the offer of a loan and Mr. Hill, too, was enabled to contribute.

Ex-Officio Visitors

The first director of the National Park Service was Stephen Mather, self-made millionaire, who had been born and educated in California and had worked as a reporter on Dana's New York *Sun* before becoming a big-time borax manufacturer in Chicago, philanthropist, mountain climber and zealous conservationist. When he wrote a letter of complaint in 1914 to Franklin K. Lane,

Secretary of the Interior, about the operation of the national parks, Lane responded: "Dear Steve, if you don't like the way the national parks are being run, come on down to Washington and run them yourself." Mather accepted the challenge and took over the job early in 1915.[29]

With his assistant, Horace Albright, later to succeed Mather as director, he set out in July of that year on a tour of the parks with the purpose of arousing public interest in them and of learning at first hand of their conditions and needs. It was the 11th of September, 1915 before they arrived on the west side of Glacier with the plan of conferring briefly at park headquarters on administrative problems before taking off across the continental divide by way of Gunsight Pass. As they were driving with Superintendent Ralston from park headquarters at Fish Creek to Apgar, they came across a man whose car was stuck in the muddy road. They stopped, helped to extricate him, and he was most appreciative. His name was Burton K. Wheeler, then U.S. Attorney for Montana, and later a member of the United States Senate for many years. Wheeler, a longtime summer resident at Lake McDonald never forgot the favor nor those who supplied the help.[30]

They arrived that afternoon at the Lewis Hotel, near the head of Lake McDonald, where their horses and outfits were waiting. Unfortunately, snow had been falling for some time and was beginning to drift. Those familiar with local conditions advised them to call it off, and they were about to do so when Mather heard that Frederic A. Delano, vice-governor of the Federal Reserve System and former president of the Wabash Railroad, had gone out over Gunsight with his two daughters that morning. That settled it. Delano, an old Chicago friend of Mather's, as well as the uncle of Franklin Delano Roosevelt, would be getting laughs the rest of his days with a story of following two girls over the mountains in weather that intimidated Steve Mather. They took off in the storm.

Back-breaking work got them to Sperry Chalets where they passed the night. The next morning, after dismissing an urge to turn back, they got to Gunsight Pass and pressed on, spending the second night at Going-To-The-Sun Chalets on Lake St. Mary. The third day took them over Piegan Pass to the Many Glacier Hotel, tired but pleased that their perseverance had given them an insight into some of Glacier's problems. Still more difficulty was encountered, however, when they undertook to complete their journey to the Park's eastern entrance by automobile and had to be towed out of the mud by relays of two-horse and four-horse teams.[31] They concluded that the hotels and chalets built by the Great Northern were excellent, but that the roads and trails left a great deal to be desired, a situation which Mather undertook to remedy when he returned to Washington.

Pressures To Permit Park Grazing

During World War I, stockmen throughout the West made proposals for pasturing herds of sheep and cattle in various of the national parks. These rather thinly camouflaged get-rich-quick schemes appeared to be based upon patriotic motives, to wit, the need for meeting national food requirements. Despite vigorous opposition by Mather, the stockmen enlisted political support with considerable success. At one juncture they had secured authority to open up Yosemite Park to grazing by 50,000 sheep, and the floral slopes of Mt. Rainier were similarly threatened. The incomparable wild gardens of Glacier were equally close to disaster when the Penfold Sheep Company, with the help of Senator Thomas J. Walsh, succeeded in persuading Secretary Lane to authorize their use of the Park's open spaces for grazing purposes.

Lane delegated Albright to make the arrangements, and the latter went to Montana where he tried unsuccessfully to dissuade the sheepmen by appealing to their finer feelings. After being rebuffed, he was sitting gloomily before the indoor campfire at the Glacier Park Hotel, waiting for a train back east, when he heard two westerners praising the Park and its wildflowers. Albright told them "You'd better go back for a last look. The sheep will have them in another season." After which he unfolded the whole story to his listeners, both from Butte. One was Bruce Kremer, vice-chairman of the Democratic National Committee, and the other was Walter Hansen, a power in meat-packing circles.

After some discussion of the problem, Hansen proposed a stratagem whereby he would make application to rent a huge section of the park for grazing cattle, which are less destructive feeders than sheep, and if Albright could jam the permit through, he would turn loose only a token herd, perhaps a carload or two. All other applications could then be denied on the ground that thousands of acres had already been leased for grazing. The plan

was a huge success because, as Albright now recalls it, "I have never thought that Walter Hansen put any cattle in Glacier Park. No reports of any were ever made."[32]

The Brooklyn Eagle Tours

Stephen Mather had many ideas in reference to publicizing the national parks. Immediately after World War I, he planned with H. V. Kaltenborn, then an editor of the Brooklyn Eagle, a series of national park tours under Eagle sponsorship. The first such tour, in 1919, was taken by 130 people, or Eaglets, and reached four national parks—Rocky Mountain, Yellowstone, Glacier and Mt. Rainier. From Denver onward, some of the Eaglets traveled in buses furnished by the park transportation companies and the title of the tour's souvenir album was **Westward Honk!** The whole event was a huge success. The Eaglets enjoyed themselves, and they were roundly saluted all along the way and in the parks.

At Glacier Park the Blackfeet Indians, inspired and encouraged by Great Northern officials, put on the war paint, danced, chanted and made speeches in Indian language. They took Kaltenborn into the tribe, naming him Mountain Chief and clapping a feather headdress on him that must have set the Great Northern back at least thirty dollars. Kaltenborn, momentarily overcome, fished in his pockets for a token of his gratitude, but the only thing he could come up with was his watch, which he gave to Chief Fish Wolf Robe. Later he confided to Horace M. Albright, who had been present at the ceremony, that the watch was a prized Swiss item that "chimed to tell time in the dark, and showed the moon phases." Albright bought the watch back from the Indian for fifteen dollars and returned it to the grateful Kaltenborn. Four subsequent flights of Eaglets accompanied Kaltenborn into the national parks and helped to dedicate several of them.[33]

Champion Visitors

One of Glacier's greatest admirers was Mrs. Frank Oastler who, by 1954, had established a record of spending 1197 days in the Park. She had first come to the area in 1912 with her husband, the noted New York surgeon, conservationist, naturalist and wildlife photographer, when they undertook a 24-day pack trip with Tom Dawson, well-known pioneer guide. Thereafter they returned almost every summer, hiking the trails, climbing the peaks and spending much time at the Many

Glacier Hotel. While visiting the Park in the summer of 1936, Dr. Oastler kept an appointment with George Ruhle, the Chief Naturalist of the Park, to climb Mt. Lincoln. While on the trail, he suffered a heart attack and, although Ruhle managed to get him down the mountain and he was able to travel to Many Glacier, he died there two weeks later as the result of a second attack.

His widow continued, nevertheless, to return each season, spending as much as 59 days a summer at Many Glacier. She contributed $3000 for construction of the Oastler Shelter which stands near the boat landing at Lake Josephine.[34] Dr. Oastler's framed photograph, above his poem "Outdoors," still hangs in the library of the National Park Service Administration Building at West Glacier.

No story of Glacier Park personalities would be complete without a few words about its most frequent and amazing visitor, Mel Ruder, for more than a quarter of a century the editor and publisher of the Hungry Horse News, weekly newspaper based at nearby Columbia Falls, Montana. In the course of providing detailed coverage of Glacier Park events, Mel is in and out of the Park scores of times each year. A skilled photographer, his classic and often sensational pictures of his favorite subject, from the air, the trails and the highways, feature every edition of his delightful publication. His newspaper accomplishments have been widely recognized, bringing him the Pulitzer prize in 1965, the Edward J. Meeman Conservation Award for journalism, twelve National Editorial Association awards covering various phases of journalism, and the Sioux Award of his alma mater, the University of North Dakota, in 1964 for "distinguished service and outstanding achievements." No national park has ever had a more competent or dedicated chronicler.

Notes For Chapter 18
[1]Visitor totals for the mid-1970's approached the million and a half level with each succeeding year showing an increase.
[2]"Through The Years In Glacier National Park," by Donald H. Robinson, at pages 79-80. It is interesting to note that Princess Ileana, a granddaughter of Queen Victoria, as well as a one-time Archduchess of Austria, now lives at Ellwood City, Pa. As the Very Reverend Mother Alexandra, she has founded an Eastern Orthodox Monastery in a mobile home in a trailer park in Toledo, Ohio, moving it in 1973 to 100 acres of land at the Ellwood City location. A biography of her mother by Terence Elsberry entitled "Marie of Romania: The Intimate Life of a Twentieth Century Queen," was published in 1973.
[3]"Through The Years," supra, at page 82.
[4]In "Blackfeet And Buffalo," at pages 110-121, James Willard Schultz tells of the Baring visit to the St. Mary country, placing the date as August, 1889. Another source suggests that a story of their visit, also by Schultz, had originally appeared in Field And Stream Magazine for December 30, 1886 and January 6, 1887.
[5]"Through The Years," supra, at page 81.
[6]Idem, at pages 82-83.
[7]Idem, at page 82.
[8]This information is contained in documents preserved in the National Park Service library at West Glacier.
[9]"Through The Years," supra, at pages 81, 102. In his article entitled "A Mind's Eye Map Of America," published in the National Geographic Magazine for June, 1920, at page 501, Franklin K. Lane described his visit to the St. Mary region. He has also visited the west side of the Park in 1913, staying at the ranger station at the head of Lake McDonald, according to Mrs. Cora Hutchings in an interview appearing in the Hungry Horse News for May 12, 1972.
[10]"Through The Years," supra, at page 19.
[11]Article in Sunset Magazine by Rufus Steele, Volume 34: 475-485, at pages 482-483.
[12]See story in the Hungry Horse News for September 24, 1971, recalling the visit of FDR as reported at the time by the Daily Inter Lake, of Kalispell.
[13]See the 1948 edition of the "Drivers' Manual" at page 21 (see note 15, Chapter 6, supra).
[14]Article in National Geographic Magazine for May, 1956, entitled "Many Splendored Glacierland," by George W. Long, at page 618.
[15]As reported by the Hungry Horse News for 5/12/72. According to an article on the Royal Canadian Mounted Police, appearing in the 1948 edition of "Drivers' Manual" at page 75 (see note 15, Chapter 6, supra), Hoover also visited the Waterton Park in September, 1937 and while there made a call at the RCMP barracks at Waterton Village where he is said to have been delightfully entertained.
[16]As reported in the Hungry Horse News for 7/31/70.
[17]"Through The Years," supra, at pages 19, 23 and 31.
[18]National Geographic Magazine for June, 1950, at page 756.
[19]For many years both McClintock and Schultz made occasional visits to the Park, walking the trails and visiting with old Indian friends nearby.
[20]"Through The Years," supra, at page 79.
[21]"Adventure Trails," by John Willard, at pages 85-86.
[22]Information supplied by Hugh Black, St. Mary, Montana.
[23]See story in the Hungry Horse News for January 5, 1973.
[24]"My Experiences And Investment In The Bad Lands Of Dakota And Some Of The Men I Met There," by A. C. Huidekoper, at page 24 (published in Baltimore in 1947, but written in 1924). The Dakota operation of the Eatons was under the name of the Custer Trail Cattle Company, with headquarters a few miles south of Medora and a few miles north of Theodore Roosevelt's Maltese Cross Ranch.
[25]Booklet entitled "Eaton's Ranch And Howard Eaton's Horseback Trips," published in 1922 by the Eaton Brothers of Wolf, Wyoming. See, also, "Steve Mather Of The National Parks," by Robert Shankland, Alfred A. Knopf, 1951, at page 90.
[26]Published by Houghton Mifflin Company in 1916.
[27]Letter of Horace M. Albright dated October 24, 1974.
[28]Idem.
[29]"Steve Mather Of The National Parks," supra, at page 7.
[30]Letter of Horace M. Albright dated 1/30/75.
[31]Idem. See, also, "Steve Mather Of The National Parks," at pages 80-81.
[32]Letter of Horace M. Albright dated 1/30/75. See, also, "Steve Mather Of The National Parks," supra, at pages 203-204.
[33]See "Wilderness Defender" (biography of Horace M. Albright) at pages 119-120. See, also, "Steve Mather Of The National Parks," supra, at pages 94-95.
[34]Great Falls Tribune, September 26, 1954.

President Franklin Roosevelt and Senator Wheeler at Two Medicine in 1934
Courtesy National Park Service, West Glacier, Montana

Secretary and Mrs. William Gibbs McAdoo about to start for Cracker Lake, August, 1918
From author's personal collection

Crown Prince Olaf and Princess Martha with Park Superintendent Libby during visit to park June 3-5, 1939
Courtesy National Park Service, West Glacier, Montana

The Howard Eaton party with the Garden Wall for a background—Howard Eaton in central foreground
Photo by Hileman

PART III.
EXPLORING
INTERNATIONAL TRAILS
Chapter 19
SCENERY OF THE
SWIFTCURRENT

The natural fascination that every international boundary possesses is enhanced when a segment of it is also the line of demarcation between two great national parks, and is further accentuated when it happens to be bordered on either side by some of the most rugged terrain and superb scenery in the world. In the case of Waterton-Glacier, headquarters of the Canadian park are only 5 miles north of the border, while Many Glacier, "inland capital" of the American park, is only 12 miles south of it. Less than 20 miles, as the eagle flies, separate these two scenic centers; and within this international zone, as it were, there is more than enough sensational scenery, all accessible by excellent trails, to keep the willing traveler busy for weeks.

On the United States side of the line, the great Swiftcurrent complex of peaks, cirques, valleys and lakes is one of the most spectacular on the continent, if not in the world. Situated in an area extending about seven miles in either direction, it comprises ten sparkling lakes, seven challenging peaks, six glaciers or icefields, four principal valleys plus a hanging valley or two, and three notable mountain passes, together with an extraordinary medley of trails that makes almost all of these fascinating features readily available. Nowhere else in Glacier is such a smorgasbord of scenic attractions spread before the delighted visitor.

In the center of all this beauty lies Many Glacier Hotel, "Show Place of the Rockies," with Swiftcurrent Motor Inn and Campground only a mile away.[1] The hotel has been described as the "hub of the Park, with trails of beauty radiating like spokes in all directions." To the south and east of this heart of Glacier's trail system, it is 55 highway miles to the nearest point on the railroad, the Glacier Park Hotel at the Park's eastern entrance. In the opposite direction, only nine airline miles beyond the head of the most northerly arm of the Swiftcurrent Valley, lies Canada.

Many Glacier Hotel, more than a sixth of a mile in length, is draped along the shore of one of the Park's most enchanting bodies of water, Swiftcurrent Lake. The hotel's great west windows face a panorama that embraces a 140° sweep of peaks of the Lewis Range, stretching from classic Mt. Gould and the Garden Wall on the left through Mt. Grinnell, spectacular Mt. Wilbur and the Pinnacle Wall to Mt. Henkel and Mt. Altyn on the right, all seemingly so near that one could almost reach out and touch them. The broad west verandas provide a vantage point from which those unable to utilize the trails may drink in at one draught more concentrated scenic beauty than at any of the Park's other hotels or motor inns.

Orientation

The Swiftcurrent Valley may, for convenience, be likened to a huge right hand, with the Sherburne Reservoir serving as the wrist, and with Swiftcurrent Lake and Many Glacier Hotel resting in its upturned palm. On such an imaginary basis, the thumb would be represented by the Appekunny Basin, while the fingers would extend, respectively, toward (1) Iceberg and Ptarmigan Lakes, (2) the Swiftcurrent chain of lakes and pass, (3) Grinnell Lake and Piegan Pass, and (4) Canyon Creek and Cracker Lake.

In each of these directions there is a trail and a worthwhile trip.[2] On each trail is a mountain lake, sometimes a chain of them, while three of the trails lead over spectacular passes.[3] There is little similarity or repetition, since each arm of the great system of valleys has an individual flavor. In fact, the Swiftcurrent Valley provides more variety than any other section of either park, despite the fact that even the longer trails can usually be round-tripped in a single day. The exceptions, of course, are those that lead out of the Swiftcurrent and into other parts of the Park.

The "Thumb"

The Appekunny Basin is a hanging valley lying between Mt. Altyn and Appekunny Peak on the north side of the Swiftcurrent Valley.[4] It is reached by a foot trail that leaves the automobile road about a mile east of Swiftcurrent Falls, shortly after the road has passed a lonely, rock-walled grave dating back to the days of Altyn, the old mining town which was located nearby. Following the east bank of Appekunny Creek, the trail leads to the base of attractive Appekunny Falls rushing over a hundred-foot cliff through a zone of weakness caused by the Lewis Overthrust.

Here, by a series of short, steep switchbacks to the right of the falls, the trail ascends to the lower section of the basin at an elevation of 6100 feet and continues for a mile or so before fading out. The lower walls of the basin are composed principally of green Appekunny argillite, colorfully topped in places by sections of red Grinnell argillite. The trees are dwarfed and stunted, but the area is ablaze with a profusion of flowers in July and August.[5] For experienced climbers, it is possible to continue westward to an upper basin containing lovely Natahki Lake,[6] a typical mountain tarn fed by melting snow and ice-cold springs; then to climb by a series of grassy ledges to the saddle between Mt. Henkel and Mt. Altyn, returning to the hotel by way of the southern slopes of the latter.

The "Index Finger"

At the head of the most northerly of the Swiftcurrent valleys is Iceberg Lake, a pocket edition polar sea put up in a deluxe binding. This is one of the most popular trails in Glacier, due not alone to the oddity of the lake and the beauty of its setting, but also to the fact that it is one of the best built trails in the Park. Distance from Many Glacier to the lake is six miles, the rise in elevation is from 4861 feet to 6000 feet, and the roundtrip can be made on foot in either half a day or a day, depending upon how leisurely the visitor wishes to be.

A great, horseshoe-shaped amphitheatre forms the setting for Iceberg Lake. This unusual cirque has been excavated from the northwestern face of Mt. Wilbur by an ancient glacier as neatly as though it were bored by a mammoth augur. The encircling cliffs of the Iceberg Wall rise perpendicularly three thousand feet above the lake — among the most imposing precipices in the Park. For only a few minutes each day, when the sun is at its zenith, can its rays reach all parts of the enclosure.

It was this scarcity of sunlight that made it possible for the Iceberg Glacier, backed up against the southwest wall of the amphitheatre

and fronting directly on the blue waters of the lake, to come into existence at an elevation of barely 6000 feet. In 1920 the ice pack was nearly one hundred feet thick, but with the warming climate of the next few years, its glacial ice had disappeared by 1940. Nevertheless, it still gathers winter's snows to its bosom, and in the warmer days of summer massive hunks of ice and snow of every conceivable shape break loose and tumble into the lake, the numbers varying with the temperature. The warmth of July and August transforms the lake into a sapphire sea, filled with a miniature navy of grotesquely shaped alabaster ships sailing hither and thither.

On The Shores Of The Lake

Along the water's edge is a rock rampart, thrown up by the action of expanding lake ice during countless ages. The open, park-like portion of the amphitheatre is a fairyland of flowers during the summer. Beside patches of snow are audaciously blooming the glacier lily, heliotrope, buttercup, shootingstar, paintbrush, bear grass and many others. Tiny nearby meadows are literally blue or crimson with thousands upon thousands of nodding wildflowers. To the left and right of the open lake run faint trails which lead up the mountainside toward prospect holes, the work of some ambitious miner of a bygone decade, and reminders of the time when the mining fever led men to this region.

The lake's name was given to it in 1890 by George Bird Grinnell,[7] although its first white visitor may have been Hugh Monroe in the early 1850's.[8] The lake, half a mile across and 149 feet deep at its center, is said to be gradually filling up with rock debris tumbling down from the surrounding walls.[9] Temperature of the water during the summer seldom exceeds 42°, which many naturalists believe may be too cold to provide adequate food for fish life.[10] Along its shores, however, thrive a multitude of Columbia ground squirrels and, in season, an abundance of bloodthirsty black flies.

This vicinity is the favorite haunt of the elusive Rocky Mountain goat. High up on the rocky battlements, safe from predatory invasions of bear or coyote, he has mapped out his own complete set of private trails. Paths which scarcely seem to offer a foothold of any sort are blithely traversed by this sure-footed ungulate in his daily journeys about the cliffs. A favorite route leads up along the Pinnacle Wall until it passes through a deep indentation called Iceberg Notch which gives access to gentler slopes leading down to Ahern Pass, on the continental divide. Considerably north of the Notch is a hole near the top of the Pinnacle Wall that can be seen from the veranda of the Many Glacier hotel in the late afternoon. This hole is about four feet in height, eight feet in width, and six to eight feet through from one side to the other.

Trail to Belly River

A branch of the Iceberg trail leads to Ptarmigan Lake and tunnel. It leaves the main trail at a point about four miles from Many Glacier Hotel, just above Ptarmigan Falls on Wilbur Creek, and leads ultimately to the Belly River region. Ptarmigan Lake is small, circular, less than a quarter of a mile in diameter, deep blue in color, with a very beautiful setting of cliffs on all sides except to the south. Here is an open vista of mountains, the summits of Grinnell and Wilbur standing out prominently under the noon-day sun. The ledges of the falls, the lake bed, and the cliffs for some 800 or 900 feet above the lake are of red argillite. Even though the elevation is 6500 feet, 500 feet higher than that of Iceberg Lake, it is inhabited by small brook trout, since its location brings it more summer sunshine.

From the lake the trail continues northward, climbing the Ptarmigan Wall by two long switchbacks over the talus slopes until it reaches the 183-foot tunnel near its summit. This tunnel and the trail on either side of it were constructed in 1931 to shorten the distance from the Swiftcurrent Valley to the Belly River Valley. The views to the north and south from the tunnel are spectacular, inviting the photographer to film some of the finest panoramas in the entire Park.

The "Middle Finger"

The second of the valleys in the Many Glacier area is the avenue leading to Swiftcurrent Pass. The feature of this trail lies not so much in its chain of charming lakes and its wonderful flowers, but rather in its spectacular switchbacks and sheer headwall, with waterfalls cascading thousands of feet from the snowfields in the old glacier basin above. On no other pass in the Park is the approach so sensational or the view so inspiring.

From Many Glacier this memorable trail winds westward past Fishercap and Redrock Lakes, the latter named for the red argillite surrounding it. At its head is Redrock Falls, above which there is a mile-long body of water called Bullhead Lake, apparently a name conferred in mining days. Above the lake, clinging precariously to the north face of Mt. Grinnell, hangs the snow-filled cirque of the old Swiftcurrent Glacier, a goat-inhabited area.

The towering headwall of the valley presents a seeming impasse; but just as further progress seems impossible, the trail begins a picturesque ascent by a series of long switchbacks, zigzagging up the escarpment lying to the north of the glacier. The switchbacks become more abbreviated as the trail rises and, as the horses slowly pivot on the hairpin turns, they are soon strung up the mountainside in units, each above the other.

As elevation is gained, all the little lakes in the Swiftcurrent Valley, which had previously gleamed through the trees of the valley floor, one by one take their places, now fully revealed, in the vista toward the east. Across the valley, the snow in the old glacial cirque glistens, while down the cliff below it fly a dozen little torrents and falls. The vivacity of their eager movements seems almost to impart life to the cold rock itself.

Nine-Lake Look-out

The scenic climax comes at the "chimney," a jutting promontory some two-thirds of the way up the Pass trail, about the outer face of which a passageway for the trail has been blasted. This point was called the "Devil's Elbow by old-time wranglers since horses were sometimes lost there in the days before the trail was widened. The view from this point is one of the most impressive in the Park, and certainly the most comprehensive afforded by any trail in the Swiftcurrent Valley. Nine blue lakes can be counted, the most distant being Duck Lake, twenty miles or more to the east. On the dim horizon are the hazy outlines of the Sweetgrass Hills, over a hundred miles away.

The summit of the Pass is 7186 feet above sea level. Not more than a mile beyond lies the Granite Park Chalet at an elevation of 6600 feet. From Many Glacier, the total rise to the summit is approximately 2300 feet, and snow frequently lingers on the Pass all summer. Goats are often seen on Swiftcurrent Mountain to the north, and a trail to the fire lookout at its summit rises another 1000 feet and affords a view even more sumptuous than that from the trail itself.

The Garden Wall Trail

Linking Swiftcurrent Pass with Logan Pass is an unique trail that hugs the western rim of the continental divide. Although not within the perimeter of the Swiftcurrent-Grinnell complex of valleys, it is separated from them for much of its length only by the relatively narrow summit of the Garden Wall, from which it takes its name. This unusual highline route is unquestionably one of the most popular and, in the opinion of many, one of the most spectacular, in the Park.

The trail is not a lengthy one (7½ miles) and lies entirely above timberline. It is reasonably level, since its elevation of 6600 feet on departure from Granite Park is almost the same as on its arrival at Logan Pass; in between, it varies but little more than 600 feet either way from that level. Much of it has been carved from the precipitous cliffs that rise a thousand feet or two above it, and at some points it has been hewn from the igneous rock and associated algal band that are so frequently visible in the Park. As it winds over the open slopes, it passes through lush stands of beargrass and other flowers, over occasional snowbanks, and through sheep and goat country. Its attraction lies not so much in the trail itself, however, as in the spectacular panorama which it affords of many peaks, brilliant with their colorful rock strata, and the great McDonald Valley lying to the southwest.

The trail was built during the summer of 1918 to provide an alternate route from Many Glacier to Going-To-The-Sun Chalets, as Sun Point was then known. Because construction was not completed until September, only two parties traveled over it that year. The first was that of William Gibbs McAdoo, then Secretary of the Treasury, and his wife, the former Eleanor Wilson, daughter of President Wilson. Although work on the trail was still unfinished in the latter part of August, it was possible for their party to get through by walking over one short section of the trail. The second party left Many Glacier on September 8th, and consisted of myself, Bertha Hosford, the Many Glacier nurse, and Edith Middleton, wife of the Many Glacier engineer. It was an unforgettable experience for all of us, but particularly for myself, since it represented the first leg of a long journey that was to take me the next day to Belton by way of Gunsight Pass, and finally back to my native North Dakota in time to register for the selective service draft on September 12, 1918.

The "Third Finger"

An exceedingly important valley in the Swiftcurrent complex is that leading toward Piegan Pass and Grinnell Glacier. Situated in this valley, proceeding southwest from Many Glacier Hotel, is a trio of lakes, commencing with Swiftcurrent, followed by Josephine and Grinnell, and encircled by a network of paths, each of which renders more accessible some particular part of the area.

The upper trail along the base of Mt. Allen is the shortest route to Piegan Pass and Morning Eagle Falls. Moss-carpeted, it leads through dense timber with occasional open areas, the result of avalanches, that reveal the whiteness of Grinnell Glacier, the blue of Lake Josephine and the ragged skyline of the majestic Garden Wall. Four miles above the hotel is a confluence of the upper and lower trails. For another two miles the merged trail plays hide-and-seek with impetuous Cataract Creek, until confronted by a great ledge of rock which spans the valley and spills the waters of the creek precipitately down its broad face. This is Morning Eagle Falls, an Indian name suggestive of its down-pouring foam and spray. Far aloft, draining the basin between Mt. Gould and a smaller peak overlooking Grinnell Lake, is delicate Feather Plume Falls. Although its tiny ribbon of water reaches the ground on quiet days, it may be blown up over the lip of the falls when the wind is gusting.

Special Coloration

The stretch of upland valley from the timberline to Morning Eagle Falls is one great flower garden during July and August. Along the base of the towering Garden Wall, and flanked to the east by the buttresses of Mt. Allen and Mt. Siyeh, is what has been called "The Garden Of Heaven."[11] This is probably the most glorious riot of color in the Swiftcurrent chain of valleys and perhaps in all of Glacier Park. The trail continues upward to Piegan Pass and to the St. Mary Valley beyond, traversing attractive Preston Park en route.

By retracing steps to the junction of the trails and following the lower path, one soon arrives at Grinnell Lake. A tiny meadow beside the lake is an equally beautiful, although somewhat smaller version of the Morning Eagle flower garden. Attention is centered, however, on the exceptional setting of the lake, occupying the remarkable cirque formed by the curving base of Mt. Gould and the Garden Wall. It is nearly a vertical mile from the surface of the lake to the tip of the grey gable of Mt. Gould. From the great shelf above, on which lies Grinnell Glacier, three streams catapult themselves more than a thousand feet to the oval lake below. As the trail crosses

Grinnell Creek, the milky coloring of the water, due to the presence of glacier-ground silt, may be observed. Beyond the lake, the trail begins the long climb to Grinnell Glacier, as will be described later.[12]

The "Little Finger"

The Cracker Lake trail into the fourth of the Swiftcurrent valleys, offers a characteristically beautiful symphony of forest and flowers, lake and glacier, cliffs and canyon. The well-known Chicago artist, Oliver Dennett Grover, once declared it "the most beautiful trail, the most beautiful lake, and the finest combination of colors" he had ever seen.[13]

From Many Glacier the trail proceeds southeast to Cracker Lake Canyon where it first encounters Canyon Creek. This captivating little torrent leads the trail a merry chase for five miles, although it is crossed but once. Its boulder-studded rapids and eddying pools are the unsuspecting hiding-places of many a gamy trout. Shady glens, great beds of ferns, and green banks of wild parsnip, ragwort and wild currant line the way. The evergreens grow closely, becoming not fewer, but smaller and more stunted, as the trail nears its upper end. Overhead loom high on either side the canyon walls, as yellow Altyn limestone, green Appekunny argillite and red Grinnell argillite are successively passed.

Reposing at the foot of huge Mt. Siyeh, like a patch of fallen blue sky, lies Cracker Lake. The exquisite turquoise blue of this mountain lake is one of the most perfect bits of coloring in Nature. The milk-white of the glacial waters, the height of the surrounding cliffs, and the reflected blue of the sky-dome, all combine to create the softest, warmest robin's egg blue that ever graced a lake.

Magnificent Mt. Siyeh towers almost perpendicularly above the upper end of the lake—a sheer four thousand feet. Emblazoned high on its face is the black band of diorite so characteristic of the Siyeh rock formation seen throughout the Park.[14] On a shelf, some little way up the cliff, is the hanging Siyeh Glacier, with its huge terminal moraine. It may be reached by a clamber over the glacial debris. Mt. Siyeh is one of the six 10,000 foot peaks in the Park yet, like Mt. Cleveland, it is not on the continental divide.

The Park In Capsule Form

Craker Lake lies at an elevation of 5800 feet, with the abandoned shaft of the old Cracker Mine still visible above its east shore. Gone, however are the remains of the ore crusher, once quite an attraction to visitors to the area, but razed by Park authorities in the early 1930's. The original trail to the lake was largely destroyed by spring floods in 1935, and a new one was constructed in the fall of 1937.

The crowning glory of Cracker Lake's beauty is the profusion of wild flowers that cover its nearby slopes in summer months, bloom-bedecked as though Nature had generously spattered them with the harmonizing tints of her great paintbrush. At an elevation that has made of the pines pitiful cowering things, the flowers bloom undismayed. In special prominence are the blues of the gentians and forget-me-nots, the yellows of the columbines and buttercups; while the brilliant crimson and scarlet of the fire-weed and Indian paintbrush vie with the deeper hues of the dark red argillite rock.

Botanically and geologically, this brief journey takes the visitor from the Transition through the Canadian and Hudsonian zones into the Arctic-Alpine, all within less than seven miles, and with a rise of less than 1100 feet in elevation, since arctic-alpine plants are found at the head of the lake.[15]

Even more interesting is the fact that in the course of this short trip to Cracker Lake, the Park itself may be seen in capsule form: The position of the Lewis Overthrust and all the principal rock formations that are found in the Park; timber in all stages from normally perfect trees to twisted and stunted snags; silvery threads of water from high cliffs, almost splashing the trail; some of the steepest and most spectacular cliffs in the Park; wonderful beds of flowers and ferns; glacial moraine and debris along the way, including a fine terminal moraine not excelled in the Park; a lake of charming location and color; an abandoned mine of historic interest; marmots, mountain sheep and goats often to be seen; and, finally, a 10,000-foot mountain from a 5800-foot elevation.[16]

Notes For Chapter 19

[1]See Chapter 16, supra, entitled "The Great Log Lodges," at pages 132-133.

[2]The trail to Appekunny basin, the "thumb," is for foot travel only.

[3]The three passes are Swiftcurrent, leading to Granite Park, Piegan, leading to Lake St. Mary, and the Ptarmigan tunnel route to the Belly River Valley. While there is an attractive lake (Natahki) in the Appekunny Valley, it is located in an upper basin to which as yet no trail has been constructed.

[4]The basin, waterfall and creek all bear the Indian name of James Willard Schultz, who spelled it "Apikuni."

[5]Its proximity to Many Glacier, its hundred-foot waterfall, and its dramatic evidence of the Lewis Overthrust in the vicinity of the cataract make this trail attractive to the hiker.

[6]Named for the Indian wife of James Willard Schultz.

[7]Elrod's Guide & Book of Information" (1924 edition), by Morton J. Elrod, at page 100.

[8]See "Signposts Of Adventure," by James Willard Schultz, at page 149.

[9]"Elrod's Guide," supra, at page 101.

[10]At any rate there are no fish in Iceberg Lake, in spite of the relatively low elevation and the legend to the contrary about the furbearing trout, as described in Chapter 9, supra, entitled "The Original Inhabitants," at page 79.

Surface temperature of the water in July and August was found to be 42° by A. S. Hazzard, Ph.D, of the Michigan Institute For Fisheries Research, who so reported in an article entitled "Fish And Fishing Waters Of Glacier National Park," appearing at page 163 of the 1948 edition of the "Drivers' Manual" (see note 15, Chapter 6, supra). "Elrod's Guide," supra, at page 101 gave the temperature as 39°. J. Gordon Edwards, who recorded the temperature once a week for an entire summer found it to be 4° Centigrade (between 38° and 39° Fahrenheit) both at the surface and one foot below the surface.

[11]"Elrod's Guide," supra, at page 120.

[12]See Chapter 20, infra, entitled "Ankle Excursions Out Of Many Glacier," at pages 165-166.

[13]"Elrod's Guide," supra, at page 102. Elrod states that Grover spent an entire summer at Many Glacier.

[14]For a description of the Siyeh formation, see Chapter 2, supra, entitled "A Romance In Rocks," at page 18.

[15]See discussion in Chapter 8, supra, entitled "Million-Acre Flower Garden," at page 63. Also, see "Elrod's Guide," supra, at page 105.

[16]"Elrod's Guide," supra, at page 105.

The author at Many Glacier in 1918
From author's personal collection

Swiftcurrent Lake and Falls, with Many Glacier Hotel and Mt. Gould

Photo by Mel Ruder

A bighorn ram pays a visit to the Many Glacier Hotel
Courtesy Burlington Northern

Many Glacier Hotel, Swiftcurrent Lake and Falls
Courtesy Burlington Northern

Chapter 20
"ANKLE EXCURSIONS" OUT OF MANY GLACIER

Glacier Park has been called a paradise for hikers. This is a particularly apt description of the Swiftcurrent region, where the variety of trails, the briskly comfortable summer climate, the invigorating atmosphere, with its scent of pines and faint aroma of wild flowers, and the spectacular alpine beauty at almost every turn, make journeys by "shanks mare," or as the cowboy guides used to say, "ankle excursion,"[1] unforgettable experiences.

Within easy reach of the Many Glacier Hotel is every kind of hiking adventure, from a leisurely stroll on level trails to the most challenging of mountain climbs, and from a short self-guided tour around Swiftcurrent Lake to a ranger-guided hike to Grinnell Glacier. The trails are safe, well marked, and inviting even to those who have done little walking for months or years.

In the Swiftcurrent area, the principal trails available to both riders and hikers have been previously described. However, there are also many points of interest which are only reachable on foot, attractive spots to which there are no beaten trails for the horses, but which may be reached by the willing hiker. Then, too, as J. Gordon Edwards says in the opening sentence of his delightful book about climbing in the Park, "The mountains of Glacier National Park are ideal for the assaults of nontechnical (or non-acrobatic) climbers."[2] Some of these hikes, both the easy and the more strenuous, warrant a place in this or any story of the Park's attractions.

Around The North End Of The Lake

Among interesting "ankle excursions" out of Many Glacier, one of the shortest and easiest is that from the hotel to its satellite facilities across the lake, the Many Glacier Campgroud and the Swiftcurrent Motor Inn. This is a two-way proposition, of course, since an estimated two-thirds of the valley's visitors are patrons of the campground and inn. The distance between these facilities and the hotel is approximately one mile by the trail or road that skirts the north end of the lake, inviting a leisurely stroll in the cool of the long Montana summer evenings.

Every guest of the hotel will want to visit the area of the motor inn and campground. On the left, as he approaches, is the latter with its 117 camp sites, and nearby the Many Glacier Ranger Station, representing park administrative headquarters for the area. On the right, a bit farther on, are the motor inn and its cabins, operated in conjunction with a general store, coffee shop and gift shop. It is from this location that the trail to Swiftcurrent Pass takes off, and nearby also is an outdoor amphitheatre utilized for evening talks by the ranger naturalists.

Conversely, curiosity alone will impel every camper and motor inn guest to visit the great hotel and its environs, so attractively visible across the lake and so readily reachable by the trail or road along the lake's north shore. Once there, he should hike around the structure, continuing from the front entrance toward its south end, then west to the lake, north along the shore and past the boat landing to the power house at its north end. The distance of a full half-mile around its perimeter will provide him with a better concept of the size and setting of this impressive "inland capital" of the Park.

Triple Cascade

Over Swiftcurrent Falls, only a few rods north of the hotel entrance, pours every drop of water flowing out of eight lakes of the upper Swiftcurrent Valley. The falls are comprised of three cascades with a total drop of 90 feet, the upper section being virtually spanned by the highway bridge to the hotel. Fish from the Hudson Bay streams could originally come to the foot of these falls; however, none were ever able to ascend them, and all fish in the lakes above have been planted.[3]

From the hotel, the hiker can reach the upper falls by following either the highway or the lake shore. There is no path that permits a descent into the gorge alongside the falls, but it is easy to retreat a few rods to the old road (opposite the junction of the road leading to the parking lot and that to the hotel entrance) and to follow it down to the site of the old bridge, passing en route a secluded glade with fireplace and logs suitable for an evening campfire. From the old bridge site will be gained an excellent view of the attractive little gorge that the upper falls have cut in the yellow Altyn limestone.

Just below the upper falls, on the south side, is a cave still occupied by a family of pack rats that were already in residence when I first came to Many Glacier in 1918.[4] Another inhabitant of the gorge is a water ouzel or dipper, a slate-colored bird that likes to live by a waterfall, and will dive under the water and clamber over the rocks with ease. Generations of these short-tailed "water-wrens" have nested near the upper falls,[5] and I have watched them many times as I fished the pool below the lower cascades. A dim trail leads on to the bottom of the lower gorge, eventually fading out completely.

Around The Lakes

One of the most delightful trails in the Many Glacier area is that around Swiftcurrent Lake, the first portion of which is designated as a self-guiding nature tour. Descriptive leaflets are available at each end of the self-guided section, describing the features along the route. The complete trip is about 2½ miles in length but, as the early guides used to say, the city folks for whom such a jaunt is too long and tiring can always walk half-way around and then return.

From the hotel, the trip can be undertaken in either direction, but preferably by heading south along the old wagon road that after half a mile brings the hiker to the boat company's winter boathouse.[6] Here the trail emerges briefly on the lake shore, and after a short distance through the pines, reaches a log footbridge across the stream that connects Lakes Josephine and Swiftcurrent. After crossing the bridge, the trail passes the upper dock for the Swiftcurrent launch and continues to a junction with the west side trail. At this fork, the right hand turn is again taken and the trail continues along or near the west shore of Swiftcurrent Lake until it crosses the creek by the same name, with its sparkling bed of multi-colored pebbles, by another log bridge near the

campground, approximately a mile from the hotel, by way of the north end of the lake.

A more extended version of this little tour will enable the hiker to encircle both Swiftcurrent and Josephine, this being accomplished by not crossing the first foot bridge mentioned above, but instead following the Josephine outlet to the lake itself and to the Oastler Shelter near the boat dock. Thereafter it is simply a matter of bearing right around the south end of the lake until the junction has been reached at the west side of the isthmus between Josephine and Swiftcurrent. From this point the trail should be followed north along the west side of Swiftcurrent Lake as described in the preceding paragraph.

It is difficult to exercise restraint in describing the beauties of Josephine, regarded by many as the Park's loveliest lake. The views from various points along its perimeter are unsurpassed, with every glimpse of the Garden Wall and Grinnell Glacier clinging to its seemingly perpendicular walls a classic picture. As some one said long ago, "Josephine is a scenic symphony with all the richness of a Maxfield Parrish landscape."

The Josephine Mine

Visible from the boat landing at the head of Josephine Lake is a tiny, gray-green mound on a narrow shelf high on the south side of Grinnell Point. This is the ancient ore dump of the abandoned Josephine Mine, erstwhile property of Parley Stark, for whom Stark's Peak, now Grinnell Point, was originally named. Despite the fact that a shaft was driven horizontally into the mountain, presumably around 1900, no payload of its ore was ever brought down or processed. As late as 1950, an old ore cart still sat on the rails outside the shaft and an ancient bellows and hand drill lay nearby, but today all are wrecked or missing.[7] Title to the property is now in the government, having been acquired in November, 1973 through a friendly condemnation suit.

Although not marked, the trail to the mine is easily found and is one of the most scenic in the Many Glacier area. The mine lies on the grassy slopes about half-way up the south side of Grinnell Point. It takes off from the Grinnell Glacier trail at a spot well above Grinnell Lake, and with the aid of switchbacks angles back toward the Point for approximately two miles. It is possible to return to Josephine Lake by way of a grassy ledge that descends diagonally toward the east; however, the top of the diagonal ramp is hard to find from above and there is no other possible route of descent through the cliffs.[8]

The Silent City

One of the most fascinating points of interest in the Many Glacier area used to be the old boom town of Altyn, less than two miles east of the hotel. Around the turn of the century, coincident with the rush of prospectors and settlers into Swiftcurrent Valley upon its being opened to settlement and mining development, Altyn sprang up almost overnight as a supply and social center. Among the mining claims developing considerable activity in the area were the Cracker Mine at Cracker Lake, the Josephine Mine, with its seven owners, including Parley Stark, Scott Stark and O. S. Main, and the Ptarmigan group of mines on Appekunny Mountain. The town was located at the lower end of Canyon Creek, near its confluence with Sherburne Lake. It was named after Dave Altyn, one of those having an interest in the Cracker Mine.[9]

As of September, 1900, Altyn boasted a weekly newspaper, "The Swift Current Courier," a general store (in a two-story building), two restaurants (meals, 50¢), two saloons, including that of Adlam & Thomson, "The Pioneer Liquid Purveyors of Swift Current District," two barbershops, one in a tent and one in a saloon, a meat market, a saw mill and a Chinese laundry. A stage line ran regularly between Altyn and Blackfoot, just east of Browning.[10] No one knows how many inhabitants there were, but it is said that there were more than a hundred buildings, as well as many tents.

Like mining camps in general, the existence of Altyn was brief, perhaps more so than most. In September, 1900, the Courier confidently stated: "With nine hundred and ninety-nine chances to win against one to lose, there is little room to doubt the destiny of Swift Current as the richest camp in the country."[11] Within two years, however, every mine had disappointed its owners and Altyn had become another ghost town.

When I used to wander through its deserted streets in the summer of 1918, the shells of some 30 to 35 buildings were still standing, all considerably battered by the elements. One could trace the old saloons, and it was said that an old faro table had been carried away as a souvenir about a decade before. Remains were

visible of an old blacksmith shop and an ancient stable, no doubt serving the needs of the stage line. Many of the structures could not be identified and were presumable dwellings.

When the mines proved non-productive, the little community simply gathered its belongings and departed. The grassy flats near the creek became as silent as they were before, though many habitations remained to mark this as a spot where men had once lived. The site now lies beneath the waters of Sherburne Reservoir, but for many a year only the lonely coyote skulked about the deserted outskirts, the wild flowers perfumed the once dusty streets, and the swallows nested in the vacant rafters of the ancient structures of the "silent city."

Ascending Mt. Altyn

Perhaps the most easily climbed of the peaks in the Many Glacier area is Mt. Altyn, rising to an elevation of nearly 3200 feet above the level of Swiftcurrent Lake. A fine foot trail to the summit was constructed in the summer of 1922, with many long and short switch-backs serving to reduce the gradient to the point where it was but little steeper than the ordinary horse trail.[12] It scurried through the shale, circled around outcropping ledges and scrambled up ravines some 2600 feet to the "saddle" between Mts. Altyn and Henkel. From there another gentle ascent of 600 feet to the eastward brought the climber to the peak's nearly 8,000-foot summit. Only traces of the old trail now remain, but the sturdy hiker can still find his way to the big cairn at the summit, working his way from a point near the north end of the lake, directly below the "saddle," and up the grassy slopes toward it.[13]

The views from the summit are rewarding, with ten lakes and the Sherburne Reservoir visible. Swiftcurrent Lake seems to be almost directly below, and the hotel with its slate roof lies like a huge, grey caterpillar along its shore. Mts. Wilbur, Gould, Allen, Grinnell and Henkel are all loftier, but in the intervening gaps rise the outlines of distant purple ranges that lie beyond. Appekunny Basin is to the northeast, and the view over the plains of the Indian Reservation stretches a full hundred miles to the eastward.

For the average hiker, the ascent may take up to four hours, but the descent can be accomplished in a fraction of that time. Where the shale seems thickest, it is often possible to vault down through the loose material at a great rate and without exertion, especially with the aid of an alpenstock.[14] Thoroughly experienced climbers may elect to vary their return to the point of departure by following more difficult terrain to Mt. Henkel toward the west, or Appekunny Basin to the north and east.[15]

Following Scenic Goat Trails

A new and different type of alpine adventure has been pioneered by J. Gordon Edwards, former ranger-naturalist and outstanding mountaineer of the Glacier Park Rockies. Having climbed all of the Park's challenging peaks, he has taken to investigating the pathways followed by the goats in the Many Glacier region, as well as elsewhere in the Park. In the course of so doing, he has discovered many skyline routes that are as thrilling and as scenic as the summits themselves. These, of course, are unmarked routes that in many cases have been found as the result of much trial and error. To preserve for the benefit of others, the results of his explorations in the Park's high country, Edwards has prepared instruction sheets that carefully spell out almost every step on each route.[16]

Several of the most scenic goat trails are in the Iceberg-Ptarmigan sector. One leads, for example, from the Ptarmigan tunnel to Ahern Pass, approximately four miles, of which Edwards says: "Scenically, this route is perhaps the greatest trail in the entire Park." Other routes include the "short-cut" from Many Glacier Hotel to Iceberg Lake via the Shangri-la bench north of Mt. Wilbur; the spectacular trip from Ptarmigan tunnel to Red Gap Pass, plus another three miles of game trail leading from Red Gap to the summit of Yellow Mountain; and the high traverse route from the slopes above Many Glacier to the Snow Moon Basin, situated at an elevation of 6600 feet on Mt. Allen.

More Goat Trails

Other interesting routes include the traverse of the trailless Blackfoot Glacier Basin from Jackson Glacier to Almost-A-Dog Pass; from Triple Divide Peak to Red Eagle Pass; from Logan Pass to Sperry Chalets; from Logan Pass to Gunsight Lake; from Fifty Mountain Camp to Jefferson Pass (and on to Francis Lake); from Ahern Pass to Chaney Glacier (via Ahern Peak and Ipasha Glacier overlook); and from Fifty Mountain meadows to Stoney Indian Pass via Chaney Glacier and Sue Lake (or via the north shoulder of Cathedral Peak). While none of these hikes should be undertaken except by those capable of Class 2 to 4 climbs, they do make available to those with these qualifications the routes to some of the world's great scenery.

During the summer of 1973, according to Edwards, a hitherto unknown phenomenon was discovered in the Kennedy Creek valley, to wit, a huge cavern located on the southwestern slopes of Yellow Mountain, a hundred feet above the north shore of Poia Lake. Its easily found, but very tight entrance leads some four or five hundred feet into an impressive chamber with small stalactites and a 40-foot waterfall. The cave has a second passage, more vertical in character; however, if there be other entrances to the cave, they have not, as yet, been located.

A Trip To The Garden Wall

Grinnell Glacier is presently the largest in the Swiftcurrent region, as well as in the Park.[17] Because of its size, its relative accessibility, and its location in the midst of some of the Park's most magnificent scenery, it has become the most popular of the Park's trails out of Many Glacier, as well as the most visited glacier in the Park. Incidentally, it is now reachable only by "ankle excursion," since it is one of the trails designated by the Park Service to be used, on a trial basis, for foot travel only.[18]

The glistening whiteness of Grinnell Glacier is visible for many miles back on the automobile highway leading into the Swiftcurrent valley. From the hotel veranda, its gleaming splendor is impressive and alluring. The trail of six miles is not difficult, and can be varied by joining the ranger-guided tour that leaves the Many Glacier boat dock each morning when the weather is good. This tour combines hiking with rides on the launches that ply on Swiftcurrent and Josephine Lakes, an arrangement that saves a total of four miles on the roundtrip.

From the dock at the head of Lake Josephine, the hike begins by a westerly crossing of the isthmus between Lakes Josephine and Grinnell, and starting up a steady grade along the flank of Mt. Grinnell above the lake. As elevation is gained, the views of the glacier and the Garden Wall become increasingly thrilling; and as the trail continues to rise, the views downward and backward toward Grinnell, Josephine and Swiftcurrent Lakes, with the Sherburne Reservoir in the distance, become breath-taking.

Glacial Reconnaissance

As the glacier is approached, lateral moraines are seen to flank it on either side, an indication of the former depth of the glacial ice. Several acres of drift face the lower glacier across an intervening pond of meltwater. From this pebbled drift, however, one can feel the chill of the ice-pack and sense the immensity of the magnificent cirque and its contents.

There are really three glaciers in the immediate view. These are the upper, or Salamander (so-called because of its shape), situated on a high shelf of the majestic Garden Wall; the Grinnell Glacier proper, occupying the lower, or main, part of the great cirque; and, finally, the petite Gem Glacier, about a quarter of a mile in length and breadth, and perched on a notch at the very summit of the Garden Wall in such a way as to be visible from both sides of the continental divide. To the south is the roof-like eminence of Mt. Gould, and to the north the lofty ridge of Mt. Grinnell.

As the ranger leads the hikers out on the glacier, they have an opportunity to see at close hand its fissures, crevasses and the astonishing amount of rock debris upon its surface as well as the poles by which the amount of annual forward movement of the ice-pack is measured. From the Salamander a melting torrent drops a sheer 350 feet to the glacier below, eroding a yawning pocket in its surface. High on the ramparts of the Garden Wall is a deep notch where goat trails abound, and to which experienced mountaineers sometimes climb, continuing on to Granite Park, or accomplishing the same feat in reverse by crossing Swiftcurrent Pass and climbing to the summit of the Garden Wall from the trail on its western face.

Endangered Species

What is the future of the three glaciers of the Garden Wall area? Geologists tell us that in prehistoric times the Grinnell arm of the Swiftcurrent Valley, like most of the other eastern Park valleys, was filled wall to wall with a river of ice, possibly successive ones, that ultimately scoured it out to the level of its present chain of paternoster lakes. As the climate gradually warmed, these enormous ice packs disappeared, but the continental divide, with its higher elevation and cooler temperatures, made possible the continued existence or subsequent formation of glacial ice on the shelf above Grinnell Lake. There it has remained to this day, industriously enlarging its cirque, and eroding the wall behind it into the sensational cliffs that are now the Garden Wall.

When George Bird Grinnell, for whom so much of this scenery was named, first visited the glacier in 1887,[19] he did not realize that even then it might be well into a deglaciation phase of its existence. The first official estimate of its size, made in 1901, was 525 acres,[20] most of which seemed to be there when I first viewed it in 1918. However, by the time that Grinnell last revisited his glacial namesake in 1926, at the age of 77, it had definitely begun to retreat, and by 1950 the shrinkage had amounted to nearly 40% of the 1901 bulk.[21] These figures had reference to the combined area of the upper and lower parts of the glacier which, by 1938, had become completely separated.

Since 1950 the further decreases have been rather modest, and experts feel that the situation may have become fairly well stabilized. As for the little Gem Glacier, now in all probability, like the former Iceberg and Swiftcurrent Glaciers, no more than a huge bank of snow and non-glaciated ice,[22] it seems to have changed but little in bulk and contour, perhaps by reason of its considerably higher elevation. The future of all three will depend, of course, upon climatic changes in the area during the decades ahead, but hopefully the years of recession have ended.[23]

Notes for Chapter 20
[1]For the origin of this colorful term, see Chapter 17, entitled "The Dude-Wranglers," at page 140, supra.
[2]"A Climber's Guide To Glacier National Park," by J. Gordon Edwards, at page 21.
[3]"Elrod's Guide And Book Of Information," (1924 edition) by Morton J. Elrod, at page 86.
[4]"Wild Animals Of Glacier National Park," by Vernon Bailey, at pages 53-54, gives a detailed description of this family of woodrats.
[5]Idem, at pages 188-190.
[6]Built at the site of the old sawmill destroyed in 1925. See Chapter 13, supra, entitled "Godfather To Glacier," at page 113.
[7]Letter dated 7/13/72 from J. Gordon Edwards, former ranger-naturalist at Many Glacier and author of the book "A Climber's Guide," supra. During the early 1950's Edwards met a man who gave him to understand that he was Parley Stark, and they discussed the mine at length. The man insisted that there was enough silver in the ore to pay for processing it; however, according to Donald Robinson, Assistant Chief Naturalist of the Park, an assay of ore samples secured from the mine by the Park Service showed no silver and very little copper. The mysterious stranger was not Parley Stark, since Stark was born in 1859 and died in 1936. For more information about the mine, see Chapter 23, infra, entitled "People Problems," at page 184 and note 19.
[8]"A Climber's Guide," supra, at page 85. A letter from its author, dated 7/13/72, describes how he discovered and reopened the old mine trail about 1954, the first part of which was actually a part of the original trail to Grinnell Glacier.
[9]"Through The Years In Glacier National Park," by Donald H. Robinson, at page 39.

[10]All of this information comes from the columns of the Swift Current Courier's first issue, published at Altyn on Saturday, September 1, 1900. It contained four pages and spoke in glowing terms of the great future of the area. The only known original of this issue was recently discovered in the Western History Department of the Denver Public Library, but reprints are now available for 25¢ each from the Glacier Natural History Association at West Glacier. Whether the issue in question was the only one ever published, or whether copies of later issues were never preserved is unknown; but the historic pages of thie first edition contain a wealth of information concerning the "glory days" of old Altyn.

[11]This was the final paragraph from the lead article on the Courier's front page, under multiple captions, as follows:

COPPER IS KING!
No Doubt Now About The Permanency
And Productiveness
Of The Swiftcurrent Mines
THE GROWTH OF ALTYN NOW ASSURED
Immense Bodies Of Pay Ore on the Gangue
Concentrator
To be Kept Running—Developments in the
Mountains Roundabout

[12]"Elrod's Guide", supra, at page 91.

[13]"A Climber's Guide, supra, at page 85.

[14]"Elrod's," supra, at page 91. The author of this book had that pleasure in 1924.

[15]"Elrod's Guide," supra, at page 98.

[16]These instructions are in mimeographed form and may be obtained, when available, through the Many Glacier Ranger Station.

[17]For additional information on Grinnell Glacier, see Chapter 6, supra, entitled "The Fascinating Glaciers," at page 47.

[18]This regulation of the Park Service was made effective at the beginning of the 1972 season, as reported by the Hungry Horse News for May 26, 1972.

[19]Article entitled "The Crown Of The Continent," by George Bird Grinnell, appearing in Century Magazine for September, 1901, at page 670. See, also, "Early History of Glacier National Park," by Madison Grant, at page 10.

[20]See Chapter 6, supra, entitled "The Fascinating Glaciers," at page 47.

[21]Idem, at page 47.

[22]J. Gordon Edwards, author of "A Climber's Guide," supra, states that he has been all over the Gem, sliding down the steep slopes and walking along the narrow ledge of rock east of the lower edge of the snow. He saw no crevasses, and does not believe there is any ice in it.

[23]See Chapter 6, supra, entitled "The Fascinating Glaciers," at page 48.

Ranger Sedlack and a class of sixth graders at Virginia Falls

Photo by Mel Ruder

Hikers resting on the shore of beautiful Lake Josephine

Photo by Walt Dyke, courtesy Burlington Northern

Chapter 21
GLACIER'S CANADIAN NEIGHBOR

Across the international boundary to the north of Glacier, and linked with the latter by lake launch, by mountain trail and by automobile highway lies its Canadian counterpart, Waterton Lakes National Park. Rising abruptly from the prairies in the southwest corner of Alberta, it represents a continuation of the geological features that distinguish its sister park. It is one of Canada's nineteen national parks that form a chain of nature sanctuaries extending from Mt. Revelstoke in British Columbia to Terra Nova in Newfoundland.[1]

Historically, the Park takes its name from the lakes that occupy the main valley; and these, in turn, were named in honor of Charles Waterton, the eccentric English ornithologist, by Lieutenant Thomas W. Blakiston, who led a section of the Palliser Expedition to that area in 1858.[2] Mt. Blakiston, the Park's tallest peak perpetuates his name. Also among the early visitors to the region were the international boundary survey parties of 1861 and 1874.[3] The former completed the survey from the Pacific Coast to the summit of the continental divide, and constructed a monument there. The survey from the Lake of the Woods in Minnesota up the eastward side of the divide was completed in 1874.[4] Prior to these various visits, the area had been the domain of the Blackfeet, the Kootenais, and the Crees.

First step in the creation of a park in the area was taken on May 30, 1895, when a township and a half, which included the Waterton Lakes, was ordered "set aside for a Forest Park."[5] This was the Kootenay Lakes Forest Reserve which, much increased in size, became the Waterton Lakes National Park in June, 1911. It was without supervision until March, 1910 when John George "Kootenai" Brown, one of those who had originally urged its establishment, was appointed Forest Ranger in charge of the Reserve; and he continued to serve as acting superintendent of the park from the time of its creation as such in 1911 until his replacement in August, 1914 at the age of 75.

Brown had first come to the Waterton valley in 1865 from Wild Horse Creek, now Fort Steele, British Columbia, over South Kootenay Pass. He became the area's first settler in 1877, its first landowner in 1891, and made a living there for himself and family in various capacities for nearly four decades. His one-time importance in the area is attested by the presence on one of the main streets of Waterton Townsite, the small community in which park headquarters are located, of a cairn dedicated to the memory of "Kootenai" Brown, "frontiersman, pioneer, gentleman." His was an adventurous career that had spanned three continents and four nations, as a youth in Ireland, British Army officer in India, buffalo hunter in Dakota, mail carrier and scout for the United States Army, trader, trapper and guide in the Waterton Lakes and northern Glacier Park areas.[6]

Present administration of the park is under the direct supervision of a resident superintendent who, in turn, is subject to the direction of the Department of Indian Affairs and Northern Development of Canada. The park wardens correspond to the rangers of Glacier Park, having the powers of a police constable and authority to enforce all park regulations. However, responsibility for the maintenance of law and order within the park still rests with the Royal Canadian Mounted Police.

Differences Between The Two Parks

Although the Waterton Lakes Park is really a geographical and geological extension of Glacier Park, there are many interesting and substantial differences between them. For example, Glacier has something like four dozen glaciers, while Waterton has none. Glacier straddles the continental divide, while Waterton lies entirely east of it. Glacier has more than 1,500 square miles and approximately 1,000,000 acres of territory, while Waterton has

203 square miles and less than 130,000 acres. Glacier's northern border coincides with the international boundary for 36 miles, as against 23 for Waterton.

In the opposite direction, it is more than 53 miles from the international boundary to the most southerly point of Glacier, as compared with a maximum north and south dimension of 14 miles for Waterton. In elevation, Glacier ranges from 3,150 feet above sea level at the confluence of the Middle and North Forks of the Flathead River to 10,400 feet at the summit of Mt. Cleveland; while the range for the Canadian park is from 4,050 feet at Waterton Lake, to 9,600 feet atop Mt. Blakiston. Interestingly, Mt. Cleveland lies close to the border, and looms as an impressive landmark from many viewing points in Waterton Park.

The Park is reached on pavement from Glacier Park by way of the Blackfeet Highway and the Chief Mountain International Highway,[7] the distance from Many Glacier being only 47 miles. Excellent paved roads also lead to Canadian points, such as Calgary (158 miles) and Lethbridge (72 miles). From the south end of Upper Waterton Lake a good trail leads to Granite Park Chalet, only 20 miles over Flattop Mountain, and Lake McDonald may also be reached via that route (followed in early days by prospectors and trappers seeking to replenish supplies), or by way of Brown Pass, Bowman Lake and the North Fork Road.

Services and Facilities

The principal hostelry of Waterton Park is, of course, the attractive Prince of Wales Hotel;[8] but other accommodations are obtainable at Waterton village. Available there are most of the customary services of a modern community, including motels, shops, garages, restaurants and churches, together with a $750,000 swimming pool, a motion picture theatre, and a dance pavilion. Although the townsite is Park property and thus belongs to the Canadian Government, private ownership of houses, stores and other buildings is permitted. The Park is officially open on an all-year basis, but from a practical standpoint its season is about the same as that of Glacier and the population dwindles to a handful after the tourist season ends.

The village itself is built on a delta deposited by Cameron Creek. It is believed that most of this alluvium was brought down while the Cameron and Alderson Glaciers were still present up the valleys. The grinding of the Waterton Glacier against Bertha Mountain was responsible for the sharp bank over which Cameron Falls now cascades in the townsite area. The light green streaks running down nearby Mt. Bertha are the result of great snow-slides which swept the trees from their pathways as they thundered at express train speed down the slopes.

From the boat pier at the village, one may board the good ship **International** for a cruise up the lake with its competent lady skipper-spieler. As it rides the deep blue water, good views are obtained of the snow avalanche-scarred slopes of Mt. Bertha and of the 20-foot swath that marks the 49th parallel and the international boundary. The launch pauses briefly at the United States end of the lake, where it sometimes takes on hikers from Many Glacier, 32 rugged trail miles away.

Nature's Handiwork

Waterton's geology is very much the same as that of Glacier. Its mountains are of extremely ancient origin, comprising gigantic strata of sedimentary shales and sandstones, aggregating more than a mile in thickness. The older rocks were uplifted and displaced horizontally to the eastward by the same Lewis Overthrust that reorganized the Glacier Park landscape. These various geological formations possess distinctive purple, red, green and grey coloration attributable to chemical changes in the minute particles of which they were composed. Seen everywhere is the glacial sculpturing that has produced prominent cirques, rock-basin lakes, U-shaped valleys, hanging valleys and sparkling waterfalls.

Within the Park's modest perimeter lie more than 20 mountain lakes. Over 100 miles of well-kept trails are available for hiking or riding, most of them radiating from the village. All of the trails lead through alpine valleys and beside picturesque mountain tarns, usually winding up a mountainside and past waterfalls to the lakes. On either side of the trails are brilliantly colored wildflowers, and the lakes with their emerald shades form a striking contrast to the dark green of the pine forests and the multi-hued slopes of the surrounding peaks. There are many snowfields throughout the park, but no genuine glaciers.

The Principal Lakes

The most conspicuous feature of Waterton Park is its main chain of lakes; and its heart is Upper Waterton Lake, a gleaming sapphire set among rugged mountains. Both countries share this jewel, for it spans the international boundary and separates the Lewis and

Livingston ranges. Seven miles in length and averaging a width of half a mile, the lake has a maximum depth of 450 feet. It occupies part of a valley that has been considerable deepened and widened by valley glaciers; in fact, a hanging valley formed by this deepening was responsible for Cameron Falls.

Rising more than 100 feet above the Canadian end of the lake is a treeless bluff surmounted by the Prince of Wales Hotel. Dwarfed by the nearby mountains, the Swiss chalet-type structure looks from a distance like a Hansel-and-Gretel cottage. Its huge lobby windows, looking southward down the lake, command one of the West's most dramatic views, and provide camera fans with limitless opportunities for unforgettable pictures.

The Waterton chain is comprised of three bodies of water. The magnificent upper lake is the one that crosses the international boundary. Linking it with the first lower lake is a stream whimsically called the Bosphorus, while that connecting the two lower lakes is known as the Dardanelles. It is along the west shore of one of the lower lakes, a sign pointing to it from the main highway a few rods away, that the burial plot of "Kootenai" Brown and his two wives (successive, not simultaneous) is located.

Cameron Lake

Apart from the entrance routes, the principal road within Waterton Lakes National Park is the Akamina Highway, a scenic ten-mile drive

Cameron Falls in Waterton Lakes National Park
Photo by Walt Dyke, courtesy Burlington Northern

High above Waterton Lake stands the Prince of Wales Hotel
Photo by Walt Dyke, courtesy Burlington Northern

WATERTON - GLACIER INTERNATIONAL PEACE PARK

Gatewey to Waterton-Glacier International Peace Park
Photo by Frances R. Hanna

that rises more than 1,000 feet from the level of the townsite to that of Cameron Lake. Along the way are seen the remnants of Discovery Well, sometimes called "Oil City," where the first discovery of oil, though it proved to be in non-commercial quantities, was made in Alberta. The highway ends on the very shores of beautiful Cameron Lake, also situated astride the international boundary, and almost due west of the village.

Next to the views from the foot of Upper Waterton Lake, that from the shore of Cameron Lake looking south toward the Herbst Glacier on the slopes of Mt. Custer, both on the Glacier Park side of the line, is one of the grandest in the Rockies. Perhaps the most southerly 200 yards of Cameron Lake lie on the United States side of the border. This is an especially interesting part of the Waterton Park for two reasons. Since the lake is bordered on the west by the continental divide, its waters flow ultimately to Hudson Bay via the Waterton Lakes and the North Saskatchewan, while waters that drain westward from the divide through Akamina Brook and Kintla Creek eventually reach the Pacific through the North Fork of the Flathead and the Columbia rivers. Also the boundary line between Alberta and British Columbia intersects the international boundary along the ridge of the continental divide just to the west of Cameron Lake, creating there a triple boundary point.

Canyons And Colors

The same fantastic rock coloring that is to be seen everywhere in Glacier Park is frequently encountered at Waterton. For example, the colors of the rock formations of the gorge leading to Cameron Lake, mostly the yellow-browns of the lower Altyn formation, are visible from a number of viewing points along the Akamina Highway. Similarly, the reds and maroons to be viewed at Red Rock Canyon, but at close range, can be only described as gorgeous.

At Red Rock Canyon a popular, self-guided nature tour follows an easy course up one side of the canyon and back down to Blakiston Falls. Signs along the route explain how the canyon was formed, and how the visible ripple marks and mud cracks beside the footpath confirm the fact that these sediments were formed in very shallow water at the bottom of an ancient sea. Some of the muds at the bottom of this sea contained iron compounds which rusted, on long exposure to the air, to form the red mineral hematite that is seen on the canyon walls. Greenish bands within the red ones also contain iron minerals, but were not oxidized to the same extent as the reddish areas. The several hundred feet of this red sedimentary rock is known as the Grinnell formation, and of course it is equally prominent in Glacier Park.[9]

Boundary Trails

The most scenic of all Waterton trails is that to Crypt Lake lying high in a hanging valley on the international border to the east of the Waterton chain of lakes. The lake lies in a U-shaped amphitheatre, or cirque, gouged out of the head of Hell Roaring Canyon, with the cliffs at its rear on the United States side of the line. The lake has no way out of its hidden valley except through an underground stream and a tremendous waterfall. The view, of course, is incomparable, but the hiker who wishes to see it must crawl on hands and knees through a man-made tunnel, climb a ladder of stone steps, and traverse a sheer ledge. Fortunate, indeed, are those who dare to make the trip to this enchanted mountain tarn.

The principal route across the international boundary is the 9-mile trail from Waterton village to the head of Waterton Lake along the west shore of the latter. Just south of the border, a branch of it runs up West Boundary Creek and, after paralleling the boundary for several miles, turns back into Canada where it branches to Cameron Lake and the Carthew Lakes. Other trails out of Waterton village lead to British Columbia by way of Akamina, South Kootenay and Sage passes.

The other principal trail across the international line is that leading into the Belly River Valley. It runs from the Chief Mountain International Highway along the route of an old wagon road into the Belly River ranger station, at which point it branches in several directions. A second, but rarely used, trail, taking off from the Blood Indian Reserve, follows the North Fork of the Belly River through sensational scenery to Miche Wabun Lake, approximately four miles south of the border.

Fauna And Flora

Much of Waterton Lakes National Park is in the transition zone between the prairie and montane life zones, making it one of the most interesting areas in the country from a botanical standpoint. Plants characteristic of both the plains and the mountains grow in profusion throughout the park, and the flowers present an ever-changing carpet of color for most of the summer season. Prominent among the flora are the same flowers found in Glacier, including the avalanche and mariposa lilies, the wild rose and wild geranium, the gaillardia, larkspur, columbine, aster, Indian paintbrush, and even the distinctive bear grass.[10]

As is the case with Glacier, the Waterton Park provides a sanctuary in which all wild creatures are protected from hunting and trapping. Larger mammals characteristic of the park include both black and grizzly bears, cougar, moose, elk, mule deer, bighorn sheep and mountain goats. Smaller fauna include the lynx, wolverine, bobcat, marten, weasel, badger, beaver, snowshoe hare and a number of varieties of ground squirrels. In a paddock near the park's north entrance is maintained a small herd of plains bison.[11]

International Peace Park

Separated as the two parks are by only the width of an imaginary line, yet joined together by a magnificent body of international water, it is only natural that there should be a special bond of friendship between the peoples of the two areas, particularly since the parks themselves were almost identical in significance and were set aside with the same purposes in mind. This special unity had first been recognized in 1910 when Senator Penrose, during the course of the debates upon the bill to establish Glacier Park, stated, "This park will be international in character."[12]

In recognition of these circumstances and wishing to commenorate the friendly relations existing between the people of the United States and Canada, the Rotary Clubs of Montana and Alberta met in joint session on July 4, 1931 at the Prince of Wales Hotel in Waterton Park. They passed a resolution initiating the movement to establish what was to be known as the "Waterton-Glacier International Peace Park," a movement that led shortly to the introduction of a bill by Congressman Scott Leavitt of Montana authorizing the United States to participate in the establishment of a park that would be joint in name and spirit, but not in ownership or administration. After its passage by both houses and signature by President Hoover, and similar legislation had also been enacted by the Canadian parliament, the International Peace Park became a reality in 1932.[13]

In 1947 a cairn was built on each side of the international border at the Chief Mountain Customs area, commemorating the establishment of the joint park. At this time, appropriate ceremonies were held by Rotary Clubs and officials of both parks, dedicating the monuments for all time to the friendly relationship that exists between the two nations.[14] The association formed by the original Rotarians meets annually on alternate sides of the border to renew their pledge of friendship and to foster good will throughout the world.[15]

Notes For Chapter 21

[1] According to the 1969 bulletin issued by the Canadian Minister of Indian Affairs and Northern Development entitled "Canada's Mountain National Parks," the Canadian system comprises the largest complex of national parks in the world.

[2] "The Papers Of The Palliser Expedition," edited by Irene M. Spry, at page 578.

[3] See Chapter 11, supra, entitled "Advent Of The White Man," at page 90.

[4] Idem.

[5] "Kootenai Brown, His Life And Times," William Rodney, published 1969 by the Morriss Printing Company, Ltd., in Victoria, B.C., at page 173. See pages 192-211 of the same text for details of the Park's development and of Brown's further service therefor.

[6] "Kootenai Brown," supra, is a well researched and authentic biography of Brown's life and adventures. It reports that he was the area's first settler (page 213), its first land owner (page 166), its first park warden (pages 192-194), and its first park superintendent (pages 198-199). An interesting, but less authentic account of his career will be found in an article entitled "Kootenai Brown, Colorful Tales Of A Waterton Pioneer," by G. Adelle Rackette, appearing at pages 46-51 of the 1948 edition of the "Drivers' Manual" (See note 15, Chapter 6, supra).

[7] See Chapter 15, supra, entitled "Roads And Highways," at pages 123-125.

[8] See Chapter 16, supra, entitled "The Great Log Lodges," at page 134.

[9] See "Notes For A Self-Guided Tour Of Red Rock Canyon," published by the Waterton Lakes National Park administration. Also, see Chapter 2, supra, entitled "A Romance In Rocks," at page 18.

[10] See folder on Waterton Lakes National Park, issued by the Director, National and Historical Parks Branch, Ottawa.

[11] Idem.

[12] "Through The Years In Glacier National Park," by Donald H. Robinson, at page 94.

[13] Action on behalf of the United States was taken by the 72nd Congress through its enactment of Chapter 157, Laws of 1931-1932 as of May 2, 1932 (The bill was HR 4752 by Leavitt).

[14] "Through The Years," supra, at page 97. For a detailed story of these ceremonies and how the International Peace Park came into existence, see article on that subject by S. H. Middleton, of Cardston, Alberta, at pages 52-56 of the 1948 edition of "Drivers' Manual" (see note 15, Chapter 6, supra).

[15] See folder on "Waterton Lakes National Park" issued by the Director, National and Historical Parks Branch, Ottawa. According to the Hungry Horse News for July 14, 1972, the date for the 1972 meeting was July 22-23 at the Glacier Park Hotel, with the president of Rotary International, Roy D. Hickman, of Birmingham, Alabama, as the featured speaker. Odd-year meetings are held at the Prince of Wales Hotel at Waterton, with Alberta clubs acting as the hosts.

Spectacular view of Waterton Lake and Prince of Wales Hotel looking south toward the United States

Courtesy Burlington Northern

Looking south on Waterton Lake from bluff on which stands the Prince of Wales Hotel
Courtesy Burlington Northern

PART IV.
PARK ADMINISTRATION
AND PROBLEMS

Chapter 22
THE GUARDIANS OF
GLACIER

Administration of the national parks is under the control of the National Park Service, a division of the Department of the Interior. The Service was created in 1916 and charged with responsibility for the national parks, monuments and similar reservations. Under the organic legislation, its function was defined as being "to conserve the scenery and the natural and historic objects and the wildlife therein and to provide for the enjoyment of the same in such manner and by such means as shall leave them unimpaired for the enjoyment of future generations."[1]

Headquartered in Washington, D.C., the Service has eight regional offices, a planning and service center in Denver, and a host of field areas throughout the United States, as well as in Puerto Rico and the Virgin Islands. Service headquarters in Glacier Park are in a functional and attractive building at West Glacier. Its three stories supply office space for the superintendent and his administrative personnel, including the chief ranger and chief naturalist, as well as a record room and an excellent library of publications dealing with subjects of special interest to the Park.

Early Administration Of The Park

Following its establishment in May, 1910, progress toward making Glacier a useable park was painfully slow, partly due to the inadequacy of congressional appropriations. Major William R. Logan, who had accompanied the Pumpelly Expedition through the region in 1883, was named "Superintendent Of Road And Trail Construction," effective August 8, 1910, and became the Park's first superintendent as of April 1, 1911.[2]

From the beginning, the new superintendent was confronted with almost insurmountable problems. 1910 was the heaviest "fire year" in the area's history, either before or since, with more than 100,000 acres of forest land consumed. Such trails as existed were practically unfit for use, and suitable administrative quarters did not exist. However, the next two years witnessed a great deal of activity in the way of trail building, construction of a suitable headquarters complex at Fish Creek, and the erection of ranger cabins along Park boundaries.[3]

The Park Rangers

Logan had organized a corps of rangers in the fall of 1910, with Henry Vaught as Chief Ranger. The others were Joe Cosley, Dan Doody, Bill Burns, "Dad" Randels, and a man named Pierce. This force was expanded to 16 men in 1912, with each man assigned a sector of the Park boundary to patrol, and particularly to be on the alert for poachers and forest fires. The cabins were primitive, the Montana winters severe, and the hazards and hardships of lone patrols were almost unbelievable.[4]

Those were the days when the Glacier Park ranger could be any resourceful outdoorsman, with plenty of courage and stamina. Not so today. The latest federal service regulations require a park ranger to be a versatile individual, a combination, in fact, of the abilities of ranger, naturalist, historian and archeologist. Minimum qualifications include a college degree or its equivalent in experience. Recruitment is from such academic backgrounds as park and recreation management, field-oriented natural sciences, history, archaeology, police science, business administration, and other subjects bearing a relationship to park management activities. Despite these rigorous requirements, the job is a popular one and there is usually a waiting list of top-quality candidates.[5]

The backbone, so to speak, of Park Service operations in every national park is its corps of park rangers. Their duties are to manage public use of, and to protect the forest, land and water resources and wildlife in the national park system. This includes directing, controlling and assisting park visitors; planning and conducting programs of public safety, including law enforcement and rescue work; planning and carrying out conservation efforts to protect plant and animal life from fire, disease and heavy visitor usage; setting up and directing interpretive programs, such as slide shows, guided tours and displays; and performing a variety of other technical and administrative assignments directly related to park operations.[6]

Organizational Set-Up

Top official of the Park is its superintendent. For administrative purposes, it is divided into the Hudson Bay District (everything east of the continental divide) and the West Lakes District (the Pacific side). The various services for each are headed up by a supervisor as follows:

District Ranger—in charge of visitor protection and services, and of ranger personnel.

District Facility Manager—in charge of roads, trails and maintenance personnel.

District Naturalist — in charge of Seasonal Ranger Naturalists during the summer.

These supervisors are responsible, respectively, to the Chief Park Ranger, Supervising Civil Engineer and Chief Park Naturalist.

There are fewer than twenty permanent rangers, some of whom have specialized assignments, such as Fire Control, Bear Control and Mountain Rescue operations. There is also a Research Biologist whose duty it is to plan, coordinate and carry out scientific research in reference to the Park's plant and animal communities (ecosystems) as a basis for effective management, conservation and interpretation of these communities and their individual parts.[8]

Seasonal And Special Assignments

With the coming of summer, the Park's need for ranger-power expands greatly, and a substantial number of seasonal rangers and ranger-naturalists are added to the staff. Many of the former are stationed at Park campgrounds, over which they exercise supervision. The corps of Ranger-Naturalists works with the two permanent Naturalists to assist the visiting public in understanding and appreciating the Park. Many of these are college professors and graduate students, and not a few of them are women. They provide information, act as hike leaders, and give evening talks, sometimes illustrated with slides. Naturalist-conducted all-day hikes are made daily to Iceberg Lake, Grinnell Glacier and Sperry Glacier, in addition to many shorter walks to other points. Ranger-Naturalists are also stationed at such points as Sperry Chalets, Granite Park and Logan Pass to assist in interpreting those areas for visitors.

Among specialized assignments, one of the most difficult is that of mountain rescue work, over which Ranger Robert Frausen has been in charge for many years. He trains other rangers in rescue techniques, and leads them personally when dangerous situations arise on the glaciers or peaks. It was he who directed the discovery and evacuation of the bodies of the five young climbers who perished on Mt. Cleveland in December, 1969. An official warning had unfortunately gone unheeded.[9]

Enforcement Activities

The Glacier Park rangers cooperate with immigration and customs officials, as well as with the Border Patrol and the wardens of Waterton Lakes National Park. During the travel season, two of the rangers act as customs officers at Waterton Lake. On criminal matters they are able to call upon the office of the Federal Bureau of Investigation at Kalispell for assistance. They have had some trouble with poachers, mainly in respect to elk on the east and south sides of the Park. There has also been some difficulty with drug pushers, although this has been minor in view of the large number of young people employed in the area each season.[10]

Because of the heavy influx of visitors, it is necessary that surveillance of certain areas be seasonally maintained. Hence the assignment of motor patrolmen to "ride herd" over the traffic on Going-To-The-Sun Highway.[11] Similarly, an experienced ranger patrols the northern backcountry on horseback to check on compliance with Park regulations, as well as to note trail conditions, to pack out litter, and to help people who may be in distress.

Things Rangers Used To Do

The duties of the ranger have varied somewhat through the years. There was a time, for example, because of the fact that the Park was bounded on the north by Canada, and prohibition laws had been enacted by both Montana and the United States, when it became profitable to smuggle Canadian liquor across the border. Rangers were not always successful in excluding it, although they combatted the traffic valiantly. With the repeal of prohibition in the 1930's, they were relieved of this unpleasant and onerous assignment.

There was also a time when their duties included predator control, and it was deemed desirable to reduce the numbers of mountain lions, bobcats, wolves and coyotes, this being

175

another policy that has become obsolete. The predator-eradication assignment of 50 years ago fell to the lot of a veteran ranger named "Chance" Beebe. "Chance" was a master of woodcraft, as well as a skillful hunter. One of his official assignments was the trapping of coyotes and wolves in the Cut Bank valley, a project on which he established a record of some 67 scalps. It was Beebe, also, who put an end to the career of the monster grizzly that over a period of decades, before and after the turn of the century, had made the valley of the Cut Bank an area of danger for Indians and whites alike.[12]

Northern Outpost

In the Park's early days, the loneliest assignment for any of its rangers was in the Belly River Valley. Because of the fact that the stream flowed northward, the only easy means of exit from the valley was by way of Canada. The Park Service maintained a rather primitive ranger station there, manned by a ranger named Harry Hockett, who had given up a lucrative wholesale drug business in Missouri to go into forestry in the western country, later coming to Glacier Park. For the five years preceding 1924, he had the Belly River assignment because he loved the life and the wilderness.

Being without telephone communication with the outside world, his only information was that which he could obtain by radio. To get his mail in the wintertime required a two-day roundtrip, since the nearest human being was located more than 10 miles away by snowshoe and the nearest village 20. However, for company he had his faithful dog Pat and a trio of horses; and looked forward to the day when the promise of a telephone and new cabin might come true.

Winter Perils

With the coming of modern means of transportation, all rangers are now stationed during the winter at West Glacier headquarters, except for one man at Polebridge, one at Walton, two at St. Mary, and one or two at East Glacier. However, in the days when rangers were stationed throughout the year at such points as Belly River and Many Glacier, these assignments meant hazards and hardships, as well as loneliness, during the long Montana winters. The ranger had certain rounds to patrol and had to spend much time on snowshoes or skis. There were many close brushes with death, such as the harrowing experience of Ranger Ben Miller who was

Chief Ranger Charles B. Sigler, November, 1975
Photo by Mel Ruder

swept away by an avalanche while on patrol in February, 1933, but lived to tell the story.[13]

In November of the same year, Ranger Elmer Ness, stationed at Belly River, started out on a 4-day patrol that would take him over Gable Pass. Near the 7000-foot summit of the pass, he slipped on an ice-glazed slope and was catapulted onto a large, protruding rock. Despite the agonies of a splintered hip socket and a double fracture of the pelvis, he managed to drag himself the 3½ miles back to the ranger station, an ordeal that required three days and two nights. A year later, after seven weeks in the hospital and a lengthy convalescence, he was again able to resume his patrol duties.[14]

Early Ranger Experiences

Before the Park was established, the area was under the jurisdiction of the United States Forest Service, and the entire territory now comprising Glacier Park was handled by only two or three rangers. One of these, Frank S. Liebig, continued to serve as a ranger in the area after it became a park. When he originally started work in 1902, his instructions were "to look for fires, timber thieves, which were plentiful along the Great Northern Railway, and for squatters and game violators."[15] His headquarters were at the head of Lake McDonald and his duties included periodic patrolling of the area under his supervision. A graphic description of the territory which it was necessary for him to cover was given by him in a Forest Service publication article many years later.[16]

"In 1905 or 1906, I made a roundtrip across the Rockies and back via Flattop Mountain and down to Waterton Lake, where the million-dollar Prince of Wales Hotel is now. At that time there was only a dim trapper's trail to follow and a trapper's hut to stay in overnight; but as a rule I preferred to stay in my small tent, which I always carried on my pack horse. On these trips I stayed quite often overnight with the Mounties in the barracks at Pincerton. These redcoats were sure a fine class of men and helped me out on several occasions. I was treated like I belonged to them, and they were much interested in our affairs.

"One overnight stopping place used to be at Babb's near the foot of lower St. Mary's Lake and back into the good old U.S.A. Here we had a small sawmill near the lake and I had to check up on the timber and stumpage. At the narrows of upper St. Mary's another old hut provided shelter for the night. Sometimes I stayed in the old mining town of Altyn if I returned over Swiftcurrent Pass. By St. Mary's Lake I came out over Gunsight Pass and Sperry Glacier Basin and thence to Lake McDonald."[17]

Red Poachers

Liebig's scariest adventure as a ranger was the result of getting word that a band of Canadian Cree Indians had crossed the border on the North Fork of the Flathead River with 10 or 12 lodges and 40 dogs, and were killing moose and smoking the meat. With Ranger Frank Herrig and a homesteader named Frank Guduhn, he moved north until the Indians were located near Kintla Creek. A large amount of meat was draped over some poles with a fire underneath. As they approached the site, guns in hand, they were met by men and dogs while the squaws and children scurried into the tepees. Liebig ordered them to leave by the next morning or he would shoot their dogs which were valuable to them in the killing of big game. But by mid-morning there were no signs of departure, and the chief said they couldn't move for a week until their meat had been cured. At this point, shots rang out and two of the dogs hit the dust. As Liebig tells the story:

"Ranger Herrig couldn't stand it any longer, and wanted to mop up all of the dogs. I got ready for action also, thinking that the Indians sure would get even with us. So I hollered to Herrig and Geduhn to hold their fire for a minute to see what the Indians had to say.

Everything was confusion in the camp and I thought lead would be flying in our direction any second. Then the chief hollered and told me they would move immediately. The lodges went down, and in three hours they were on the trail up the North Fork and across the Canadian border. We hung around for several days, but the Crees stayed away."[18]

Trapper Turned Ranger

Prominent in the early days of the Park was a character named Joe Cosley. In the mid-1890's he had come to the Waterton Lakes-Belly River region, where he followed the occupations of guide and trapper. Soon after Glacier became a national park, he served several years as a ranger in the Belly River Valley.[19] He it was, so it has been said, for whom Crossley Lake and Crossley Ridge in the northern part of the Park were named, the spelling being corrupted from "Cosley" to "Crossley" in the course of map-making.[20]

After serving in the Canadian army in World War I, Cosley returned to his old haunts in the Belly River-Waterton Lakes sector, acting as a guide for visitors in the summer and surreptitiously following the occupation of a trapper in the winter. When the rangers objected to the latter, he simply moved across the border into the North Flathead region of southeast British Columbia, but still close to Glacier. From that haven, he continued to make occasional forays into the high valleys of Glacier, making a fine catch of beaver and muskrat and slipping back into Canada before he could be apprehended. The rangers stalked him unsuccessfully for years; finally, however, he was to receive his come-uppance.[21]

Ranger Turned Poacher

In 1929 the ranger in the Belly River area was Joseph Heimes, and on May 4th of that year he found evidence of beaver trapping, and followed the tracks to the poacher's camp. There he found the owner missing, but noted the hind quarters of a beaver hanging on a pole over the fire, several traps, and three muskrat hides cached between bed blankets.[22] He returned that evening to find Cosley himself and put him under arrest after a struggle. With the help of another ranger, Cosley was taken over Gable Pass on snowshoes,[23] then down to East Glacier and by Great Northern to Belton, at the opposite end of the Park, where his trial was held on May 7th. He pleaded guilty, was fined $100, and given a 90-day suspended sentence. His rifle, traps and muskrat hides were confiscated and he was released at 3 p.m. that same day after two friends had taken care of paying the fine.[24]

Some two hours later park officials were tipped off that Joe, having borrowed a pair of snowshoes, had departed with a friend in the latter's car for Avalanche Creek, to which point the Logan Pass road had been cleared of snow, and was planning to return to the Belly River to retrieve his cache of beaver pelts. They telephoned to Clarence Willey, ranger at Lake McDonald, but Cosley had already passed that point and had a comfortable headstart. When he reached the snow above Avalanche Creek, he put on his snowshoes, racing up the McDonald Valley to Ahern Pass, and down to the Belly River where he picked up his beaver pelts and continued into Canada.[25]

The next morning Rangers Heimes and Hansen traveled by train to East Glacier, thence by automobile to Cardston in Canada, and on west toward Waterton Lakes Park, finally hiking into Joe's camp in the Belly River Valley, only to find him gone without a sign.[26] He had snowshoed from above Lake McDonald over dangerous Ahern Pass to the Belly River at the age of 59 in less than 20 hours, a feat at any age. With his furs he had made good his escape to Alberta and departed from Glacier Park, never to return again.[27]

The rangers of today do not have to deal with the likes of Joe Cosley. Neither do they have to eliminate park predators, nor to intercept liquor smugglers seeking to cross the border. They do, however, have a multiplicity of routine duties, not the least of which is coping with the whims and foibles of the million and more members of the vacationing public that annually throng Park trails and camps. And they are still confronted with most of the old park problems, as well as a few new and challenging ones. These seem logically to fall into three general categories that will be discussed in some depth in the next three chapters.[28]

Notes For Chapter 22

[1] See 1968 bulletin of the National Park Service entitled "Careers in the National Park Service," at page 4. Date of approval of the creational Act was August 25, 1916.

[2] "Through The Years In Glacier National Park," by Donald H. Robinson, at page 56.

[3] Idem, at page 57.

[4] Idem, at page 58.

[5] See bulletin dealing with the same subject as that in Note 1 above, but issued in mimeographed form in 1972 by the Park Service.

[6] Idem.

[7] Letter from William J. Briggle, Superintendent of Glacier National Park, dated July 15, 1973.

[8] Idem.

[9] Interview with Ruben O. Hart, then Chief Ranger, on 7/10/70.

[10] Idem.

[11] See Hungry Horse News for 7/3/70.

[12] McClintock in his book "The Old North Trail," at pages 44-45, recites the Blackfoot legend of the dreaded "Medicine Grizzly Of Cut Bank Canyon" and relates terrifying encounters with the beast by both William Jackson and McClintock himself. According to McClintock, the grizzly's footprints measured 13 inches in length, were six inches broad at the heel and seven inches across the toes. For the story of how Beebe finally slew the monster "after an exciting episode of relentless pursuit in which man and beast matched wits and interchanged roles in stalking each other," see Ruhle's handbook entitled "Roads And Trails Of Waterton-Glacier National Parks," at page 97.

[13] For a more complete report on the adventure of Ranger Ben C. Miller, see page 187 of Chapter 24, infra, entitled "Environmental Problems."

[14] The experience of Ranger Ness has been vividly described by himself in an article entitled "On Patrol," appearing at pages 105-107 of the 1948 edition of the "Drivers' Manual" (see note 15, Chapter 6, supra).

[15] Article entitled "Early Days In The Glacier Park Country," by Frank S. Liebig, appearing in the Spring Edition of "Montana West," at page 7.

[16] Idem.

[17] Idem, at pages 8 and 9.

[18] Idem, at pages 7 and 8.

[19] "Kootenai Brown, His Life And Times," by William Rodney, at page 207.

[20] "Through The Years," supra, at page 110.

[21] See article entitled "Cosley, Trapper And Guide Extraordinary," by Julia Nelson of Mountain View, Alberta, appearing in the "Canadian Cattleman" for August, 1953. See, also, article by Ranger Joseph F. Heimes entitled "Capture of Joe Cosley," appearing at pages 107-111 of the 1948 edition of the "Drivers' Manual" (see note 15, Chapter 6, supra).

[22] Idem.

[23] Heimes had hoped to be able to take Cosley to Waterton and thence by automobile to Cardston, Alberta, to East Glacier, and to Belton where the U.S. Commissioner was located. However, when he called the Royal Canadian Mounted Police for permission to use the Waterton route, the reply, was "The minute he steps over the line he's a free man." So, with the aid of Ranger Tom Whitcraft (later Glacier's chief ranger), Cosley was taken to Babb over Gable Pass on snowshoes, thus avoiding the necessity of crossing the Canadian boundary. (Interview with Heimes appearing in the Hungry Horse News, May 23, 1975).

[24] See articles referred to in Note 21.

[25] Idem.

[26] Idem. In 1929, when this adventure occurred, the highway over Marias Pass had not been completed, and construction of the Chief Mountain Highway had not yet been undertaken.

[27] See articles referred to in Note 21. However, a third and considerably different version of this tale is to be found at pages 39-42 of Andy Russell's 1971 book entitled "Trails Of A Wilderness Wanderer." As Russell tells the story, there is no mention of Cosley having been apprehended by the Glacier Park rangers, and they had merely been tipped off to his plans at a time when he had gone to Kalispell to make a deal for his pelts. Russell, however, got his details of the episode from a friend of Cosley, who presumably got it directly from Joe; hence it makes him out to be the hero, rather than the villain, as in the Julia Nelson and Ranger Heimes versions.

[28] Of the greatest concern to the modern Glacier Park rangers are what may be described as people problems, environmental problems, and grizzly bear problems. These, respectively are the subjects of the final three chapters of the book.

Park Ranger station in a setting of natural beauty
Photo by Walt Dyke, courtesy Burlington Northern

Ranger station and "Snowflake" at Waterton Lake, looking north
Photo by Mel Ruder

Chapter 23
PEOPLE PROBLEMS

The national parks have to deal with most of the problems that are created by people everywhere, as well as a few special ones contributed to by circumstances peculiar to the parks. In Glacier National Park man-caused problems fall into three principal categories: those incident to enforcement of both general laws and special park regulations; the nuisances caused by inexperience or foolhardiness of visitors and employees in making use of park areas; and the problems created by privately owned property within park boundaries.

Fortunately, major crime is a rarity in most of our national parks, and this is especially true of Glacier, remote as it is from our great centers of population. With but few exceptions, moreover, the hordes of sightseers who flock to the area during its brief season are on a holiday, and are seldom impelled by other than recreational motives. Such crimes as homicide, rape, burglary, mugging and grand theft are non-existent.

Inevitably, of course, there are misdemeanors and infractions of various kinds, of which the ordinary visitor does not become particularly aware, that are bound to occur wherever there are enforceable rules and regulations. Laws applicable to automobile use, as well as the possession of forbidden substances, have to be enforced. Violations of Park regulations include the killing of game, feeding the bears, carrying firearms, building fires in unauthorized places, camping in non-designated locations, and discharging firearms within the Park. Those charged with offenses are arraigned before a United States magistrate or in federal court, depending upon the character of the offense.

Dangers To Personal Safety

A different set of problems grows out of the use of park premises for recreational purposes in such a way as to cause injury or the danger of injury to the user himself, and sometimes to require aid from Park Service personnel. In most cases, the occurrence can be traced to inexperience, combined at times with poor judgment and a certain degree of foolhardiness. It is inexperience, of course, that leads to misconceiving the dangers by reason of snow on the trails, the perils inherent in glacial ice, and the lack of security afforded by the shale rocks that compose so much of the Park's high country. The danger is greatly increased by traveling without companions who, in case of accident or injury, can assist or go for help. For those who undertake conquest of the peaks, there are additional hazards from lightning and avalanche.

Strangely, the trait of foolhardiness in use of park facilities is not necessarily limited to those unacquainted with our national parks. One of the most flagrant examples of a deliberate flaunting of safety considerations occurred in September, 1915, when Stephen Mather, director of national parks, apparently impelled by rather flimsy considerations of personal pride,[1] took off from Lake McDonald Lodge over Gunsight Pass by saddlehorse in a snow storm, contrary to all advices from local people familiar with conditions. He and his party were successful in getting through, but one can readily imagine the headlines and the damage to the Park's image had they perished in the course of such a reckless exploit.

To a large extent, the mishaps that occur on Glacier's trails or mountain slopes befall members of the younger generation, including the seasonal employees of the park concessionaires. In fact, much more of a threat to the young people in the parks than bears or automobiles is the venturesome spirit that takes them off well beaten paths and leads them into hiking or climbing situations with which they do not have the ability to cope. Carried away by the delightful trails and seemingly safe mountains and streams, a few are wont to take imprudent risks and sometimes pay with their lives.

Incidence Of Fatal Injuries

Mishaps to those making use of saddle horse facilities in Glacier Park have been virtually nil. But according to records of the Park, hiking or climbing fatalities average about one per season. At least, this was the rate during 1966-1969, when there were four deaths attributable to trail accidents. Two of these were in 1966 and involved entirely unrelated accidents to priests, one of whom lost his footing and fell off the edge of the road near Logan Creek, while the other fell over a small cliff on the slopes of Mt. Oberlin. In 1967, a 20-year-old was fatally injured descending Mt. Custer, while another death occurred in 1969 as the result of a fall on Mt. Altyn.[2]

Too often the obituary column claims its victims from among the youngsters, visiting or working in the Park for the first time, who take to the high trails, the alpine slopes and other perilous places. For example, in 1960 Frederick Steinmetz, aged 18, of Detroit, Michigan, an art major at Assumption College in Windsor, Ontario, slipped off a cascade at the headwaters of Kennedy Creek, located some miles to the northeast of Many Glacier Hotel. He had been working as a clerk at the Swiftcurrent Motor Inn, and embarked on his fatal excursion on his day off.

It was in 1955 that June Johnson, of South Euclid, Ohio, came to a tragic end when she inadvertently plunged a thousand feet down the slopes of Mt. Altyn, near the Many Glacier Hotel. On June 18, 1963, Jerome Delaney, aged 19, son of a former mayor of the city of St. Paul, while visiting in the Park fell to his death from Mt. Pollock near Logan Pass. Delaney was wearing moccasins, while his two companions were shod in tennis shoes. He plummeted 1,000 feet when a shale ledge gave way.

Catastrophe On Cleveland

Perhaps the Park's greatest tragedy took place during the Christmas holidays of 1969 when five young men undertook to scale Mt. Cleveland, the Park's highest peak. All were from Montana, including Ray Martin, aged 22, of Butte, James Anderson, aged 18, of Big Fork, Jerry Kanzler, aged 18, of Bozeman, Mark Levitan, aged 20, of Helena, and Clare Pogreba, aged 22, of Butte. They had last been seen on December 27, 1969, as they left Waterton Lake, avowedly bound for the summit of Mt. Cleveland.[3]

When they had not returned within a reasonable time, search efforts began and continued to January 8, 1970, when weather and avalanche danger forced their termination. However, surveillance was carried on as weather permitted during the winter, and some of the party's gear, such as a camera, slicker, pack and hat, were found at points which

indicated that they had been attempting to scale the peak's west wall. The search was resumed in May, 1970, without success. With persistence, however, a team of rangers and others with mountaineering experience was finally able to recover the bodies of all five climbers. Two of them were found on June 28th and the others on July 2nd. In reconstructing the tragedy, it was thought likely that they had been higher on the mountain when struck by an avalanche and swept down to the 7,500-foot level.

The bodies had been buried in solid ice and were extricated with great difficulty. When Jim Anderson's body was located, they were able to identify him by his calendar watch, which had stopped on December 30th. When picked up, the watch started running again. He had been an Eagle Scout, an all-around athlete in high school, a four-year bandman playing the cornet, and member of the chorus. He had organized the Mission Ski Club and had enrolled at Montana State University with the idea of becoming a geologist.[4]

After locating the first two bodies, it was possible to follow the climbing ropes which connected them. It appeared that their deaths had been due to the tremendous fall down the mountainside. The discovery and recovery of the bodies entailed a great deal of skill and hard work by the search party, as well as a cost of more than $25,000 to the government. It was the most extensive search effort in Glacier Park history.[5]

Injuries And Rescues

Other accident victims have been more fortunate. On July 30, 1969, Mary Ellen Acheson, aged 19, of Missoula, Montana, was injured in a fall from the Pinnacle Wall. Due to severe injuries, she was unconscious or only semiconscious for nearly a month, but miraculously recovered after a long convalescence. On August 18, 1969, Lisa Cheri Westmoreland, aged 21, of Regina, Saskatchewan, a summer employee at the Prince of Wales Hotel, undertook to hike from Gunsight Lake toward the Jackson Glacier. On suffering a fall, she went down a water course about 50 feet and was ultimately rescued by helicopter. The latter was fortunately available, having just brought Senator Strom Thurmond, of South Carolina, from Great Falls to Babb. The senator participated in the rescue.[6]

Another dramatic rescue took place on June 15, 1969, when Sheri Munnerlyn, aged 22, University of Texas senior from Amarillo,

Texas was hiking on a trail above Appekunny Falls with her fiance. She fell 20 feet and slid another 50, coming to a stop in shale. It required nearly two hours to bring the bleeding girl by stretcher down the Appekunny switchbacks. Her injuries included a compound fracture of the right shoulder and arm, together with assorted sprains, bruises and lacerations.

A not so dramatic "rescue" was necessitated when a 17-year-old hiker participating in a church-affiliated trail outing on July 20, 1971, became ill in the vicinity of Ptarmigan Lake, seven miles from the Many Glacier Hotel.[7] He developed convulsions, apparently from the smoking of lichens, i.e., fungus plants growing on rocks or trees along the trail. It required eight men to carry him by stretcher to the nearest road, which happened to be that near the Swiftcurrent Motor Inn, where the rescue party arrived with him at five the following morning. The cost to the government was over $100.

The Older Generation

Not all of the mishaps are due to youthful lack of discretion, of course. Late in June, 1972, Robert Miller, aged 57, of Philadelphia, left St. Mary, apparently intending to hike to Lake McDonald over Gunsight Pass, which was not scheduled to be open to foot traffic until mid-July. Between Gunsight Lake and the Pass, he slid and tumbled about 100 feet, suffering a broken wrist, head injuries and other damage. Fortunately, he was able to hike the long miles back to St. Mary, from which point he was taken to the hospital at Cardston, Alberta; otherwise, he might have become merely another statistic in the "missing persons" file.

On July 29, 1971, Norman Rabbers and his son Tom, aged 16, of Glen Ellyn, Illinois, were both injured while climbing at the 7200-foot level of Rising Wolf Mountain above Two Medicine Lake. When the pair did not return to the Two Medicine Campground, Mrs. Rabbers notified the rangers who started up the mountains shortly after daybreak. They presently came upon Tom, hobbling along on two broken ankles and seeking help for his father who had suffered a skull fracture and concussion. It was necessary to use a helicopter to evacuate them to Two Medicine for transfer to the hospital at Browning.

Stranded Climbers

Sometimes the situation is one not involving injuries. For example, on July 19, 1970, Paul Merrill, aged 16, of Boston, Massachusetts, was on the slopes of Mt. Pollock near Logan Pass, with five other youths from the "Encampment For Citizenship" at Great Falls. Two of them made it to the summit; the other four turned back and young Merrill became stranded on a steep slope. A rescue team went up the mountain to a point above the lad and, with the aid of ropes, assisted him to safety.

Similar rescues occur not infrequently. In 1955, rangers went to the aid of three teen-aged youths who had hitchhiked from St. Paul, Minnesota, had climbed over a ridge from Lower Lake St. Mary to Boulder Creek, and had become stranded there. Rangers did the same in June, 1956, for a man and his son who had gone from the parking lot at Logan Pass over the snow to the Hidden Lake Overlook, leaving mamma waiting for them in the car.

In June, 1970, still another rescue operation was initiated by the disappearance of Randy Johnson, aged 18, of Gambrills, Maryland, and Manny Perry, aged 17, of Tucson, Arizona. The two boys, second-year employees at the Lake McDonald Coffee Shop, left there intending to climb Mt. Cannon from Logan Pass. Darkness overtook them on the cliffs and, when they failed to return that night, a rescue party had to be organized. Fortunately, the lads were sensible enough to wait for daylight to descend to the Avalanche Campground, but they had created a problem by undertaking their climbing adventure without advising anyone of their plans.[8]

Disappearing Hikers

Not all of those who become lost are found again. Such missing persons are usually lone hikers who depart from a well marked trail and suffer a heart attack or serious injury in a seldom visited area, from which they lack the strength to get back to safety or assistance. Such a missing person was young David Wilson, student at Ohio Wesleyan University, employed in the summer by the National Park Service. Wilson left a note on July 22, 1962, saying that he was going to climb Going-To-The-Sun Mountain, but he was never seen again. He had, of course, violated a cardinal mountaineering rule of never undertaking such a venture alone.

An even more puzzling disappearance was that of Dr. F. H. Lumley, research scientist from Ohio State University, aged 27, who undertook to hike the well-marked trail from Goathaunt Camp at the head of Waterton Lake to the latter's north end, less than ten miles away. This was in August, 1934 and he was never heard from again. The trail was neither long, steep nor hazardous, but again the situation was that of a lone hiker.

Most mysterious of all was the disappearance of two young men, the Whitehead brothers, of Chicago. In the summer of 1926 they left Granite Park Chalet high on the continental divide to hike to Lake McDonald and Belton. Since that day no trace of them has ever been found, although thousands of dollars were spent in the search. Many theories have been advanced as to their fate, but no official explanation has ever been arrived at.

Mishap On Sperry Glacier

There have been some spectacular rescues involving glacier accidents over the years. One of these, taking place about 1906, while the present park region was under the jurisdiction of the Forest Service, was the subject of a graphic report by Frank S. Liebig, then a Forest Service ranger.[9] Liebig had just reached the Sperry Basin after riding over Gunsight Pass one afternoon, when people came running over to tell him that a woman had fallen into a crevasse on Sperry Glacier and they didn't know how to get her out. In the meantime they had sent a man to Lake McDonald for ropes. When Ranger Liebig got to the crevasse, he could see the woman wedged in the ice some 30 feet down, lying almost horizontally, and seemingly lifeless.

Anchoring a rope above and sliding down to the level of the woman, Liebig tried unsuccessfully to pull her loose. Then with an axe he chopped niches on either side of the ice on which he could plant his feet to get a better leverage. Finally he was able to dislodge her and get a rope around her waist. She was pulled to the surface and carried down to the camp where a big fire was going with "lots of hot coffee and lots of hot brandy." As Liebig himself tells it,[10] in his not too grammatical way:

"A doctor came up towards morning and pronounced the woman O.K. Some men and women filled her up all night with hot brandy until she was glorious drunk. We sure had a late breakfast the next day. All thought I had done a wonderful job. The woman never even said thank you for getting her out of the glacier. She surely would have been dead if she had stayed in the ice all night."

History Repeats Itself

In 1971, some 65 years later, Ronald Bruce Matthews, aged 32, a native of Big Mountain, Montana fell into a crevasse high on the slopes of Sperry Glacier. Matthews, a ski instructor, and three friends from Whitefish with similar skills, had hiked to the campground below Sperry Chalets on August 14, 1971. On the 15th, a Sunday, they hiked to Sperry Glacier and climbed Gunsight Mountain. On the return, they were planning to ski down snow-covered portions of the glacier since they regarded the skiing conditions as good.[11]

Near the top of the ridge, however, Matthews fell and went plunging several hundred feet down the steep glacial slopes into a huge crevasse located in what is called the "bergschrund" part of the glacier. His companions immediately went into action, two going to the crevasse and another to the Chalets to summon help. Within an hour a mountain-trained rescue crew was en route to the scene aboard a helicopter piloted by Bob Schellinger, bringing ropes and equipment. The craft was skillfully landed on a narrow snow ledge above the crevasse. Two of the rescue team "roped up" and rappelled into the aperture, risking collapse of the snow and ice from above, reaching Matthews as quickly as possible, and getting him out of the 40-foot-deep crevasse in record time.[12]

Despite the tremendous rescue effort, the victim did not survive. Dr. R. Wade Covill, Columbia Falls physician who was brought to the scene by helicopter, examined Matthews and diagnosed the fatal injuries as probable fractures of the skull and other bones, together with lung damage. He was of the opinion that death had been due to injuries, rather than exposure. The other members of Matthews' party paid high tribute to the Glacier Park rangers composing the rescue team and to Pilot Schellinger, saying, "These park men really know what to do on a glacier."[13]

Calamity In Other Forms

The waters of Glacier Park must be regarded as more treacherous than those in non-mountainous areas because of their icy temperatures and often turbulent cascades. We have already seen how Frederick Steinmetz suffered fatal injury in 1960 when he lost his footing and was carried over a cascade on Kennedy Creek. Equally unfortunate was Kenneth Gelston, whose body was never recovered after he had the ill luck, in June, 1964, to make a misstep and tumble 100 feet over St. Mary Falls while taking a picture.

Lakes and streams of the Park also claim their share of victims. Robert B. Personett, aged 23, of Half Moon, Montana, drowned on June 28, 1970 in the North Fork of the Flathead River. The rubber raft in which he was traveling with four companions smashed into a log jam, deflated and sank in the fast-moving waters of the river. Having no life-jacket, Personnett was unable to survive; but his four life-jacketed companions made their way to a small island and were rescued.[14] Only a few days later, on July 5, 1970, Neil Fisher, aged 9, son of Mr. and Mrs. Mike Fisher of Havre, Montana, disappeared while playing along the banks of the lower McDonald Creek below the Apgar bridge. There were no witnesses to the accident but his body was recovered from the stream the following day.

Waters of the Park can also be lethal to members of the fair sex. On July 5, 1972, Perihan North, aged 46, wife of Seasonal Naturalist Warren North, of State University, Arkansas, drowned near the east end of Upper Lake St. Mary.[15] When she failed to return from a lone boating trip in a rubber raft, a search was made. Her raft was found with oars in place, her life jacket and purse in the raft. After further search, her body was discovered in four or five feet of water about a quarter of a mile from the raft.

Alienated Lands In The Park

A major problem for Glacier Park administrators lies in the fact that there is a substantial acreage of privately held lands within the boundaries of the Park.[16] These, however, represent a major reduction from the 21,986 acres of state, county and private lands that lay within its borders when Glacier was established as a park in 1910. These non-federally owned lands date back to pre-Park days, and to the homesteads acquired and mining claims staked out prior to the turn of the century.

Whenever opportunities present themselves and funds are available, the Park Service and its friends have been buying up these properties. An important acquisition during 1969 was that of the McFarland Ranch located six miles north of Polebridge on the North Fork of the Flathead River, with its ranch buildings and air strip built by the Montana Aeronautics Commission.[17] Another even more important step in the right direction was the exchange in 1953 of more than 10,000 acres of forested lands within the Park owned by the State of Montana for federal lands of equal value in eastern Montana. A ceremony was held in the Park in July 18, 1953 to dedicate this exchange of lands and to celebrate the end of a 30-year struggle to bring it to fruition.[18]

Unfortunately, as time goes on, the values of these privately owned tracts increase, and the potential cost of acquisition rises. Most of them are in the Lake McDonald area and along the North Fork of the Flathead, and consist of resort properties, stores, shops, summer homes and a few ranches. On the eastern slopes, private ownership has been limited to a few old mining claims. Originally numbered in the hundreds, nearly all of such claims have been lost through failure to do the necessary assessment work, or to keep up tax payments.

Swiftcurrent Valley Lands

Among the legendary mining claims in the Many Glacier area is the old Josephine Mine, comprising 95.07 acres situated on Grinnell Point above Josephine Lake. Not until 1973 did this ancient claim pass into government ownership.[19] Even better known is a tract of 68.13 acres situated on the shores of Cracker Lake,[20] locale of the old Cracker Mine, and reachable only by trail. It has changed hands two or three times in recent years, and has become something of a controversial issue in northwest Montana.

It was in July, 1969 that two alert women of Cut Bank, Montana, after paying some $44.65 in delinquent taxes on the 68.13 acres at Cracker Lake, obtained ownership through a tax deed.[21] Soon after this coup, the ladies offered the property to the National Park Service for $6,800, but when the latter did not respond with sufficient celerity, they sold the property for that price to Robert M. Graham, son of a seasonal park ranger, and Michael T. Fitzgerald, who formerly held a job on Park trails. These young men in turn conveyed partial interests to others.[22]

Public indignation was aroused in November, 1971 when advertisements by a Great Falls real estate firm offered the property for sale for $92,500, stating—

"HEAVEN ON EARTH on 68 acres in Glacier National Park with 1210 feet on Cracker Lake; virgin acres of alpine meadow accessible by trail and near Many Glacier Hotel."[23]

An illustrated leaflet contained a picture of the property over the caption:

"The rugged beauty of the Glacier Park wilderness as seen from the real estate that is for sale. An ideal site for recreational development."[24]

Further Developments

When friends of the Park became aware of what was taking place, indignation continued to mount. Alarmed residents of Columbia Falls wrote to United States Senator Metcalf about the situation and the Hungry Horse News editorially deplored the potential victimization of the American taxpayer and urged early condemnation by the federal government.[25] Senator Metcalf took the matter up with J. Leonard Volz, Director of the Park Service's Midwest Regional Office which has jurisdiction over Glacier Park.[26]

Advices from Volz indicated that the Park Service had in April, 1970 given the two Cut Bank ladies a conditional offer to buy the acreage at the $6,800 price named by them, but was informed that it had already been sold.[27] On making contact with the new owners early in 1971, Volz requested and received permission to appraise the property, a prerequisite to any purchase under the applicable statute. The appraisal was made, followed by a Park Service offer to pay the amount found to be the fair market value, and by the owners' refusal of such offer.[28]

The situation has thus reached an impasse where it is likely to remain so long as the owners persist in their bold gamble to achieve an unconscionable capital gain.[29] The applicable law permits them to decline to sell except at their own figure;[30] however, they may find that their advantages under the law are offset by certain disadvantages in the way of public opinion and governmental control over the uses to which such a property could be put. Any prospective purchaser would be unlikely to sink a large sum into property on which commercial development would almost certainly be banned.

As long as the matter remains unresolved, the owners will be unable to put the property to any beneficial use, their investment will be producing no income, and there is always the possibility that mounting public indignation might lead to an amendment of the statute under which such abuses are possible. In the meantime, along with other facets of the "alienated lands" problem, the Cracker Lake situation will continue to be a thorn in the side of the National Park Service and a source of deep distress to all lovers of Glacier as a wilderness park.

Notes For Chapter 23

[1] See Chapter 17, supra, entitled "Visitors: Distinguished And Otherwise," at pages 152-153.

[2] Interview on 7/10/70 with then Chief Ranger Hart.

[3] Hungry Horse News for 7/3/70.

[4] Idem, for 7/10/70.

[5] Idem, for 7/3/70.

[6] Idem, for 6/26/70.

[7] Idem, for 7/23/71.

[8] Idem, for 6/26/70.

[9] Article in magazine entitled "Montana West," Spring Issue, 1970, at pages 7-10, reprinted from Volume I, "Early Days In The Forest Service," Region I, Missoula, Montana.

[10] Idem, at page 9.

[11] Hungry Horse News for 8/20/71.

[12] Idem.

[13] Idem.

[14] Idem, for 7/3/70.

[15] Idem, for 7/7/72.

[16] As of 10/1/75, according to Robert B. Lunger, Park Realty Specialist, 21,014.42 of the original 21,986 privately or state owned acres had been acquired through purchase, exchange or condemnation, leaving only 971.58 acres in non-federal ownership, including 35.86 in county roads dedication and 5.63 owned by the state. Most of the privately owned tracts lie west of the divide, with 842 acres being controlled by only 12 owners.

[17] Hungry Horse News for 4/2/71. After a study of the uses to which the property might be put, the ranch buildings were torn down or removed.

[18] "Through The Years In Glacier National Park," by Donald H. Robinson, at page 102.

[19] According to a letter dated 11/22/74 from Robert B. Lunger, Park Realty Specialist, the Josephine claim was acquired by the government on 11/16/73 through a friendly condemnation suit against the heirs of Remi Choquette. The latter had acquired it, according to a letter dated 11/1/74 from Erling Evenson, of the County Assessor's Office at Cut Bank, Montana, by a deed dated 7/29/30 from Parley Stark and Etta Myrl Stark, as directors of the Josephine Copper Mining and Smelting Co.

[20] Hungry Horse News for 12/10/71.

[21] Idem.

[22] Idem, for 12/10/71 and 7/28/72.

[23] Idem, for 4/30/71 and 12/10/71.

[24] Idem, for 12/10/71.

[25] Idem, for 4/30/71, 5/21/71 and 12/10/71.

[26] Idem, for 4/23/71.

[27] Idem, for 4/23/71, setting forth letter dated 4/13/71 from J. Leonard Volz to Senator Metcalf.

[28] A letter from Superintendent William J. Briggle dated 8/24/72 indicated that the owners were still asking "92,-500, which is ten times the appraised value." However, a letter dated 11/22/74, from Robert B. Lunger, Park Realty Specialist, stated: "A new appraisal has been ordered on the Cracker Lake property and negotiations will be conducted with the owners in the near future. The Park Service has no plans to condemn this property."

[29] By the provisions of the law which established the Park as such in 1910, condemnation can be resorted to only when there is concrete evidence that activities adverse to the intent and purpose of the area are being undertaken.

[30] According to Mr. Volz, the evidence which will warrant condemnation must consist of "surveys, plats, advertisements and other similar items." While there have been advertisements of the Cracker Lake property, apparently the real estate activity has not reached the point where it might serve as a sufficient legal basis for condemnation. This information was also contained in the Volz letter of 4/13/71 to Senator Metcalf appearing in the Hungry Horse News for 4/23/71.

Chapter 24
ENVIRONMENTAL PROBLEMS

In biblical lore, the four horsemen of the Apocalypse were said to have been War, Famine, Pestilence and Death. In Glacier National Park, their counterparts are forest fire, flood, avalanche and pollution. The Park is blessed with marvelous evergreen forests that can burn like tinder, with a wealth of water that, given excessive rainfall, can turn into raging torrents, with tremendous accumulations of winter snow and ice that can break loose without warning and thunder down a mountainside, and with fragile landscape and wilderness facilities that are susceptible, like those of Yellowstone and Yosemite,[1] to damage through pollution and ecological erosion.

Of these four problems, the first three have been more or less in operation since the dawn of time; the fourth only since the advent in the area of man, the polluter without peer. In respect to the latter, one has only to recall the horde of prospectors for minerals and oil that over-ran the Swiftcurrent Valley and parts of the western slopes of the region around the turn of the century, leaving their marks indiscriminately on valley and hillside. In departing almost as abruptly as they had come, they were oblivious to the clutter left in their wake. No one worried about such things in those days.

Nor were their predecessors, the Blackfeet, Nature's neatest groundkeepers. George Bird Grinnell reports that when he first visited the Swiftcurrent Valley in 1887, he came to "a large grassy park below the falls, where Indian hunting-parties make their permanent camps." In describing the scene, he said ". . . everywhere about this park may be seen the sites of old Indian camps, with rotting lodgepoles, old fireplaces, and piles of bone and hair, showing where game had been cut up and hides dressed."[2] Apparently the red man had established a pattern which too many of his white brethren were content to follow.

Juggernaut Of The Mountains

Long before the future park was ever glimpsed by human eye, it served as a repository for the twin forces of ice and snow, potential ingredients of that frightening phenomenon called an avalanche. Like its fellow disasters, flood and forest fire, an avalanche can be extremely terrifying; unlike them, its reign of terror is a matter of moments only, rather than of hours or days. An avalanche is a creature of the mountains, born of a marriage between high elevations and steep slopes, with the law of gravity serving as midwife at the fateful moment.

Although the principal component of both may be ice, the glacier and the avalanche are antonyms in the matter of movement. Even more so than the snail, the glacier represents the classic symbol of the ultra-deliberate. The avalanche, on the other hand, is a self-propelled juggernaut, traveling at express train speed. Few are the people who have ever been able to escape from the path of a down-coming snowslide or avalanche. Either you happen to be in its line of descent and become a statistic, or you are outside its path and are lucky.

"Avalanche" is a name that has been associated with the Glacier Park locale ever since the day in June, 1895 when Professor Lyman B. Sperry and his party penetrated the tangled forests between Mt. Brown and the present Mt. Cannon and camped in a basin which he described as a "precipitous mountain pocket or valley, rivalling in striking features and general impressiveness the far-famed Yosemite."[3] They agreed, because of the number of avalanches seen and heard during their stay, that "avalanche" would be a most appropriate name for the basin and its "little gem of a lake."

Sperry observed "the tell-tale remains of an immense avalanche which many years ago cut a swath about a mile in length and twenty rods in width down the southern slope, sweeping the forests into the lake . . . The bark and tops of the trees then uprooted have disappeared, and the diminished trunks, huddled together at the outlet of the lake, are solemn witnesses of the terrible avalanche which thundered down these steeps perhaps a century ago. The southeastern part of the basin is kept almost entirely destitute of vegetation by the frequent and destructive avalanches which sweep that region. Two exhibitions of their power were given us during our June visit."[4]

When Part Of A Glacier Itself Falls

Possibly the most dramatic and extraordinary avalanche ever to descend a mountain slope in what is now Glacier Park happened not long before the visit of Professor Raphael D. Pumpelly to the upper Nyack Valley in August, 1883. On studying the glacier which now bears his name, situated on a lofty shelf on the north side of the valley, he was surprised to note that a huge piece was missing from one side of its front face, a piece that he estimated to have been a quarter of a mile in length and breadth respectively.

Continuing eastward, his party soon entered an amphitheatre about two miles wide, at the head of which was situated a 2000-foot cliff topped off by the front face of the glacier, itself another 500 feet in height. It was then that they realized what had happened to the mysteriously missing section of the glacier, and Pumpelly has related it in his memoirs as follows:

"The missing block of ice was now accounted for. It had plunged down the 2500-foot wall and its acquired impetus had carried it several hundred feet up the opposite slope of the cirque, plowing a broad swath through a dense forest of large Douglas firs whose trunks and branches, still holding their bark, lay in every position, like giant jackstraws. A few years ago Professor L. B. Sperry . . . sent me a photograph on which appears evidence that it (the glacier) breaks off regularly in great square blocks, as in my time."[5]

Highway Catastrophe

Avalanches of snow, commonly called snowslides, also occur with some degree of frequency in the mountains of both Waterton Park and Glacier Park. On Logan Pass, in Glacier, the descending highway to the west is built through a section where the snow drifts each winter to a depth of 70 feet or more. When it is time to get the road open in the latter part of May or early June, its depth is still close to maximum, and it takes the equipment many days to clear a pathway through for the automobile highway. Even when a channel has been carved out, the spectacular wall of snow still looms up more than 50 feet above the road at its upper side, and no one can be entirely sure that a part of it may not suddenly give way.

Just such a catastrophe happened on May 26, 1953. Tulips and fruit trees were in bloom in the Flathead Valley, but up on the continental divide the great drift was still partially blocking the road to Logan Pass. As a road crew was busily working in the area, a huge part of the snowbank unexpectedly broke loose and buried all four men and their rotary plow. Within a short time, Foreman Ray Price happened along and saw the slide covering the highway for about 300 feet, while the men and their plow were nowhere to be seen.

With the aid of a crew dispatched from headquarters after a telephone call by Price, the shovelers soon uncovered Fred Klein partially buried some 400 yards down the slope, but alive. That evening Foreman Jean Sullivan was found miraculously alive, though unconscious, after being buried in the snow for eight hours. The other two men, William Whiteford and George Beaton, were killed, the body of the latter being located early the next morning with the aid of a bloodhound. Sullivan and Klein were among the few who have stood in the path of an avalanche and lived to tell the tale.[6]

A similar, though less tragic, incident occurred in February, 1933, when Ranger Ben C. Miller, then stationed near Essex, was moving on snowshoes along the side of Scalplock Mountain. A sudden avalanche of snow rolled him 200 feet down the mountain and buried him deeply. After a 25-hour struggle to get rid of his snowshoes and back-pack, he was finally able to extricate himself. Fortunately, his only injuries consisted of a few minor sprains and frost bites.[7]

Conflagrations Of Consequence

Fire has played a ravaging role in the history of the Park, yet, strangely enough, through all the annals of pre-Park days, no mention is to be found of any major forest fire, and rarely have there been reports of any minor ones. To a degree, this is understandable, in view of the rare intrusions of humans into the area during the 19th century. Nevertheless, it is rather astonishing that no substantial areas were burned over as the result of lightning-lit blazes.

The region became a national park in May, 1910, and the August of that year will be remembered from the Dakotas to the Pacific Coast as one of devastating prairie and forest fires, with the sun smoke-darkened over much of the northwest.[8] The new park found itself beleaguered by blaze after destructive blaze before it had a regular fire-fighting force or adequate funds with which to combat the many conflagrations. Hardly had its first superintendent, Major Logan, taken over his new duties when he was obliged to devote most of his time to this one activity, and he found himself greatly handicapped by lack of equipment and manpower, as well as by lack of trails and roads of any consequence.[9] Nearly all of the fires were on the Park's western slopes and Frank Liebig, previously a ranger in the area for the Forest Service, was the fire boss. Before the autumnal rains mercifully put an end to the devastation, more than 100,000 acres, or one-tenth of the Park's total acreage, had gone up in smoke.[10]

Fortunately, most of the "burns" occurred in the wilderness areas rather than in more scenic sections where visitors were to be most numerous in years to come. The largest of the conflagrations was in the territory just south of the Canadian boundary and above Kintla Creek, where a total of 23,000 acres burned, mostly as the result of dry-lightning storms. One large fire in the southeastern part of the Park destroyed much of the forestation of the upper Ole Creek drainage, and continued over the continental divide to the vicinity of what is now East Glacier.[11]

Trouble Strikes Again

The Park's so-called "fire-years" have fortunately been spaced rather well apart, depending upon varying weather patterns and the number of lightning storms. After the debacle of 1910 came a breathing spell of a full decade until 1920, when three smaller fires devastated a total of 2,000 to 2,500 acres, all on the western slopes with 80% of the "burn" being on Dutch Creek. By this time, of course, park authorities were somewhat better equipped to make early

discovery of fires, and to control those that did get under way.[12]

1926 was a bad "fire-year," with trouble beginning before the travel season opened, and continuing most of the summer. A total of more than 50,000 acres were burned as the result of more than 23 different blazes, the worst being in the Lake McDonald-Apgar Mountain sector. National Park Service Director Albright came to the Park in August and personaly assumed direction of fire-fighting activities. The number of men on the fire lines exceeded 700 at one time during the protracted struggle.[13]

The fire situation then remained relatively quiescent until 1929 when the notorious Half-moon Fire began on August 16th on private logging operations about ten miles southwest of the Lake McDonald area. Fanned by high winds and low humidity, it escaped the territory of the Half-moon Logging Company and spread rapidly on both sides of the Middle Fork of the Flathead River toward Belton and Lake McDonald, and continued eastward almost to Nyack before it was stopped. Fortunately, Park Headquarters, Belton and most of Apgar escaped destruction.[14]

This holocaust consumed more than 50,000 acres of Park forests, as well as another 50,000 acres outside the Park. The total firefighting cost was $300,000, of which Glacier's share was $244,000. Fire control agencies from all over the northwest were called upon for assistance, and National Park Service Fire Control Expert John Coffman took over direction of the battle commencing on August 22nd. The area burned included the route of the highway from West Glacier to the foot of Lake McDonald, now covered by new growth lodgepole pines replacing the imposing redcedars and hemlock that formerly stood there.[15]

On The Eastern Front

Practically all of the fires up to this time had been on the west side of the continental divide, but on August 6, 1935 an extensive fire broke out in the Park's northeastern sector. Having its inception in a campfire on Kennedy Creek, it spread with the aid of a high wind to the east, burning more than 550 acres within the Park, including the Kennedy Creek Ranger Station. After crossing into the Blackfeet Indian Reservation, it burned another 2650 acres there.[16]

Commencing on the day after the start of the Kennedy Creek fire, a lightning-lit blaze erupted on Boundary Creek west of Waterton Lake. Getting out of control on August 9th, it headed eastward toward the Waterton Townsite and Lake. When it was finally stopped through the cooperation of fire-fighting crews from both parks, it had burned to within a mile and a half of the town, including two and a half miles of timber along the west shore of the lake. The loss of forested area in Waterton Park was estimated at 1,244 acres, and that in Glacier at approximately 1,000.[17]

Apart from the Ole Creek blaze of 1910, the only other conflagration to extend its course over both sides of the continental divide was the catastrophic Heaven's Peak fire of August, 1936. It was on the 19th of that month that lightning struck a tree on the slopes of Heaven's Peak, west of the Garden Wall, kindling a small fire. It was promptly fought and apparently stopped after about 200 acres had been destroyed. However, high winds on August 31st swept the blaze up the west side of the divide to Granite Park, across Swiftcurrent Pass, and by 8:00 p.m. on September 1st, it was roaring down the Swiftcurrent Valley toward the Many Glacier Hotel.[18]

The hotel was only saved by heroic measures, with men posted upon its roof with wet brooms ready to extinguish any flying embers that might sail across the lake. However, the chalets on the slopes of Mt. Altyn, as well as 31 of the Swiftcurrent Cabins and the ranger station, were entirely consumed. A fortunate shift in the wind enabled the weary fire-fighting crews to halt further progress. Nevertheless, more than 7,500 acres, including a large part of one of the Park's most beautiful valleys, had been burned.[19]

The Record Improves

Other bad "fire-years" have occurred since 1936, but they have been relatively few and none has affected the more frequently visited scenic areas. In 1940, over 20 fires were set by lightning, burning a total of approximately 1,000 acres on the western slopes. In 1945, 280 acres were burned on Curley Bear Mountain. In 1958, 33 fires, mostly caused by lightning, destroyed over 3,000 acres, the largest being 2,500 acres on Coal Creek in the southern part of the Park.[20] In 1967, a fire on Huckleberry Mountain destroyed 8,859 acres and another, known as the Flathead fire, burned over 3,109 acres.[21] Also, a very destructive holocaust in August, 1967 grew out of a long-smoldering snag on the east ridge of Heaven's Peak. Nearly two weeks later, a strong wind sprang up and swept the fire down across the Mc-

Donald Valley and up to tree-line above the Going-To-The-Sun Highway. Only good fortune prevented a repetition of the 1936 catastrophe. However, every one of these blazes, except for the Curley Bear fire, was west of the continental divide, and the total destruction for the entire period of more than three decades was but a fraction of the acreage burned over in such single years as 1910, 1926 and 1929.

The achievement of such a record represents a combination of good management, good weather and good luck. The suppression program of the Park Service is under the supervision of a ranger designated as the fire control officer. At strategic lofty locations throughout the Park are lookout towers, each manned during the season of high hazard by a live-in fire-watcher or married couple brought in by helicopter when trails are still snow-blocked. Their duty is to spot incipient fires and to get immediate word to the fire-fighting crews. More than 300 miles of special fire trails give access to these towers and to locations particularly useful from a fire suppression standpoint. By these various means it has been possible not only to lengthen the intervals between the so-called "fire years" but also to reduce the annual burned acreage to practically zero during some years.[22]

Progress Toward Fire Control

From the statistics given it would appear that park authorities have been gaining the upper hand in their long fight to control this deadly threat to environmental integrity. However, the present fire control officer, Ranger Colony, points out that weather conditions play a major part in the picture, and that such factors as a multiplicity of lightning storms, dry years, lack of rain at times when fires are burning, and high winds which fan the flames, are beyond human control. Also to be considered is the fact that during long fire-free periods, burnable material tends to accumulate within the forests, making them more vulnerable.

Nevertheless, in reviewing the Park's fire history, several encouraging facts are evident. While the fires have been numerous and the burned areas extensive, aggregating around 240,000 acres, or close to one-fourth of the Park's entire acreage, yet never has there been a loss of human life. Most of the territory burned has been on the more heavily forested western slopes and off the beaten track for the majority of Park visitors. Moreover, it should be noted that Mother Nature, **mirabile dictu,** has been able to restore damage from the great fires of a generation or more ago so expeditiously and well that their effects are not now such as to detract materially from the pleasure of today's casual observer.

Water Hazard

The danger of floods in Glacier Park is not a serious one. Only twice in Park history have its waters gotten out of hand, and only once have they burgeoned into a flood of major proportions. The year was 1964 and the snows of the preceding winter lay deep in the upper valleys and high cirques when, on a Sunday, the 7th of June, torrential rains began to fall on both sides of the continental divide. Precipitation on June 8th ranged from four to eight inches in the southern section of the Park, and it was estimated that as much as twelve inches had fallin in some parts of the snow-covered mountain slopes.

At the upper levels the warm rains had a powerful effect on the accumulated snows, causing them to melt at an unprecedented rate, and filling every rivulet and stream to the brim with melted snow. On the west side of the Park, the West Glacier bridge was wrecked, as well as the old bridge upstream, thus wiping out the means of getting to Lake McDonald and Logan Pass. The Lake itself received such a volume of water from McDonald Creek that the dining room and grill at McDonald Lodge were seriously damaged.[23]

On the east side of the divide, the dam across the Lower Two Medicine collapsed, inundating the little ranches of the Blackfeet Indians below it, and drowning nine of a group attempting to escape the deluge in a truck. Elsewhere, 25 Blackfeet perished when the Swift Dam in the Heart Butte area was swept away. The heaviest 24-hour rainfall in its history was recorded at Waterton Townsite, causing the Waterton Lakes to rise four feet in less than three hours.[24]

Fifteen miles of Highway No. 2 over Marias Pass were devastated, and the Essex and Walton bridges were washed out.[25] The damage was estimated at $6,000,000[26] and the route was not fully open to traffic, despite the efforts of a 200-man crew, until the end of July.[27] The Great Northern Railway line, paralleling Highway No. 2, also suffered extensive damage, more than six miles of track being washed away or, in some places, being left suspended in mid-air. The main line was out of service for three weeks.[28]

Despite the heavy loss of life on the Blackfeet Reservation, there were no deaths in the Park itself. There was, however, vast property damage, particularly to highway installations and the Going-To-The-Sun Highway was closed to traffic until June 29th to permit extensive repairs.[29] Total damage within the Park was estimated at $4,000,000 for the restoration of buildings, utilities and minor roads,[30] as well as 24 trail bridges and many trails.[31] Travel through the Park was disrupted during the early part of the season, and the total number of visitors was more than 200,000 below the average for the two preceding years.[32]

Pollution And Erosion

Environmental problems in Glacier Park were largely ignored until the nation-wide ecological awakening of the late 1960's brought a painful recognition of their presence and gravity. It was at about this same time that the visitor-volume began to pass the million mark annually, overtaxing many existing facilities, including trails, campgrounds, back country camping sites, and the means of disposing of sewage and garbage.

Particularly was the wear-and-tear of overuse evident in the Logan Pass area with its fragile alpine meadows. With 5,000 or more visitors a day, sewage was beginning to pollute the headwaters of St. Mary Lake, and vegetation along the trail to the Hidden Lake Overlook was commencing to suffer from the encroachment of careless hikers and thoughtless flower pickers. Affirmative steps to improve the situation have included arranging for sewage to be trucked out of the area, and for the construction of a board walk six to eight feet in width for a part of the distance to the Overlook.[33] A ban was placed upon the use of camper trailers on the Going-To-The-Sun Highway in 1971;[34] and other restrictions will be imposed in the future upon the use of heavy vehicles if deemed necessary.

Elsewhere in the Park protective measures have had to be taken. A number of campground sites have been closed for a season to give them a rest and the vegetation a chance to make a comeback. Certain trails have been closed to other than hikers because of the erosion incident to horse travel. In the back country, restrictions have been placed on the number of people and horses that may utilize certain locations on an overnight basis, while at other locations overnight camping has been banned altogether. The building of wood fires in a number of areas is no longer permitted, and rules require those who pack in to pack out their garbage from the back country. Restrictions have been placed upon the number of fish that can be caught, to obviate the need for constant re-stocking and to discourage nearby residents from making special trips to the lakes of the Park for the purpose of stocking home freezers.[35]

Fluoride Invasion

There is rather conclusive evidence to indicate that one area of the Park has suffered damage from chemical pollution emanating from beyond its borders. The source of the difficulty is a large chemical plant located at Columbia Falls, a few miles west of the Park's southwestern corner. Its emissions of fluorides have run as high as 7,500 pounds per day, a part of which was being carried by prevailing winds through a saddle in Teakettle Mountain to the Park. There, according to studies made by the United States Forest Service and by the Director of the University of Montana Environmental Studies Program in 1971, they have produced substantial injury to trees, vegetation and animals.[36] In fact, data from these studies indicated that the chemical was being passed up along the food chain, and that substantial damage persisted even after the plant's volume of emissions had been materially reduced.[37]

The important thing in the fight against ecological damage to Glacier Park is that those in a position to do something about it have made it their business to recognize pollution and erosion wherever they appear, and to adopt positive measures designed to hold the line and, if possible, reduce their volume. As a matter of fact, the entire environmental picture is an optimistic one in the Park. Not only are the various ecological problems being dealt with realistically and firmly, but the outlook on natural dangers and disasters is equally encouraging. Forest fires have been greatly reduced in number and extent, floods are rare, and avalanches continue to be interesting phenomena, but not a menace to life or limb. For the knowledgeable visitor, these are facts that throw light upon a seldom publicized phase of the Park's background and personality, facts that can add spice to his acquaintance with, and understanding of, its many attractive features.

Notes For Chapter 24

[1] Article in Newsweek Magazine for July 19, 1971, at page 47, entitled "Parks Under Siege."

[2] Article entitled "The Crown Of The Continent" by George Bird Grinnell, appearing in the Century Magazine for Sept., 1901, at page 669.

[3] Article in "Appalachia," Volume VIII, No. 1, January, 1896, by Lyman D. Sperry, entitled "In The Montana Rockies," at page 58.

[4] Idem, at page 65. Sperry's nephew, Alfred L. Sperry, who became a lawyer, accompanied his uncle on a number of visits to the future Park in the 1890's, and in 1932 published a little volume of his recollections entitled "Avalanche," illustrated with many pictures taken by the party photographer.

[5] "My Reminiscences" by Raphael Pumpelly, Volume II, at pages 642-43, published in 1918 by Henry Holt & Co.

[6] Hungry Horse News for 12/11/70. In addition to those of ice and snow, the Park occasionally features another kind of avalanche, to wit, mammoth rock slides. On July 31, 1972, a section of the northeast face of Chief Mountain broke away and rumbled down the slopes. Witnesses 17 miles away, according to the Hungry Horse News for 8/4/72, reported that the bulk of the falling rock was so great as to produce a noticeable change in the profile of the mountain. Also, see the News for 8/11/72.

[7] The story of Miller's ordeal is told in detail in his own words in an article entitled "Thrilling Stories About Rangers," appearing at pages 104-105 of the 1948 edition of the "Drivers' Manual" (see Note 15, Chapter 6, supra).

[8] For an excellent story of the 1910 holocaust, see article in the September, 1974 issue of American West Magazine by James G. Bradley, entitled "When Smoke Blotted Out The Sun, The Most Destructive Forest Fire In American History—Idaho, 1910." See, also, "Through The Years In Glacier National Park," by Donald H Robinson, at page 83.

[9] Idem, at page 83.

[10] Idem, at page 83.

[11] Idem, at pages 83-84.

[12] Idem, at page 84.

[13] Idem, at page 84.

[14] Idem, at page 84.

[15] Idem, at pages 84-85.

[16] Idem, at page 85.

[17] Idem, at page 85.

[18] Idem, at page 85.

[19] Idem, at page 85.

[20] Idem, at page 86.

[21] Information from National Park Service records supplied on 8/20/72 by Ranger William M. Colony.

[22] In 1971, according to the Hungry Horse News for 7/14/72, there were only nine fires in the entire Park, with total destruction of one acre, an almost incredible record. But even as such outstanding results are being obtained, the value of traditional fire suppression programs is being questioned on the ground that they are likely to have "serious deleterious ecological consequences." The whole subject is under study by National Park Service scientists. See the Hungry Horse News for 11/29/74.

[23] Hungry Horse News for 6/12/64.

[24] Idem, for 6/19/64.

[25] Idem, for 6/12/64.

[26] Idem, for 9/4/64.

[27] Idem, for 7/31/64.

[28] Idem, for 6/20/64.

[29] Idem, for 7/3/64.

[30] Idem, for 6/19/64.

[31] Idem, for 7/17/64.

[32] "Through The Years in Glacier National Park," by Donald H. Robinson, at page 127.

[33] Hungry Horse News for 8/7/70, 6/25/71.

[34] Idem, for 7/23/71.

[35] Idem, for 7/22/71, 7/7/72.

[36] Idem, for 12/10/71.

[37] Idem, for 8/18/72.

Chapter 25
BEAR PROBLEMS

Not since the sinking of the Titanic have America's newspaper readers recoiled with such horror as on August 14, 1967, when they were greeted by reports of the savage mangling and killing of two lovely young women by enraged grizzly bears in the mountains of Glacier National Park.[1] For a time, such headlines as "Night of Terror"[2] and "Grizzlies Kill Girls" shoved war stories, race riots and traffic deaths off the main line of the news.

Hardly had the recounting of full particulars of the gruesome tale subsided when throughout the press and leading magazines of the country, as well as among the citizenry generally, a tremendous controversy began to rage over the question of whether grizzlies and humans should continue to co-exist in the national parks.[3] The Park Service was besieged with heavy criticism, as well as a large amount of unsolicited advice, as to what it should have done, and ought to be doing about the situation.[4] Every bear expert in the country, from Andy Russell to Gairdner Moment, broke into print on the subject, adding his particular fuel to the flames.

Not only was there intense distress and revulsion over the fact that two attractive young women had become victims of the mightiest beast in the national parks, but there was vast puzzlement among experts and tyros alike over the question of why, after nearly sixty years of freedom from lethal encounters with *Ursus horribilis*[5] in Glacier Park, tragedy should strike twice on the same August night in different locations, both victims being park employees, both feminine and 19, and both being attacked while in their sleeping bags at a campground with others under circumstances involving no provocation by those attacked or their companions.

The story giving rise to the headlines of August, 1967 has been told and re-told a number of times.[6] The action took place in two areas of Glacier, both on the western side of the continental divide, but several miles apart. Granite Park is a mountain chalet situated at an elevation of about 6500 feet near Swift-current Pass, while Trout Lake, at an elevation of 3880 feet, lies approximately seven miles northwest of Lake McDonald.

Tragedy Number One

Among those arriving at Granite Park on the late afternoon of Saturday, August 12, 1967, were Roy Ducat and Julie Helgesen, both employed at the lodge at East Glacier, she in the laundry, he as a busboy. His home was at Perrysburg, Ohio, and although only 18, he was already a sophomore at Bowling Green University, majoring in biology. Julie was 19, a native of Albert Lea, Minnesota, and prominent in school activities while in high school. She was now a sophomore at the University of Minnesota.

Julie and Roy had been at East Glacier for nearly two months when they had opportunity for a special week-end holiday. Packing their gear, including lunches from the Lodge kitchen, they hitchhiked to Logan Pass, then hiked the eight miles of Garden Wall trail to Granite Park. They arrived at about seven o'clock, but it was nearly eight before they finally decided to spend the night at the official campground, where there were a few other sojourners. They had been warned of the danger of bears, but laughed and said they were not afraid. After all, no one had ever been killed by a bear in Glacier Park. Nevertheless, Roy carefully buried the remnants of their meal a few hundred feet away. Then they got into their sleeping bags and soon fell asleep.

About 12:45 a.m. the pair was awakened by an investigative bear which savagely attacked both of them, then carried Julie screaming into the darkness. Despite the severity of his wounds, Roy managed to arouse others in the campground area, and word of the attack was relayed to the Chalet several hundred yards up the trail. When the impact of the message was realized, a search party was formed and warily proceeded with flashlights to the campground.

Rescue Operation

There they found Roy Ducat in a semi-conscious condition and bleeding badly from his wounds. After he was given first aid, members of the party carried him up the trail to the Chalet, while Ranger-Naturalist Joan Devereaux (now Joan Watson, having married Ranger Tom Watson in 1971) succeeded in contacting Park Fire Headquarters by two-way radio, advising them of the attack, and requesting aid and medical supplies. Headquarters responded that a helicopter would arrive in twenty or thirty minutes with supplies and an armed ranger. When it arrived, Roy Ducat was loaded into it and flown to the hospital at Kalispell, where he was under surgery for three hours.

Then Ranger Gary Bunney, armed with a heavy-duty Winchester, and several volunteers set out in the three a.m. darkness for the campground. On reaching it, they cautiously fanned out in a number of directions, since they had no means of knowing in which direction the grizzly had made off with Julie. Finally to the left and down the slope they heard a faint cry and hastened in its direction. They came upon the girl lying on her face, covered with blood and barely alive. Gently they gave her first aid, and by means of an improvised stretcher got her back to the Chalet and onto a makeshift operating table where she was ministered to by three physicians who happened to be guests at the Chalet. It was 4 a.m. when another guest, Father Connolly, baptized her, gave her absolution for her sins, and she breathed her last. In a few moments, the helicopter was on its way with her body, winging through the darkness to Kalispell.

Nightly Show At Granite Park

What Julie Helgesen and Roy Ducat did not know, not that it would necessarily have affected their course of action, was that the vicinity of Granite Park was a grizzly bear hangout, that regularly each evening around dusk, two or more grizzlies would appear in the gully at the rear of the Chalet where its garbage was dumped, and feed there for half an hour or longer, that this had become a "showtime" for Chalet guests[7] and even on a few occasions for some of the Park's rangers and ranger-naturalists. Nor had they heard of the old sow with two cubs that had sometimes been seen about the garbage dump after the other bears had departed, or that their tracks had been noted, especially in the mornings, in the same vicinity.

Early in August, the spectators at the regular evening performance had included a ranger-naturalist, his wife, and two members of the Park headquarters staff at West Glacier. They had heard reports that grizzlies were making nightly appearances at the Chalet and decided to hike up after work and see for themselves. When they arrived at Granite Park, they were told that two bears had been showing up every evening, and that the tracks of another adult bear with cubs were often seen in the vicinity of the dump in the morning. They were rewarded by seeing the two regulars approach the garbage pit around ten p.m. and eat their fill. As they were leaving around midnight for the return hike, they were attracted by noises in the vicinity of the dump, and upon investigation, found it occupied by a large grizzly and her two cubs, busily feeding on the leftovers. Then they hastened back to West Glacier, feeling rather fortunate to have seen, not one or two, but five of the great animals in the course of a single brief visit.[9]

Tragedy Number Two

The helicopter with Julie's body had hardly taken off from Granite Park shortly after four in the morning when the scene of action shifted to the Trout Lake area, some ten miles to the west of Granite Park. Five young Park concessioner employees had hiked in with their overnight gear, intending to spend the night in the area. The group consisted of three young men and two girls.

Two of the boys were brothers, Ron and Ray Noseck, from Oracle, Arizona. Ray, aged 23, was a dental student at the University of Louisville in the wintertime and the manager of a service station near Lake McDonald Lodge in the summer season. His brother Ron, aged 21, also a dental student at Louisville University, was employed as a waiter at the Lodge at East Glacier. Their dates for the trip were Denise Huckle, aged 20, a room clerk at East Glacier, and Michele Koons, aged 19, employed in the gift shop at Lake McDonald Lodge. Both girls were college students, Michele being a sophomore at California Western University, near her home in San Diego. The fifth member of the party was 16-year-old Paul Dunn, of Edina, Minnesota who had accepted a job as busboy at East Glacier Lodge, in the course of a visit to the Park with his parents. He had been invited along on the trip by his fellow-employee at East Glacier, Ron Noseck.

With them on the trail over the slopes of Mt. Stanton was Squirt, an abandoned puppy that had been befriended by Denise and brought along on the trip, strictly against park regulations. They had crossed a little plateau, after an ascent of nearly 2,000 feet, and hiked down the trail toward Trout Lake. They had originally planned to continue another two miles to Arrow Lake, but decided against it when they encountered a couple of fishermen who told how they had been treed in that area the previous day by a troublesome bear. However, even this news did not particularly dampen their ardor. Getting run up a tree was a part of the fun and adventure of Glacier Park, and they knew that no one had ever been killed by a bear in the Park.

The Camp At Trout Lake

So they set up camp on the shore of the lake, near the logjam at its end. Michele remained at the camp with the dog while the others fished until eight o'clock. Then while they were cooking hot dogs around the campfire, Michele spotted a bear in the nearby trees. They hastily retreated down the shore some fifty yards, as a scrawny brown grizzly invaded their camp, appropriated their food, strolling leisurely from dish to dish before taking its departure.

When they were able to return to their camp, the terrified youngsters found that practically all of their food had been eaten. They considered returning to Lake McDonald, but were deterred by the inky darkness and the fact that they had only one flashlight. They decided instead to move their camp to another location farther down the shore. There they gathered old logs and built themselves a cheerful fire which they determined to keep burning throughout the night. They arranged their sleeping bags in a semi-circle about the fire and fell into a nervous slumber.

Grizzly Invasion

Well after midnight they were awakened by disturbing sounds that caused them to rebuild the fire to a more reassuring level. At times the sound seemed to come from the shallow water below the camp, and again from the woods above. They placed a sack of cookies overlooked by bruin in the earlier foray on the edge of a log, from which it disappeared in a few minutes. At 4:30 a.m., when the fire had died down again, the camp was suddenly invaded by a bear that began sniffing at the sleeping bags. Paul Dunn leaped out of his, and hastily climbed a nearby tree from which he was able, by the dim light of the campfire, to survey the scene below.

The camp was now in a frenzy as the others tried to escape the marauder. Ron Noseck helped Denise into a tree and threw the dog up to her. Ray played dead in his sleeping bag as the bear sniffed at him and moved on; then rolled out of the bag and raced to a tree, calling to Michele to do the same. When the zipper to her bag became stuck, the bear began tearing at her arm. As the others watched helplessly, the bear dragged her into the woods, sleeping bag and all, and they heard her scream, "Oh, my God, I'm dead!"

With the coming of dawn about six a.m., the four survivors climbed down from their trees and wearily stumbled back over the trail toward Lake McDonald and the ranger cabin near its north end. A ranger-led rescue party, including Ron Noseck and Paul Dunn, rushed back to Trout Lake. There, at the end of a trail of blood, bits of sleeping bag and clothing, they found Michele's badly mangled body, not much over 100 feet from the camp.[10]

The Tragedy At Okotomi Lake

There had been one earlier grizzly encounter in Glacier that had shaken the Park and the country by its strange circumstances and unprecedented ferocity. This had occurred on July 18, 1960, when Alan Nelson and Edomo Mazzer, both ranger-naturalists in the Park, decided to hike on their day off from Rising Sun Campground on the shore of Lake St. Mary to Okotomi Lake. They took with them Smith Parratt, the ten-year-old son of another ranger naturalist. At the lake they met Gote Nyhlen and Brita Noring, two school teachers from Sweden, and all five started the return trip together about 3 p.m.

As they rounded a turn in the trail, Mazzer saw a grizzly with two cubs and ran back, shouting to the others to climb trees. All but Smitty Parratt succeeded in gaining the safety of trees, but when Alan Nelson saw Smitty being mauled by the old sow, he jumped down and charged her. She left Smitty and attacked Alan, who couldn't get back up the tree fast enough. After biting a huge chunk out of his thigh, she went on to pull Brita out of her tree and maul her badly, although the most severe injuries had been inflicted on the boy. The attack lasted only minutes, then the bear and her cubs vanished. The first of three rescue parties brought by the uninjured men reached the site at 7:45 pm. and before the evening was over, all of the victims had been evacuated and taken by ambulance to the hospital at Cardston, Alberta.[12]

Brita Noring and Nelson, although painfully injured, recovered rather rapidly. Smitty Parratt lost his left eye, and suffered severe puncture wounds of the chest, a collapsed right lung, double fracture of each of five ribs, a compound fracture of the right upper arm, extensive scalp lacerations, and a compound fracture of facial bones. To reduce the terrible facial and scalp scars required a series of twelve operations in the next three years, and these were followed by still others designed to reconstruct the left tear duct and to improve his appearance.

Although not originally expected to live, the plucky lad recovered from his five-year ordeal to the point where he became an Explorer Scout, won a high school letter in the 660-yard run, played the saxophone in the school band, made a straight A average, and was selected by the faculty as the outstanding freshman of the year. Even after the accident he continued to return to the Park every summer with his family, his love of Glacier as strong as ever.[13]

Five Questions Posed By The Twin Attacks

Both before and after these incidents there have been other grizzly attacks in Glacier, which it would serve no purpose to describe. Suffice it to say that, except for the 1967 incidents, none had a fatal ending, and none had involved a raid by a grizzly bear, definitely identified as such, upon a camp site, campground or sleeping bag occupant.[14] Except for the 1960 incident, no attack was ever made upon a ranger-guided party, and except for Smitty Parratt, no Glacier visitor ever suffered wounds of extreme severity. Nearly all of the attacks that have occurred were unprovoked, and most of them were perpetrated by a mother grizzly with cubs.

With an increase in the number of Park visitors through the years, and a correspondingly greater frequency of ursine encounters, there came also a greater appreciation of the dangers involved. Particularly was it realized that a primary part of the problem lay in failure to perceive that with bears, as with humans, familiarity breeds contempt; and that such contempt was being engendered by the feeding of the great quadrupeds, and by their resultant familiarization with human beings, human locales and human food. Early steps were taken to minimize these contacts by the elimination of hotel garbage dumps, by prohibiting the feeding of bears by visitors, and by the removal of so-called "bum bears" from the scenes of their begging to remote wilderness areas of the Park.

No intensive studies of the bear problem were made, however, and by 1957 the annual visitor-volume to Glacier had reached the 700,000 level; by 1967, it was hovering around the million mark. Thousands of these visitors were flooding the trails and marching through the wilderness backcountry, bringing human food and distributing human garbage wherever they went. The enforcement of rules designed to minimize the bear hazard became more difficult and, at some locations at least, the providing of garbage feasts for neighboring bears was still passively tolerated.

When the twin tragedies of August 13, 1967 burst upon a stunned world, including Park officialdom, it triggered a massive reaction to the problem, and a review of the measures that could and should be taken to insure that there would be no recurrence of such fatalities, and that bear encounters would be reduced to a minimum. As a result of the hue and cry across the country, the situation received a thorough airing, making it evident that there were at least five questions for which answers were sorely needed.

Related Or Unrelated?

Could it be that two grizzly attacks in the same national park on the same night, both on 19-year-old girls in sleeping bags, both unprovoked and both fatal, were matters of mere coincidence? Although not the most important of the five questions, this is certainly the most perplexing and intriguing. Never in the history of Glacier had any life heretofore been sacrificed, nor apparently had it been seriously considered that any would be. To be asked to believe that the two events were totally unrelated boggles the mind.

Preliminarily some consideration had been directed toward the question of whether the situation had involved one bear or two; but this was quickly resolved when the geography was examined and it was realized that the two attack sites, though separated by only nine airline miles, were thirty trail miles apart, with an 8000-foot mountain ridge in between. It **had** to be two bears.[15] But if two bears were involved, what could have been the coordinating factor, if such there was? Why the same night, and not far from the same hour? Why, indeed, after 57 years of co-existence unmarked by any fatality and with relatively few attacks, should there happen, almost simultaneously, not one, but two deaths? What might the odds be against occurence of such a double tragedy?

When statistics became available, they only served to intensify the mystery and more definitely to point the finger at eerie coincidence. On the basis of computerized calculations, the odds against one such killing in a single night were reported to be 1,000,000 to 1, with the odds against two the same night rocketing to 1,000,000,000,000 to 1.[16] Of course, what comes out of a computer depends entirely upon the input, which in this case would have to include a base figure of zero deaths in Glacier for the first 57 years of its existence.

Astronomical Odds

But other statistics produce the same result. During the 1960's the average of five bear injuries per year in all national parks inhabited by such animals represented one injury for each 1,500,000 visitors, or 0.0007 per cent.[17] Another approach would be to compare the number of bear-induced fatalities in Glacier for the decade of the 1960's with its visitor-volume for the same period, and this would produce odds of approximately 4,175,000 to 1, or 0.00024 per cent.[18] Whatever the statistical method used, it provides no answer to our question.

While some experts have simply declined to accept such an explanation as reasonable, [19] Andy Russell, an acknowledged expert on the grizzly and its behavior, said that he was as sure as any man could be that the happenings of August 13, 1967 represented nothing more than sheer coincidence.[20] This was also the opinion of most of those qualified to express one, including Ruben Hart, then the Chief Ranger at Glacier.[21]

It is believed by some that the simultaneity of the two incidents can be understood only through a recognition that man and the grizzly have been on a collision course from the time they first came in contact with each other on the North American continent, that by 1967 man with his offensive smell and antagonistic ways had been pushing the grizzly farther and farther back into his limited space, and that the conditions of that summer at certain places in the Park made an explosion of the growing tension inevitable.[22] While this theory is a plausible one, even its proponents concede that it was pure coincidence that two grizzlies chose a few hours of a single night to strike two victims who had much in common.[23]

Cause Or Causes Of The Attacks?

Whether or not the events of the night of August 13, 1967 were purely coincidental in character, what were the reasons that brought about their occurrence? At the outset this, too, seemed to be a question for which there was no very good answer; and many were the theories tentatively advanced with a view to explaining why two bears, as if on prearranged signal, killed two girls. Those considering the matter took note, of course, of the fact that both of the guilty animals were females, and that the one at Granite Park had cubs, often a circumstance connected with such attacks. But even though the female is more deadly than the male, bears with cubs had never previously taken human life in Glacier, and the bear at Trout Lake **had no cubs.**[24]

Rabies as a possible cause was ruled out in both cases by official tests made upon the bodies of the offending bears[25] which, of course, had been promptly slain after the attacks. The factor of weather was suggested, since it had been a season of unusually high temperatures, of thunder, lightning and raging forest fires; and other animals have been known to become restless under the influence of such phenomena.[26] Potential aggravation from these sources was negatived, however, by opinions on grizzly behavior and reactions.[27] Such things as cosmetics and perfume were suspected, since the victims were young and feminine; and even the possibility of female odors was cited, since one of the girls was known to have been menstruating at the time, and the other was apparently about to.[28]

One rather unusual theory was predicated on the fact that both girls had been dragged away from their camp sites in their sleeping bags. It was hypothesized by two of Glacier's top naturalists that since bears have been learning to open packaged food, perhaps they thought the sleeping bags were packages; that possibly sleeping bags themselves might worry a bear, or it might become alarmed upon finding a strange cocoon with something warm and alive inside.[29] Not enough is really known about grizzly behavior to rule out each and every one of these ingenious theories completely, [30] but the fact remains that, without any of them, there is a simple and sufficient answer to the question of causation in each of these cases.

Midnight Visitors

In reference to the Granite Park attack, the evidence indicated two very pertinent causative factors. To begin with, the killer bear was a female with cubs and the responsibility for keeping them fed. More importantly, however, the chalet personnel had followed a nightly pattern of dumping garbage in the gully some 50 yards behind the chalet, where the grizzlies would come at a regular hour each evening to feast, usually with an audience of spellbound humans only yards away.[31] The old female and her cubs did not ordinarily appear until around midnight; nevertheless, she had been seen there and undoubtedly had become accustomed to human surroundings, odors, and food, and possibly had come to rely upon the latter as a source of sustenance.

This was the unhappy background of her August 13th behavior. Who knows but that the garbage on that night, and perhaps for two or three previous nights, had been so thoroughly picked over by earlier foragers as to leave little or nothing for the old female, thus driving her to seek other sources of food for herself and cubs, or perhaps enraging her to the point where she became sufficiently irrational to lay aside her normal fear of man? The whole picture was in violation of the most basic rule of bear management, to wit, that against feeding them or providing them with inducements to hang around areas inhabited or frequented by humans.

Activities Of The Rogue Bear

As to the Trout Lake attack, the evidence is different, but equally clear. It had been a long hot summer, and the berry crop on which the bears are wont to depend for food was rather scant. All season long a skinny, odd-shaped female grizzly had been haunting the area of Arrow Lake and Trout Lake. As far back as the latter part of June, this animal had been raiding the camps of visitors to the sector, opening cans of food, ripping into packs and first-aid kits, and destroying other gear. For the next several weeks, it not only continued these tactics, but began to harass hikers to and from Lake McDonald, following a few yards behind for considerable distances and frightening them. The bear's strange behavior was repeatedly reported to park authorities.[32]

This bizarre animal not only invaded camps with great regularlity, but it refused to be scared away by yelling or stone throwing. It methodically slashed packs into small pieces, bent the frames, and gobbled up any available food. The report of an encounter between two Columbia Falls youths and this skinny brown grizzly even appeared in the Hungry Horse News for August 4, 1967. When the camp of a girl scout troop from Kalispell was invaded by the same bear, destroying their food and belongings, they fled the scene. However, one of the girls paused long enough to take a picture of the rogue bear, a picture which appeared on the front page of the Daily Inter Lake, Kalispell's newspaper, on Thursday, August 10, 1967.[33] By this time, its operations in the Trout Lake area had become a matter of general information.

When, later on, the nefarious activities of the Trout Lake bear were skillfully pieced together by a master reporter, it became apparent not only that she had been waging a campaign of guerrilla warfare against the campers of the area for a period of nearly two months prior to the events of August 13th, but that she had grown bolder and bolder with each passing week.[34] The only wonder was that her persistent hit-run tactics had not sooner culminated in tragedy.

The Grizzlies Must Go?[35]
The Anti-Grizzly View

In the light of tragic experience in Glacier and Yellowstone, is it advisable for bears and people to continue to co-exist in the national parks?[36] There is a considerable body of informed opinion holding that such co-existence is not practicable.[37] No one has gone so far as to urge the outright extinction of the grizzlies, but they have taken the position that these great omnivores are exceedingly dangerous animals, the most dangerous, in fact, on the North American continent; that as such, they should be excluded from the national parks and be permitted to continue their existence only in wilderness areas unfrequented by man, such as parts of Alaska and northwest Canada.[38] One eminent biologist feels that the Park Service should make up its mind whether it wants to run a park for people or for bears; and if it seems important to conserve the grizzly, there are other suitable habitats.[39]

Those who share this view feel that the danger to humans from a status of co-existence is too great, and that sooner or later the 1967 tragedies will be repeated with increasing frequency. These individuals hold that while, statistically, the number of people injured or killed by bears is small, this is not a valid reason for permitting the continuance of a dangerous condition.[40] They suggest that while very few people have ever been injured by falling from the top of the Washington Monument, this did not deter the National Park Service from putting up a protective guard rail.[41]

Others point out that space is one of the prime needs of a grizzly, and that the "lower 48" states no longer have the space he requires; that if he is denied running room, and humans continue to come into ever-increasing contact with him, the grizzly will inevitably maim and kill. They assert that no matter what steps the Park authorities take to improve the conditions for co-existence, a few summers may pass without serious injury, but sooner or later standards will slip, complacency will develop, and human error will recur. Then along will come another peculiar grizzly, like the one at Trout Lake, or one that has become dependent upon people-provided food, like the one at Granite Park, and "more human life will be sacrificed, almost as certainly as tamaracks lose their needles and beavers eat aspen bark."[42]

The Grizzlies Should Stay?
The Pro-Grizzly View

"Should the huge bears be allowed to roam free in U.S. national parks or should they be resettled in government-owned wilderness inaccessible to the public?" Thus was the sixty-four dollar question phrased by Science Digest Magazine in its October, 1969 article, the opening line of which began "The great grizzly controversy roars on."[43] From a review of publications on the subject, it is apparent that the pro-grizzly faction outnumbers the antis considerably, the results running about three in favor of the bears to one against. An attitude survey of public opinion, conducted within a year or two following the Glacier Park fatalities, on the question of whether grizzlies should be eliminated from the national parks, showed only 104 of out of 3420 responses supporting such action, or less than 3%. What the public did favor was more effective management of people, bears and garbage.[44]

The National Parks Magazine editorialized that "Hard as it may go against man's more selfish instincts, the grizzly has a right to the fragment of existence left to it. The future will not thank us should we commit genocide on such an animal."[45] Another writer opined that "To destroy all bears would be unthinkable. But with campers flooding our woods, we must learn how to live with the animals whose land we invade."[46]

Preservation Of The Grizzlies

Eldon G. Bowman, formerly a seasonal ranger in Glacier Park, has stated that on the basis of his experience over several summers of field work, "people and bears can use the same area with risks reduced to an acceptable minimum. We have come full circle back to what the public wants and expects in regard to the parks, the wilderness and grizzlies. These big bears can and should be preserved in their natural settings, available for those who will make the effort and run the risks inherent in the wilderness to see them."[47]

Other writers have indicated their preference for retention of the grizzly provided certain steps be taken to insure visitor safety. David Niven, for example, suggests that wilderness areas should be limited to day use, with the possible exception of people who walk or take pack horses on back country trails. He adds: "There should be more roads and people should be required to view the animals from their cars" as is done "in the great parks of Africa, where parkland is considered the home of the animals which the people visit."[48]

Andy Russell asserts that "summer hikers and campers using our national parks and wilderness country can travel the trails in grizzly country with almost complete safety. To those who might say that is not enough, I would reply that complete safety is not found anywhere in a man's life."[49] He makes it clear, however, that such a statement presupposes that steps will be taken to provide for disposal of all park garbage through universal use of adequate incinerators, to institute firm enforcement of the regulations forbidding the feeding of bears within the parks, and to bring about thorough indoctrination of all hikers, campers and wilderness travelers in respect to the big bears, their habits and reactions.[50]

Jean George concluded that "In the final analysis, it appears that man and grizzly **can** co-exist in our wilderness parks—but co-existence raises problems similar to those of managing traffic: it means more regulation and less freedom, to achieve greater safety. It also means enforcement of all regulations by the National Park Service."[51]

A similar conclusion was reached by Roger Caras who insisted that the bear danger in Glacier had been over-dramatized by the widespread publicity accorded the events of August 13, 1967, and the correspondingly emotional over-reaction which followed on the part of many. In an effort to place the matter in proper perspective, he commented that "In truth, bear watching in an area administered by our National Park Service is one of the safest things a person can possibly find to do on a vacation. Flying, diving, swimming, boating, baseball, football, home carpentry and taking a shower are all more dangerous."[52]

Steps Toward A Solution?

What measures, if any, are being put into effect by Glacier Park authorities to cope with the grizzly problem? In response to this fourth question, it is now highly encouraging to be able to report that the National Park Service has adopted an aggressive and well-designed program for control of the bear-people relationship. Former Chief Ranger Ruben Hart outlined it as follows:[53]

(1) An educational program for visitors and hikers, including weekly lectures by naturalists at key points in the Park, and the publication of detailed information in reference to grizzlies, and of instructions on the Park's "Pack-in, Pack-out" policy.[54]

(2) Strong warnings to visitors against having anything in camp or on the trail that will attract a hungry bear, and against doing anything of an antagonistic or bear-baiting character.

(3) Abolishment of bear dumps and substitution of incinerators.

(4) Use of bear-proof garbage cans throughout the Park.

(5) Respecting the habitat of the bears by scheduling no new trails in the wilder areas.

(6) Capturing and transporting nuisance bears to more remote areas, after tagging them for future identification.

(7) Eliminating the incorrigibles when they persist in their unsatisfactory conduct.

Enforcement is also being stressed. Visitors apprehended in the act of feeding bears are brought before the United States commissioner and fined. Likewise, the "pack-in, pack-out" policy is being enforced on the trails. A horse patrol by ranger personnel is part of a program to keep the back country clean;[55] also assigned to back country patrol have been other rangers with special qualifications, such as degrees in ecology and veterinary medicine. Trail crews are charged with the responsibility for cleaning up any campground debris and picking up roadside litter. Modern vehicular garbage-carrying equipment has been acquired in order to make possible morning and evening pickups, with the objective of eliminating overnight carryover of garbage.[56]

The number of grizzlies in the Park is estimated at 200, thus providing each with a theoretical range of 8 square miles.[57] At park headquarters a map is maintained with a pin for the location of each grizzly sighted, the purpose being to keep tab on bear whereabouts. A check is also maintained on black bears seen. Warnings are posted and sometimes there are trail closures after grizzly sightings. Nuisance bears are captured by four-man crews using a tranquilizer gun, then transported by helicopter to a remote back country location, while still in a temporarily immobilized condition.[58] Handling the problem bear effectively represents a very important phase in the over-all program for handling the bear problem.

Since 1967 there have been very few injuries and no deaths in the Park attributable to bears. In commenting on the situation, Park Biologist Cliff Martinka said: "I feel one can no longer point to a grizzly bear in this park that is in any way tied to man for his food source. Glacier has a natural free-ranging population of grizzlies. These animals are interested in avoiding man."[59] In other words, the aggressive Park Service program to bring the grizzly program under control has been paying substantial dividents, making it possible to comply with the mandate of Congress that parks be preserved in their natural state, **unimpaired,** for the enjoyment of future generations.[60]

Silvertip grizzly on the move

Photo by Mel Ruder

Magnificent Menace Or Natural Resource?

What do grizzly bears mean to a wilderness park? And what would we lose if these big bears were to disappear from our parks? For one thing the grizzly is part and parcel of the wilderness eco-system, with a vital place in the delicate balance of plant and animal life. Like many predators, he feeds on the weak and the sick, culling the unfit. He helps to regulate the numbers of small rodents which have a habit of over-populating their habitat and damaging the vegetation on which other forms of life are dependent.[61]

Additionally, it should be recognized that the grizzly is as much a wonder of our land as the Grand Canyon or Old Faithful. Of himself, he is an unique natural resource — a magnificent, ferocious, unpredictable beast with a rare power to kindle the imagination and quicken the pulse.[62] His is a dignity and power matched by no other on the North American continent. For many, the opportunity to share a mountain with him for a while is a privilege and an adventure like no other.[63]

And, finally, not the least of the values added by the grizzly to a wilderness park is verisimilitude. Wilderness means challenge, self-reliance and risk; it must include significant elements of all of these or it has no excuse for being set aside and preserved. The big bears represent an inherent part of that wilderness and of the risks which it includes. They are a symbolic, as well as an actual, sign that there is still some authentic wilderness left.[64]

Notes For Chapter 25

[1]The double tragedy occurred between midnight and dawn on the morning of August 13, 1967, too late to appear in the Sunday editions of that date.
[2]Caption for the news report by Time Magazine for 8/25/67.
[3]The classic story of the cases is "Night Of The Grizzlies," by Jack Olsen, distinguished not only because of its comprehensive book-length treatment, but also by reason of its penetrating analysis and fascinating style. Published in hardcover form by G. P. Putnam's Sons, 254 pages, 1969, and as a paperback by New American Library, 175 pages, 1971.
[4]See, for example, article entitled "Menace In Our Northern Parks," by Emmett Watson, appearing in Sports Illustrated Magazine for 10/30/67; article entitled "Human Injury Inflicted By Grizzly Bears," by Stephen Herrero, appearing in Science Magazine for 11/6/70; and article entitled "People Versus The Grizzlies," by Andy Russell, in Field And Stream Magazine for March, 1968.
[5]**Ursus horribilis,** the scientific name for the grizzly bear was used in the reviews of these cases by Time Magazine in its 8/25/67 issue at page 19, by Newsweek in its 8/27/67 issue at page 26, and by the National Parks Magazine in its December, 1969 issue, at page 22.
[6]The most detailed report is by Olsen in his "Night Of The Grizzlies," supra. Less comprehensive stories appear in W. J. Schoonmaker's book entitled "The World Of The Grizz-

ly," published in 1968 by J. B. Lippincott Co., at pages 162-165; also in articles entitled "People Versus The Grizzlies," supra, in "Menace In Our Northern Parks," supra, and in "Glacier Park's Great Grizzly Bear Mystery," by E. D. Fales, Jr., appearing in Popular Mechanics Magazine for November, 1968.
[7]This fact is also reported by Gairdner B. Moment in his article entitled "The Reader's Turn," appearing in Audubon Magazine for September, 1969; also by Andy Russell in his article entitled "People Versus The Grizzlies," supra.
[8]"Night Of The Grizzlies," supra, at pages 79, 80 and 88.
[9]Idem, at pages 96 and 97.
[10]"Glacier Park's Great Grizzly Bear Mystery," supra, at page 220.
[11]"Grizzly: The Story of Five Hikers," an article by Albert Ruffin appearing in Life Magazine for 8/27/65.
[12]Idem.
[13]Idem. Concerning this incident, it was reported in the article entitled "Menace In Our Northern Parks," supra, at page 71, that the Parratt case was settled out of court by the government on 10/24/66 for $100,000, thus matching an earlier judgment for the same amount obtained by Joseph Williams, a 20-year-old employee of the Swiftcurrent Motor Inn, on account of an attack by a grizzly occurring on 6/18/59 on Mt. Altyn.
[14]Seasonal Ranger J. Randy Bednorz had an encounter on August 4-5, 1972 with a bear at Lincoln Lake, suffering minor injuries. In view of the fact that it climbed a tree after him, it seems unlikely that it was a grizzly. See Hungry Horse News for 8/11/72.
[15]Article entitled "Glacier Park's Great Grizzly Bear Mystery," supra, at page 220.
[16]"Night Of The Grizzlies," supra, at page 243.
[17]"Human Injury Inflicted By Grizzly Bears," supra, at page 94. This article contains a comprehensive bibliography of the literature on the subject up to November, 1970.
[18]The number of Park visitors for the 1960 decade approximated 8,350,000.
[19]"Night Of The Grizzlies," supra, at page 243.
[20]"People Versus The Grizzlies," supra, at page 60.
[21]According to "Menace In Our Northern Parks," supra, at page 71, then Chief Ranger Hart said: "This whole thing, the coincidence of two attacks at almost the same time, leaves us at a loss."
[22]"Night Of The Grizzlies," supra, at page 244.
[23]Idem.
[24]"Glacier Park's Great Grizzly Bear Mystery," supra, at page 220.
[25]Idem. See, also, "Menace In Our Northern Parks," supra, at page 74.
[26]"Glacier Park's Great Grizzly Bear Mystery," supra, at page 220.
[27]"Menace In Our Northern Parks," supra, at page 74.
[28]"Glacier Park's Great Grizzly Bear Mystery," supra, at page 220.
[29]Idem. See, also, "People Versus The Grizzlies," supra, at page 115.
[30]"Menace In Our Northern Parks," supra, at page 74.
[31]"People Versus The Grizzlies," supra, at page 115. See, also, the report of Gairdner B. Moment in his article entitled "The Reader's Turn," supra, at page 109, in which he related his personal experience at Granite Park on the evening of 8/12/67.
[32]"Night Of The Grizzlies," supra, at pages 52, 63, 65 and 68.
[33]Idem, at page 76.
[34]Idem, at pages 39-69.
[35]Caption of article in Science Digest Magazine for October, 1969.
[36]As phrased by Jean George in article entitled "Grizzlies, The Magnificent Menace," appearing in the Reader's Digest for August, 1969, at page 118, the question is "Can man and grizzly bear co-exist in our national wilderness parks?"
[37]Article entitled "Bears, The Need For a New Sanity In Wildlife Conservation," by Gairdner B. Moment, professor of biological science at Goucher College, appearing in

Bioscience Magazine for December, 1968, echoed in the National Observer for 2/24/69.

[38]As pointed out by Herrero in "Human Injury Inflicted By Grizzly Bears," supra, at page 594: This radical proposal is clearly contrary to the obligation stated in the statutes of the acts under which American and Canadian national parks were established to preserve and protect native wildlife."

[39]"Bears, The Need For A New Sanity in Wildlife Conservation," supra, and see comment thereon by Herrero in his article entitled "Human Injury Inflicted By Grizzly Bears," supra, at page 594.

[40]"The Reader's Turn," supra, at page 108.

[41]Idem.

[42]"Night Of The Grizzlies," supra, at page 253.

[43]"Grizzlies Must Go?", an article appearing in Science Digest for October, 1969.

[44]"Human Injury Inflicted By Grizzly Bears," supra, at page 598.

[45]National Parks Magazine for December, 1969, at page 22.

[46]"Glacier Park's Great Grizzly Bear Mystery," supra, at page 220.

[47]Article entitled "The Grizzly In The National Parks," by Eldon G. Bowman, appearing in American Forests Magazine for July, 1969, at page 55.

[48]Article entitled "Is It Going To Be The Bears Or Us?" by David Nevin, appearing in True Magazine for August, 1969.

[49]"People Versus The Bears," supra, at page 116.

[50]Idem, at pages 116 and 151.

[51]"Grizzlies, The Magnificent Menace," supra, at page 119.

[52]"In Defense Of The Grizzly," an article by Roger Caras appearing in the Audubon Magazine for May, 1969, at page 54.

[53]Interview with former Chief Ranger Hart on July 10, 1970.

[54]Idem. An excellent pamphlet entitled "In Grizzly Country" has been given to visitors commencing in 1969; and a leaflet covering the "pack-in, pack-out" policy has been issued by the Glacier Natural History Association for free distribution to Park visitors.

[55]Interview with former Chief Ranger Hart on July 10, 1970. This patrol was initiated by the same ranger who wrote the article entitled "The Grizzly In The National Parks," supra, appearing in the American Forests Magazine for July and August, 1969.

[56]Interview with former Chief Ranger Hart on July 10, 1970.

[57]Article by Clifford J. Martinka entitled "Population Characteristics Of Grizzly Bears In Glacier Park," reported in the Hungry Horse News for December 31, 1971.

[58]Interview with former Chief Ranger Hart on July 10, 1970. This program is in the capable hands of Ranger Art Sedlack, former park naturalist. The transporting of grizzlies to remote sections of the Park has not proven to be as effective a program as had been hoped, although bear-caused injuries in the ensuing five years were limited to three rather minor ones and no deaths. Presumably, alternative procedures will be utilized if it is felt that the helicopter transfer procedure is not accomplishing its purpose. See Hungry Horse News for 8/13/71.

[59]Hungry Horse News for 7/24/70.

[60]"The Grizzly In The National Parks," supra, for July, 1969, at page 17.

[61]"Grizzlies, The Magnificent Menace," supra, at page 60.

[62]Idem.

[63]"Grizzly Country," by Andy Russell, at page 60.

[64]"The Grizzly In The National Parks," supra, July, 1969, at page 18.

Grizzly sow with cubs
Courtesy National Park Service, West Glacier

Tranquilized grizzly
Courtesy National Park Service, West Glacier

Tranquilized grizzly being placed in culvert trap for removal to remote wilderness area
Courtesy National Park Service, West Glacier

Grizzly being released from trap after transfer to remote area

Photo by Mel Ruder

BIBLIOGRAPHY

Albright, G. A. — "Official Explorations For Pacific Railroads, 1853-1855," U. C. Press, 1921.

Albright, Horace M. — Letter dated January 20, 1975 to the author.

Albright, Horace M. and Taylor, Frank J. — "Oh, Ranger."

Alden, William C. — Pamphlet entitled "Glaciers Of Glacier National Park," published in 1914 by the Department of the Interior.

Alt and Hyndman — "Rocks, Ice And Water, The Geology of Waterton-Glacier Park," published in 1973 by Mountain Press Publishing Company in cooperation with the Glacier Natural History Association.

Arrowsmith — "Map of all the New Discoveries in North America," based upon information supplied by Peter Fidler.

Bailey, H. E. — Article entitled "How The Trees Came To Glacier Park" from "Glacial Drift," Volume V for July-August, 1932.

Bailey, Vernon and Florence Merriam — "Wild Animals of Glacier National Park," published in 1918 by Department of the Interior.

Baring, Robert — Statement with respect to beauty of St. Mary region (1889).

Bauer, E. A. — Article entitled "Glacier: The Park With Everything" in Field And Stream Magazine for June, 1964.

Blakiston, Lieut. Thomas — "Further Papers Relative To The Exploration of British North America."

Borah, Leo A. — Article entitled "Montana: Shining Mountain Treasureland" in National Geographic Magazine for June, 1950.

Bowman, Eldon G. — Article entitled "The Grizzly In The National Parks," appearing in American Forests Magazine for July, 1969.

Bradley, James G. — Article entitled "When Smoke Blotted Out The Sun, The Most Destructive Forest Fire In American History—Idaho, 1910," appearing in the September, 1974 issue of the American West Magazine.

Briggle, William J. — Letter dated August 24, 1972 in reference to Cracker Lake Mine property.

Brown, Dee — Introduction to Grinnell's "Pawnee, Blackfoot and Cheyenne," describing Coolidge presentation of Roosevelt medal to Grinnell.

Bureau Of Outdoor Recreation — "Continental Divide Trail Study Report," issued in 1971.

Burpee, Lawrence J. — "Pathfinders Of The Great Plains: A Chronicle Of La Verendrye And His Sons," published by Glasgow, Brock & Co. in 1922.

Byron, George Gordon, Lord — Dramatic poem entitled, "Manfred."

Campbell, Archibald — "Survey of Northern Boundary of the United States, 1878."

Campbell, Marius — Pamphlet entitled "Origin Of The Scenic Features Of Glacier National Park."

Canadian Minister of Indian Affairs — Bulletin entitled "Canada's Mountain National Parks."

Caras, Roger — Article entitled "In Defense Of The Grizzly," appearing in the Audubon Magazine for May, 1969.

Carver, Capt. Jonathan — "Three Years' Travels Throughout The Interior Parts of North America For More Than Five Thousand Miles, 1766-1768," (1802 edition) printed by Samuel Etheridge for West and Greenleaf, No. 56 Cornhill, Boston.

Catlin, George — "North American Indians," republished in 1926 by John Grant of Edinburgh, Scotland.

Chittenden and Richardson — "The Life, Letters And Travels of Father Pierre-Jean De Smet," Volume II, published in 1905, showing letter written on June 12, 1850 by De Smet to Hugh Monroe.

Christopherson, Edmund — "Adventure Among The Glaciers."

Clark, Earl F. — Article entitled "John F. Stevens, Pathfinder For Western Railroads," in American West Magazine for May, 1971.

Colony, William M. — Interview with, on August 20, 1972.

Cosley, Joseph E. — "A Short Story Of Kootenai Brown."

Coues, Elliott — "History Of The Expedition Under The Command Of Lewis And Clark."

Department Of Interior — Information Pamphlet on Glacier National Park, issued in 1924.

De Smet, Pierre J. — "Oregon Missions And Travels Over The Rocky Mountains In 1845-1846," published in 1847.

D'Evelyn, M. N. — "Over Red Eagle Pass," from "Glacial Drift," Volume VII for April, 1934.

—"Wolves In Glacier Park," from "Glacial Drift," Volume VII, June, 1934.

Director, National and Historic Parks — Folder on Waterton Lakes National Park.

Dowler, J. W. — "Lake McDonald," poem published in 1914.

Dyson, James L. — "Glaciers And Glaciation" appearing in the 1948 edition of the "Drivers' Manual," at page 230.

—"Glaciers And Glaciation in Glacier National Park."

—"The Geologic Story of Glacier National Park," published by the Glacier Natural History Association.

—"The World of Ice."

Eaton Brothers — Booklet entitled "Eaton's Ranch And Howard Eaton's Horseback Trips," published in 1922.

Edwards, J. Gordon — "A

Climber's Guide To Glacier National Park."
—"Climbing Glacier's Massive Peaks," article appearing in "The Naturalist," No. 2, at page 45.
—Letter dated July 13, 1972 in reference to the Josephine Mine.
Elrod, Morton J. — "Elrod's Guide And Book Of Information" (1924 edition).
Evenson, Erling — letter dated November 1, 1974, regarding ownership of Josephine Mine.
Ewer, John C. — "The Story of The Blackfeet," 1966, originally published by the Bureau of Indian Affairs.
—"Winold Reiss: His Portraits and Proteges," article appearing in Montana Western History, Volume XII, Number Three, Summer of 1971.
Fales, E. D., Jr. — Article entitled "Glacier Park's Great Grizzly Bear Mystery," appearing in Popular Mechanics Magazine for November, 1968.
Flandrau, Grace — "The Lewis And Clark Expedition."
—"The Story of Marias Pass."
George, Jean — Article entitled "Grizzlies: The Magnificent Menace," appearing in the Reader's Digest for August, 1969.
Glacier Natural History Association — Booklet on "Fish And Fishing in Glacier National Park," published in 1973.
Grant, Madison — "Early History of Glacier National Park."
Gray, Ralph — Article entitled "From Sunclad Sea To Shining Mountains," in the National Geographic Magazine for April, 1964.
Great Northern Railway publications — Brochure entitled "Trail Riding In Glacier National Park," published circa 1935.
Great Falls Tribune — Issue of October 20, 1889, reporting exploration of Marias Pass by Major Baldwin.
—Issue of September 26, 1954 in reference to Mrs. Oastler.
Greeley, Alfred W. — Article entitled "Glacier National Park: Crown of the Continent" in World's Work Magazine for May, 1908.

Greene, Charles K. — "Montana Memories IV."
Greenhow, Robert — "Memoir Historical And Political of the North West Coast of North America," printed in 1840 by Blair & Rives, of Washington.
—"Oregon And California," (Second edition) published in 1845 by Charles C. Little and James Brown.
Grinnell, George Bird — Article in the Scientific American Supplement for September 23, 1899.
—"Blackfeet Lodge Tales," published in 1892 by Charles Scribner's Sons.
—Notes of, preserved in records at Parks headquarters at West Glacier.
—"Pawnee, Blackfoot and Cheyenne."
—"Some Autumn Birds of the St. Mary Lakes Region," article published in 1888 in Forest and Stream Magazine.
—"The Crown Of The Continent," in Century Magazine for September, 1901, at pages 660-672.
—"To The Walled-In Lakes," article originally published under pseudonym "Yo" in Field And Stream Magazine in 1885, reprinted in Drivers Manual (1948 edition).
—"Trails Of The Pathfinders."
Hamilton, William T. — "A Trading Expedition Among The Indians in 1858," an extract from which appeared in "Montana: Its Story and Biography" by Tom Stout, 1921.
Harrod, Howard L.—"Mission Among The Blackfeet," published in 1971 by University of Oklahoma Press.
Hart, Ruben O. — Interview with, on July 10, 1970, on the grizzly problem, et al.
Harvey, George H., Jr. — Article entitled "Our First Sierra Club Outing," appearing in the Sierra Club Bulletin, Volume XII, No. 2.
Hays, Howard H. — "Drivers' Manual" (1948 edition).
Hazzard, A. S. — "Fish And Fishing Waters In Glacier National Park," appearing in Drivers' Manual, 1948 edition.
Heimes, Joseph F. — Article entitled "Capture of Joe Cosley," appearing in 1948 edition of the

"Drivers' Manual."
—Interview on the Cosley capture appearing in Hungry Horse News for May 23, 1975.
Herrero, Stephen — Article entitled "Human Injury inflicted by Grizzly Bears," appearing in Science Magazine for November 6, 1970.
Holbrook, Stewart H. — "James J. Hill," published in 1955 by Alfred A. Knopf.
Holtz & Bemis —"Glacier National Park, Its Trails And Treasures," published in 1917 by George H. Doran Company.
Horodyski, Robert — Letter dated August 16, 1973 from Dr. Horodyski, Professor of Geology at the University of California at Los Angeles.
Hudson's Bay Company — Letter from London dated May 8, 1973, with respect to the employment of Hugh Monroe.
Huidekoper, A. C. "My Experiences And Investment in the Bad Lands of Dakota And Some Of The Men I Met There."
Hungry Horse News — Published and edited as a weekly newspaper at Columbia Falls, Montana, by Mel Ruder.
Iversen, Phillip R. — Letter dated October 7, 1975.
Keller, L. Floyd — Article entitled "The Mountain Goat of Glacier National Park," published in 1948 edition of "Drivers' Manual," at page 147.
Kinley, Ray — Letter dated June 24, 1973 to the author describing the saw mill explosion in August, 1925.
Lane, Franklin K. — Article entitled "A Mind's Eye Map Of America," in National Geographic Magazine for June, 1920.
L'Assomption, Quebec Parish Church — Birth records showing date of birth of Hugh Monroe.
Laut, Agnes C. — "Enchanted Trails Of Glacier National Park."
—"Wonderland Of The Great Northwest," articles in Travel Magazine for January-May, 1926.
Lawrence, E. I. — Article entitled "A Vacation Trip Through Glacier National Park," appear-

ing in the Sierra Club Bulletin, Volume XII.

Lechleitner, R. R. — Pamphlet on "Mammals of Glacier National Park," published by Glacier Natural History Association.

Lewis, Meriwether — "History of the Expedition Under the Command of Lewis and Clark," republished in 1965 by Dover Publications, edited by Elliott Coues.

—"Journals of the Lewis and Clark Expedition," (1814 Unabridged Edition), republished in 1961 by J. B. Lippincott Company, Volume III.

Leydet, Francois — National Geographic Magazine article on Olympic National Park in February, 1974 issue, describing mountain goats there.

Liebig, Frank S. — "Early Days In The Glacier Park Country" appearing in the Spring Edition of Montana West for the year 1970, after originally appearing under the title of "Early Days in the Forest Service," compiled by the U.S. Forest Service, Region I, Missoula, Montana.

Lindsay, Vachel — Book of poetry entitled "Going-To-The-Sun," published by C. D. Appleton & Company about 1923.

Little, Richard Henry — Sketch on the wimpus appearing in his column in the Chicago Tribune entitled "A Little About Everything," appearing in August, 1911.

Long, George W. — Article entitled "Many-Splendored Glacierland" in National Geographic Magazine for May, 1956.

Lunger, Robert B. — Letter dated November 22, 1974 in reference to acquisition of the Josephine mine property.

—Records of, as Park Realty Specialist for Glacier National Park.

MacGregor, I. G. — "Peter Fidler: Canada's Forgotten Surveyor," published in 1966 by McClelland & Stewart, Ltd. of Toronto.

Martinka, Clifford J. — Article entitled "Population Characteristics Of Grizzly Bears In Glacier Park," 1971.

Mauff, John — Letter dated April 12, 1874 in reference to the time and place of the death of Dr. Frank B. Wynn.

McClintock, Walter — "The Old North Trail," republished in 1968 by the University of Nebraska Press.

Middleton, S. K. — Article on origin of International Peace Park appearing in 1948 edition of "Drivers' Manual."

Miller, Ben — Article on his experience with an avalanche entitled "Thrilling Stories About Rangers," appearing in the 1948 edition of "Drivers' Manual."

Mitchell, Guy Elliott — Article entitled "A New National Park," appearing in the National Geographic Magazine for March, 1910.

Monroe, Hugh — Interview in Fort Benton River Press on February 19, 1890.

—Interview published in the Chinook Opinion on October 29, 1892.

Moore, C. W. "Dinty" — Article entitled "Origin Of Fur-Bearing Trout" appearing in Hungry Horse News for August 25, 1972.

Moment, Gairdner B. — Article entitled "Bears, The Need For A New Sanity In Wildlife Conservation," appearing in Bioscience Magazine for December, 1968.

—Article entitled "The Reader's Turn," appearing in Audubon Magazine for September, 1969, dealing with the grizzly problem.

Muir, John — Article on national parks and forest reserves, appearing in the Atlantic Monthly Magazine for January, 1898, Volume 81: 21-22.

—"Our National Parks," published in 1901.

National Parks Magazine — Editorial in December, 1969 issue.

—Report on grizzly bear tragedy in its issue for December, 1969.

National Park Service — Bulletin entitled "Careers In The National Park Service."

—Pamphlet entitled "In Grizzly Country," given to Park visitors commencing in 1969.

—Records at West Glacier headquarters.

Nelson, Alan G. — "Wild Flowers of Glacier National Park."

Nelson, Bruce — "Land Of The Dacotahs," published in 1964 by University of Nebraska Press.

Nelson, Julia — Article entitled "Cosley, Trapper and Guide Extraordinary," appearing in the "Canadian Cattleman" for August, 1953.

Ness, Elmer — Article entitled "On Patrol" appearing in 1948 edition of "Drivers' Manual."

Nevin, David — Article entitled

"Is It Going To Be Us Or The Bears?" appearing in True Magazine for August, 1969.

Newsweek Magazine — Article entitled "Parks Under Siege," appearing in issue for July 19, 1971.

—Report on grizzly bear tragedy in its issue of August 27, 1967.

Ober, Michael J. — Article on "Skyland Camps," appearing in "MONTANA, the magazine of Western History," Volume XXIII, Number Three, Summer of 1973.

Olsen, Jack — "Night Of The Grizzlies," published in 1969 by G. P. Putnam's Sons.

Pacific Railroad Reports, Volume I, copy in Glacier National Park library at West Glacier.

Parratt, Lloyd P. — Pamphlet entitled "Birds Of Glacier National Park."

Parsons, John E. — "West On The 49th Parallel," published in 1963 by William Morrow and Company.

Pumpelly, Raphael — Volume II of "My Reminiscences," published in New York in 1918 by Henry Holt & Company.

Pyle, Ernie — "Home Country," published posthumously in 1947.

Rackette, G. Adelle — Article entitled "Kootenai Brown, Colorful Tales Of A Waterton Pioneer," appearing in the 1948 edition of the "Drivers' Manual."

Reiner, Ralph E. — "Flowering Beauty Of Glacier National Park and the Majestic High Rockies."

Rinehart, Mary Roberts — "An Appreciation Of Glacier National Park," article written especially for the United States Railroad Administration about 1920.

—"Tenting Tonight" published in 1917 by Houghton Mifflin Company.

—"Through Glacier Park With Howard Eaton" published in 1916 by Houghton Mifflin Company.

Robinson, Donald H. — "Through The Years In Glacier National Park," published in 1960 by Glacier Natural History Association in cooperation with National Park Service.

—"Trees And Forests Of Glacier National Park."

Rodney, William — "Kootenai Brown, His Life And Times," published in 1969 by Gray's

Publishing Ltd., Sidney, British Columbia.

Ruffin, Albert — Article entitled "Grizzly: The Story of Five Hikers," appearing in Life Magazine for August 27, 1965.

Ruhle, George — Handbook entitled "Roads and Trails of Waterton-Glacier National Parks."

Runte, Alfred — Article entitled "Worthless Lands — Our National Parks," appearing in the "American West" magazine for May, 1973.

Russell, Andy — Article entitled "People Versus The Grizzlies," appearing in Field And Stream Magazine for March, 1968.

—"Trails Of A Wilderness Wanderer," published in 1971.

Sanders, H. F. — Article entitled "Glacier Park," appearing in Overland Monthly Magazine for June, 1909.

Schoonmaker, W. J. — "The World Of The Grizzly," published in 1968 by J. B. Lippincott Company.

Schultz, James Willard — "Blackfeet And Buffalo," published by University of Oklahoma Press in 1962.

—"Blackfeet Tales of Glacier National Park."

—"Conception of Glacier National Park," article appearing in Great Falls Tribune for November 15, 1936.

—"Friends Of My Life As An Indian."

—Letter dated May 20, 1929 to the Glacier National Park Naturalist, and now in the Park's official files at West Glacier.

—"My Life As An Indian."

—"Signposts Of Adventure."

Science Digest Magazine — Article entitled "Grizzlies Must Go?" appearing in issue for October, 1969.

Scientific American Magazine — Article entitled "A Tunnel For Saddle Horses," issue of June, 1932.

Severeid, Eric — "Not So Wild A Dream," published by Alfred A. Knopf in 1946.

Sharp, Robert P. — "Glaciers."

Sharpe, Grant W. — "101 Wildflowers Of Glacier National Park."

Shankland, Robert — "Steve Mather Of The National Parks," published in 1951 by Alfred A. Knopf.

Singer, Francis J. — "History and Status of Wolves in Northern Glacier National Park," as reported by Hungry Horse News for January 10, 1975.

Sperry, Alfred L. — "Avalanche."

Sperry, Lyman B. — Article entitled "In The Montana Rockies," appearing in "Appalachia," Volume VIII, No. 1, for January, 1896.

Spry, Irene M. — "The Papers of the Palliser Expedition."

Standley, Paul — "Flora Of Glacier National Park."

Steele, Rufus — Article entitled "The Man Who Showed His Father," appearing in Sunset Magazine for March, 1915.

Stevens, Isaac I. — "Surveys For A Railroad Route," Volume XII, Book I.

Stimson, Henry L. — "My Vacations," privately printed in 1949.

—"The Ascent Of Chief Mountain," first appearing as a chapter in "Hunting In Many Lands" published in 1895 by Forest And Stream Publishing Company, New York.

Stinson, Ira S. — Article entitled "Roads and Trails in Glacier National Park," appearing in the 1948 edition of the "Drivers' Manual."

Strother, French — Article entitled "Louis W. Hill," published in World's Work Magazine for September, 1916.

Sunset Magazine — Article entitled "When We Found Glacier, We Stopped Looking" in June, 1958 issue.

Swain, Donald C. — "Wilderness Defender," a biography of Horace M. Albright, University of Chicago Press, 1970.

Swiftcurrent Courier — First and only newspaper of Altyn, published September 1, 1900.

Thompson, David — "Narrative."

Thompson, Margaret — "High Trails Of Glacier National Park," published in 1938 by the Caxton Printers, Ltd.

Tilden, Freeman — "The National Parks."

Time Magazine — News report on grizzly bear tragedy in issue of August 25, 1967.

Twiss, Travers — "Oregon Territory," published in 1846 by D. Appleton & Company.

United States Statutes — Chapter 24, Statutes of 1872, establishing Yellowstone Park.

United States Statutes — Chapter 37, Laws of 1911-1912, 62nd Congress.

United States Statutes — Chapter 157, Laws of 1931-1932, approved May 2, 1932.

United States Statutes — Chapter 226, 61st Congress, establishing Glacier National Park.

United States Statutes — Chapter 264, 63rd Congress, accepting jurisdiction of the Park from the State of Montana.

United States Statutes — Chapter 372, Laws of 1929-1930, 71st Congress.

United States Statutes — Chapter 384, 61st Congress, containing first appropriation for construction of Glacier Park trails.

Vaught, L. O. — Letter to M. E. Beatty, Chief Park Naturalist, dated February 24, 1948, in records of Park Headquarters at West Glacier.

Veach, Sr., William — "An Early Trip Into Glacier Park," from "Glacial Drift," Volume VIII, April, 1935.

Volz, J. Leonard — Letter dated April 13, 1971 in reference to status of Cracker Mine property.

Waters, Dr. Alvin W. — Article entitled "The Last Of The Glidden Tours," published in the March, 1963 issue of "Minnesota History."

Waterton Lakes National Park Administration — "Notes For A Self-Guided Tour of Red Rock Canyon."

Watson, Emmett — Article entitled "Menace In Our National Parks, appearing in Sports Illustrated Magazine for October 30, 1967.

Wiecking, H. R. — Article entitled "The Glacier Park Hotels, Chalets and Cabin Camps," appearing in the 1948 edition of the "Drivers' Manual."

Willis, Bailey — Article entitled "Along The Northwest Boundary" in World's Work for July, 1902.

—Article entitled "Stratigraphy And Structure, Lewis And Livingston Ranges, Montana," published on November 15, 1902 in the Bulletin of the Geologic Society of America, Volume 13.

Yard, Robert Sterling — Book of the National Parks.

INDEX

213

THE AUTHOR,
WARREN L. HANNA

An attorney with many books on California law to his credit, Warren L. Hanna, recently retired, has been a man of diverse interests. *Montana's Many-Splendored Glacierland* has been dear to his heart, being sometimes in the background and often in the foreground of his life for more than six decades. On the back cover of this book is the moving story of the two women who encouraged him to carry on the research and writing for this book.

Born in Iowa and raised in the Sheyenne River Valley of eastern North Dakota, he got his early education in the schools of Valley City, where his father was city superintendent of schools during the years 1899-1946. His A.B. degree was obtained at age 18 from the University of North Dakota, and his J.D. and M.B.A. from the University of Minnesota. In the summers of 1918 and 1920 he worked at the Many Glacier Hotel in Glacier National Park where he was in charge of the transportation/information desk. It was there that he met Claire Miller, the girl he was to marry in 1921.

They went to California in September, 1924, where Hanna worked for the Southern Pacific Railroad Company and other concerns until 1931. He then accepted a position as workers' compensation judge (then called referee) with the California Workers' Compensation Appeals Board, and devoted nearly 12 years to this work.

In 1936, as a sideline, he began to edit and write books on California law, featuring principally the field of workers' compensation, in which his 4-volume work has long been regarded as the "bible" in California. Under the name of Hanna Legal Publications, he published a variety of law books, all of which he edited or wrote, until he sold his publications in 1959 to Matthew Bender & Company, third largest law book publisher in America. During his publishing years, more than half a million books bearing his name reached the shelves of California bench and bar.

In the meantime, Hanna collaborated with a friend in 1943 in the founding of a law firm specializing in insurance law. By the time Hanna retired from practice in 1983, the firm of Hanna, Brophy, MacLean, McAleer & Jensen numbered 67 attorneys with branch offices in Oakland, Santa Rosa, Sacramento, Redding, Fresno, Bakersfield and San Jose. Among American law firms that specialize in the practice of workers' compensation jurisprudence, it is undoubtedly one of the largest, if not the largest.

Among his non-compensation interests is that of Sir Francis Drake in California, and he published in 1979 a book on that subject entitled *Lost Harbor*. More recently he has published a biography entitled *The Life and Times of James Willard Schultz*. Other works shortly to be published are *Stars Over Montana: Men That Made Glacier Park History* and *Life Among The Blackfeet, A Compilation of Early Articles by Schultz and Edited by Warren Hanna*.

Hanna has received many honors and awards. From his alma mater, the University of North Dakota, he received its Sioux Award in 1967 followed by an honorary doctorate in 1970. In 1974 he received the California Manufacturers Association award "as the man who has done the most for workers' compensation in California during the years 1949-1974." In 1983, his national fraternity, Alpha Sigma Phi, gave him its Distinguished Service Award.

Obviously, the author of *Montana's Many-Splendored Glacierland* is a man who uses his time well and happily. With his wife, Frances, he resides in the Berkeley hills overlooking the Golden Gate. There they built their home in 1961 where they are active socially and in local club affairs. They have two daughters living in northern California and a third in Washington, D.C., as well as several grandchildren.